The Nazi Persecution of the Gypsies

The Nazi Persecution of the Gypsies

Guenter Lewy

OXFORD
UNIVERSITY PRESS
2000

OXFORD
UNIVERSITY PRESS

Oxford   New York

Athens   Auckland   Bangkok   Bogotá   Buenos Aires   Calcutta
Cape Town   Chennai   Dar es Salaam   Delhi   Florence   Hong Kong   Istanbul   Karachi
Kuala Lumpur   Madrid   Melbourne   Mexico City   Mumbai
Nairobi   Paris   São Paulo   Singapore   Taipei   Tokyo   Toronto   Warsaw

and associated companies in
Berlin   Ibadan

Copyright © 2000 by Guenter Lewy

Published by Oxford University Press, Inc.
198 Madison Avenue, New York, New York 10016

Oxford is a registered trademark of Oxford University Press

Library of Congress Cataloging-in-Publication Data
Lewy, Guenter, 1923–
The Nazi persecution of the gypsies / Guenter Lewy.
p.   cm.
Includes bibliographical references and index.
ISBN 0–19–512556–8
1. Gypsies—Nazi persecution.   2. World War, 1939–1945—Atrocities
3. Gypsies—Germany—History—20th century.
I. Title.
D804.5.G85L49   2000   940.53'18'08991497—dc21   98-52545

Acknowledgment is made to the following sources for permission to use
previously published material: Sage Publications, Ltd., for the article "Himmler
and 'Racially Pure Gypsies,'" in *Journal of Contemporary History*, vol. 34, no. 2
(April 1999), pp. 201–214; the *National Interest*, for the article "The Travail of
the Gypsies," in the Fall 1999 issue.

3 5 7 9 8 6 4 2
Printed in the United States of America
on acid-free paper

Contents

Preface   vii

Introduction: A History of Oppression
and Maltreatment   1

I. The Prewar Years: A Three-Track Policy

1. Track 1: Harassment Stepped Up   17
2. Track 2: Crime Prevention   24
3. Track 3: Confronting an "Alien Race"   36
4. The Special Case of the Austrian Gypsies   56

II. A Tightened Net (1939–1942)

5. "Security Measures" and Expulsions   65
6. Creating Social Outcasts   84
7. Detention and Deportation
from the Ostmark (Austria)   107
8. The Killing of "Spies" and Hostages
in German-Occupied Europe   117

III. A Community Destroyed (1943–1945)

9. Deportation to Auschwitz   135
10. Life and Death in the Gypsy Family Camp
of Auschwitz   152
11. Gypsies in Other Concentration Camps   167
12. Gypsies Exempted from Deportation   181

IV. After the Disaster

13. Victims and Perpetrators   199
14. Conclusion: The Course of Persecution Assessed   218

Abbreviations and Glossary   229
Notes   232
Bibliography   275
Index   297

Preface

To this day the persecution of the Gypsies under the Nazi regime remains one of the most neglected chapters in the history of that fateful era. Although there are hundreds of works that examine all aspects of the Nazi onslaught on the Jewish people, the fate of the Gypsies is the subject of only one book in the English language. Published in 1972, Kenrick and Puxon's *The Destiny of Europe's Gypsies* represented a welcome attempt to make up for decades of neglect, but the book fell short of a satisfactory treatment. It was based on a limited range of sources and was marred by mistranslations and factual errors; its analysis, compressed to a mere 125 pages, was marked by undue simplifications. A revised edition that appeared in 1995 was further abbreviated and omitted all documentation. The publisher explained that footnotes and references had been removed to help make the book a better read for older schoolchildren.

During the last twenty years or so German authors have begun to tackle this long-slighted subject, though most of these studies are monographs of limited scope. Some works are excessively polemical and are part of what in Germany has been called "militant history." They are superficial and fail to describe and analyze the actual chain of events in all their historical complexity. It was not until late 1996 that Michael Zimmermann's *Rassenutopie and Genozid* appeared, a comprehensive scholarly work and the first book that does justice to the intricacies of Nazi policy toward the Gypsies.

There are many reasons for the prolonged failure to pay attention to this topic. The suffering of the Gypsies was overshadowed by the massive tragedy of the Jewish people, which received extensive coverage during the Nuremberg trials and in the documentary record created by these lengthy proceedings. By contrast, the persecution of the Gypsies was barely mentioned and not a single Gypsy was called to testify before the various tribunals. During the years that followed, numerous Jewish survivors wrote about their tribulations, although very few Gypsies related their experiences. Hardly any Gypsies belonged to the intellectual class. Moreover, some of the most basic tabus of Gypsy culture regarding ritual purity and sexual conduct had been violated in the concentration camps, and survivors therefore were reluctant to talk about what had happened. Subjects such as compulsory sterilization could hardly be discussed at all. Inquiries by outsiders were hampered by the suspicion with which Gypsies have traditionally regarded the non-Gypsy world—the result of centuries of harassment and persecution.

To an important extent, this book is based on documentary materials gathered in twenty-nine German and Austrian archives—federal, state, local and others such as the Institute for Contemporary History in Munich and the Central Office for the Prosecution of Nazi Crimes in Ludwigsburg. The most important single source consulted in Germany consisted of nearly a thousand files on individual Gypsies compiled by the German police. Such records have been preserved in only three state archives—in Potsdam, Magdeburg and Düsseldorf. Not meant for outside consumption, these files provide a detailed and highly informative picture that is indispensable for a proper understanding of the course of persecution. Many misconceptions about the Nazi treatment of the Gypsies are due to an exclusive reliance on decrees issued in Berlin and a failure to ascertain how these policies were implemented at the local level. In addition to information about the actions of the authorities, these records also contain much valuable material about the attitudes and reactions of the victims.

Other primary sources were consulted at the National Archives and the archive of the U.S. Holocaust Memorial Museum in Washington. The literature on the subject by now includes a limited number of memoirs. Despite the fallibility of all such recollections, the testimony of these survivors helps put the actions of the persecutors into perspective. The heart-rending stories of their ordeal remind us of the human tragedies obscured by the bureaucratic language of official documents.

In the interest of a treatment in depth, this book focuses on the Gypsies of Germany and Austria and of territories incorporated into the Third Reich such as the Czech Republic (known as the Protectorate of Bohemia and Moravia) and Alsace-Lorraine. I also discuss actions taken against Gypsies in areas under German military administration in the Baltic states, the Soviet Union and Serbia because of the important light they throw on the overall character of Nazi policy.

The Gypsies are an elusive people who have been romanticized as well as vilified. For example, commenting on Isabel Fonseca's book *Bury Me Standing: The Gypsies and Their Journey*, Richard John Neuhaus, editor of the magazine *First Things*, recently charged in an intemperate outburst that the Gypsies "are, with exceptions, a lazy, lying, thieving, and extraordinarily filthy people" who are "exceedingly disagreeable people to be around." On the other hand, different observers have praised their music and their close-ness to nature. Some contemporary German writers consider the Gypsies and their less inhibited ways a valuable challenge to what they see as the reg-imented lifestyle of modern society, preoccupied with technological effi-ciency and material wealth. The same attitude has led to an insistence on certain "politically correct" ways of looking at the history of the Gypsies, including a new nomenclature. Thus instead of the traditional word *Zigeuner* (Gypsy), which is considered pejorative, most Germans today use the terms "Sinti" and "Roma." These names refer to the tribe to which the majority of German Gypsies belong (the Sinti) and to the Gypsies of southeastern European origin (the Roma). In fact, there is nothing pejorative per se about the word "Zigeuner," and several Gypsy writers have insisted on the unin-terrupted use of the term in order to maintain historical continuity and express solidarity with those who were persecuted under this name.

There remains the pleasant duty of acknowledging my gratitude for the generous assistance I have received from many quarters. Sybil Milton, for-merly senior historian at the U.S. Holocaust Research Institute, was most helpful to me when I first set out to work on the subject of this book. A fel-lowship from the American Council of Learned Societies and a stipend from the German Academic Exchange Service (DAAD) made possible five months of research in the Federal Republic of Germany. The archivists and librarians there were cooperative and supportive, and the same holds true for the personnel of the National Archives and the U.S. Holocaust Memor-ial Museum in Washington. I have also benefited from exchanges of views and assistance in obtaining documents from scholars working on the history of the Gypsies and related fields, in particular Christopher Browning, Lud-wig Eiber, Hans Hesse, Martin Luchterhandt, Hansjörg Riechert, Gesine Schwan, Wolfgang Wippermann and Michael Zimmermann. Stephen Miller and Michael Zimmermann read an early draft of this book, and I thank them for their constructive criticism. I am indebted to Chrisona Schmidt for an outstanding job of copyediting. Needless to say, none of the above individuals or institutions are responsible for the opinions and con-clusions reached here, which remain my personal responsibility.

Washington, D.C
November 1998   G. L.

The Nazi Persecution of the Gypsies

Introduction

A History of Oppression
and Maltreatment

The persecution of the Gypsies by the Nazi regime represents but a chapter in a long history replete with abuse and cruel oppression. Ever since the Gypsies appeared in central Europe in the early fifteenth century, they have been expelled, branded, hanged and subjected to various other kinds of maltreatment. Indeed, in some parts of Europe the vicious tribulations experienced by this minority continue unabated to the present day. As a result of this history, many Gypsies are reluctant to acknowledge their ethnic identity, and statistics about the number of Gypsies in the world are therefore notoriously unreliable.

Gypsies in German Lands: Early Years

The people known today as Gypsies speak a multiplicity of dialects, all derived from Sanskrit with borrowings from Persian, Kurdish and Greek. Analysis of this language, known as Romani, and other evidence have established with considerable certainty that the Gypsies left the Indian subcontinent more than a thousand years ago, probably in several waves, and gradually migrated through Persia, Armenia and Turkey to Europe. We do not know what brought about this exodus; the Gypsies are an unlettered people who have neither written nor oral histories relating their past. For the fourteenth century, their presence is documented in Greece, where they were known as Atsinganoi or Atzinganoi; the German Zigeuner, the French Tsiganes, the Italian Zingari and similar names in other languages derive from this Byzantine appellation. From the year 1417 on, chronicles mention their movement through the Hanseatic towns and other parts of Germany.

The same year, the German emperor Sigismund issued a group of some one hundred Gypsies a letter of safe conduct. Traveling in extended family groups, these nomads made their living by providing specialized goods and services. They wove baskets, repaired kettles, sharpened scissors, traded in horses, performed music, trained animals; their women danced and told fortunes. In order to sell their products and perform their trades they had to keep moving from place to place.[1]

Presenting themselves as pilgrims and penitents, Gypsies at first were well received and accepted private or public alms. The story they told is handed down in several versions. According to some accounts, they claimed to hail from Egypt and were doing penance for having abandoned for some years the Christian religion. Others relate that they claimed to be expiating the sins of their forefathers who had refused to help the Blessed Virgin and the Christ Child on their flight to Egypt. Still others speak of penance in memory of the flight of Jesus.[2] The Gypsies were therefore frequently called Egyptians; the name Gypsies in English and Gitanos in Spanish is a distorted form of this word. Very soon, however, tensions developed between the indigenous, sedentary population and these dark-skinned, foreign-looking wanderers. Their dedication to a life of penance was being called into question, and instead they were now often denounced as heathens. No longer considered penitent Christians, their begging drew resentment. Many accounts mention that "they were excessively given to thievery."[3] There were charges of sorcery, witchcraft, child stealing and spying. Gypsies were said to be noisy, dirty, immoral, deceitful and generally asocial. Their self-proclaimed ability to see into the future both attracted and terrified.[4]

With the Turks expanding into the Balkans, in 1497 the legislature of the Holy Roman Empire accused the Gypsies of spying for the Turks and in the following year ordered their expulsion from all German lands. This decree was reenacted several times, and similar ordinances soon followed in individual German territories, though enforcement appears to have been lax. The theme of the stealing and dishonest Gypsies now appeared regularly in chronicles of the times, and even outstanding humanists such as the seventeenth-century Jacobus Thomasius concluded that these black-looking heathen foreigners, speaking a strange tongue, were not fully human.[5] Jealous craft guilds, seeking to maintain local monopolies, sought to limit traditional Gypsy occupations such as metalworking and the manufacture of baskets. As a result of these restrictions, Gypsies increasingly resorted to begging and stealing, reinforcing a stereotype that had accompanied them all along. Some formed or joined criminal gangs that preyed especially upon the rural population.

A policy of rejection now became the norm. With the spread of the Reformation, pilgrims lost their earlier lofty status, and begging too came under sharp attack. Although local parishes were prepared to support their indigenous poor, foreign beggars were routinely sent away. "Settled people," observes Angus Fraser, "on the whole, do not trust nomads; and in a European society where the majority were pressed into a life of piety, serfdom and drudgery, Gypsies represented a blatant negation of all the essential values and premises on which the dominant morality was based."[6]

The fortunes of the Gypsies worsened after the Thirty Years' War. This disastrous conflict, centered in Germany, uprooted tens of thousands. When it ended in 1648, vagrant hordes of dispossessed peasants and disbanded soldiers strode through the land begging and stealing. Some Gypsies too formed robber bands, numbering fifty to one hundred members, who stole for their sustenance. The most famous of these Gypsy brigands was Jakob Reinhardt, who was hanged in 1787 along with three other Gypsies. In response to this chaotic situation, the German princes enacted a flood of legislation, some of it specifically directed against Gypsies. Between 1497 and 1774, there were 146 edicts against Gypsies in German lands; about three-quarters of the anti-Gypsy measures identified for the years 1551–1774 were issued within the hundred years following the Thirty Years' War.[7]

Enforcement of these edicts suffered from the absence of an effective police force, but increasingly more stringent and ruthless penalties sought to make up for the weak power of the state. In 1652, the Elector of Saxony, George I, declared Gypsies to be outlaws in his land; in 1711, Augustus I of Saxony ordered that violators were to be flogged, branded and, on second appearance, put to death. In 1710, Prince Adolph Frederick of Mecklenburg-Strelitz commanded that captured Gypsies were to be confined for life at hard labor; older males and women over twenty-five were to be flogged, branded and expelled. Children under ten were to be handed over to good Christian families for a proper upbringing. The forcible removal of young children was practiced in other states as well. The archbishopric of Mainz decreed in 1714 that Gypsies and other thievish vagrants were to be executed without trial for practicing an itinerant way of life; women and grown children were to be flogged, branded and banished or put for life into workhouses. In 1725 King Frederick William I of Prussia ordered that Gypsies over eighteen, both male or female, be hanged without trial. An edict issued in 1734 by Ernst Ludwig, the Landgrave of Hesse-Darmstadt, provided that Gypsies had to leave his land within a month; those disregarding this order would forfeit life and possessions. A reward was put up for catching or killing a Gypsy. In 1766, Carl Theodor, Count Palatine by Rhine, proclaimed that Gypsies and other such vagabonds were to be arrested and punished; those found in his territory a second time were to be hanged without further trial, their bodies being left on the gibbet as a warning to other offenders. Those professing ignorance of this law were to be branded on the back with a gallows and banished.[8]

A few raised their voices against these extreme penalties. The cathedral chapters of Speyer, Worms and Mainz argued that Gypsies and the like were "after all human beings and could not dwell between heaven and earth."[9] But by and large, vagabonds were seen as ipso facto criminals and punished severely. Gypsies were caught in a tide of repression against vagabondage and begging. Their status as rootless people was itself an aberration that had to be corrected by the power of the state. Only gradually did the forces of enlightenment sweeping Europe change the cruelty of the law and thus bring about an amelioration in the status of the Gypsies.

In order to survive, Gypsies sought to make the most of the loopholes in this system of oppression. They took advantage of the multiple jurisdictions and different legal codes existing in the various German states. Some found more than one godfather for their children; others, practicing a long-existing skill, forged passports and thus obtained the coveted license to practice an itinerant trade (*Wandergewerbeschein*), required from the first half of the nineteenth century on. Their musical talent apparently played an important role in their winning a measure of tolerance.

Modern Times: Regulation and Harassment

In a society that was becoming increasingly urbanized and industrialized, Gypsies had to abandon some of their old trades, and many became impoverished and dependent on local welfare. Still, they resisted becoming wage laborers as well as they could. Industrial production displaced the making of articles for hawking and many turned to peddling machine-made goods bought from wholesalers, moving from village to town. Most of them became sedentary during the winter months, but, following seasonal occupations, they continued their independent and nomadic way of life during the summer.

Attracted by economic opportunity and relative prosperity, a new wave of Gypsies from the Balkans and Hungary entered central Europe in the second half of the nineteenth century; their Romani speech was heavily influenced by Rumanian. The majority of Gypsies who had lived in German-speaking lands for several centuries continued to be known as Sinti, but alongside them there now existed a new group who called themselves Rom. This influx of more dark-skinned foreigners coincided with the spread of racial consciousness in Germany. In a time of important biological advances, the French Count Gobineau's *Essai sur l'inègalitè des races humaines* (1853–1855) had a marked impact in Germany. Gobineau argued for the superiority of the "Aryan race," those who spoke Indo-Germanic languages, and he assigned inferior status to persons of mixed ancestry, or *Mischlinge*. Similar ideas were put forth by Englishman Houston Stewart Chamberlain in his book *Die Grundlagen des neunzehnten Jahrhunderts*, published in Germany in 1899.[10] Alongside the view of the Gypsies as primitive but idyllic people propagated by the Romantic era, there now emerged a far less benevolent picture of the Gypsies—a racially inferior group whose presence in Germany jeopardized the purity of the Germanic race. Italian criminologist Cesare Lombroso supported this judgment. In his book *L'uomo delinquente* (1876) and in his later German work *Die Ursachen und Bekämpfung des Verbrechens* (1902), Lombroso maintained that Gypsies were shiftless, licentious and violent people who tended toward crime on account of their racial makeup.[11] Less than half a century later, these ideas led to a wave of brutal persecution of the Gypsy people.

Racist thinking may have influenced those who framed rules and laws regulating the life of German Gypsies during the second half of the nineteenth century, but racial considerations were generally of minor importance in the regulations they created. In order to encompass all of the many different types of beggars and vagabonds found in Germany, the authorities stressed conduct rather than race—a peripatetic lifestyle, conducting an itinerant trade and moving one's personal belongings in a caravan. In addition to Gypsies, these criteria led to the inclusion of the *Jenische*, whose origin is not fully known. These so-called white Gypsies were of local extraction. In addition to German, they spoke their own dialect known as Rotwelsch or *Gaunersprache* (language of rogues). Hence the regulations encompassed Gypsies and Gypsy-like itinerants.[12] As we shall see later, even the Nazis, despite their preoccupation (not to say obsession) with racial ideas, for a long time continued to use this formula. They too sought to catch in their net all types of vagabonds, whether Gypsy or not.

The main aim of the regulations issued by the German states during these years was to halt the influx of foreign Gypsies, especially members of the Roma tribes from the Balkans. Leading the way in 1885, Bavaria issued a measure specifically directed against Gypsies. The decree called for strict control of the identity papers carried by Gypsies, canceling whenever possible the licenses issued to itinerant traders and restricting the issue of new such licenses. Gypsies whose citizenship was in doubt could be arrested and kept in jail until the state to which they belonged accepted them. Those apprehended were made liable for the costs of any arrest, legal proceeding or expulsion. Another measure issued in 1889 frankly acknowledged that the purpose of these harassing controls was to deter Gypsies from itinerating in Bavaria.[13]

In 1899 Bavaria established at police headquarters in Munich an office for coordinating actions against Gypsies. Local police were now required to report the appearance of Gypsies and other itinerant groups to this *Zigeunerzentrale* (Central Office for Gypsy Affairs). The reports had to include the nature of the identity papers they carried, how many animals, especially horses, the itinerants had, from where they had come and in which direction they had moved, and whether the police had taken any measures against them. Not taking any action had to be justified. Prosecutors were asked to report all legal proceedings and convictions of Gypsies and other vagabonds. The local offices registering births, marriages and deaths (*Standesämter*) similarly had to provide copies of their records. Summaries of all of these reports were carefully catalogued in a special alphabetical file. Other German states also supplied names and photos, and by 1925 this data bank included more than 14,000 names from all over Germany. Very soon too the Zigeunerzentrale not only recorded information received but began to collect it. It also began to suggest measures against Gypsies. As a result of such a suggestion, from 1911 on all Gypsies in Bavaria were fingerprinted.[14]

The head of the Bavarian Zigeunerzentrale was one Alfred Dillmann. In 1905, Dillmann issued a compilation of all the data collected until then in a publication called *Zigeunerbuch*. In addition to all relevant laws and administrative regulations affecting Gypsies, the Gypsy Book included 3,350 names and more detailed information about 611 persons; 435 individuals were classified as Gypsies, 176 as Gypsy-like itinerants. It identified 477 persons having a criminal record, most charged with petty crimes such as begging, not having a license

Zigeuner=Buch

herausgegeben zum amtlichen Gebrauche im Auf=
trage des K. B. Staatsminiiteriums des Innern vom
Sicherheitsbureau der K. Polizeidirektion München.

Bearbeitet von

Alfred Dillmann,

Oberregierungsrat bei der K. Polizeidirektion.

München 1905.
Dr. Wild'iche Buchdruckerei (Gebr. Parcus).

Title page of the
Zigeunerbuch *issued by the*
Munich police in 1905. From
Zigeunerbuch *(Munich,*
1905). COURTESY OF
BAYERISCHE STAATSBIBLIO-
THEK, MUNICH.

to carry on an itinerant trade or theft. The book was printed in an edition of
7,000 copies. Bavarian authorities received a free copy; others in Germany and
in neighboring states who wanted the book had to pay one mark.[15]

Other German states too tackled what was referred to as the "Gypsy
plague" (*Zigeunerplage*). In 1903, the Interior Ministry of Württemberg promulgated a Struggle against the Gypsy Nuisance decree. The issuing of
licenses for itinerant trade could now be limited, roving bands were to be
accompanied by the rural police until they could be handed over to the police
in the neighboring district, children of school age were to be taken from their
itinerating parents and made to attend school.[16] Another decree of 1905 forbade traveling in hordes; one local authority interpreted "horde" as any
group of persons that included two or more individuals not part of a family.[17]
Similar measures were adopted in other German states. The pattern of control and regulation was so pervasive that it was difficult for Gypsies not to
collide with the law. Whether it was making camp in the open, lighting a fire
at the edge of a forest, or grazing horses, the nomadic way of life itself almost
inevitably led to the violation of some legal norm. Altogether, these provisions were clearly designed to make nomads abandon their peripatetic
lifestyle; they constituted harassment that aimed at making the life of Gypsies

and other itinerating people so unpleasant that they would not want to live in Germany.[18]

As mentioned earlier, the fact that the German states had no uniform legislation dealing with the Gypsy "problem" made it somewhat easier to evade the most stringent controls. Each jurisdiction sought above all to get rid of its own Gypsies as quickly as possible; in practice this meant that Gypsies were continuously being pushed across borders. In order to put an end to this situation, in 1911 the Bavarian Ministry of Interior invited representatives of Preussen, Saxony, Württemberg, Baden, Hesse and Alsace-Lorraine to a conference to discuss united action. The conference met in Munich December 18–19, 1911; its deliberations were based on a lengthy memorandum prepared by the Munich police. Not surprisingly, the conferees had differences of opinion, beginning with the question of who was to be regarded a Gypsy. The conference working paper had stressed that there existed few pure Gypsies and that it was therefore the Gypsies' way of life, their occupation and nomadic lifestyle, and not membership in a tribe or race, that should be the decisive criterion. Other conferees considered this definition too broad. Eventually agreement was reached on a compromise formula: "Gypsies, in the eyes of the police, are those who are Gypsies according to the teachings of ethnology as well as those who roam about in the manner of Gypsies."[19]

The conferees were not authorized to decide on concrete measures to be taken, and the outbreak of World War I further diverted attention. During that conflict, the fear of spies and the demands of the war economy, which required a sedentary population, created new hardships for Gypsies. Additional restrictions were enacted that forbade traveling and imposed more rigid requirements of reporting to local authorities; some of these measures continued in force after the end of the war. Attempts to achieve a unified stand on matters concerning the Gypsies were also kept up. But this aim was not achieved, and in 1926 Bavaria became the first state to issue not just administrative regulations but to enact legislation dealing with Gypsies.

On July 16, 1926, acting over the objections of the Social Democrats and Communists, the Bavarian legislature approved the Law for the Combating of Gypsies, Travelers and the Work-Shy. A memo by the Ministry of the Interior that accompanied the draft legislation explained that travelers (*Landfahrer*), or Gypsy-like itinerants, had been included in the law because they had become even more of a nuisance than those belonging to the Gypsy race on account of their large numbers. Including the travelers would make it clear that Gypsies were not being subjected to special legal provisions solely because of their birth status, an action that would have violated Article 109, the equal protection clause of the German constitution.[20]

According to the new law, those who wanted to itinerate with wagons and caravans needed a permit from the police. This permit was valid for only one year and could be revoked at any time. Traveling with children was forbidden, except when adequate provision had been made for the children's education. Taking along horses, dogs and animals that served commercial purposes required a police permit. It was forbidden to travel or camp in "hordes," a

Gypsy caravan in a gravel-pit near Munich in 1920. COURTESY OF KESTER ARCHIV.

horde being any group of individuals or several families. Camping was permitted only in places assigned by the local police; campers had to register with the police and had to deposit their identity cards and permits for the duration of their stay. For those with a criminal record, the authorities were empowered to assign special travel routes, forbid them to stay in specific localities or assign them a particular place of residence. Foreign Gypsies or foreign travelers were subject to these provisions even in the absence of a criminal record. Persons above the age of sixteen who could not provide proof of regular work could be put into a workhouse for up to two years; this term could be renewed.[21]

The implementing regulations for the new law issued by the Ministry of the Interior provided additional details and definitions. "The concept 'Gypsy,'" it was stated, "is generally known and does not require further explanation. The teachings of ethnology determine who is to be regarded a Gypsy." Travelers were not Gypsies racially or tribally, but conducted themselves like Gypsies; their itinerant trade was presumed merely to conceal a dishonest way of life in the manner of the Gypsies. The permit for traveling was given only to those who had a license for carrying on an itinerant trade, which according to earlier decrees required proof of a permanent residence. No permit to travel was to be issued when there were grounds for believing that the applicant would seek to provide for his sustenance by begging, poaching, illegal fishing and the like. The regulations pointed out that the law was not directed against honest traders with a permanent residence who had to itinerate in the exercise of their calling.[22]

Inasmuch as the Bavarian law imputed a dishonest way of life to all Gypsies it certainly was based more on prejudice than fact. On the other hand, the inclusion of non-Gypsy travelers indicated once again that the primary purpose of these legal restrictions was to penalize a certain lifestyle rather than persecute an ethnic group of people on account of their racial origin. The aim was to regulate and discourage conduct that rightly or wrongly was associated with the Gypsies.

In 1926, the long-standing aim of the Bavarian government to achieve a national policy with regard to the Gypsies met some success. On August 16, a committee of the German Criminal Police Commission (DKK), a coordinating body, adopted a set of guidelines prepared by the head of the Munich police that was to serve as the basis for an all-German program of action. These guidelines, largely taken from the 1911 conference memo, were included in a new draft agreement between the German states on the "struggle against the Gypsy plague," which was approved by representatives of the German states in Berlin in April 1929. The Zigeunerzentrale of Munich was to function as a clearinghouse not just for Bavaria but for all of Germany. Local police authorities were encouraged to see to it that individuals who had completed their jail term were handed back to them so that they could be expelled or sent to a workhouse.[23]

Goaded by Bavaria, several German states now issued additional regulations. A decree of the Prussian Ministry of the Interior of November 3, 1927, required that all "nonsedentary Gypsies and Gypsy-like itinerants" above the age of six be fingerprinted. Non-Prussian governments were urged to adopt the same practice,[24] and most German states indeed soon followed suit. On April 3, 1929, the parliament of Hesse approved a comprehensive Law for the Fight against the Gypsy Nuisance that was patterned largely on the Bavarian law of 1926.[25] "All in all," one observer correctly concludes, "the Weimar Republic had done a good deal of spadework for the regime which would succeed it."[26]

Pressure to act against the Gypsies came not only from the police but also from the German population itself, especially in the cities where during the winter months many Gypsies rented lots for their caravans or put them on municipal property. The well-documented case of Frankfurt/Main can serve as an example, though similar events took place in other cities.

Following repeated complaints and petitions demanding action against the Gypsies, on November 19, 1928, the city council of Frankfurt debated a proposal to move some forty Gypsy caravans from a part of town known as the Gallus quarter to a less-populated area. Their current site was said to be filthy, smelly and lacking canalization. The children attending the schools of the district, the school authorities pointed out, were so dirty and emitted such a strong odor that plans had been considered for separate classes and for providing them with a daily bath and clean clothing. The money for these services unfortunately was not available. After considerable delay, caused by the difficulty of finding a location that would not draw protests from neighbors, in September 1929 the city administration set up what was officially called a "concentration camp for Gypsies" north of the city at the border with the state of Hesse. Though fenced in, camp inhabitants could come and go at will and there was no permanent guard. The establishment of this camp led to two unforeseen results. First, only one large Gypsy family agreed to move to the new site, and the police refused to relocate the other Gypsies who were German citizens and had valid and paid-up leases for their lots. Second, the town of Bad Vilbel, a well-known spa in Hesse that was close to the camp site, protested vigorously. Property values were said to be endangered; the farmers of the area feared thefts from their fields and orchards and soon put in claims for losses attributed to the Gypsies.

At a meeting of the Frankfurt city council on January 28, 1930, several delegates demanded more police patrols and supported the payment of compensation to the aggrieved farmers. The Communist delegate asked for better treatment of the Gypsies and, to general laughter, held up the example of the Soviet Union which, he said, had succeeded in turning these nomads into useful citizens. A National Socialist delegate accused the Gypsies of being parasites who did not pay taxes and lived on welfare payments. He ended his lengthy speech with the demand that the Gypsies be expelled from Frankfurt and sent back to wherever they had come from. Higher state authorities meanwhile took the side of Bad Vilbel and demanded that the camp be closed down. Sanitary conditions were said to be disastrous, a finding corroborated by an inspection of the camp held in May 1930. There was no well for drinking water and only one part of the camp was paved; no school was available for the sixteen children of the Gypsies. The problem eventually solved itself when the last Gypsies left the camp.[27]

Roots of Hostility

There can be little doubt that much of the enmity and outright persecution experienced by the Gypsies throughout their history has been rooted in prejudice and xenophobia. The Gypsies were different and that fact alone created problems for them. Their nomadic way of life was often romanticized; they were said to lead a carefree existence that was noble in spirit and close to nature. At the same time, Gypsies also drew the suspicion and hostility of their sedentary hosts. As in the case of the Jews, Gypsies were accused of every conceivable misdeed and crime, and this stereotyped view of Gypsy life is reflected in our language. "He lies like a Gypsy" is a European proverb. In many languages the words "Jew" and "Gypsy" are equivalent with haggling and usury. In English, to "gyp" is to swindle or cheat, a gypsy moth is a parasite whose larvae feed on the foliage of trees, and a gypsy cabdriver is someone who picks up passengers without a proper taxi license.[28]

Some students of Gypsy life have acknowledged the presence of some negative behavioral traits but explain them as the result of discrimination and poverty. Unable to obtain land and having no fixed abode, Gypsies had to rely on begging. "Forbidden to do business with shopkeepers," writes the American Gypsy scholar Ian Hancock, "the Roma have had to rely upon subsistence theft to feed their families; and thus stealing has become part of the stereotype. Forbidden to use town pumps or wells, denied water by fearful householders, uncleanliness becomes part of the stereotype."[29]

Yet prejudice alone, I submit, is not a sufficient explanation for the hostility directed at the Gypsies over the centuries. Whether they result from exclusion and poverty, or other factors, certain characteristics of Gypsy life tend to reinforce or even create hostility on the part of the populations among which they move or dwell. These traits, customs and attitudes are reported not only by their enemies but also by well-meaning observers, sympathetic anthropologists and, at times, by Gypsies themselves. Such reports appear in the earliest accounts of their appearance in Europe, and they can be found in the most recent works dealing with the life of the Gypsies.

As a result of a long history of persecution, Gypsies harbor a deep-seated suspicion of non-Gypsies, referred to as the *gadzé*. Hence to lie to a *gadjo* is perfectly acceptable behavior and carries no stigma. Through centuries of experience in avoiding the prying questions of curious outsiders, notes the American anthropologist Anne Sutherland who professes her "admiration and respect for the Rom people," Gypsies "have perfected the technique of evasion to an effortless art. They delight in deceiving the *gajo*, mostly for a good reason, but sometimes just for the fun of it or to keep in practice."[30] Jan Yoors, who lived with Gypsies for many years, relates that they practiced the art of the falsehood without self-consciousness. "In Romani they said, *'tshat-shimo Romani'* (the truth is expressed in Romani). It was the Gaje who, by forcing the Rom to speak a foreign language, made the Gypsies lie. The Rom said, *'Mashkar le gajende leski shib si le Romeski zor'* (surrounded by the Gaje the Rom's tongue is his only defense)."[31] Gypsies, writes their self-described friend Martin Block, are "masters in the art of lying and pretending innocence, when there is a question of misleading a 'gadzo' or non-gypsy. The police know this at their cost."[32]

Beyond finding it extremely difficult to get Gypsies to give true evidence, the German police, from the nineteenth century on, were frustrated that Gypsies, in addition to their real name in Romani, very often had several non-Gypsy names. These names were created when a Gypsy eloped to marry, was stopped by the police, or escaped custody or deserted from the army. The number of names correlated with the number of difficult situations a Gypsy had encountered. Police officials, therefore, had to spend time seeking to unravel the personal history of their arrested suspects. Judges too, of course, had to know whether a person was a first offender or had a criminal record. Needless to say, none of this endeared the Gypsies to the authorities or others who were taken in by a false identity.

The Gypsies' easy resort to and highly developed skill in stealing was another source of strong enmity. "Stealing from other Rom is wrong," observed Sutherland, "but it is not necessarily wrong when it is from the *gaje*;

although one should not be too greedy."[33] His friend Putzina explained to
Yoors that "stealing from the Gaje was not really a misdeed as long as it was
limited to the taking of basic necessities, and not in larger quantities than
were needed at that moment. It was the intrusion of a sense of greed, in itself,
that made stealing wrong."[34] Hence, picking up some wood from the forest
was no misdeed, for if not gathered it would rot; putting a few horses to pas-
ture overnight in someone's meadow was not that bad for grass would continue to grow. Altogether, Gypsies considered the world of nature as a kind of
public domain, and this included the "stray" chicken encountered on the village path. An English Gypsy, Manfri Wood, recalls regularly poaching with
grown-ups as a youngster before World War II. "We all believed that three
things belonged naturally to all men: the wood that lies on the ground, the
birds and beasts that live in the forest and on the heath and the fish in the
water. These were all free for the taking and no man had any right to deny
another the privilege of the taking." Wood owned a dog trained to catch
chickens. "Wherever we travelled and whatever part of the country we were
in, we always had chicken for dinner as long as this bitch was alive."[35] The
Jenische Engelbert Wittich reported the same attitude: taking a chicken or
goose from people who had so much more than the Gypsies was not considered a matter of consequence.[36] Women were known to carry under their
long skirt a special bag for hiding their booty.

According to a Gypsy legend, which is told in many different versions,
before the crucifixion of Jesus a Gypsy stole the fourth nail, intended for
Jesus' heart. In gratitude, God gave the Gypsies a heavenly license to steal
from the *gadzé*. Regardless of whether this story is considered an authentic
Gypsy narrative or an invention of their enemies, the legend reflects accu-
rately a widespread attitude among Gypsies toward the non-Gypsy world.[37]

Another way of extracting money from non-Gypsies was fortune-telling. A
favorite scheme involved "finding" a miniature human skull (actually the head
of a small pigeon) in an egg, a sign of a curse that could be alleviated by
depositing a large sum of money in a cloth. This cloth, in turn, had to be kept
by the fortune-teller overnight. The person defrauded never again saw either
the money or the Gypsy perpetrating this confidence trick.[38] Variations on
this scheme consisted of driving out spirits from sick cattle or praying for the
health of a sick person, naturally for a substantial payment of money. As late as
1954, a Gypsy fortune-teller was able to extract DM 7,200 (about $5,000)
from a seventy-one-year-old German woman on the pretense that by burying
money she could bring back a son missing in Russia.[39] It is the simple-minded
mentality of the rural population, argues a contemporary German author, that
enables the Gypsies to trick them out of large sums of money. But, he goes on,
it is difficult to reproach them for exploiting the almost incredible naïveté of
their victims.[40] Persons defrauded by these kinds of schemes are unlikely to
accept such exculpations that blame the victim rather than the perpetrator.

Other routines appear to be timeless and universal. Both the Belgian Jan
Yoors, writing about Gypsies in France during the 1930s and 1940s, and
Isabel Fonseca, who spent much time with Gypsies in the Balkans during the

Inside the caravan of a Gypsy family in Munich in 1947. COURTESY OF FOTOARCHIV O. SCHMIDT.

late 1980s, describe the "scratching scheme": Several Gypsy girls, badly dressed and unkempt, would enter a butcher shop while scratching their scalp and arms as if for lice. Continuing this demonstrative scratching with vigor, they would then touch meat, hams or sausages with their dirty little hands. Sometimes they were chased away, but more often they would be given the soiled articles at a very low price or for nothing. Once out of the store, the scratching stopped abruptly, but by then it was too late for the merchant to retrieve his goods.[41]

Gypsies observe numerous tabus that guard against contamination by what is considered *marime*, or unclean. Thus dishes are not washed in the same vessel used for washing clothes; there are strict rules about washing various parts of the body. Unfortunately, many of these rules are more concerned with maintaining ritual purity than cleanliness. Polluting dirt can be visible, but it must be a clear distance from the clean. Thus feces outside a home are acceptable whereas indoor toilets, close to food, are shunned; the chemical toilets in modern caravans often remain unused for the same reason.[42] Isabel Fonseca tells of a rich Gypsy in the newly independent Republic of Moldova who had built himself a palace. There were nine turrets, three grand salons and balconies over an inner court, but there were no bathrooms or toilets.[43] Not surprisingly, non-Gypsies who do not know why Gypsies prefer a hedge to a communal lavatory or flush toilet in their home interpret this conduct as filthy and violating all sanitary principles.

The same goes for other aspects of housekeeping. Gypsies take excellent care of the inside of their wagon or caravan, which often show dazzling displays of china, mirrors, carpets and elaborate formica ceilings. The outside, on the other hand, is generally indescribably dirty. Rubbish is tossed out the windows or is simply swept out the back door. The backyards of houses inhabited by Gypsies frequently are full of litter and junk.[44] Gypsies are aware of the sanitary norms of the society in which they live but simply do not share the values of that society. Neighbors and health authorities naturally take a dim view of such practices, which confirm the prevalent stereotype of Gypsies as slovenly and dirty.

These, then, are some examples illustrating the juxtaposition of stereotype and reality. On the other hand, many of the other accusations leveled at the Gypsies originate in myth and simple prejudice. Gypsies are *not* promiscuous; indeed, their sexual mores are quite strict. They do *not* steal children, a charge that probably arises from the fact that the generally dark-looking Gypsies sometimes have blond offspring. Killing may occasionally result from a tribal feud or blood revenge, but Gypsies generally do *not* commit murder. Though highly skilled at stealing, few Gypsies commit burglary. Open houses might be victimized, but Gypsies have a superstitious fear of closed doors and windows as well as of evil spirits that wander about at night. Hence most thefts are carried out during the day and without the use of burglary tools or force.

By and large, then, Gypsies are not a violent people, and many stories attest to their generosity, strong sense of family loyalty and friendship. Crime statistics in regard to German Gypsies before and during the Nazi regime are not very reliable. One study of Gypsy crime in Upper Bavaria in 1938 found that 75 percent of Gypsy men and 84 percent of women had a criminal record,[45] but most of these violations involved the disregard of various restrictive ordinances and theft. Most basically, the misdeeds of individuals cannot cast guilt upon an entire group of people. Moreover, many of the negative traits and social practices described above did not hold true for the sedentary and occasionally prosperous Gypsy population. Some Gypsies had assimilated to their German environment and practiced ordinary crafts or trades; not a few had intermarried or lived with German partners. Yet during a time when large numbers of Gypsies still followed a seminomadic way of life, many aspects of their social organization and lifestyle clashed with the values of their sedentary surroundings. Many Germans regarded them with a mixture of fascination, fear, distrust and rejection. By and large, therefore, Gypsies were a highly unpopular (not to say despised) minority. When the Nazis intensified the harassment and persecution practiced by earlier regimes, most of their neighbors remained superbly indifferent. Worse, as we shall see, pressure for stepping up the harsh treatment meted out to Gypsies came not only from the top Nazi leadership but also from the party's rank and file and from the German population itself.

Part I

THE PREWAR YEARS:
A THREE-TRACK POLICY

When Adolf Hitler became chancellor of Germany on January 30, 1933, Gypsies constituted a small minority of approximately 26,000 people of no particular interest to the Nazi leadership. That indifference changed gradually and largely as a result of pressure from below. In a political and social climate that stressed law and order, Gypsies, long regarded as asocial and given to crime, drew increased hostility. Many of them were itinerants and as such did not fit into the new society of stable social relations that the Nazis sought to build. They were said to not accept the value of regular work and were accused of being a burden upon welfare agencies. Last but not least, many Gypsies' dark complexion marked them as an alien group and inevitably drew the attention of those who desired a racially pure state rid of all foreign elements. In response to these concerns, as we shall see in the next three chapters, the regime started to give increased attention to the "Gypsy problem."

Gypsy policy evolved along three tracks, each approach following the other more or less consecutively. First, local and state authorities intensified the measures of control and harassment they had used in previous years. Second, from about 1937 on, the regime's plans for the prevention of crime took special note of Gypsies and subjected them to intense scrutiny and, at times, incarceration in concentration camps. Third, racial legislation enacted against the Jews in 1935 came to be applied also to Gypsies. Beginning in 1938, decrees issued against the "Gypsy plague" made explicit mention of the alleged racial inferiority of the so-called *Zigeunermischlinge* (Gypsies of mixed ancestry). Much of the incoherence of Nazi policy toward the Gypsies arises from the fact that the three tracks of Nazi policy toward the Gypsies overlapped and at times conflicted with each other. Thus, for example, the criterion of social adjustment sometimes could override racial origin. It is also important to note that despite the increased use of racial rhetoric, many Nazi measures directed against the Gypsies continued to include Gypsy-like itinerants, the so-called white Gypsies (Jenische). Although they were of German origin and were not Gypsies racially, they lived and conducted themselves like Gypsies.

1

Track 1: Harassment Stepped Up

During the first three years of the Nazi regime, the treatment of the Gypsies did not change very much. The decrees and laws legislated during the Weimar Republic continued in force and new and similar measures were adopted. As we shall see later, some of the laws enacted by the new regime, such as the sterilization law of July 14, 1933, and the law against dangerous professional criminals of November 24, 1933, affected Gypsies somewhat more than the general population. However, this legislation was not aimed specifically at the Gypsies.

Controls and Surveillance Continued

In March 1933, a coordinating body of the German states approved the policy statement on the "struggle against the Gypsy plague," drafted in 1929 and mentioned in the introduction. This step did not lead automatically to a uniform national policy, but several states did enact laws and regulations as suggested by the compact. Thus on August 10, 1933, Bremen adopted the Law for the Protection of the Population against Molestation by Gypsies, Travelers and Work-Shy. The legislation and the implementing regulations, issued on October 27, 1933, generally followed the Bavarian law of 1926.[1]

On May 23–25, 1934, allegedly in response to repeated complaints from the population,[2] the state of Baden conducted an unannounced search of all Gypsy dwellings. The decree ordering this operation stated that "Gypsy-like itinerants (half-Gypsies and travelers)" were to be treated like Gypsies.[3] The search yielded a count of 1,019 persons, 568 of them under the age of twenty. False papers and weapons were confiscated, and in sixty-one cases charges were brought for various violations of law. A year later, Karl Siegfried Bader, a state official, reported on the situation in Baden at a meeting of the International Criminal Police Commission in Copenhagen, Denmark. All Gypsies and Gypsy-like itinerants required special identity cards with pictures and fingerprints. They were not allowed to travel in "hordes," and licenses for the itinerant trade were issued only to those who had a permanent domicile. As a foreign element, Bader concluded, Gypsies would never become full-fledged members of German society. Those who violated law and order could expect no consideration; incorrigible elements, he noted, might have to be sterilized.[4] In January 1937, new instructions were sent to the police of Baden for the "fight against the Gypsy nuisance," which called for strict enforcement of all relevant laws and regulations.[5] Pursuant to this exhortation, and in a case repeated often in other locations, two Gypsies in the district of Mosbach were sentenced to fourteen days in jail for traveling in a "horde."[6] Similar orders for more aggressive action against Gypsies were issued in the states of Thuringia, Württemberg and Bavaria.[7]

As in the past, the *Zigeunerzentrale* (Central Office for Gypsy Affairs) in Munich was well ahead of everyone else in suggesting measures for attacking "the Gypsy problem" and in pressing for united action. The Bavarian legislation of 1926, as a memo to the Bavarian Ministry of the Interior dated March 28, 1934, pointed out, had proven itself and was well suited to serve as the basis for an all-German law. Such a law was badly needed, because the various states did not act in a uniform manner, despite the adoption in principle of the 1926 guidelines for police action against Gypsies. As a result, the practice of expelling Gypsies from one location to another continued. One of the special merits of the Bavarian law, the memo stressed, was its inclusion of "work-shy travelers" who, on account of their large numbers, constituted a greater threat to law and order than the Gypsies; the number of those considered Gypsies in a racial sense was small.[8] In another memo to the Ministry of the Interior, dated August 30, 1935, Munich police officials argued that the time had come for more radical measures. Those belonging to the Gypsy race, who constituted a foreign element in the population, should be expelled from the country, either by direct force or by eliminating their ability to make a living; German travelers should be made sedentary. Much time, energy and work could be saved, it was maintained, by attacking the evil at its roots and implementing the principles it recommended throughout Germany.[9]

Authorities in Berlin, meanwhile, were moving in the same general direction. On June 6, 1936, the German and Prussian minister of the interior issued a decree concerning the "fight against the Gypsy plague," which called for a stepped-up effort. Foreign Gypsies were to be prevented from entering Germany; those found in the country were to be expelled. German Gypsies and travelers, the decree ordered, should be made sedentary so that the police could more easily control and supervise them. The concrete measures to be taken followed the Bavarian model,[10] but in the absence of an all-German police force the minister could do no more than recommend that the other German states issue the necessary implementing instructions to their police forces. One of the recommendations acted upon involved staging raids "from time to time" on Gypsy camps.

The German states had demonstrated their ability to act cooperatively in regard to the problem of beggars, and this model of united action was now to be extended to Gypsies and travelers. The first roundup of beggars and vagabonds, carried out with the assistance of Nazi storm troopers, occurred in September 1933, and additional sweeps took place during the following months. At first, in conformity to traditional practice, those arrested would receive a stiff warning or be brought before a judge and sentenced to several days in jail.[11] Occasionally, "disorderly elements" were also sent to concentration camps, especially Dachau, though this practice at first drew occasional criticism. Franz von Epp was a longtime member of the Nazi party who, on March 9, 1933, on orders of Hitler, set up a Nazi government in Bavaria. In March 1934 he expressed the view that too many of the 2,200 inmates of the Dachau concentration camp were asocial elements who should be handled by the courts.[12] By early 1935, the rigorous measures employed to clear the streets of beggars had been largely successful, helped undoubtedly by the improved economic situation.

From the beginning, raids against beggars occasionally also targeted Gypsies; after the decree of June 1936 the Gypsies were included more systematically. A circular issued by the Bavarian Ministry of the Interior of June 22 directed that operations against beggars, held in accordance with the decree of June 6, include Gypsies and travelers.[13] The *Landrat* (chief magistrate) of Esslingen reported to the minister of the interior of Württemberg on April 13, 1937, that an operation against beggars held on April 3 had led to the arrest of sixteen persons on charges of begging and vagrancy. No Gypsies had been found in the district on the day of the operation, but Gypsies did appear from time to time, protected by a license to conduct an itinerant trade. The official suggested that Gypsies no longer be issued these licenses, since they served only to facilitate begging. "With the help of such measures, employed with determination," he concluded, "it should be possible to stop the Gypsy plague, the ultimate aim being the extermination of these parasites."[14]

On July 8, 1937, a sweep was held simultaneously in several cities of the Ruhr district. In the city of Dortmund, the chief of police reported a week later, a total of 146 Gypsies and Gypsy-like itinerants living in twenty-three caravans, had been counted. There were seventy-six males and seventy females; eighty-one were children under the age of fourteen. All of them were German citizens; one was a member of the Nazi party. Eight Gypsies had regular employment, and seven were supported by welfare, whereas the rest consisted for the most part of unemployed musicians. Two women had an itinerant trade license and peddled notions. A search of the caravans and camping places had not yielded anything untoward, though several children had incomplete identity cards. The chief of police ended his report with the recommendation that similar operations be conducted again in the future, and, if possible, simultaneously for all of Germany.[15]

In the city of Bochum, the raid of July 8 included sedentary Gypsies. Many of these, the chief of police noted in his report, lived in caravans. Although most of the inhabitants of these wagons were properly registered with the police, such persons could give no assurance of being permanent residents; for the sake of public safety, they therefore had been included in the search operation. Altogether 131 Gypsies had been counted, of whom 42 were found not to be registered. Seventeen had no identity cards. The Bochum chief of police too concluded that the operation had been a success and suggested that it be repeated yearly.[16] A similar operation took place on August 5, 1938, and yielded very similar results. In Dortmund, apart from problems with incomplete identity cards, no violations of law were discovered and no "wanted or suspicious persons were encountered."[17]

The operations targeted against Gypsies and Gypsy-like itinerants described above continued a pattern of control that had been in use for many decades. The rhetoric describing these sweeps at times became a bit more heated. More radical measures were said to be needed, and some officials talked of sterilization and even extermination of "the parasites." Still, none of this represented anything terribly new. As we shall see in a subsequent chapter, such ideas, taken from the teachings of racial hygiene, had been widely discussed in the 1920s; proposals for the elimination of "inferior" elements had been put forth since the turn of the century. Moreover, words such as "extermination" did not necessarily mean physical killing. Hitler, for example, had often spoken of the "extermination of Germandom" in the Austro-Germanic empire, but the context indicated that he meant by this no more than the process of de-Germanization or a policy of slowly squeezing out German elements and traditions.[18] Eventually, extermination did indeed assume a far more deadly meaning, but in the years 1933–1937 few thought of such radical measures—either against Jews or against Gypsies. For the time being, the treatment of the Gypsies essentially still remained "harassment as usual."

Municipal Gypsy Camps, 1933–1938

The presence of Gypsy caravans in the inner cities had long been a source of irritation for the people there as well as for municipal authorities. Gypsies would spend the winter months in these temporary camps; in many cases they put their caravans on rented lots that lacked sanitary facilities and other amenities, and the people living in the vicinity resented these uninvited neighbors and their different lifestyle. In the introduction, I discussed the situation in Frankfurt/Main in the later 1920s that led to the establishment of a "concentration camp" for Gypsies. After 1933, an additional motive for setting up such camps was the new regime's policy of urban renewal—an endeavor to clean up the inner cities and liquidate unauthorized shacks and huts. All of these Gypsy camps, it should be stressed, were created by municipal authorities rather than by state governments or the central government in Berlin.

In a response to an inquiry from his counterpart in Frankfurt, in March 1937 the police chief of Cologne described the Gypsy camp in his city as an arrangement that had proven itself. The camp, near Venloer Street, had been established in 1935 by the municipality of Cologne. It was large enough to hold about three hundred caravans, though the actual occupancy at any one time was no more than fifty to sixty caravans with about four hundred to five hundred persons. The administrator of the camp was a former member of the SS, but the camp resembled a vacation campsite more than a concentration camp. The administrator assigned lots to newcomers and collected the rent, which on the average was RM 3 a month per caravan. He also maintained a list of the occupants and made sure that they were registered with the police, a requirement that all Germans had to fulfill (such registration continues to be required in Germany and most European countries). In order to maintain public quiet and law and order, the police chief concluded, it had not become necessary to install a special police post in the camp.[19] The authors of an essay on the Cologne Gypsy camp published in 1991 add a few additional details. The camp was set up for occupants of caravans who had been living on public lots or had rented space from private owners. Those without a caravan of their own could obtain quarters in two old camp barracks. The majority of Cologne Gypsies occupied private apartments and were not affected by the establishment of the Gypsy camp. However, those receiving welfare payments had to move to the camp if they wanted to keep their financial support.[20]

Following repeated complaints from the population and from local Nazi party leaders, the city of Frankfurt established a new Gypsy camp near Dieselstrasse in the summer of 1937. When plans for this camp became known, those living nearby protested, but their complaints were overruled. By January 1938, the camp held 122 persons, most of them apparently poor and needy. Some of the inmates in the new camp lived in their own caravans; for those without caravans the welfare office of Frankfurt bought second-hand moving vans and converted them into dwellings. Negotiations were under way to move to the camp several Gypsy families living in the city in private apartments as well as unemployed carnival actors, presumably "white Gypsies." The camp was supervised by two police officers each of whom was on duty twenty-four hours at a time. The inhabitants of the camp were counted each morning and evening. Since the Gypsies could no longer live from begging, fortune-telling or stealing, the welfare office reported on January 17, 1938, those in need received welfare payments. They were, however, lower than regular welfare payments made to needy fellow Germans. Efforts were made to find work for those without employment.[21]

The city of Düsseldorf set up a Gypsy camp in July 1936. Fourteen of the families moved there were from a large squatter camp known as the "wild settlement Heinefeld," which had been closed down; twenty-eight families were from similar locations. The primary motive here appears to have been a desire to rid the city of elements widely regarded as belonging to the *Lumpenproletariat*. On a large lot at the edge of town near the Höherweg the city erected four barracks for families, with each married couple having one room. A fifth barrack was built for single persons. Eventually Gypsies living in caravans were also brought there. The camp had a camp leader, an armed member of the SS, who was assisted by a police officer. The occupants of the camp could come and go at will, but they had to check in and out. A count was taken every morning. Nonresidents were not allowed to enter the Gypsy camp.[22]

In 1929, Berlin, Germany's capital, had a Gypsy population of 1,600 persons.[23] Here too the presence of Gypsy caravans had drawn criticism. The occasion for removing them was the staging of the Olympic Games in Berlin in the summer of 1936. All caravans were moved to a camp outside the city in order to reinforce Berlin's appearance as a model city and impress foreign visitors. Some Gypsies living in regular apartments were included in the measure. On July 16, 1936, about six hundred Gypsies were escorted by the police to the suburb of Marzahn, today a run-down former East German satellite city. At the time, the city of Berlin owned a lot there that had previously been used to dispose of sewage. The site was located next to a municipal cemetery, which further violated Gypsy ritual conventions. The camp at first had about 130 caravans; those without caravans were put up in barracks discarded by the Reich Labor Corps *(Reichsarbeitsdienst)*. Since these barracks did not have room for all those who needed shelter, some camp occupants had to sleep in the open. The camp had only three sources of water and two toilet facilities. There was no electricity and many dwellings could not be heated. Because of overcrowding and poor sanitary conditions, disease was rampant. Until March 1938, the welfare authorities reported 170 cases of illness requiring hospitalization. There were several outbreaks of communicable diseases such as diphtheria and tuberculosis; in March 1939 the municipal department of health diagnosed 40 percent of the camp inmates as afflicted with scabies.[24]

In 1937, an administrative barrack was added. It contained two "warming rooms" and a room for the delivery of babies, as well as quarters for the police guard and the camp administrator. By September 1938, the number of Gypsies in the camp had risen to 852. Three more barracks were built that year, but overcrowding continued and several families had to sleep on the ground under caravans. A school with five grades was organized in a barrack put up in 1938.[25] Despite the harsh conditions in the camp, a report of the Berlin municipality issued in 1937 made the self-serving observation that the hygienic situation represented an improvement over previous sites and noted that the Marzahn camp would serve as the place of residence for Gypsies moving to Berlin in the future.[26]

Similar municipal Gypsy camps existed in Kiel, Freiburg im Breisgau, Fulda, Magdeburg, Hannover and several other German cities. The degree of compulsion associated with them varied; some were fenced in, others were not. The occupants of these camps were not "inmates." They could vote with their feet if conditions did not suit them, and the number of persons in these camps indeed fluctuated widely.[27] In some cases, as in Karlsruhe, the authorities limited the time that owners of caravans could stay in the camps, for they did not want to attract Gypsies who would spend the entire winter in their city.[28] Altogether, only a part of the total Gypsy population lived in these camps. Many Gypsies continued to live in their private houses or apartments. Some cities with substantial Gypsy populations such as Hamburg and Munich had no municipal camps at all.

After war broke out in 1939, as we shall see in a later chapter, the character of these camps changed. Freedom of movement was eliminated, supervision was tightened and the occupants were subjected to compulsory labor. However, during the early years of the Nazi regime, the Gypsy camps discussed here served primarily to rid the cities of unwanted caravan dwellers, as did the "concentration camp" that was set up in Frankfurt/Main in 1929. The municipal Gypsy camps during the years 1933–1938 fit into the pattern of harassment and control, albeit stepped up and intensified, typical of the pre-Nazi period in Germany.

2

Track 2: Crime Prevention

The Nazis' rise to power was helped by widespread concern in German society about moral decay and the spread of crime. Much of the apprehension about the alleged crime wave resulted from sensational media reporting. The Nazis took advantage of public anxieties and presented themselves as the champions of law and order. They would end, they pledged, the constitutional restrictions that had tied the hands of the police and led to the coddling of criminals. After Hitler assumed power in January 1933, the new government soon adopted measures that promised to attack the problem of crime "at its root." Gypsies were one of several groups caught in a steadily widening net of presumed criminals.

Preventive Police Custody

The Nazis' new, more aggressive approach to crime first targeted so-called professional criminals and habitual sexual offenders. In addition to more severe sentences and castration, the Law against Dangerous Career Criminals of November 24, 1933, allowed unlimited "preventive police custody" for individuals twice convicted of a crime. Under the law, the decision for detention was to be made by the courts, but, starting in early 1935, the police, acting on its own, sent such "habitual criminals" to Dachau and other concentration camps. "Political criminals" sent there for "protective custody" consequently found themselves in the company of actual criminals, aggravating the tribulations experienced by political inmates in the dreaded camps. Subsequent decrees expanded the population targeted by the "prevention of crime," which came to include beggars, vagabonds, prostitutes, pimps, and the work-shy. Criminality gradually became a social category, and Gypsies, reputed to be asocial elements, soon became enmeshed in the new measures.[1]

Nazi ideology contributed an increased emphasis on the hereditary character of crime to police work. Solving the problem of crime and achieving a society without criminals, it was believed, required purging German society of racially inferior elements, for the roots of crime, more often then not, lay in the prevalence of bad racial stock. Such ideas became increasingly popular in police circles, and so did the shift to preventive crime fighting. Members of the detective force or criminal police (*Kriminalpolizei* or *Kripo*) in particular had long been interested in instituting preventive custody for habitual offenders, and most of them happily accepted the increased powers granted the police. In early 1935 Arthur Nebe became head of the Prussian Kripo and later assumed an important role in developing Nazi policy toward the Gypsies. He was among those who welcomed the switch to a preventive approach to crime. Several former colleagues recall that Nebe embraced the concept of preventive custody with enthusiasm. After the 1936 Berlin Olympic Games Nebe received a medal for successfully preventing crime during the games, attributed to a large roundup of "the usual suspects."[2] Equipped with arbitrary powers of arrest and detention, the criminal police gradually functioned more and more like the Gestapo, the secret political police. Despite an image of apolitical professionalism, the Kripo proved more acceptable to the Nazis than any other branch of the police; very few of its members needed purging after 1933.[3] When Kripo officers eventually received SS rank, this designation merely formalized a status most of them had earned through loyal and often enthusiastic service to the Nazi state.

The concept of crime had been expanding since 1933. On December 14, 1937, Minister of the Interior Wilhelm Frick, a party stalwart, issued a decree, Preventive Crime Fighting by the Police. The decree provided for two ways of preventing crime and protecting society. First, the police were authorized to put professional criminals and repeat offenders under systematic supervision. The police could now prohibit such individuals from leaving their place of residence without permission, oblige them to report to the police at regular intervals, and prohibit them from driving a car, using certain kinds of public transportation or owning weapons. Second, the police were given the right to take certain individuals into preventive custody. In addition to regular criminals, this provision included those "who, without being professional and habitual criminals, endanger the general public by their asocial conduct."[4] This definition was repeated in the implementing regulations issued on April 4, 1938, which construed as "asocial" all those who "demonstrate by their conduct, even if it is not criminal, that they are unwilling to adapt to the life of the community." Hence "asocial" were (1) persons who by repeatedly committing petty crimes violated the system of order established by the national socialist state, "for example, beggars, vagrants (Gypsies), prostitutes, alcoholics, those with contagious diseases, especially venereal diseases, who refuse treatment," and (2) persons without a criminal record who sought to escape the duty to work and became dependent for their support on the public, "for example, the work-shy, those who refuse to work, alcoholics." Preventive custody was to be used "primarily against asocials without a permanent residence."[5]

According to the implementing regulations, those taken into preventive custody were to be sent to concentration camps; the duration of their stay there was unlimited. Applications for the imposition of preventive custody were to be submitted by the local Kripo to the head office of the criminal police in Berlin. That office made the final decision regarding both the initiation and the termination of preventive custody; a review was to take place every twelve months.[6] No legal remedy was provided for these decisions. Given the elastic nature of the concept of "asocial," anyone without a permanent residence or a clear source of income could be caught in this dragnet. That this was indeed the intent of the decree was confirmed by Himmler in a circular of May 13, 1938. The old border between Germany and the recently annexed Austria had been abolished and there were no longer any passport requirements. In order to prevent Gypsies and Gypsy-like itinerants from moving at will across the former border, Himmler suggested that, if no other legal provision could be found, the authorities consider using the section of the decree of December 14, 1937, that provided for the imposition of preventive custody on those who endangered the general public by their asocial conduct.[7] In short, this decree represented a catchall measure that could be used against practically anyone whose conduct did not please the Nazi state. Not all measures aimed at preventing crime need violate the rule of law, but the system introduced here was clearly irreconcilable with any conception of due process.

Reorganization of the German Police

On June 17, 1936, Hitler appointed Heinrich Himmler head of the German police; henceforth he carried the title Reichsführer der SS und Chef der deutschen Polizei. Combining the SS with the police in effect gave a party organization control over a key state function and provided the SS with new powers of intimidation and terror. When Himmler assumed sole control of Germany's entire apparatus of repression, he was thirty-six years old; his right-hand man, Reinhard Heydrich, was thirty-two. Formally, Himmler was subordinated to Minister of the Interior Frick, but in practice the new head of the German police could do as he pleased. In August 1943 the superior status of the Reichsführer was given formal recognition when Himmler was made minister of the interior and Frick was given the consolation prize of head of the Protectorate of Bohemia and Moravia.[8]

Upon his appointment, Himmler divided the police into two departments: the Order Police (*Ordnungspolizei*), which carried out the traditional functions of the uniformed police force, and the Security Police (*Sicherheitspolizei*), which included the Gestapo and Kripo. "In the national socialist German state," Kripo head Nebe reflected later, "it is obvious that the struggle against the political enemy and against the asocial criminal must be directed by one

Heinrich Himmler and Reinhard Heydrich in 1938. COURTESY OF AP/ WIDE WORLD PHOTOS.

authority."[9] The Security Police, combining Gestapo and Kripo, was led by SS Group Leader Heydrich who continued as head of the SS Sicherheitsdienst (SD), the Nazi party's security service that collected domestic intelligence and maintained ideological control. Shortly after the beginning of the war, on September 27, 1939, Security Police and SD were combined in the new Reich Main Security Office (*Reichssicherheitshauptamt*, or RSHA), an arrangement that institutionalized Heydrich's control over these two police forces. Aligning complementary party and state agencies created a powerful new tool for persecuting those deemed to be enemies of the Nazi state.[10] The reorganization of the police was to have repercussions also for the Gypsies.

On September 20, 1936, the head office of the Prussian Kripo assumed responsibility for criminal police operations in all of Germany; on July 16, 1937, it was renamed Reich Criminal Police Office (*Reichskriminalpolizeiamt*, or RKPA). In an article published in 1938, RKPA chief Nebe stressed that the Kripo had to protect the state not only against criminals but also against "all asocial individuals." The reorganized German criminal police, Nebe promised, "will operate in the spirit of genuine National Socialism and will fulfill its tasks without fault."[11]

The RKPA had a special department in charge of preventive crime measures; a separate bureau dealt with Gypsies.[12] On May 16, 1938, a Himmler decree announced that, effective October 1, 1938, the Central Office for Gypsy Affairs (*Zigeunerzentrale*)[13] in Munich would be moved to Berlin and reconstituted in the RKPA as Reich Central Office for Combating the Gypsy Nuisance (*Reichszentrale zur Bekämpfung des Zigeunerunwesens*). The task of this office was "to compile information on all Gypsies in Germany and to decide on all measures necessary for combating the Gypsies."[14] By the time the Munich Gypsy office was transferred to Berlin, it had 33,524 files covering the following types of individuals:

1. 18, 138 Gypsies and Gypsy *Mischlinge* (persons of mixed ancestry)
2. 10,788 Gypsy-like itinerants (*nach Zigeunerart umherziehende*)
3. 4,598 others, including sedentary persons conducting an itinerant trade[15]

Since June 5, 1936, under an authorization issued by the German Ministry of the Interior, the Munich Gypsy office had served as liaison with the newly established International Central Office for Combating the Gypsy Nuisance in Vienna.[16] That function too was now taken over by the RKPA.

Operation Work-Shy

It did not take long for the new police apparatus to be put to use. On January 26, 1938, Himmler ordered the Gestapo to take action against the work-shy. The decree acknowledged the jurisdiction of the Kripo for preventive crime measures but noted that on account of the heterogeneous character of the population involved the Kripo was not yet ready to act. Those asocial elements unwilling to work, on the other hand, represented a clearly defined group, and the Gestapo was therefore ordered to proceed against them and take them into "protective custody" to be served in concentration camp Buchenwald. The arrest of the work-shy was to be a one-time action.[17]

It should be noted that this is the only known instance of the Gestapo's involving itself directly in matters concerning "asocials." The system of protective custody, authorized under an emergency decree issued on February 22, 1933, was generally used by the Gestapo only against political enemies of the regime. Apparently it was utilized here against asocials because in a tightening labor market Himmler was anxious to put everybody to work without delay, and at this time he saw the Gestapo as the most appropriate instrument to achieve this goal.

In the spring of 1938 the SS opened the first of its economic enterprises located in or near concentration camps in Sachsenhausen and Buchenwald. Hitler and Speer had decided that bricks and stone for the reconstruction of Berlin and other major cities could be produced by the inmates of the concentration camps, and Himmler and his chief of administration, Oswald Pohl, eagerly embraced this plan, which opened up a new source of influence and income for the SS.[18] In a lecture given about a year later, SS–Oberführer Greifelt, Himmler's liaison person to the Four Year Plan, acknowledged the role that economic considerations had played in the action against the work-shy:

> The tight situation in the labor market necessitated the imposition of work-discipline for the country. Hence persons who were unwilling to participate in the working life of the nation and who were merely scraping by as work-shy or asocials and making the cities and main road unsafe had to be dealt with by coercive means and set to work. Following the lead of the "Four Year Plan" department, the Gestapo took energetic and vigorous steps in this matter.[19]

The decree ordering the Gestapo into action defined the work-shy as all men of working age whose ability to work had been established by a medical examination but who had refused work without justification in two instances or had left a place of employment without a compelling reason. Local labor exchanges were instructed to establish the identity of the work-shy by April 3, 1938 and to transmit the names to the Gestapo. In addition to relying on this source of information, the secret police, working in cooperation with other appropriate authorities such as welfare offices, was to make its own inquiries. Between April 3 and 9, the work-shy were to be taken into custody. Unless the arrested persons could justify their idleness by reason of sickness or a special family situation, they were to be sent to concentration camp Buchenwald, with the continuation of their incarceration to be evaluated every three months.[20]

The implementing instructions issued locally stressed that only men able and willing to work were to be seized. "Not suitable are drinkers, old vagrants, professional or habitual criminals, Gypsies and similar elements."[21] Postponed because of the plebiscite on the Anschluss (annexation of Austria) scheduled for April 10, the action began on April 21 and was ordered to be concluded by April 30. The names of those who could not be seized by that date were to be handed over to the Kripo.[22]

We know little about the results of this first action against the work-shy. According to one account, the Gestapo arrested some 1,500 "asocials."[23] Apparently the SS leadership was not pleased with the performance of the Gestapo, for on June 1 Heydrich issued an order for a new and more sweeping operation to be carried out by the Kripo during the week of June 13–18. The decree of December 12, 1937, on preventive crime fighting, Heydrich wrote, had given the police extensive powers to proceed not only against professional criminals but also against all asocial elements who were a burden on society and harmed its well-being. "However, I have had to note that so far the decree has not been applied with the necessary severity. The rigorous implementation of the Four Year Plan requires the participation of all those able to work and does not tolerate that asocial persons shirk work and thus sabotage the Four Year Plan." The decree, therefore, ordered that each Kripo district office (they numbered fourteen in 1938) take into preventive custody at least two hundred male asocial persons who were able to work. Especially to be targeted were vagrants, beggars (even if they had a permanent residence), "Gypsies and Gypsy-like itinerants if they have not demonstrated a readiness to take up regular employment or have a criminal record," pimps and others with a criminal record involving violent acts. Also to be seized were male Jews who had been sentenced to a jail term of more than one month. Those arrested were to be sent to concentration camp Buchenwald. The total number taken into custody was to be reported to the RKPA by June 20.[24]

By the summer of 1938, the labor shortage had become quite serious. The Kripo did not want to be accused of contributing to a failure of the Four Year Plan, and it responded with a wave of arrests that occasionally went beyond the instructions received. Some of those seized, the RKPA admonished the district offices on June 23, had been work-shy in the past but were now regularly employed. Their arrest, therefore, was not authorized and they were to be released forthwith.[25] This time around, then, the results were far better than expected; according to Greifelt, Himmler's liaison to the Four Year Plan, by 1939 the concentration camps held more than 10,000 individuals categorized as asocials.[26] Buchenwald had received 4,600; the rest were sent to other camps such as Sachsenhausen, Dachau, Flossenbürg and Mauthausen. In Flossenbürg and Mauthausen the SS had just begun to operate large stone quarries, and the new arrivals were put to work in a literally back-breaking routine that led to many deaths. According to non-Gypsy inmates who survived, the treatment meted out to the "asocials," their camp uniform marked with a black triangle, was harsh and brutal. In the hierarchy of the SS they ranked very low, only above Jews and homosexuals. Their stay in the camps was designed to "educate" them and make them into worthy members of what the Nazis called the German people's community. Many did not survive this schooling, which was accompanied by systematic brutalities. The asocials had a mortality rate higher than the political or criminal inmates of the camps.[27] On the other hand, the new inmates were to be treated in such a way that they could serve as a labor force in the new SS economic enterprises. Each of the work-shy seized was examined by a physician who had to certify that the person arrested was "suitable for camp and work."[28] Then as later, the tension between these two functions of the concentration camps remained unresolved.

The proportion of Gypsies among those arrested as asocials during Operation Work-Shy in June of 1938 is not known, though a few figures are available from some localities. In Aachen, eleven Gypsies were arrested during the week of June 13–18 and sent to the concentration camp Sachsenhausen.[29] In Dortmund, eight of a total of sixty male Gypsies were seized.[30] In the district of Verden near Bremen, fifteen persons were arrested as work-shy, four of them Gypsies.[31] In Cloppenburg, near Bremen, thirty-five men were seized; eleven of them were Gypsies.[32] In the greater Hamburg area, about one hundred Gypsies were arrested and sent to Sachsenhausen.[33] We also have a few relevant statistics from the camps, though they are not complete because Gypsies were generally registered as asocials. Buchenwald had almost 8,000 inmates in 1938, about 4,600 of whom were labeled as work-shy;[34] as of February 2, 1939, there were said to be 107 Gypsies in Buchenwald.[35] In Sachsenhausen the camp held 4,887 inmates listed as work-shy on November 24, 1938; 371, or 7.6 percent, of these were Gypsies.[36] Operation Work-Shy was clearly targeted against those the Nazis considered asocial and was not directed specifically against Gypsies.

Police files on individual Gypsies preserved in the state archives of Magdeburg and Düsseldorf enable us to look beyond mere statistics and to gain some insight into the human tragedies involved. They also show that as a result of the prevailing hostility toward Gypsies, often the mere fact that someone was a Gypsy without a steady place of residence or job resulted in their being labeled a criminal and subjected them to preventive custody in a concentration camp. Thus, for example, Wilhelm L. was arrested as "work-shy (Gypsy)" on June 13, 1938, and sent to Buchenwald. The police report justified his classification as work-shy on the grounds that "he does not want to have a steady and regular job and prefers to engage in business."[37]

Perhaps still adhering to an old sense of professionalism, Kripo officers sought to convince themselves that they were arresting criminals and not just asocial persons. Hence the reports sent to the RKPA in Berlin included a description of the life of the arrested person that was called "criminal life history." This could create the paradoxical situation, exemplified by the case of Georg A., a twenty-one-year-old unemployed Gypsy, that a life story headlined "criminal life history" ended with the sentence, "So far he has not been involved in any criminal activity here." A. was sent to Buchenwald on June 14, 1938.[38] The same ending is found in the "criminal life history" of Karl P., a twenty-three-year-old Gypsy musician, whose "criminal" conduct consisted of the fact that he had never had steady employment. He ended up in Sachsenhausen and was still there as of November 1942, more than four years later.[39]

Some of those arrested in June 1938 were incarcerated even longer, often being moved from camp to camp. Josef F., born in 1909 in Hungary, was seized because he had neither a fixed place of residence nor steady employment. On the arrest form, the reason for his apprehension was given as "Gypsy (work-shy)." He was sent to Sachsenhausen, Mauthausen, Dachau, and eventually back again to Sachsenhausen. The last date of record there is September 9, 1944.[40] We do not know whether he lived to see the liberation of the camps. Wilhelm L. was a musician born in 1891 who had a wife and five children. His first destination was Buchenwald; from there he was transferred to Natzweiler in 1942, then to Dachau in 1943, and eventually back to Natzweiler. He was still alive on April 1, 1944; his subsequent fate is not recorded.[41]

Albert L. was a fifty-year-old Gypsy peddler who was arrested on June 13, 1938. His "criminal life history" accused him of never having worked in his life. "He has always been wandering about the country and therefore falls under the decree about work-shy persons." According to the notation by the examining physician, L. was "suitable for camp and work." He died in Buchenwald on October 9, 1942, of "acute heart failure." According to standard practice, his next of kin were informed that the body of the deceased could not be returned to them "for hygienic reasons." His ashes were available upon written request.[42] The sixty-seven-year-old Maximilian L. escaped being sent to a concentration camp in 1938. His medical examination found him to be unsuitable for work because of high blood pressure. However, his reprieve was only temporary. In March 1943, L., by then seventy-two years old, was sent to Auschwitz.[43]

Some of the Gypsies arrested during Operation Work-Shy did have criminal records. Michael L., who was married with four children, had a total of twenty-five convictions, among them begging, vagrancy, theft, fraud, embezzlement, robbery, and causing serious bodily injury. He was sent to Buchenwald and was still being held on May 26, 1943.[44] The criminal record of thirty-nine-year-old musician Gustav L. included desertion from the army in 1918, theft, and illegal possession of a firearm. On account of an injury incurred during his military service in World War I he was found to have limited work capabilities. He too was sent to Buchenwald where he died on August 19, 1942.[45] We do not know how many of the Gypsies taken into preventive custody in June of 1938 had a criminal record. Needless to say, even those who were truly hardened criminals should not have been subjected to the life of torment that was the lot of the concentration camp inmates. Moreover, as we have seen, the main purpose of Operation Work-Shy appears to have been the procurement of slave labor rather than the prevention of crime. All of the concentration camps established for the "asocials" in 1938 were set up in conjunction with newly opened economic enterprises operated by the SS.[46]

On April 6, 1939, the RKPA informed the Kripo offices that on the occasion of Hitler's birthday on April 20 they intended to free "a considerable number of inmates under preventive custody." The local offices were asked to submit lists of candidates for release.[47] However, the number of Gypsies who benefited from this amnesty was small. In Sachsenhausen, for example, not a single Gypsy was included among the 954 "asocials" released.[48] In a circular issued on June 18, 1940, the RKPA explicitly excluded Gypsies from consideration for release.[49] Still, as can be learned from the police files that have been preserved, some of the Gypsies arrested during Operation Work-Shy were eventually set free. Although the ultimate decision on releasing an inmate in preventive custody was in the hands of the RKPA in Berlin, local Kripo offices could make recommendations. Thus when a family applied for the release of a father, husband or son, the local Kripo office sometimes supported such an application; in other instances they opposed it.

August L. from Quedlinburg was thirty-eight years old when he was arrested on June 13, 1938. At the obligatory medical examination, he claimed to be suffering from a kidney and bladder disorder, but the examining physician merely diagnosed him as malnourished and L. was sent to Sachsenhausen. In October of the same year, his wife applied for his release, and neither the mayor of Quedlinburg nor the Kripo of Magdeburg expressed any objection. L. was set free on August 25, 1939. Before leaving the concentration camp, he had to sign a standard form promising not to talk about the life of the camp, and not to say or write anything against the National Socialist state and its institutions, and stating that he had subscribed to the declaration voluntarily.[50]

Thirty-one-year-old Gypsy musician Josef S. from Cologne had been arrested on June 14, 1938, and sent to Sachsenhausen. His mother submitted a petition for his release to Hitler, which remained unanswered. On December 31, she wrote to the Gestapo in Berlin. Her son, she pleaded, was sorely missed by her as well by his wife and their four children. He was a good boy who had thought that he could support his family by playing music. "Because of this he has indeed put himself outside of the *Volksgemeinschaft* [the people's community], to which he, as a German, belongs." The mother was confident that from now on her son would "earn his daily bread by working honestly and conscientiously with his hands" and that he would not violate any laws. If her son could be released, she concluded her letter, she would "express her appreciation by gratitude and loyalty to the Führer. Heil Hitler." S. was set free on July 3, 1939.[51]

Such applications from family members were not always successful. Twenty-two-year-old Gypsy musician Karl L. had been arrested as work-shy on June 13, 1938, and sent to Buchenwald. On February 16, 1940, the official in charge of Gypsy affairs at the Magdeburg Kripo office supported the mother's request for his release. Workers were urgently needed for road repairs. Moreover, he added, "it is to be assumed that the above named will now condescend to accept steady work." This application was turned down in Berlin, however, and more than two years later, on October 15, 1942, the mother sent her letter directly to concentration camp Natzweiler. My son, she wrote, "has been incarcerated for four years and four months. I am sick and not able to work and therefore cannot support myself." She received no welfare payments; another son had already died in custody. "My son is willing to accept work here and support me."

That request too was ignored. By the time the desperate mother submitted her next application in February 1943, another son had died in a concentration camp. This time she addressed herself to Dr. Ritter, the Berlin official in charge of researching the racial characteristics of the German Gypsy population (there is more about him in chapter 3). Included in her letter was a request for the release of her husband. My son and my husband, she pleaded, have been in custody for four and a half years. Two other sons had died in concentration camps. She was now living on the meager earnings of two other children who were crippled; there was not enough food to go around and her sickness was getting steadily worse. Neither her husband nor her son had a criminal record. Both of them were willing to work. "I am confident that my husband and my son have learned this in the camp." This letter too failed to produce results. On March 2, 1943, L. was transferred from Natzweiler to Dachau. From there he was sent to Buchenwald on September 25, 1944. Whether he or his father survived these tribulations is not known.[52]

In the case of fifty-one-year-old Simon L. from Quedlinburg, the wife's request for the release of her husband had the support of the mayor and the Kripo of Magdeburg. She was even able to enlist a lawyer, which was highly unusual in this type of case. In a letter sent to the Kripo of Magdeburg on July 31, 1939, two attorneys from Osnabrück inquired why L. had been taken into preventive custody since, according to the prisoner's next of kin, he had no criminal record. A brother had been released a few days ago, and L. too could find work immediately. When these interventions failed to produce results, the wife appealed to Hitler and Himmler, but these applications too led nowhere. On May 12, 1941, in a letter to the RKPA, the Kripo of Magdeburg once again argued for the release of L. He had been in preventive custody since June 13, 1938, and his incarceration must have had an impact on him. The labor market being what it was, the prisoner could undoubtedly find work immediately. The wife could not work on account of a heart condition, and she and her two children had to subsist on a monthly welfare payment of RM 28.85; all three were undernourished. The release of the husband, therefore, would provide a remedy for the dire condition of this family. The RKPA turned down this recommendation. "The conduct of the husband in the work and reeducation camp," they replied on May 26, "provides no assurance that his future behavior will be unblemished." About seven months later, another petition by the wife drew the same response. On October 14, 1942, L. died in Sachsenhausen.[53]

At times, the local Kripo office opposed the release of a prisoner. The twenty-three-year-old musician Karl P. had been arrested on the grounds that he was a street musician who had never held a regular job. Regulations, issued by Heydrich on March 1, 1939, provided that persons who itinerated from place to place in order to make a living as peddlers, horse traders or musicians were no longer to be regarded as asocial simply on account of their itinerant lifestyle.[54] The Kripo of Magdeburg took note of this change in the definition of who was to be regarded as asocial or work-shy but opposed the release of P. anyway. It must be assumed, they informed the RKPA in Berlin on April 12, 1939, that P. will continue to roam around the countryside "without aim or plan and will use his musical playing simply as a cover for begging."[55]

In December 1940, the RKPA agreed to the release of prisoners in preventive custody who had volunteered to remove duds (unexploded bombs). One of those who benefited from this provision was the thirty-seven-year-old musician Dewald P. who had been arrested on June 14, 1938. His "criminal life story" described him as an illiterate person without a trade who had moved around with his family and made a living presenting shows. "So far he has not been involved in any criminal activity here." P. was classified as "work-shy" and sent to Sachsenhausen from where he was released on December 21, 1940. Upon his return to Magdeburg, he was put under police supervision. His file lists him as having died in Auschwitz on March 13, 1944.[56]

Some wives and mothers traveled to Berlin in order to plead in person the case for the release of their husbands or sons before the RKPA. On June 28,

1938, the RKPA wrote the local Kripo offices that the appearance of these women jeopardized the public health of the capital. "I request to see to it that the movement to Berlin stops. Otherwise I will find it necessary to order preventive custody also for these persons."[57] Local police offices too were annoyed by family members who kept showing up with requests for the release of their loved ones. On March 10, 1942, Auguste L. was summoned to the Kripo of Magdeburg and was forced to sign a statement in which she acknowledged having made a nuisance of herself by her repeated visits to the office. She now realized, she declared, "that my husband cannot yet be released. I understand all this and in the future will conduct myself accordingly." The problem solved itself for the Kripo officials when L. and other members of her family were deported to Auschwitz on March 1, 1943.[58]

It appears that the arrests of Gypsies in 1938 did not draw any adverse reaction from the population. As I have noted, some local officials supported release applications submitted by family members. But only one case is known of an individual who actually took the initiative to plead for Gypsies who were being held in preventive custody. That person was a Protestant pastor in Magdeburg, Reverend Witte. In November 1938, Witte submitted several petitions to the RKPA in Berlin requesting the release of Gypsies who had been arrested during Operation Work-Shy. The text of these petitions is not preserved, but we know that the local Kripo opposed the discharge. Still, in the case of Josef S., a father of four children, the RKPA ordered that the inmate be freed from custody anyway.[59]

The imposition of preventive police custody on Gypsies during Operation Work-Shy in 1938 represented a significant escalation of persecution. An undeterminable number of men, probably several hundred, were branded as asocial (most of them on account of their itinerant lifestyle), and were sent to concentration camps. Some of them were released within a year, but many others stayed in the camps for years on end. Not a few of the prisoners were killed by guards whose hatred for "asocials" had been specifically encouraged; others died as a result of systematic mistreatment or inadequate medical care. It is significant that during Operation Work-Shy Gypsies were not targeted specifically on racial grounds; they constituted merely one segment of a far larger population known as the asocials. Nevertheless, many Gypsies perished as a result of measures designed on the one hand to break and reform the personality of individuals considered asocial and on the other to provide slave labor for the new SS economic enterprises. Operation Work-Shy certainly had very little to do with the prevention of crime, the ostensible reason for the incarceration imposed. It constituted a new level of arbitrary persecution and oppression.

3

Track 3: Confronting an "Alien Race"

On December 8, 1938, Himmler issued a decree entitled Combating the Gypsy Plague that spoke of a need to tackle the Gypsy problem in terms of the "inner characteristics of that race." This was the first decree directed against Gypsies that made explicit reference to race, but, of course, Himmler's introducing racial terms into the debate over what to do about the "Gypsy nuisance" was hardly surprising. Many Gypsies had a dark complexion, which had long given rise to charges that they represented a foreign element. Hence, it was only a question of time before the Nazis' policy of cleansing Germany of non-Aryan elements would come to include the Gypsies. Although they were originally from India and therefore presumably of Aryan origin, Gypsies certainly did not resemble the typical "Germanic" (Nordic) type. As I have noted, for the first few years of the Nazi regime, anti-Gypsy measures had been justified primarily on social grounds. Gypsies and Gypsy-like itinerants, it had been asserted, were given to crime and generally represented an asocial element. Now the notion that Gypsies constituted an alien and inferior race was added, introducing a powerful new catalyst for anti-Gypsy agitation.

From Racial Hygiene to Nazi Racism

The idea that physical characteristics are an indication of inherent worth was propagated by many European thinkers during the nineteenth century. Complexion, posture, color or type of hair and shape of the head, it was believed, enabled scientists to determine whether an individual belonged to one racial group or another. The human races, in turn, were ranked, and some were seen as more valuable than others. Men such as Count Joseph Arthur de Gobineau (1816–1882) and Houston Stewart Chamberlain (1855–1927) argued that all cultural achievements had been the work of the "Aryans" and warned them against interbreeding with members of inferior races. Alongside these outright racist ideas existed the discipline of eugenics, which sought to improve the human race by controlling reproduction and limiting marriage to the physically and mentally fit. For Francis Galton (1822–1911), the man who coined the term "eugenics" (being well born), improving the human race meant improving mankind, though he too wanted the more "suitable" races or strains of blood to have a better chance of prevailing over the less suitable. In Germany, physician Wilhelm Schallmeyer (1857–1919) argued for the need to secure the biological capacity and racial quality of the German people. This was to be achieved by licensing marriage and by sterilizing those of "lesser hereditary value." Schallmeyer, however, denied the existence of pure races and made no attempt to rank the various groups within the white race.[1]

The term "racial hygiene" is attributed to another German physician, Alfred Ploetz (1860–1940). In 1895 Ploetz published a book in which he argued for the superiority of the German race, and he lived long enough to receive a professorial appointment at the University of Munich from Hitler personally in 1936. Although not an anti-Semite, Ploetz advocated a crude form of Social Darwinism. In order to keep the superior Germanic people healthy, he suggested, a caucus of physicians should preside over every birth deciding whether or not each newborn would be allowed to live.[2] A student of Ploetz, Dr. Fritz Lenz, occupied the first chair for race hygiene at the University of Munich, established in 1923. Neither Ploetz nor Lenz equated fitness with any particular race as did the ideologues of the growing militant nationalist movement. The two doctors were concerned with what they saw as the harmful effects of certain social institutions and the social and economic costs of protecting the weak. They wanted to promote the reproduction of the fittest and most socially valuable. At the same time, both men eventually joined the Nazi party and became supporters of Nazi racism. As historian George Mosse has put it, "The mainstream of eugenics and of racial hygiene did not lead directly into Nazi policy, though it indirectly helped to make it possible." For men such as Ploetz and Lenz the Nazi movement proved irresistible. "The heady prospect of a nation willing to make its race fit to survive wiped out any blemishes this process might entail."[3]

Social Darwinism appealed to the nationalists. They liked the emphasis on struggle and the dominance of hereditary over environmental factors. Particularly in Nazi ideology, nature rather than nurture was the key to the development of human excellence or failure. The diversity of mankind was rooted in biology. What made a Jew a Jew or a Gypsy a Gypsy was something in the blood. Hence, once a Jew, always a Jew; once a Gypsy, always a Gypsy. Since hereditary traits could not change, they had to be neutralized and that, ultimately, could only mean radical measures such as compulsory sterilization, nonvoluntary euthanasia or physical annihilation. Racial hygiene thus provided a pseudoscientific rationale for the denigration, and eventually the extermination of those deemed unfit to survive.[4]

Hitler's thinking was decisively affected by the teachings of racial hygiene. While Hitler was in jail, serving his prison term for the failed Munich putsch of November 8, 1923, Munich publisher Julius Lehmann, one of his early and ardent supporters, sent him a copy of a textbook on human heredity and racial hygiene by Erwin Baur, Eugen Fischer and Fritz Lenz.[5] When Lenz later reviewed Hitler's *Mein Kampf*, published shortly after Hitler's release from prison, he correctly claimed that Hitler had incorporated parts of this textbook into his book.[6] *Mein Kampf* mirrors ideas taken from this and other books on racial topics that Hitler read during his incarceration. He denied the equality of the races, demanded the subordination of inferior and weaker races to better and stronger ones, attributed the decline of civilizations to the mixture of blood, and advocated preventing the reproduction of so-called sickly or criminal elements. Hitler reserved his special ire for the Jews, whom he denounced as the absolute enemy of the Aryan race.

Mein Kampf does not mention the Gypsies, in whom Hitler appears to have had no interest. At most, he regarded them as a minor irritant. During his twelve years as the ruler of Germany, Hitler referred to Gypsies only twice, in brief remarks that were made in connection with the issue of Gypsies serving in the military. The fact that Hitler was largely unconcerned about the "Gypsy problem" helps explain why Jews and Gypsies were ultimately treated so differently. The Jews, for Hitler and the Nazi movement, were the incarnation of evil, a powerful people who quite literally threatened the existence of mankind. The Gypsies, on the other hand, were seen as a plague and a nuisance; few in number, they could be handled with more or less traditional measures. The sharply escalated persecution of Gypsies that took place during the last three years of the war in part was the result of pressure from the lower ranks of the Nazi movement, who considered the war a good opportunity to get rid of the Gypsies. It also represented the culmination of endeavors by the criminal police, assisted by its own "Gypsy experts," to solve the "problem" of the Gypsy *Mischlinge* (Gypsies of mixed ancestry), labeled asocial, by way of deportation, incarceration and sterilization. However, even then, as we shall see later in this book, no plan ever emerged to annihilate all Gypsies analogous to the "Final Solution of the Jewish Question."

The Sterilization Law of 1933

The Nazis' assumption of power in January 1933 gave them the opportunity to translate their eugenic and racial theories into practice, and the sterilization of the hereditarily sick and insane was the first item on this agenda. An extensive lobbying campaign for such a law had been under way for years. Members of the medical profession, in particular, agitated for the sterilization of the genetically "unfit," though an occasional voice was also heard demanding sterilization on wider grounds. In a book published in 1925, professor of psychiatry Robert Gaupp included Gypsies among those "mentally and morally sick" who, he suggested, should be sterilized.[7] In 1928 a public health physician (*Medizinalrat*) in Saxony, Gustav Boeters, suggested the compulsory sterilization of the unfit and inferior, including vagabonds and Gypsies.[8] In the drive for sterilization, advocates of racial hygiene were joined by bureaucrats worried about the ever increasing cost of caring for the insane and feeble-minded in state institutions. In 1932 a law that provided for the voluntary sterilization of certain classes of genetically defective individuals was drafted in Prussia and received the support of both racist and nonracist eugenicists. Due to the political turmoil that afflicted the Weimar Republic during its final days, this draft law never became legislation, but interest in such a law remained high.[9]

The Law for the Prevention of Genetically Diseased Offspring was adopted on July 14, 1933, and took effect on January 1, 1934. On the surface, it was a eugenic measure with no racist or specifically National Socialist connotations. It made no provision for sterilization on racial or social grounds. The law was based in part on the American Model Eugenic Sterilization Law developed in 1922[10] and on the Prussian draft law of 1932. Unlike the Prussian draft, however, the new legislation provided for compulsory sterilization of individuals who, according to medical knowledge, were likely to pass on to their offspring a serious physical or mental disorder. This included schizophrenia, inherited mental retardation, epilepsy, blindness, deafness or other serious bodily deformities as well as severe alcoholism. Anyone acting in an official capacity who learned of the existence of such an illness was required to submit an application for the sterilization of the afflicted individual. These applications were to be acted upon by special genetic health courts (*Erbgesundheitsgerichte*) composed of one judge and two doctors.[11] Decisions could be appealed to a superior genetic health court, but no figures are available on the total number of successful appeals. In one jurisdiction, the appellate genetic health court rejected sterilization orders in 7.8 percent of the cases.[12] According to another local sample, appeals lasted an average of nine months and were successful in 25 percent of the cases.[13] It appears that some physicians and judges maintained their professional integrity whereas others became ideological zealots.

During the 1920s and early 1930s, the sterilization of persons with severe inherited diseases was endorsed in many countries, including the United States. In Sweden, large-scale sterilizations were carried out on those accused of leading an "asocial way of life" well into the post–World War II period. This group included the Tattars, nomads who were said to be descended from Swedes and Gypsies.[14] However, in no other country did the number of sterilizations come even close to the number performed in Nazi Germany. In the United States, by the end of 1931, twenty-four years after the first sterilization law had been enacted, a total of 12,145 sterilizations had been performed.[15] In Nazi Germany, on the other hand, during the first year of the sterilization law alone, 43,775 persons were sterilized.[16] In 1936, in response to considerable unease in the population, Hitler forbade the publi-

cation of these figures. Reliable estimates put the total number of sterilizations up to the outbreak of the war in 1939 at 290,000–300,000.[17]

The German sterilization law was enacted as a eugenic measure, but it
found broader application. In 1937, on secret orders from Hitler, about five
hundred black children (referred to as the *Rheinlandbastarde*), the offspring of
black French occupation troops and German women, were sterilized. The
action was carried out by the Gestapo working in collusion with the genetic
health courts.[18] Gypsies too found themselves caught in the net, for the courts
increasingly accepted asocial conduct as proof of hereditary disease. Whether
this treatment of the asocial is discrimination or racism is probably irrelevant.
It is clear that the sterilization of those labeled as asocial, including the Gypsies, represented an important new step in the persecution of this group.

Minister of the interior Frick, in a circular issued in January 1937, coun-
seled against putting too much reliance upon intelligence tests. Examining
physicians were advised to pose questions regarding the "occupational life of
the individual, his surroundings and whether he has stood the test of life."[19]
Criteria of social worth were likely to catch nonconforming types such as
Gypsies in particular, and in several cases Gypsies were sterilized for such reasons. An application seeking the sterilization of a young pregnant Gypsy
woman in Bremen stated that "she is dirty and a strong smoker." In addition,
she had been convicted of theft and fraud. In another case a physician supported his application with the argument that the individual concerned, a Gypsy
who made his living as an actor, was not known in the area. "His relatives live
in a small second-rate caravan and are typical Gypsies—work-shy and unreliable."[20] This particular sterilization order was ultimately overturned by the
appellate genetic court, but many other Gypsies were not so fortunate.

Other reasons specified on applications for sterilization include many
types of "social failure"—nonobservance of the duty to attend school,
enrollment in a school for problem children, lack of an occupation, unemployment, following a Gypsy lifestyle, welfare dependence, divorce, having
several illegitimate children, and the like. The sterilization law, theoretically
a eugenic measure, in practice became a tool for the persecution of an
allegedly asocial group.

Being asocial was equated with a special form of mental disorder called
"moral mental retardation." In 1936, a researcher in the racial hygiene division of the Reich Department of Public Health, Fred Dubitscher, analyzed
450 cases that carried this diagnosis. In many instances moral mental retardation had been diagnosed when there was no deficit in intelligence; nevertheless, Dubitscher concluded that sterilization had been justified. These cases,
he explained, involved individuals who had demonstrated complete indifference to moral values. Among the offenses that could indicate such an asocial
outlook were theft and vagrancy.[21] Another kind of retardation without obviously inferior mental ability was called "disguised mental retardation." In a
study published in 1937, Gypsy specialist Robert Ritter described a type of
children who were able to display "a certain independence and cunning and
especially were quick talkers." This kind of disorder "which carries the mask

of cleverness we will characterize most appropriately as disguised mental retardation."[22] Needless to say, such an approach allowed mental retardation to be established in almost any kind of case. The categories of moral and disguised mental retardation became instruments to sterilize "asocial" individuals about whom no proof of a genuine mental deficit was available.

Available figures indicate that "hereditary mental retardation" was the most frequently cited disorder in sterilization proceedings. In the university hospital of Göttingen, 58 percent of all women were sterilized for this disorder.[23] In Hamburg, 46 percent of all cases involved this diagnosis.[24] Other sources indicate a percentage as high as 60 percent.[25] Physicians and researchers acknowledged that the heritability of mental retardation was not proven, but, arguing that they could not wait until full certainty was achieved, they used the disorder as a reason for sterilization anyway. We do not know how many Gypsies were among those sterilized for the various kinds of mental retardation, nor do we have figures on the total number of Gypsies sterilized under the sterilization law of 1933. According to one recent estimate, based on extrapolations from available local and regional statistics, about five hundred Gypsies were sterilized in 1933–1939. Such a figure would indicate a higher percentage of sterilized among the Gypsies than for the population as a whole.[26]

On August 31, 1939, shortly after the outbreak of war, the Ministry of the Interior ordered that applications for sterilization be submitted only when there was the "most urgent" need to prevent the creation of offspring.[27] There were several reasons for this order. The first and official reason was that in time of war it was necessary to save precious medical manpower and to reduce administrative proceedings to a minimum. However, another motive was also at work. Considerable unrest had developed among the population, especially among Catholics, about the scope and implementation of the sterilization policy. Party organizations, alarmed at the negative reaction from sterilized individuals and their families, had demanded to be included in the decision-making process involving the sterilization of party members. There was also alarm over the number of deaths resulting from this procedure.[28] Finally, the beginning of the war saw the start of the euthanasia program, a far more radical policy for ridding Germany of its "defective" individuals. Hence, between 1939 and 1945 the number of sterilizations declined drastically. In Frankfurt, for example, only 6.4 percent of all the sterilizations carried out between 1934 and 1944 took place after the start of the war,[29] in Göttingen, 11.2 percent were carried out between 1940 and 1945,[30] and in Bremen the percentage of sterilizations during wartime was 12.4.[31]

For the Gypsies, however, the onset of war brought about an increase of tribulations, including a sharp rise in sterilizations from 1943 on. Many of those exempted from deportation to Auschwitz in 1943, as we shall see, had to submit to sterilization, and this second phase of sterilizations for the Gypsies abandoned all pretense of eugenic purpose. The clear intent had become the elimination of offspring from a group of perfectly healthy men, women and children.

The Nuremberg Racial Laws

During the first few years of the Nazi regime, there prevailed a precarious balance between the Nazi party and the state bureaucracy; the development of racial policy took place within this setting of bureaucratic competition. The Ministry of the Interior included the Advisory Committee for Population and Race Policy, which was involved in drafting a law designed to exclude Jews from full citizenship rights as early as July 1933. In the Nazi party the Office of Racial Policy *(Rassenpolitisches Amt)* had been set up on May 1, 1934, and this office too worked on the construction of racial programs and laws. On September 15, 1935, at the conclusion of the annual party congress in Nuremberg, Hitler announced two anti-Jewish laws, which were soon interpreted to cover Gypsies as well.

The Law for the Protection of German Blood and Honor, regulating sexual relations between Germans and Jews, was the first in a series of laws and decrees dealing with the issue of alien blood *(artfremdes Blut)*. The law forbade both marriage and extramarital sexual relations between "Jews and German citizens of German and related blood." It was followed by the Law for the Protection of the Hereditary Health of the German People of October 18, which imposed the obligation of a marriage license certifying that the partners were "fit to marry" according to genetic and racial criteria.[32] On November 15, the first decree implementing the Nuremberg law of September 15 extended the ban on interracial marriages to all cases in which "one had to expect progeny that would endanger the purity of the German blood."[33] Finally, a decree issued by minister of the interior Frick on November 26 identified others besides Jews who polluted the German blood: "Gypsies, Negroes and their bastards."[34] Another decree by Frick, dated January 3, 1936, repeated this provision, but allowed marriages between Germans and Gypsies "with only a quarter or less of alien blood."[35] In 1938, several Gypsies are said to have been sent to concentration camps for having sexual relations with persons of German blood,[36] but full enforcement of the ban on such interracial sexual contacts did not begin until the war years when the life of Gypsies came under more rigorous scrutiny. We know of no show trials charging Gypsies with "racial defilement" *(Rassenschande)* as there were for Jews.

The second Nuremberg law with an impact on the Gypsies was the Citizenship Law. Approved on September 15, 1935, the law limited German citizenship to those of "German or related blood."[37] This law too made no specific mention of Gypsies, but in an article published at the end of the year Frick made it clear that alien races other than Jews were also covered. Since Jews were not of German blood, he wrote, no Jew could become a German citizen. "However, the same goes for the members of other races whose blood is not related [*artverwandt*] to the German blood, for example for Gypsies and Negroes."[38] An authoritative commentary on the new racial legislation published in 1936 noted that persons of "alien blood" could not become German citizens. "Ordinarily, only Jews and Gypsies are persons of alien blood in Europe."[39] One consequence of this interpretation of the law was to deprive Gypsies of the right to vote. Acting on a decree of the minister of the interior issued on March 7, 1936, local authorities now revised the voters lists and removed both Gypsies and part-Gypsies (*Zigeunermischlinge*) from the rolls.[40]

The first two important racial laws of the Nazi state did not mention Gypsies, undoubtedly reflecting the limited importance of the Gypsy issue. For the Nazis, essentially, there existed only one racial problem in Germany, the Jews, who were regarded as the sworn enemies of the Aryan people and a mortal threat. In 1933 there were about 525,000 Jews in Germany, many of them holding important positions in German society. The Gypsies, on the other hand, numbering a mere 26,000 or so, represented a strictly marginal element. As two officials of the Ministry of the Interior put it in a quasi-official treatise published in 1938: "The racial problem for the German people is *the Jewish question*, since only the Jews are numerically significant as members of an alien race in Germany." Other foreign races residing in Germany, they concluded, in comparison to the Jews, "are of little significance."[41]

The Research Institute for Racial Hygiene and Population Biology

A recurring problem that arose in connection with the enforcement of various laws and decrees directed against the Gypsies was determining who counted as a Gypsy. This issue became especially acute after the enactment of the Nuremberg Laws, which used racial criteria. Membership in the racial category "Jew" was based on the religious affiliation of parents and grandparents. However, no such simple criterion applied to Gypsies who were Christians and in many cases intermarried with the local population. Some had become sedentary and were not easily identifiable as Gypsies. In order to solve this problem, the Ministry of the Interior in the spring of 1936 ordered the establishment of a research institute in the Reich Health Office. The central task of this institute, located in Berlin and called *Rassenhygienische und bevölkerungsbiologische Forschungsstelle*, was to collect information about Germany's nonsedentary population, especially Gypsies and Zigeunermischlinge. These data were to be used by the Kripo and other official agencies in addressing the "Gypsy problem." In addition, the information collected was to be used in formulating a law dealing with the Gypsy issue, which had been under discussion since early 1936. Physician Robert Ritter became the head of the institute and was soon regarded as the government's leading expert on the Gypsies.

Born in 1901 in Aachen, Ritter had a doctorate in educational psychology as well as in medicine. He had a particular interest in child psychology and in 1934 obtained his specialist certification in child psychiatry. Apparently Ritter came to the subject of Gypsies through his work on antisocial youth and the biology of criminality (*Kriminalbiologie*), a field of study that considered crime to be rooted in the hereditary characteristics of individuals and

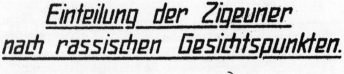

Einteilung der Zigeuner nach rassischen Gesichtspunkten.

Scheme for the racial classification of Gypsies according to the "racial makeup" of their four grandparents. COURTESY OF BUNDESARCHIV BERLIN.

Die rassische Zugehörigkeit eines Zigeuners wird nach der rassischen Zugehörigkeit seiner 4 Grosselternteile bestimmt.

Reinrassiger Zigeuner ist derjenige, dessen 4 Grosseltern sämtlich Zigeuner waren (Ziffer 1).

Die Person, bei der ein Grosselternteil zur Hälfte oder zu einem Viertel Zigeuner oder deutschblütig war, die übrigen drei Grosselternteile Vollzigeuner gewesen sind, gilt noch als reinrassiger Zigeuner (Ziffer 2-4).

Die Person, die unter ihren Grosseltern weniger als 3 Vollzigeuner zu Vorfahren hat, gilt als Zigeunermischling (Ziffer 5-32).

Die Person, bei der ein Grosselternteil zur Hälfte oder zu einem Viertel zigeunerischer Abstammung war, die übrigen drei Grosselternteile aber deutschblütig gewesen sind, gilt als Nichtzigeuner (Ziffer 33 und 34).

groups. Although his political leanings were nationalistic, he never joined the Nazi party.

Ritter's team included the anthropologists Adolf Würth, Gerhard Stein and Sophie Ehrhardt. Also on his staff was Eva Justin, a trained nurse, who had worked with Ritter at the University of Tübingen and who received her doctorate in anthropology with a dissertation on Gypsy children in 1943.[42]

Robert Ritter taking pictures in a Gypsy camp, around 1938. COURTESY OF BUNDESARCHIV
KOBLENZ.

Organized in small groups, the investigators toured cities and countryside,
educational institutions and Gypsy camps, prisons and concentration camps
in order to collect material on Gypsies and Gypsy-like itinerants. Local police
and other officials were under orders to render all possible assistance. The
investigators searched in civic registries and municipal archives, in police files
and court records. They took photographs and anthropometric measurements as well as blood samples, and they interrogated individuals about their
background. Some of them are said to have spoken the Romani language.
Interviewees who were reluctant to cooperate were threatened with arrest and
incarceration in a concentration camp. The information collected was subsequently arranged in genealogical tables; some of these scrolls are said to have
been eighteen feet long and to have included hundreds of names. In a presentation offered at the International Congress on Population, held in Paris in
1937, Ritter proudly told of a clan he had been able to follow back over two
and a half centuries and through eight to ten generations.[43]

By 1939 the Gypsy archive built up in Ritter's institute had information on
over 20,000 individuals. In addition to the data collected by Ritter and his
associates, the archive was able to draw on the files of the *Zigenerzentrale*
(Central Office for Gypsy Affairs) in Munich. The task of classifying the
entire German Gypsy population was expected to be completed in two years.
"Already now," Ritter wrote in a report published in 1939, "the archive is of
the greatest value in meeting the needs of race improvement and of the
Criminal Police. It serves as a source of information regarding all questions

Eva Justin, an assistant of Ritter, measuring the head of a Gypsy woman, around 1938.
COURTESY OF BUNDESARCHIV KOBLENZ.

concerning Gypsies and their descendants for all state authorities, the organs
and formation of the party, and especially the departments of public health.
In addition to these practical results, the collected information also provides
ample material for the drafting of a Gypsy law."[44]

Among the sources consulted by Ritter and his assistants were church registers. These records went back several hundred years and contained information on baptisms, marriages and deaths. Some church archivists made special efforts to help track down members of alien races. Following the
adoption of the Nuremberg Laws, archivist Karl Themel of the Evangelical
Church in Berlin mobilized 150 helpers and created an alphabetical index for

all baptisms in Berlin between 1800 and 1874. Every member of the national community *(Volksgenosse)*, Themel wrote, now "has the duty to become aware of his blood-link to the German people and to prove this link."[45] Part of the cost of this large undertaking was paid by the Evangelical Church synod of Berlin. Within this larger index, Themel constructed a special section, a "baptism index for those of alien blood," which listed "Jews, Gypsies and Negroes." Copies of all entries in this special index, Themel insisted, had to be sent to the Reich Office for Genealogical Research, the agency authorized to certify that someone belonged to the Aryan race.[46] We do not know how many other archivists went out of their way to track down those of alien blood, but Ritter noted in 1937 that church registers were indeed very useful.[47] As late as 1942, when the Gypsies' situation had worsened considerably, the record indicates that a Catholic priest supplied the Kripo with information from parish files.[48]

In addition to classifying individual Gypsies, Ritter also set out to undertake a systematic study of the "Gypsy problem," the results of which were to serve as a basis for policy and legislation. The Gypsies in Germany, Ritter concluded, were a primitive people who belonged to an alien race *(artfremde Rasse)*, though entirely pure Gypsies hardly existed any more. For many generations German Gypsies had intermarried with the *Jenische* (the "white Gypsies") and other asocial elements in the population. This process had accelerated in the years since World War I when Gypsies had become subject to various restrictions. They were no longer allowed to travel through the countryside in hordes; begging and fortune-telling were punished. Hence now the great majority of Gypsies came to live in barrack colonies and similar dwellings for the poor on the outskirts of the major cities. They shared these quarters with the Jenische with whom they increasingly intermarried. As a result, Ritter maintained, there had emerged a population of parasites who lacked ambition and were work-shy. Many of them had become habitual criminals. They constituted "a highly inferior *Lumpenproletariat*." Those who still traveled around were racially purer and had a lower rate of criminality, but even they had become a nuisance on account of their begging and stealing.[49]

All previous attempts to solve this problem, Ritter argued, had failed, since Gypsies could not be made truly sedentary. Pushing them from one state to another was no solution either, for they always returned sooner or later. Police actions dealt only with symptoms. Coping with the "Gypsy problem" required solutions based on knowledge of their racial peculiarities and on the insights of the biology of criminality. Itinerant Gypsies were the most manageable; the purer the race of Gypsies the easier it was to supervise them. "Here we know clearly that we are dealing with primitive nomads of an alien race whom neither education nor penalties can make into sedentary citizens." They should be allowed to follow their own way of life, Ritter suggested, though they had to remain separate from the rest of the population. Travelers who followed an honest occupation and for whom roaming about was "in the blood" also did not present too many difficulties. To force them to become sedentary would deprive them of ways of making a living and subject them to

challenges they could not meet. The most difficult problem was that of the
Zigeunermischlinge and Jenische, considered a population of criminal clans
and asocial elements. The only solution for these groups was to prevent their
uncontrolled moving around, by confining them in "closed colonies" and sterilizing all those who could propagate. "The Law for the Prevention of Genetically Diseased Offspring could be used in most cases, since these asocials in
their majority suffer from partial or disguised mental retardation."[50]

Ritter approached the "Gypsy problem" through the biology of criminality,
a discipline that had been around since the 1890s. During the 1920s many German students of crime flocked to this field. The Society for the Biology of
Criminality came into being in 1927 with Adolf Lenz as president. Studying
identical twins among prison inmates and other data, practitioners of this
branch of knowledge concluded that criminality was hereditary, especially
since criminals tended to mate with each other. One influential investigator
summed up his findings in a book entitled *Crime Is Destiny*.[51] Criminals were
born rather than made. Hence, since a hereditary criminal disposition could
not be rehabilitated, it had to be neutralized, and that meant locking up criminals and sterilizing them. Ritter shared these views. "The aim of our work, he
wrote in 1939, "is to demonstrate with an exact methodology that sociological
manifestations have their root in biology, i.e., in the final analysis in the laws of
heredity."[52]

More than fifty years later, there is still no agreement on the causes of
crime, though the view that there is such a thing as "born criminals" or a
"crime gene" is rejected by practically all students of the subject. Twin studies
of criminal behavior, like other empirical methods, have weaknesses that pre-
clude a precise quantitative outcome. Some personality traits associated with
criminal behavior such as intelligence, impulse control and aggressivity are to
some extent heritable, and this affects the likelihood that certain individuals
will engage in criminal activity.[53] However, this does not mean that environmental factors can be disregarded. Biological predispositions are activated by
circumstances. Constitutional factors interact with familial and other social
experiences; nature and nurture work together in a complex pattern of interaction. "Our knowledge of this interaction," conclude two scholars, "is not
yet good enough to permit anyone to say with confidence how much of the
variation in the law-violating behavior of people can be attributed to genetic
and how much to environmental factors."[54]

Obviously, therefore, there is no scientific justification for branding an
entire group of people as asocial or criminal on the basis of allegedly unalter-
able biological factors. Even if it were true that biological factors had a large
share in determining criminal behavior, there exists no way of predicting
which individual in a particular group will become a criminal. The fact is that
the German practitioners of the biology of criminality proposed and carried
out drastically invasive strategies of crime fighting for which a scientific basis
did not exist then or today.

The conclusions reached by Ritter and his associates on the racial origins
and characteristics of the German Gypsies were based on assumptions shared

by the majority of Nazi researchers. The dominance of hereditary over environmental factors was "a dogma of Nazi ideology."[55] Ritter's findings also solved another problem—the Indian origin of the Gypsies. According to Ritter, many individuals adhered to the view that because the Gypsies originally came from India and because their language was related to Sanskrit they were to be considered "Aryan." Ritter rejected this argument.[56] Only a small minority of Gypsies—perhaps no more than 10 percent—were still racially pure; the large majority were Mischlinge. This conclusion made it possible for the Nazis to play the race card against the Gypsies. Radical measures of persecution against the large majority of the Gypsies, they could argue, were justified because the Mischlinge were both asocial and racially inferior. Indeed, in Nazi eyes these two accusations were linked: Gypsies were asocial because they belonged to an inferior race. We shall soon see how Himmler's decree of December 8, 1938, made use of these arguments.

Anti-Gypsy Agitation Heats Up

The press and other media outlets had been abusing Gypsies for decades. From about 1936 on, however, the verbal assaults escalated. An analysis of the *Fuldaer Zeitung*, for example, shows a definite increase in articles accusing Gypsies of various crimes from 1936 on.[57] Charges that Gypsies were asocial parasites now combined with racist invective. In a political climate that increasingly stressed the crucial importance of cleansing Germany of alien blood, old animosities against the Gypsies could now be dressed up in racist language. People felt free to express their anti-Gypsy sentiments more openly and more vehemently. Demands were being heard for a "final solution to the Gypsy question," though as yet nobody thought of physical annihilation. The stepped-up anti-Gypsy agitation provides strong evidence that the escalation of anti-Gypsy policy that got under way in 1938 was to an important degree a response to public opinion.

Saul Friedländer has written that during the 1930s "the German population . . . did not demand anti-Jewish measures, nor did it clamor for their extreme implementation." There was some glee in witnessing the growing degradation of the Jews, "but outside party ranks, there was no massive popular agitation to expel them from Germany or to unleash violence against them."[58] Friedländer acknowledges the difficulty of determining whether the promotion of hatred originated in the party or among unaffiliated citizens. But in the case of the Gypsies the situation is far more clear-cut. Demands for a radical solution of the "Gypsy problem" appear to have come from all quarters. They were voiced by local officials, academics, publicists, and just plain citizens. It is highly unlikely that all of these people were party members. The long history of such vilification certainly demonstrates that hostility toward Gypsies was not limited to Nazis. Advocates of harsh anti-Gypsy measures such as Ritter and Würth were not members of the Nazi party.

Ritter's views about what to do with the Gypsies have been described earlier. His colleague Adolf Würth had very similar ideas. In an article published in an anthropological journal in 1938, Würth argued that the National Socialist state would have to solve the Gypsy problem as it had solved the Jewish question. The Zigeunermischlinge, in particular, constituted a danger to the German people that "has to be repelled with all available means." Measures had to be taken to prevent their further mixing with those of German blood and to stop them from multiplying.[59]

In a study of the Gypsy colony in Berleburg (Westfalen), Robert Krämer of the University of Münster also focused on the need to prevent the further propagation of the Mischlinge, whom he called "for the most part more unpleasant people than the Gypsies." He found that they were parasites who claimed rights but recognized no duties. Their houses were primitive and dirty. The crime rate among them was high and their moral behavior was "scandalous." Although the Gypsies were considered an alien race, they were not thought to constitute as strong a danger to the German people as the Jews because they were small in number, were mentally inferior, and therefore were unable to penetrate the leading strata of society. Still, Krämer concluded, they should be made subject to the Nuremberg Laws. The protection of German blood required finding "a final solution to the Gypsy question."[60] The mayor of Berleburg, a physician, in an article published in 1937, called the Gypsies of his town a degenerate group and expressed the hope that the new Germany would find "effective means and ways in order to rid the native, German-blooded population of this Gypsy-plague."[61]

A similar plea for help during the year 1937 came from the chief of the rural police in the district of Esslingen in Württemberg. In a letter directed to the *Landrat* (chief magistrate), the officer charged that the city of Stuttgart sought to get rid of its Gypsies by issuing them itinerant trade licenses. Such licenses served merely as a cover for begging and made it impossible for the rural police to control the Gypsies effectively.

> The Gypsy is and remains a parasite on the people, who supports himself almost exclusively by begging and stealing. . . . The Gypsy can never be educated to become a useful person. For this reason it is necessary that the Gypsy tribe be exterminated [*ausgerottet*] by way of sterilization or castration. With the help of such a law the Gypsy plague would soon be eliminated. I am firmly convinced that an appreciable number of these fellows would immediately cross the border in full flight; the number of the remaining Gypsies would decrease from year to year and they would become superannuated. Such a measure would not cost the state very much money, and within a short span of time the Gypsy plague would be eliminated.[62]

Other demands for the sterilization of the Gypsies came from academics. Dr. Heinrich Wilhelm Kranz was an ophthalmologist by training who in 1933 became head of the Institute for Hereditary Health and Race Preservation (*Institut für Erb- und Rassenpflege*), a party-sponsored institution at the

University of Giessen. In an article published in 1937 in the party organ *Neues Volk*, Kranz argued that the Gypsies constituted "an asocial and criminal problem." Their key characteristics were "begging, fraud and theft in all its varieties." A resolute and uniform solution to the Gypsy problem was needed. Kranz advised that Gypsies "be eliminated [*ausgemerzt*] from the body of the people as soon as possible by way of preventing their propagation."[63]

Kranz's assistant Otto Finger studied two Gypsy clans and published his findings in 1937. Of the 174 persons investigated, Finger concluded, 136 had to be categorized as asocial; they constituted useless elements that were a burden to society. "It is unacceptable that work-shy and asocial conduct is sanctioned by the state by rewarding racially unsuitable persons for their lack of suitability with public welfare." Finger proposed that such hereditarily burdened asocial individuals be kept under lock and key, and he expressed regret that under existing legislation it was all but impossible to sterilize such parasites.[64]

The author of an article in *Volk und Rasse*, published by the German Society for Racial Hygiene, cited Finger's findings and called for eliminating the Zigeunermischlinge from the ranks of the German people. Through several generations these elements had contributed nothing positive and had been a burden on society. "We cannot allow that, as a result of too much kindness and indulgence, parasites spread among our people who are a constant threat to our national purity [*völkische Sauberkeit*]."[65]

An unsigned article about "Gypsies as an asocial group" that appeared in *Deutsches Ärzteblatt*, a publication for physicians, propagated like ideas. Gypsies constituted a plague. "They provided for themselves by being masters in lying, stealing, defrauding, and begging. Wherever they go they exploit nature and humans." All attempts to settle them had failed; moreover, German soil should not be wasted on alien vagabonds. The article proposed that the Gypsies, since they were asocial, be treated like hereditarily diseased individuals. They should be subjected to protective custody and prevented from passing on their inferior stock to succeeding generations. "The aim is: Merciless elimination [*rücksichtslose Ausmerzung*] of these defective elements of the population."[66]

Very occasionally individuals even argued that Gypsies constituted a danger to German society as great as that posed by the Jews. Public health official Dr. Carl-Heinz Rodenberg maintained that Gypsies, like the Jews, represented "a biologically foreign body" that "has a destructive influence on our body politic, integrated in terms of blood and race." They were a sociological and biological threat that should not be underestimated. From the racial point of view, the danger stemming from the Gypsies therefore was no smaller than "the danger arising from mixing with Jews."[67]

If we add to these expressions of abuse the many newspaper articles that decried the "Gypsy plague" and called for more energetic moves by the government to stem the "Gypsy nuisance,"[68] we have a picture of German thought about the Gypsies in the late 1930s. Sentiments that called for hardness and a lack of mercy represented a kind of Nietzschean element that shattered boundaries and eventually facilitated murder. We have no public opinion polls on the subject, but hostility toward the Gypsies appears to have been nearly universal. Although not everyone called for sterilization, most demanded that "something" be done about the Gypsies. In time, the "something" was given a content that turned out to be fairly close to what the various writers cited here had proposed. Himmler's decree of December 8, 1938, probably was promulgated in some measure as a response to a public opinion that was steadily becoming more radical in its view of the "Gypsy question."

The Decree for "Combating the Gypsy Plague" of December 8, 1938

A draft of the decree against the "Gypsy plague," dated March 24, 1938, had been circulating since April of that year. In a comment on this draft, the Office of Gypsy Affairs of the Munich Kripo agreed that tackling the Gypsy problem in terms of the "inner characteristics of that race [*aus dem Wesen dieser Rasse heraus*]" was important. However, Munich officials pointed out that "in addition to registering and dealing with the racially pure Gypsy and the Mischlinge it is necessary to include also those who are of German blood and roam around in the manner of Gypsies. It is a well-known fact that especially these kinds of itinerating persons collide with the law more frequently than the Gypsies."[69] A memo submitted to the minister of the interior of Württemberg on July 9, 1938, made the same point. The question of the Jenische was "especially urgent" since they were "particularly asocial and inferior from the point of view of hereditary biology."[70]

The Combating the Gypsy Plague decree, when finally issued in the name of Himmler on December 8, 1938, reflected these views as well as the input of Ritter's Research Institute for Racial Hygiene and Population Biology. Experience in fighting the Gypsy plague and knowledge gained from research on race biology, the decree began, make it appropriate that the problem of the Gypsies be tackled in terms of the "inner characteristics of that race." It had become clear that Mischlinge were responsible for most criminal offenses committed by Gypsies. Because of their strong roaming instinct, racially pure Gypsies had resisted all attempts to settle them. "It is therefore necessary that in the final solution of the Gypsy question [*bei der endgültigen Lösung der Zigeunerfrage*] racially pure Gypsies and Mischlinge be treated differently." In pursuing this goal, it was necessary first to determine the racial affiliation of every German Gypsy and of Gypsy-like itinerants.[71]

The decree therefore ordered the registration [*Erfassung*] of all sedentary and nonsedentary Gypsies as well as of Gypsy-like itinerants. Personal data concerning individuals above the age of six who belonged to these groups were to be reported to the Reich Center for Combating the Gypsy Nuisance at the RKPA in Berlin. If necessary, the police could impose custody (also known as *Identitätshaft*) in order to obtain this information. The final determination of whether an individual was a Gypsy or a Gypsy-like itinerant was to be made by the RKPA on the basis of an expert opinion [*Sachverständigengutachten*]. Hence all persons affected by this decree were obligated to submit to a racial-biological examination by such experts. The police were authorized to use compulsion to fulfill this requirement.[72]

Other provisions of the decree directed that identity papers such a passports and licenses to practice an itinerant trade be issued only after all personal data required by this decree had been obtained and the racial-biological examination had been completed. All IDs were to note whether the individual was a Gypsy, a Zigeunermischling or a Gypsy-like itinerant. Itinerant trade and driver's licenses were to be issued only after a careful check. Applications for carrying a weapon were to be denied in all cases. Traveling and camping in hordes (defined as several individuals or families) were to be prevented; local police were to regulate the duration of such camping and to collect camping fees as well as security deposits. In the case of all affected persons, the police were to determine whether the imposition of preventive custody on account of asocial conduct was indicated. "In this determination, especially severe criteria are to be invoked." Foreign Gypsies were to be prevented from entering Germany; those found in the country were to be expelled. Gypsies, Zigeunermischlinge and Gypsy-like itinerants were to be excluded from areas close to the border; sedentary Gypsies and sedentary Mischlinge were exempted from this provision. Probably in response to the complaints of large cities that they had become a refuge for those expelled from smaller towns and rural areas, the decree provided that in the future nobody was to be relocated into cities with a population of more than 500,000 inhabitants.[73]

The decree contained special orders for registrars of births, marriages and deaths and for departments of public health. Registrars were to report every birth, marriage or death of persons covered by this decree to the local Kripo; that office was to forward this information to the RKPA. Being a Gypsy, a Zigeunermischling or a Gypsy-like itinerant, the decree pointed out, created a presumption that under the Law for the Protection of the German Blood and Honor a marriage was not allowed. Hence such persons had to supply a certificate of suitability for marriage [*Ehetauglichkeitszeugnis*]. Departments of public health too were ordered to report all cases involving persons covered by the decree. Finally, the decree abolished all state regulations concerning the Gypsy problem. Similarly, all existing laws or police orders were to be modified to bring them into line with this decree. In Austria and the Sudetenland (just seized by Germany), the decree was to be applied as well as possible.[74]

Himmler's decree of December 8, 1938, included many provisions long used by the German states in restricting the life of Gypsies, such as the proscription of traveling in hordes and requiring a permit for camping. At the same time, it included new elements that marked an important milestone in the development of Nazi policy toward the Gypsies. First, continuing a trend begun with Himmler's reorganization of the German police in 1936, the handling of the Gypsies was firmly in the hands of the Kripo run by the RKPA in Berlin. The jurisdiction of the states was effectively ended, and all important decisions, down to the question of whether a certain individual was to be considered a Gypsy, were now made by the RKPA, an organization run by Nebe and dominated by Himmler's deputy, Heydrich. Second, the decree created an unparalleled data base covering the Gypsy population and those leading a Gypsy-like lifestyle. The registration of the Gypsies had been attempted with varying degrees of success since the nineteenth century, but at no time had police, civic registrars and departments of health been brought together in such a gigantic data-collecting network. Third, Himmler's decree ratified the important role played by Ritter's institute. Racial classification depended on an opinion to be prepared by "experts," and these unnamed experts were, of course, Ritter and his associates. Their work on classifying the Gypsy population, which had been going on for some time, now received formal legitimation and was explicitly linked to the work of the police.

In an important departure from previous practice, the decree of December 1938 stressed the importance of treating the Gypsy problem on the basis of race. At the same time, the decree continued the practice of going not only after those of "Gypsy blood" (pure Gypsies and part-Gypsies), but it also extended the various measures of control and discrimination, including preventive police custody for asocial conduct, to those who roamed about in the manner of Gypsies, the Jenische. Even when invoking the Nuremberg law restricting the right to marry, an avowedly racist piece of legislation, the "white Gypsies" who were of German extraction (albeit supposedly of inferior stock) were treated just like the "black Gypsies" possessed of "alien blood." Indeed, in the provision dealing with border areas, the Jenische were treated worse. Although sedentary Gypsies and sedentary Zigeunermischlinge were exempt from the proscription to live in these parts of the country, no such exemption was available for the itinerating "white Gypsies." Lifestyle rather than racial affiliation was to be decisive.

On March 1, 1939, Heydrich issued implementing regulations for the decree of December 8. The introduction stated that the German people respected foreign races, but the state, in order to safeguard the unity of the national community, had to adopt measures to solve the Gypsy problem. These included "the racial separation of the Gypsies from the German people, the prevention of racial mixing, and lastly the ordering of the life of racially pure Gypsies and of the Zigeunermischlinge." A law providing the legal foundation for these measures would have to be enacted. As we shall see later, this law was never adopted; the Nazis preferred to deal with the Gypsy problem on the basis of ad hoc decrees and case-to-case decisions by the RKPA. Such an approach gave them more arbitrary power in dealing with this heterogeneous population. The introduction ended with the affirmation of the need to ascertain first the number of Gypsies, Mischlinge and Gypsy-like itinerants. Once these numbers were known, it would "become possible to adopt further measures." Old methods of handling this problem were no longer adequate. "The Gypsy problem must be understood and solved on a national scale."[75]

The implementing regulations of March 1 provided administrative details for the December decree. Among these was a provision for the appointment of a specialist for Gypsy questions in every local Kripo office and for the establishment of a department for Gypsy affairs in every regional Kripo office. Given the tendency of bureaucratic organizations to justify their existence, there can be little doubt that the establishment of these special offices for Gypsy questions contributed to the magnification of the Gypsy problem. Extending the machinery of police control provided the Gypsy issue with far greater importance than it had possessed hitherto. The regulations also provided for new identity cards of different colors to be issued after the completion of the racial examination. Those for pure Gypsies were to be brown, for Mischlinge brown with a blue stripe, and for Gypsy-like itinerants gray.[76] Also included was a provision that an itinerant lifestyle by itself was not a reason for classifying someone as asocial, but this change, as I have already noted, appears to have been of little practical significance.

The decree Combating the Gypsy Plague of December 1938 foreshadowed the way in which Himmler eventually sought to solve the "Gypsy problem." Influenced by Ritter's views, the decree affirmed the necessity of distinguishing among "pure Gypsies," Zigeunermischlinge and Gypsy-like itinerants. In this way, the decree indeed was based on racial criteria, though it did not imitate the application of racialist principles to the Jews. "Pure Jews" were the incarnation of evil and the archenemy of mankind but Mischlinge, being only partly Jewish, were treated somewhat less severely. In regard to the Gypsies, it was the other way around. Mischlinge were considered the bad element and pure Gypsies considered less of a threat. As we shall see later, the deportation of Gypsies to the East in March 1943 made use of these distinctions.

4

The Special Case of the Austrian Gypsies

In the early hours of March 12, 1938, German troops crossed into Austria. A day later, the so-called Anschluss law made Austria a province of the German Reich, and this annexation was ratified in a plebiscite held on April 10. Austria had ceased to exist as an independent state. About 11,000 more Gypsies had come under Nazi rule.

Gypsies in the Burgenland

The great majority of Austrian Gypsies (probably close to 8,000) lived in the Burgenland, the easternmost and poorest Austrian province, which bordered on Hungary.[1] During the reign of the empress Maria Theresa (1740–1780) and under her son, Joseph II (1780–1790), Gypsies in Hungary (which then included the Burgenland) had been forced to become sedentary. In the 1930s their descendants lived a precarious existence, occupying the lowest ranks of the social scale. Some of them continued to exercise itinerant trades such as weaving and repairing kettles. Most of them lived in squalid quarters on the fringes of villages, and the more fortunate among them worked in construction and in agriculture as hired hands. High unemployment made it very difficult to find work; many subsisted on poor relief. The peasants themselves eked out a living close to the poverty line. For the Gypsies, writes one student of the history of Austrian Gypsies, "the poorest of the poor, the only way out of a hopeless situation was often begging and theft."[2]

Hostility toward the Gypsies in the Burgenland was widespread. They were seen as competitors for the few jobs available and as a financial burden on their communities. The press berated Gypsies on account of their crime rate and the miserable and primitive huts in which they lived; they were said to be parasites leading an asocial existence. There were allegations that they were infected with syphilis, which they spread to non-Gypsies while they themselves remained immune. The Anschluss made it possible to express these negative sentiments even more freely. An article in the Nazi party organ *Neues Volk* of September 1938 charged that only 850 of about 8,000 Gypsies living in the Burgenland had "a more or less regular job." All the others made a living by begging, fortune-telling, thievery and other criminal pursuits.[3] Another writer, alleging that six out of seven Gypsies in the Burgenland had a criminal record, called for something to be done about this situation.[4]

The authorities, it appears, did not need much convincing and moved against the Gypsies with dispatch. What had taken several years in Germany was accomplished in the Burgenland within a matter of months. Moreover, some of the measures adopted were harsher than those taken in the Altreich (Germany in its pre-1938 borders). For example, whereas the families of German Gypsies taken into preventive custody received financial assistance from welfare offices, a ruling issued on October 6, 1938, by the RKPA denied this support to the next of kin of Gypsies arrested in Austria.[5]

On March 17, 1938, it was announced that Gypsies would not be allowed to vote in the referendum of April 10.[6] Following decrees forbade begging, vagrancy and play of Gypsy music. Hard-working *Volksgenossen*, it was said, were annoyed by the sloppy bearing of Gypsy musicians who used their music as a cover for begging.[7] Another decree made Gypsies subject to compulsory labor at public works for ten hours a day. Almost half of their wages were to be paid to the communities in which they lived as compensation for many years of welfare relief. It is not clear to what extent these decrees were implemented in 1938. We do know that in the capital of the Burgenland, Eisenstadt, 232 Gypsies were taken into preventive custody and sent to concentration camps.[8] On May 12, twenty-six-year old Franz H. wrote to his government in Berlin and complained about the treatment the Gypsies were now receiving. He signed his letter "Heil unserm Führer, Heil Hitler," but this did not help him. He was arrested and sent to Dachau.[9]

Playing a major role in these measures was the governor (*Landeshauptmann*) of the Burgenland, Tobias Portschy, a leading member of the Nazi Party since its early days on the wrong side of the law. In August 1938, Portschy issued a lengthy memorandum in which he outlined his views of the Gypsy problem and what ought to be done about it. On account of their amazing rate of propagation, Portschy argued, the Gypsies in the Burgenland created a serious danger for the preservation of the purity of German blood. They now numbered 8,000 and in some villages already constituted a majority of the population; in about fifty years, unless something was done, there would be 50,000 of these "parasites." The Gypsies were burdened with hereditary and contagious diseases. They were professional thieves, whose lives were characterized by lying, fraud, laziness and other asocial traits. Half of them had a criminal record; 102 men and 22 women had committed capital crimes such as murder, robbery, arson and aggravated battery. Many communities in the Burgenland were under severe financial stress providing social services to this parasite population.[10]

Rejecting old remedies such as trying to turn Gypsies into farmers, Portschy called for a National Socialist solution of the Gypsy question. The most important goal was to limit the further growth of the Gypsy population, which could be achieved through sterilization, based on a liberal interpretation of the Law for the Prevention of Genetically Diseased Offspring. Furthermore, all Gypsies had to be forced to work. They were to be confined in special institutions or work camps, men and women being separated to prevent them from procreating. The most suitable work for them was cutting trees and digging irrigation canals and other flood control measures. They were to receive shelter, food and clothing, but no more than that; any further remuneration would only make it attractive for them to stay in Germany. Their right to emigrate was to be preserved. Once Germany had acquired colonies, they could be sent into these new territories.[11]

The above measures, Portschy maintained, could be realized within the framework of existing legislation. However, new "special legal norms" were also needed. Sexual intercourse between Gypsies and Germans was to be considered "racial defilement" (*Rassenschande*) and severely punished. "Those who know the Gypsies' character and understand how degraded their race is will agree that they must be treated exactly like the Jews." Gypsy children should no longer be allowed to attend primary schools. No Gypsy was to be admitted to a public hospital; medical care was to be provided exclusively by institutional or camp physicians. Gypsies were to be excluded from military service. Some people, Portschy acknowledged, would consider these proposals barbaric and inhumane. In reality, however, they were most humane, for only thus could a solution be found for the "Gypsy plague." If the Nordic people were to grant these "emissaries of the Orient" any kind of favor they would be guilty of criminal negligence.[12]

Portschy was not alone in putting forth radical proposals for solving the "Gypsy question," though his rhetoric was probably a bit more heated. Portschy's diatribe was part of a powerful and steadily growing chorus that demanded to rid the Burgenland of its Gypsies. *"Das Burgenland Zigeunerfrei!"* became the slogan,[13] and, in 1939 Himmler obliged his followers in the Ostmark by taking several hundred Burgenland Gypsies into preventive custody. In 1941, thousands more were deported to the East. The Gypsies of Austria, especially those in the Burgenland, were even more despised than the Gypsies in the rest of Germany. This gave rise to calls for quick and radical solutions to the "Gypsy plague," and the authorities in Berlin eventually provided just such plans.

On July 26, 1938, Himmler ordered that the decree of December 14, 1937, on preventive crime fighting be applied to Austria.[14] About a year later, this decree was invoked to make a decisive move against the Gypsies of the Burgenland. On June 5, 1939, the RKPA informed the Kripo regional office of Vienna that Himmler wanted the "Gypsies or Zigeunermischlinge of the Burgenland who are work-shy and asocial to a pronounced degree taken into preventive custody." The RKPA estimated that this involved about 2,000 males above the age of sixteen. Exempt were those who for some time had held steady jobs, especially in agriculture, and were indispensable for bringing in the harvest. Unlike Operation Work-Shy of June 1938, which had been limited to men, this order included women. "Wives (spouses) and other female relatives of the Gypsies and Zigeunermischlinge to be arrested are also to be taken into preventive custody, for according to past experience it is to be feared that they will engage in criminal conduct or become prostitutes and thus endanger the community. The number of female persons—fifteen to fifty years old—to be seized should not exceed one thousand." Men were to be sent to Dachau, women to Ravensbrück. The children of the arrested adults as well as breast-feeding mothers and pregnant women were to be cared for by private relief organizations; in fact many of the children ended up in the camps. The entire operation was to be concluded by June 30.[15]

According to the 1939–1940 yearbook of the RKPA, the operation against "asocials" in the Burgenland led to the arrest of 553 men and 440 women, for a total of 993 Gypsies.[16] The women were dispatched to Ravensbrück. The men, sent to Dachau, eventually ended up in Buchenwald, for in October 1939 Dachau was temporarily vacated. Other men not included in this total may have been sent to Mauthausen. The Vienna edition of the June 28 *Völkischer Beobachter* expressed satisfaction with the arrest of the Gypsies. Paraphrasing a well-known song, the newspaper story was headlined "Come, Csigany—show me how you can work."[17]

Other Measures against the Austrian Gypsies

Abolishing the border between Germany and Austria led to increased movement of Gypsies between the two parts of the Reich. In order to stop this migration, Himmler ordered on May 13, 1938, that all Austrian Gypsies above the age of fourteen be fingerprinted. One copy of these prints was to be sent to the RKPA in Berlin. "Non-sedentary Gypsies and Gypsy-like itinerants are to be told that they may not cross the border of the old Reich."[18] The Kripo of Eisenstadt, acting on its own, fingerprinted every Gypsy above the age of six.[19]

On May 23, 1938, it was announced that the order forbidding marriage between Jews and Germans included Gypsies. They too belonged to an alien race and therefore should not be allowed to marry persons of German blood.[20] An order issued on February 27, 1939, forbade Jews and Gypsies to acquire real estate.[21] Later that spring, a debate ensued over the question whether Gypsy children were to be treated like Jewish children and be barred from the public schools. The debate illustrated the rival lines of authority and jurisdiction that had developed, and the resulting confusion in the formulation of Gypsy policy.

On February 15, 1939, Kurt Krüger, an official in the Austrian Ministry of Education and a Nazi party member, inquired from the staff of the deputy of the Führer whether Gypsy children could be excluded from the public schools. A reply dated March 7 stated that "it does not seem opportune to dilute the special measures taken in regard to the Jewish question by extending them to all members of alien races and to put Jews and others of alien races on an equal footing." The Gypsy question was a special problem; in addition to its racial aspect it was also closely related to the regulation of the asocials. "I do not want to take the question of the schooling of Gypsy children out of this context."[22]

The Austrian official was not happy with this reply. On March 11 he once again addressed the office of the deputy of the Führer and invoked the authority of an official in the NSDAP Office of Racial Policy, Dr. Frerks. After an inspection tour of the Burgenland, Frerks had conveyed to him his "urgent desire that Gypsy children be removed from the public schools and be treated like the Jews." He had also told him that Krüger could consider this opinion an official position of the Office of Racial Policy. Hence, Krüger wrote, unless he received a message contradicting this view until March 15, he would issue a decree that would treat the children of Gypsies and Zigeuner-mischlinge like the children of Jews. He also proposed sterilizing all Gypsies with a criminal record. This proposal too, he wrote, was supported by Dr. Frerks, who agreed with him on the urgent necessity of halting the rapid increase in the Gypsy population. The Jews would die out after two or three more generations anyway.[23]

It appears that Krüger had second thoughts about proceeding on his own in this matter. Instead of ordering the immediate exclusion of Gypsy children from the public schools, he decided first to collect more information on the number of Gypsy children who would be affected by such a step. A report from the Steiermark, a newly constituted party district (*Gau*) in southern Austria, revealed that the ever zealous Portschy, the deputy *Gauleiter* (Nazi Party official), had already expelled about half of the 850 Gypsy children of school age from the public schools of his district. The remaining 425 children lived scattered in different locations, which made the creation of special classes for them impractical.[24]

The head of the school district of Oberwart in the Burgenland wrote to Krüger on March 29 that in his view the steadily increasing number of Gypsy children called for urgent and radical measures. Several reasons supported the exclusion of these children from the public schools. First, they were carriers of contagious diseases, they did not wash or change their clothing and they exuded a horrible smell. To put German boys and girls in the same rooms with this "pest" amounted to "racial suicide." Second, to provide instruction for the 1,078 Gypsy children in the district would require the employment of twenty new teachers, a tremendous economic burden. The money required for such a program, the official argued, could better be spent for the education of the German population. Moreover, the police probably had little interest in literate Gypsies. "This race causes them enough trouble now. One could imagine what it would be like if all of them knew how to read and write." Lastly, there were pedagogic considerations. The younger Gypsy children spoke no German and would need teachers who knew the Romani language. Finding them would be a wasted effort. Past experience had shown that most Gypsy children learned little while stealing a lot. The problem of schooling for the Gypsies, the official concluded, could be solved only within the framework of a total solution of the Gypsy problem. All Gypsies should be concentrated in several camps; then children could be instructed in reading and writing but no other subject. Four to six SA or SS men could supervise such a program. "In order that this pest disappear from the German milieu, I propose the painless but total sterilization of this race. Until they are finally disposed of one should employ them in forced labor."[25]

Austrian officials thus faced a dilemma. They wanted to rid their schools of Gypsy children, but at the same time they were not prepared to spend the money necessary for special classes for Gypsies. A solution to this predicament came about a year later when the minister of education in Berlin issued an instruction on the school attendance of Gypsy and Negro children. Following the adoption of the Citizenship Law of September 15, 1935, Gypsies had been denied the right to vote. Yet the Ministry of Education in June 1939 still referred to Gypsies as German citizens whose children had the right and duty to attend public schools, typifying the confusion in formulating racial policy. Because the number of these children in any one locality was generally small, the instruction pointed out, the establishment of special Gypsy schools was not realistic. However, "insofar as such children constitute a moral or other threat to their classmates of German blood, they can be expelled from the school." The police were to be informed about such cases.[26] School officials in the Ostmark thus were given the right to banish Gypsy children whom they considered a threat. Since these officials regarded all Gypsy children as "pests," this instruction in effect provided the solution they had been looking for: They could expel Gypsy children from the public schools without providing a costly alternative in the form of separate classes or schools.

No information is available on how many school districts got rid of their Gypsy children in this way. In Vienna all principals, prodded by school administrators, put in requests to have Gypsy children excluded on the grounds that they constituted "a threat to the moral character of the German children." These requests were of course granted.[27]

Many in the former Austria continued to demand a radical solution of the Gypsy problem. For example, on January 12, 1939, the police post of St. Johann reported to the Landrat that the rural population was calling for more energetic measures against the "Gypsy plague." People were fed up with shouldering the expense of dealing "with this itinerating race that does nothing but steal from and swindle the Germans." Among the measures being sought were new regulations forbidding the nomadic life of the Gypsies and the sterilization of serious repeat offenders. "Altogether, sterilization should be used more frequently, for this evil has to be tackled at its root."[28] Before long, as we shall see, these demands for a more radical approach to the Gypsy problem were indeed accepted by decision makers in Berlin.

Part II

A TIGHTENED NET

(1939–1942)

5

"Security Measures" and Expulsions

The accusation that Gypsies are given to espionage is very old and is based on their itinerating lifestyle and intimate knowledge of the countryside. In the late fifteenth century it was alleged that they spied for the Turks. The legislature of the Holy Roman Empire of the German Nation that met in 1497 called the Gypsies traitors and spies and ordered their expulsion from all German lands. These accusations were repeated in 1500, 1530 and 1548,[1] and the onset of modernity brought no end to such charges. At the beginning of World War I, Gypsies were expelled from the fortified area of Strassburg, located close to the French border.[2] On April 30, 1916, the Ministry of Interior of Saxony declared that Gypsies constituted a danger to the security of the Reich; their international connections and their peripatetic way of life, it was said, made them especially susceptible to espionage.[3] A military commander in Koblenz on February 6, 1917, forbade Gypsies to itinerate; in a message to the *Landräte* (chief magistrates) he warned that foreign agents used the Gypsies for espionage and sabotage and that deserters found refuge among them.[4] An order issued by the military command in Württemberg and distributed by the Ministry of the Interior on November 6, 1917, forbade Gypsies from engaging in "Gypsy-like roaming" and from camping in the vicinity of military or other facilities important for the war effort.[5]

Allegations of Gypsy espionage continued to be raised by the Nazis during the 1930s. On July 4, 1936, the Prussian Gestapo distributed a report by the Bavarian political police that noted the presence of Gypsies in the vicinity of military construction sites. "It is suspected that these Gypsies work for foreign intelligence services."[6] Members of a Gypsy band playing in Halberstadt, the Gestapo Düsseldorf reported on October 17, 1939, had been observed talking with soldiers. "Suspicion of espionage cannot be excluded."[7] None of these charges were ever proven, but this fact did not prevent the allegations from being repeated time and again.

Removal from the Western Border and other Restrictions

Restrictive measures against the Gypsies began already during the preparations for war. On July 21, 1938, the special commissioner of the Ministry of the Interior for the building of the *Westwall*, von Pfeffer, issued a decree that ordered the expulsion of roving Gypsies from the area on the left bank of the Rhine and from the state of Baden. The text of this decree is not preserved, but subsequent correspondence and instructions show that the measure exempted sedentary Gypsies. In practice events took a different course. Many local authorities, it appears, used the opportunity to get rid of all of their Gypsies, sedentary and nonsedentary, and the government of Hesse expelled even Gypsies on the right side of the Rhine. Altogether the expulsion was accompanied by considerable disarray, for no new places of residence had been prepared for these people and no city was anxious to have them. Some arrived in Berlin only to be sent back to Frankfurt/Main. The welfare office of Frankfurt complained on August 24 that forty-nine Gypsies, refused by Berlin, had been dumped on the city. Twelve of these had been kept, and the others had been moved on to Erfurt, Halle and Kassel. These cities, in turn, had sent the Gypsies back to Frankfurt. The city's Gypsy camp, the welfare office pointed out, had outrun its capacity and some of the new arrivals had to sleep in the open.[8]

Himmler took note of this chaotic situation and on August 26 ordered that sedentary Gypsies, who should not have been expelled in the first place, be sent back to their place of residence. Several months later, Himmler agreed that the Ministry of the Interior would pay the costs incurred in removing and returning these people.[9] The Combating the Gypsy Plague decree of December 8, 1938, as I have noted, reaffirmed the principle that only nonsedentary Gypsies and Gypsy-like itinerants be excluded from the border areas. In July 1939, the special commissioner for the building of the Westwall informed the Ministry of the Interior of Baden that according to information received from the Gestapo in Karlsruhe, an unusually large number of Gypsies were to be found in its area of jurisdiction. Their presence so close to border fortifications was undesirable, and he therefore asked the government of Baden to remove all itinerating Gypsies from the districts of Villingen and Donaueschingen. "Gypsies who hold a regular job are not affected by this order."[10]

The beginning of the war brought several further restrictive measures. On September 2, 1939, a decree issued by Heydrich established a border zone along the entire German frontier in which licenses to carry on an itinerant trade were valid only with a special authorization. "The roaming of Gypsies and in the manner of Gypsies in the border zone is forbidden."[11] Several days later, on September 9, instructions went out to use the most restrictive criteria in issuing itinerant trade licenses. The police were authorized to withhold this license even if ordered to issue a license by a court.[12] Police files in Düsseldorf show that applications for this all-important license were now turned down routinely. The standard phrase explaining the refusal was that the applicant would use "the itinerant trade merely as a pretense in order to follow the typical Gypsy offenses such as fortune-telling, faith healing and begging."[13] In practice this meant that numerous Gypsies were deprived of their traditional livelihood. On October 11 a decree of Himmler provided that working papers (*Arbeitsbuch*) for Gypsies, *Zigeunermischlinge* (Gypsies of mixed ancestry) and Gypsy-like itinerants were to be issued only after the Kripo had established the applicant's identity.[14]

In November 1939, Heydrich's domestic intelligence service, the *Sicherheitsdienst (SD)*, reported that Gypsies and other fortune-tellers were spreading rumors about the end of the war.[15] The same month Heydrich issued a decree against fortune-telling by Gypsy women; the term "Gypsy woman" was to be interpreted loosely. "Even persons with little Gypsy admixture are to be treated as Gypsies." Recently, the decree explained, numerous reports had been received about Gypsies who through fortune-telling had created "considerable unrest in the population." This activity harmed the German people and therefore had to be stopped. The decree therefore provided that Gypsy women convicted of fortune-telling and those under serious suspicion of engaging in fortune-telling now or in the past be taken into preventive custody. The children of those arrested were to be cared for by their families; only if they were unable to handle this task should the welfare organizations take charge of these children. In arrest reports the number of pregnant or breast-feeding women was to be highlighted.[16]

Many of the women arrested under this decree did not survive preventive custody, typically served in the concentration camp of Ravensbrück. Anna L. was a forty-seven-year-old Gypsy woman who in February 1940 was sent to Ravensbrück because of fortune-telling. She died there on May 14, 1942. Her next of kin were informed that the body could not be released for "hygienic reasons."[17] Emma K. was thirty-six years old and the mother of six children when she was arrested in June of 1940 for fortune-telling. She agreed not to engage in this activity in the future and therefore, instead of being sent to a concentration camp, was sentenced by a Magdeburg court to three weeks imprisonment. In March 1943 she and her six children were deported to Auschwitz. The fate of this family is not known.[18]

A Freeze on Mobility

The conquest of Poland in September 1939 encouraged Heydrich to make grandiose plans to deport Jews and Gypsies to the newly seized territories in the East. This area was to become a gigantic dumping ground for all undesirable elements; Germany was to be made racially pure. Hence on September 21, one week before the conclusion of the Polish campaign, Heydrich informed leading police officials and the heads of the task forces for special missions (*Einsatzgruppen*) operating in Poland that Hitler had approved the expulsion of the Jews and "the remaining 30,000 Gypsies" from the Reich. The plan, to be implemented over one year, was to settle the deportees in the eastern part of Poland, an area later known as the General Government (*Generalgouvernement*).[19]

In preparation for this expulsion, on October 17 Heydrich issued a decree providing for a freeze on mobility for Gypsies, generally referred to as the *Festsetzungserlass*. On orders of Himmler, the decree declared, the Gypsy question was shortly to be tackled on a thorough and nationwide basis. First, all Gypsies and Zigeunermischlinge were to be advised, effective immediately, not to leave their place of residence. Noncompliance was to be punished by imprisonment in a concentration camp. Second, on October 25, 26 and 27 Gypsies and Zigeunermischlinge were to be counted by local police authorities. Reports on the results were to include information on whether the persons counted had done regular work during the preceding five years, whether they had been able to make a living for themselves and their families, whether they occupied a permanent dwelling (an apartment or property) and whether one of the marriage partners was Aryan. These reports were to be completed with the utmost dispatch. The RKPA, working in cooperation with the Reich Health Office (read Ritter's institute engaged in classifying the Gypsy population), would examine these data and then issue the necessary arrest orders. Those arrested, the decree concluded, "until their final removal" would be kept in special collection camps. Plans for the establishment of such camps and for the availability of guards and vehicles for transport to these camps were to be made forthwith.[20]

The execution of this order could be swift, for most of the data needed had been collected already several months earlier under the Combating the Gypsy Plague decree of December 8, 1938. A special form, RKP 172, had been developed in the spring of 1939 that carried the heading "Count of Gypsies, Zigeunermischlinge and Gypsy-like itinerants," and the information collected at that time was now incorporated into the reports required by the new decree. A substantial number of such reports, primarily from the districts of Kassel and Fulda, have been preserved.[21] Most of the Gypsies in this part of Germany apparently led a predominantly settled life. According to the reports, the majority of individuals "do regular work." Occasionally a person maintained that he was Aryan. "W. claims to be of Aryan descent," stated a report from Kassel, "but he was unable to supply proof for this assertion."[22]

Meanwhile, however, the planned mass expulsion of Jews and Gypsies had run into an unforeseen problem that soon brought the entire operation to a halt. On October 19, the first Jews had arrived in Nisko, located southwest of the city of Lublin, which had been designated as a special territory for Jews (*Judenreservat*). RKPA head Nebe was anxious that Gypsies from Berlin be included in these transports, and on October 12 he inquired from Eichmann, in charge of arrangements, how soon the Gypsies from Berlin could be sent to the East. Lengthy delays in their departure would necessitate the construction of special camps for them, which would entail great cost and other difficulties.[23] Eichmann replied on October 16 that the first transport of Jews from Vienna would leave for Nisko on October 20. "Three to four carloads of Gypsies could be added to this transport."[24] Further transports of Viennese Jews were planned for the following weeks, and the Gypsies of the Ostmark, it was envisaged, would be put on these trains in special cars.[25] Yet nothing came of these plans, for on October 19 Himmler ordered a stop to all further transports to Nisko. The reason for this abrupt reversal was the logjam that had arisen in the absorption of ethnic Germans (*Volksdeutsche*) from the Baltic states, a large-scale operation very dear to Hitler and Himmler. In order to provide lodging and livelihood for this massive influx into West Prussia and the part of Poland annexed to Germany (the Warthegau), it was necessary to expel large numbers of Jews and Poles into eastern Poland. This effort, it was decided, had priority over all other resettlement plans.[26] The Gypsies of Germany had gained a respite.

The expulsion of the Gypsies from the Reich had been shelved, but the freeze on mobility, ordered in preparation for their deportation to the East, was not annulled. On October 25–27, the days set aside for the count, all adult Gypsies were made to sign a declaration in which they obligated themselves not to leave their present place of residence. They also had to acknowledge that if they violated this injunction they would be sent to a concentration camp. Any changes in residence required permission from the police.[27] The files preserved show that such changes were allowed only in rare cases of severe personal hardship or job relocation. On the other hand, temporary absences for the purpose of visiting a sick close relative or attending a funeral in another town were generally approved routinely. Such trips required a special permit that had to be presented to the police at the place to be visited and had to be surrendered upon return to the permanent place of residence.[28] On April 1, 1942, the RKPA forbade the issuing of these permits for travel to Berlin. Too many Gypsies, it was said, used such visits in order to plead at the RKPA for a change in various decisions taken by the RKPA.[29]

For Gypsies who had derived their livelihood from an itinerant trade, the freeze on mobility presented a serious problem. The Kripo in Munich therefore inquired in Berlin whether such persons could be granted some freedom of movement, and the RKPA agreed with this suggestion. The purpose of the October 10, decree, it was explained, was to make sure "that every Gypsy and Zigeunermischling can be reached at all times. If that fact is assured there are no objections to allowing these persons to practice their trade with a limited degree of mobility." Such traders, if not needed for other pressing work, were instructed to send a postcard to their local police authority every fourteen days, in which they would note their current address and their next destination.[30] This provision remained in force until it was canceled on March 7, 1941. The local trade, the new announcement pointed out, was able to meet the needs of the population. Moreover, it was important to employ all Gypsies and Zigeunermischlinge in regular manual labor, which these persons had always sought to avoid.[31]

The decree of October 17, 1939, ordering a freeze on mobility did not, unlike earlier decrees, mention Gypsy-like travelers who were of "German blood," and this omission undoubtedly was not an oversight. The decree thus marked a switch to a more marked emphasis on racial criteria in the formulation of Gypsy policy. For the first time, "white Gypsies" were treated better than "black Gypsies." The measure apparently was to prepare the ground for the expulsion of Gypsies and Zigeunermischlinge only; Gypsy-like travelers were not included in the planned deportation. At the same time, the old emphasis on lifestyle was also reaffirmed. The decree had asked for information about social status—ability to support a family and whether the individual was fully sedentary. Presumably, those who were socially adjusted and sedentary, that is, those who had held a regular job during the preceding five years, were to be exempted from deportation.

The expulsion of the German Gypsies into the newly acquired lands in the East had been canceled for now, but the idea did not disappear from view. Some of the key elements of Heydrich's scheme showed up in a memorandum of November 25, 1939, authored by Erhard Wetzel and Gerhard Hecht, two officials of the Office of Racial Policy of the Nazi party. That office for some time had been trying to elbow its way into the formulation of Gypsy policy. The memorandum dealt with the treatment of the population of the former Polish territories according to racial-political criteria and proposed that in addition to 800,000 Jews the General Government absorb "about 100,000 Gypsies and other alien elements" to be expelled from the Reich.[32] Himmler and Heydrich, it appears, paid little attention to this memorandum from a rival agency for which they had little use.[33] They had their own plans, which were no less radical in scope.

The Expulsion of May 1940

In October 1939, as we have seen, the logjam created by the resettlement of ethnic Germans led to cancellation of the plan to deport the German Gypsies to the East. But the measure had only been postponed. When Hitler appointed Himmler as Reich commissioner for the strengthening of German nationhood (*Reichskommissar für die Festigung Deutschen Volkstums*, or RKF) on October 7, 1939, he charged him with the task of bringing ethnic Germans back into the Reich on one hand and eliminating the damaging influence of alien population groups in Germany on the other.[34] Himmler was all too willing to handle this dual assignment. In all of Germany, he told the Gauleiter and other party functionaries on February 29, 1940, "there are [only] 30,000 Gypsies who nevertheless cause very substantial racial damage. Especially in the Ostmark there are very many of them." Himmler indicated that he would attempt to expel the Gypsies in 1940.[35] On January 30, 1940, Heydrich convened a meeting of forty-two SS functionaries to discuss resettlement policy. The SS Race and Resettlement Main Office (*Rasse- und Siedlungshauptamt*, or RuSHA) once again brought up the plan of sending

30,000 German Gypsies to the General Government. The operation was to take place after about 120,000 Poles were expelled into the General Government to make way for the resettlement of more than 100,000 Volhynia Germans (ethnic Germans from the part of eastern Poland seized by the Soviet Union).[36]

Not everyone agreed with this plan. The surgeon general (*Reichsarzt*) in the Ministry of the Interior, Dr. Leonardo Conti, who combined state and party functions in matters of health, opposed deportation on the grounds that it would achieve only a geographical change and not a real solution of the problem of the Gypsies. In a widely distributed letter written on January 24, 1940, Conti argued that the most important task was to prevent the further mixture of Gypsy and German blood, and this could only be achieved through sterilization. Expelling the Gypsies to the General Government did not really solve the problem. The expelled Gypsies would cause the authorities in the General Government great difficulties, for Gypsies learned to outwit the state. They undoubtedly would use forged papers to cross the border into Lithuania, Hungary, Slovakia and Rumania; eventually, equipped with foreign passports, they would reappear in Germany. Thus the expulsion-emigration-immigration cycle would be repeated while the number of Gypsies continued to increase. The only effective solution was to sterilize all Gypsies and Zigeunermischlinge immediately. Conti called for a conference to discuss the issue on February 7.[37]

No information about this conference has been preserved. We do know that early in 1940 Ritter held very similar views. In a report on the work of his institute, Ritter argued that the only effective solution of the Gypsy question was to put the asocial Zigeunermischlinge into work camps and to prevent their further propagation. "Only then will future generations of the German people be truly freed from this burden . . . . Every other attempted solution such as to expel Gypsies able to propagate beyond the German border to the East will be unsuccessful *in the long run*."[38]

Demands for slowing down the relocations came from the governor of the newly established General Government in the eastern part of Poland, Hans Frank. This "moody autocrat," as Hilberg calls him,[39] was not opposed to radical measures against Jews and Gypsies, but he feared a disorderly influx and altogether was less than happy about the General Government becoming a dumping ground for all kinds of undesirable elements. Frank also was locked in a bitter conflict with Himmler over who would make crucial security decisions in the General Government. Himmler demanded primary authority for his SS and police apparatus, whereas Frank insisted on the last word for himself and his administration. In this contest Frank believed that he had come out on top. He told a group of administrators from the district of Lublin on March 4, 1940, that in a meeting with Göring held on February 12, attended also by Himmler, he had been able to obtain a commitment that no expulsions into the General Government would take place without his agreement. Instead of an influx of millions of Poles, the General Government would have to absorb only 100,000–120,000 Poles, an as yet undetermined number

of German Jews, and about 30,000 German Gypsies.[40] These were the figures that Himmler and Heydrich had discussed a few weeks earlier, but, as far
as the Gypsies were concerned, even this goal was not attained.

In April 1940 the expulsion of the Gypsies, envisaged since the beginning
of the war, finally moved into the concrete planning phase. On April 27,
Heydrich issued a decree, Resettlement of Gypsies, that gave orders to start
the long-delayed process. "The first transport of Gypsies to the General
Government—2,500 persons, members of entire clans—will be sent away in
the middle of May. Included at first will be Gypsies from the western and
north-western border areas." The Kripo offices of Hamburg and Bremen
were to gather 1,000 Gypsies in special collection camps and load them onto
trains. The Kripo of Cologne, Düsseldorf and Hannover were also to collect
1,000 Gypsies, and Stuttgart and Frankfurt/Main were to gather five hundred persons.[41]

Further details were provided in implementing regulations issued the
same day. Gypsies and Zigeunermischlinge were to be seized in accordance
with the lists prepared under the decree of October 17, 1939; the total number to be deported was not to exceed 2,500. If not enough Gypsies to reach
this quota could be found in the border areas, Gypsies from the adjacent
provinces could be added. Several groups were exempted from deportation:
all frail persons, especially those over seventy years, women seven or more
months pregnant, Gypsies married to a German, Gypsies who had sons or
fathers serving in the military, Gypsies who owned substantial real estate, and
Gypsies of foreign nationality. Those seized were to be put into collection
camps for no more than three days. In these camps, Gypsies over the age of
fourteen were to be photographed and issued an identity card; those over the
age of six were to be fingerprinted. Prior to leaving the camps, all Gypsies
were to be deloused. Every person was allowed to take along up to fifty kilo
of luggage and twenty zloty (ten marks); the Polish currency was to be provided by the RKPA. Jewelery, stocks and bonds and money beyond the sum
of RM 10 had to be left behind, either with other Gypsies not subject to
deportation or in special bank accounts. The transports were to be guarded
by police; every transport was to have an accompanying physician and to be
provided with food for fourteen days. The entire operation was to be carried
out as soon as the necessary transport could be made ready.[42]

A detailed report on how the deportation was carried out in the Frankfurt
area was compiled by the Darmstadt Kripo. On May 16, a total of 199 persons were arrested "without problems": one hundred in Mainz, eighty-one in
Worms and eighteen in Ingelheim. The seized Gypsies were put on a special
train. "The cooperation of the German railroad," the report noted, "deserves
special mention." The arrested persons were taken to a collection camp
established at the Württemberg state prison of Hohenasperg. Here it was
discovered that the lists for the arrests had been compiled without consulting
the racial-biological examinations carried out by the Ritter institute in
Berlin. It was thus difficult to be sure that the arrested persons were indeed
Gypsies or Zigeunermischlinge, who were subject to deportation, and not

Gypsy expellees on the way to the train station Asperg for their journey to the General Government, May 22, 1940. COURTESY OF BUNDESARCHIV KOBLENZ.

Gypsy-like travelers. To solve this problem, Dr. Adolf Würth, a staff member of the Ritter institute, was quickly dispatched to Hohenasperg. He brought along the relevant files and carried out some further examinations. Several individuals, it now turned out, indeed were not Gypsies and they were released. In other instances, Gypsies had been arrested even though their father or son served in the armed forces, and they, too, were set free. The total number of those exempted from deportation was twenty-two.[43]

On May 22, somewhat behind schedule, the special train that was to take the deported Gypsies to the General Government was finally ready to roll. Before departing from the collection camp, those over the age of fourteen had to sign the following declaration: "I have been told today that if contrary to orders I return to Germany I shall be sterilized and taken into preventive police custody (concentration camp)." Several Gypsies at first hesitated to sign this declaration. This was the only difficulty in the entire operation, the report noted. Everything else proceeded smoothly and went according to plan. Among the minor glitches listed in an appendix was the difficulty of handling mothers who breast-fed their babies. Dealing with the new mothers and their suckling infants, some just a few days old, "involved much work." The decree had exempted highly pregnant women, but as a lesson for future deportations the police officer pointed out that "pregnant women can be transported and handled more easily than a breast-feeding mother."[44]

A collection camp for Gypsies in the Rhineland was established in Cologne. Five days later, 938 Gypsies were deported from this camp to the East on May 21.[45] Police files preserved in the state archive for Rhineland-Westphalia in Düsseldorf provide additional details about this deportation.

Here too the results of the examinations carried out by the Ritter institute apparently were not available, and this led to mistakes in the selection process. For example, Gustav L. was deported because there was a description of him in the Marienberghausen police record as "a Gypsy-like itinerant" (dated April 10, 1939). He protested his deportation on the grounds that he was not a Gypsy and was eventually allowed to return. The expert evaluation (*Gutachten*) of L., the RKPA informed the Cologne Kripo on October 20, 1941, proved that he was indeed a non-Gypsy, and his deportation therefore was in error. L. was sent a letter informing him of this decision, but the letter was returned as undeliverable. Apparently, L. by then had moved to another place of residence. His eventual fate is not known.[46]

In another case, a Gypsy who had been deported with his family insisted that he was a German citizen. Philipp S. wrote to Hitler from Poland that he hoped for help from "my Führer." He and his ancestors, he pleaded, were Germans. His letter ended "Heil Hitler," but none of this helped. The Cologne Kripo informed S. on October 8, 1940, that "according to existing regulations your application can not be approved." S. survived the deportation.[47]

Lawyers were urged not to represent Gypsies, yet a few of them did agree to help Gypsies threatened with deportation. Fritz Rebmann intervened on behalf of Johanna F., a forty-year-old woman who, he argued, was only one quarter Gypsy. Rebmann had represented the family since 1930. They were honest people who had never come into conflict with the law. Moreover, F. was the sole support for her old mother and her severely handicapped brother. In case of her deportation, both of these persons would become dependent on welfare. The intervention was successful and F. was released on May 25.[48]

In several other cases lawyers were unable to obtain the annulment of deportation orders. W. Teschendorf intervened on behalf of two Gypsy families. Some members of these families, the lawyer pointed out, had been released. The deportation of two of the men would leave behind their German wives, who were pregnant. In another case, two sixty-nine-year-olds would be deprived of their children's support and would become a burden on the state. Teschendorf stressed that he had raised only the most severe hardship cases. Such cases, he maintained, "create nothing but resentment and indignation and supply our enemies with material for anti–National Socialist propaganda. I should point out that I am a member of the NSDAP and an SA leader." Teschendorf failed in his appeal.[49]

In another case, the intervention of a lawyer was unsuccessful even though according to the deportation decree a release would have been possible. The wife of Johann G., the attorney Carl Schwengers pointed out, was seven months pregnant and thus eligible for exemption. She was the mother of five other children. The family had always been self-supporting. The appeal was rejected and the family was deported.[50]

The deportation decree provided for the exemption of parents whose sons had been conscripted into the military, but this provision too was interpreted in the narrowest and strictest manner possible. Joseph L. was supposed to start his military service on May 19. On May 18 he applied for the release of his parents, who had been seized on May 16. The application was rejected on the grounds that on the day of the arrest of the parents L. had not yet been a soldier.[51] Similarly, persons over seventy who were frail could be exempted, but few, it appears, were given the benefit of the doubt. Among the deported was a man of seventy-three; another was seventy-nine years old.[52]

The implementing regulations for the deportation decree had envisaged the possibility that those able to foot the expense at a later time might be given the opportunity to have their furniture and other belongings sent to them in the General Government. However, this provision was never put into practice. At first the property of the deported Gypsies was not touched. Apartments were sealed and their contents inventoried.[53] In Mainz furniture was stored in the basement of a municipal storage facility, but in October 1940 the chief of police complained about the expense involved, which he maintained was out of proportion to the value of the stored articles. In December the RKPA decided that vermin-infested items could be destroyed; others could be entrusted to Gypsies who had not been deported.[54] About a year later, it was decided that this property would be seized. The expropriation was justified with the help of a law of July 14, 1933, that provided for the confiscation of property owned by persons engaged in activities hostile to the German people and state. A memo of the Ministry of the Interior dated November 14, 1941, noted that the 2,500 Gypsies and Zigeunermischlinge resettled into the General Government had been following "endeavors hostile to the German people and state" and that their property therefore was forfeited.[55]

The charge that the deported Gypsies had been enemies of the German state was, of course, nothing but a convenient justification for a confiscation of property. The Gypsies had often been depicted as a plague and a nuisance, but, apart from a few isolated allegations of espionage, they had not been accused of activities hostile to the German state. Indeed, on September 4, 1940, the RKPA had informed the Office of Racial Policy of the NSDAP that the dispatch of the 2,500 Gypsies to the General Government was "a resettlement and not a punishment." Negotiations were in progress to enable close relatives to join them there.[56] The deportation of 2,500 Gypsies to the East in May 1940, as this and numerous other documents make clear, was the beginning of an intended expulsion of all German Gypsies. It had nothing to do with punishment for political activities for which the 1933 law had been enacted.

Several documents, including the RKPA letter of September 4, 1940, refer to an urgent demand of the High Command of the Armed Forces (*Oberkommando der Wehrmacht*, or OKW) to remove Gypsies from the western and northwestern border areas. On January 31, 1940, the OKW indeed had requested Himmler to issue "as soon as possible" an order prohibiting Gypsies from residing in the border zone. Whether German citizens or not, the OKW had written, they represent a thoroughly unreliable element and their presence in the border zone is therefore "intolerable from the point of view of defense."[57] This request may have persuaded Himmler and Heydrich to begin the expulsion of the Gypsies from Germany with those in the western border area, but the basic expulsion plan, as I have noted, had been made several months earlier. A reference to military security does not appear in Heydrich's decree of April 27, 1940; like the alleged hostility of the Gypsies to the German state, it may have been added after the fact. Altogether, the idea that the expulsion was based in the main on concern about military security is less than credible. If urgent military considerations, perhaps linked to the planned attack on France, were the motive for this decision, why did Heydrich wait until April 27 to issue the expulsion order? Why was it not executed until the middle of May, an entire week after the invasion of the Low Countries? Why did he limit the number of expellees to 2,500? Why did he exempt foreign Gypsies and Gypsy-like itinerants who generally were regarded with no less suspicion than the German Gypsies? Why did Heydrich send the expellees to the General Government, which was also a border zone and in which the Gypsies as potential spies probably could do more harm than in Germany where they were under close supervision? To repeat, to set a numerical target of 2,500 Gypsies and Zigeunermischlinge made no sense if the measure was based on considerations of military security. The expulsion of May 1940 is traceable to plans first announced in September 1939, and it continued to be enforced well after the changed military situation in the West no longer provided any possible justification. The quota of 2,500 is explainable only in terms of the limited availability of transport and probably Frank's insistence that his domain not be swamped by too many Gypsies all at once.[58]

The 1940 deportation measure was the first installment in a scheme to expel all German Gypsies within one year. In July 1940 the RKPA was still planning another transport to the General Government, and Kripo offices were asked to report on the number of Gypsies in their area of jurisdiction.[59] However, by September this larger plan had been abandoned. In the letter of September 4, cited above, the RKPA noted, "Further resettlements are not anticipated for now, since the reception in the General Government at the present time is encountering difficulties. The final solution of the Gypsy problem is scheduled after the end of the war."[60] A victorious conclusion of the war was expected at an early date. An RKPA memo of November 27, 1940, once again made reference to the end of all further "resettlements" of Gypsies and attributed this decision to Himmler.[61]

At first, as I have noted, the RKPA was still anticipating the possibility that close relatives who were interested in following their next of kin to the General Government would be able to do so. But by the end of the year 1940 even this very limited migration was ruled out. On December 7 the RKPA notified regional and local Kripo offices that the General Government "at the present time does not desire this intended resettlement." The leadership of the General Government, the RKPA noted, had promised to reexamine the issue again in April 1941,[62] but nothing came of this reevaluation. On August 9, 1941, the RKPA had to inform the Kripo offices that because of the war in the East moves to the General Government were no longer possible.[63]

The plan to expel 30,000 German Gypsies to the new territories acquired in the East thus had ended with the expulsion of a mere 2,500.[64] The major obstacle to the realization of this scheme appears to have been the logjam created by the forced movement of over 300,000 Poles into the General Government. Also, by the summer of 1940 Himmler probably was preoccupied with more important matters. A one-sentence memo composed in the office of the general governor, Hans Frank, dated August 3, 1940, explained the new situation succinctly: "The Reichsführer–SS und Chef der Deutschen Polizei has ordered that the evacuation of Gypsies and Zigeunermischlinge into the General Government is to be suspended until the general solution of the Jewish question."[65]

The German Gypsies in the General Government

The railroad cars heading East in May 1940 held fifty persons each. A separate car contained food that was handed out daily. The destinations varied. One transport of Gypsies put together at Hohenasperg went to the former Jewish ghetto of Jedrzejow. Another train stopped in the middle of the countryside in the General Government, and its passengers were left there to fend for themselves.[66] Still others were put into work camps and employed in agriculture, road construction, flood control or arms manufacturing. An undetermined number of Gypsies were dispersed among villages, and many had to be supported by the communities. Others eventually made their way to larger towns and found work. According to some accounts, those employed received only sustenance and many probably died of hunger, cold and disease; other reports speak of regular wages and even supplements of food for those engaged in heavy labor. In some ghettos and camps tight discipline prevailed and infractions of the rules were punished with death; at other locations the Gypsies could come and go at will.[67] At least one massacre of men, women and children is reported to have taken place near Radom.[68]

More detailed knowledge is available about the fate of the 910 Gypsies deported from Hamburg. They were sent to Belzec, located near the border of the Soviet-occupied part of Poland, where they had to build a camp and then were put to work digging antitank ditches. This camp also contained Jews and Polish Gypsies. There were no doctors and no running water; the food was inadequate and hygienic conditions were atrocious. The guards, ethnic Germans, often beat inmates accused of working too slowly. The many deaths resulted mostly from bad living conditions; there also were some killings by the guards. One Gypsy family of twenty-six from Flensburg experienced nine deaths within three months.[69]

The situation in the Belzec camp was the subject of a meeting between Frank's administrators and SS and Police Leader Odili Globocnik on July 1, 1940. An inspection of the camp had revealed "the unacceptability of the existing conditions," but there was no agreement on what to do about it. The SS, which had to pay for running the camp, was in favor of releasing and settling Gypsy women and children and those not able to work; the administrators of the General Government objected to this release on the grounds that "the Gypsies are not sedentary people, that they are given to stealing and other crimes, and that they have a high rate of venereal disease." The governor of Lublin, Ernst Zörner, finally agreed to provide some money for improving conditions in the camp, including a special dwelling for old people and women with small infants. "In order to prevent the spread of contagious diseases," Globocnik promised to supervise these improvements, "i.e., better food, a regular source of water, improvements of the toilets, of the system of canalization and the dwellings." A Jewish doctor was also to be provided.[70]

On July 18, another meeting was held. Globocnik informed the participants that he was under orders to move the 1,140 to another location. Among them, he noted, were veterans and even party members married to German women. A more important reason for this order may have been the expected completion of the antitank fortifications. After some discussion, the conferees agreed to transport the German Gypsies to Hansk, a community in the district of Chelm, where several large empty buildings were said to be available. A camp was to be established there and able Gypsies were to be put to work. This decision, it was stressed, affected only the German Gypsies in Belzec; the Polish Gypsies were to be kept in the camp and any others seized would be sent there as well. Globocnik assured Frank's administrators that no additional German Gypsies would be sent to the district of Lublin.[71]

The buildings in Hansk were part of a former prison complex called Krychow. Wooded partitions were installed to provide family quarters. Here the Gypsies were put to work in a drainage and canalization project. With the arrival of cold weather, work ceased and the SS guards departed. Many of the Gypsies now moved to the larger cities to look for any kind of employment. Some remained in Krychow, but on February 25, 1941, the camp was formally closed. During that winter, many Gypsies died of hunger, cold and disease. Some of the survivors were sent to the town of Siedlce, where the Gypsies deported from the Cologne area had preceded them. The Gypsies at first were quartered in the Jewish ghetto in the center of Siedlce, where about 15,000 Jews lived. After the Jews had been shot in August 1942 the Gypsies were moved to another former ghetto outside the town where every family had its own room. They were no longer guarded, though three policemen came by several times a day. Many Gypsies worked for the German railroad. They were paid 70–80 zloty a week and received a meal at noon. Here too there were no guards; the supervisors were railway officials.[72]

As I have noted, Gypsies in Germany generally could obtain permission to temporarily leave their place of residence in case of personal hardship. However, applications from those deported to the General Government to visit relatives in Germany were turned down almost routinely. When Stefan R. in Duisburg requested a "furlough" for his children in the General Government on account of an impending death in the family, the application was rejected by the RKPA. In a decision dated December 3, 1940, the RKPA instructed that the denial be explained in terms of a "considerable limitation" on the frequency of rail traffic.[73] On June 19, 1943, Paul S. and his wife, who had been deported from Cologne, asked for permission to return to Cologne for two weeks. The request was forwarded by the SD Radom to the Kripo in Cologne, who denied it without delay on June 21: "Their return is not desired."[74]

Before their deportation the Gypsies had been warned that anyone who returned without authorization would be sent to a concentration camp. Still, many tried to get back to Germany. Some managed to live illegally under new names in the larger cities,[75] but most were caught and sent to concentration camps. Hertha R., a nineteen-year-old Gypsy woman from Duisburg, had been sent East on May 16, 1940, and attempted to return to Germany in November 1941. When arrested in Upper Silesia, she explained that life in the General Government had been "unbearable . . . . During the one and a half years in the General Government I was unable to obtain a paid job. Since during the past winter I had suffered great distress from hunger and cold, I did not want to spend another winter there. For this reason I took the risk to return to Germany." On January 19, 1942, on orders of the RKPA, R. was sent to the concentration camp for women in Ravensbrück. On July 18, a lawyer, acting in the name of the father of the young woman, requested her release. Her subsequent fate is not known.[76]

Not surprisingly, the majority of those who defied the order not to return to Germany were young people. Karl K. was eighteen years old when he was deported with his family from Duisburg in May 1940. After less than a month he had fled the General Government, but he was arrested in Marienburg in East Prussia on June 5 and consigned to the Gross Rosen concentration camp. There he died on April 1, 1942: "shot while trying to escape."[77] Twenty-one-year-old Anton W. was seized on July 28, 1941, as he was seeking to make his way back to Germany. He was sent to Sachsenhausen but escaped on June 11, 1942. Arrested again on April 25, 1944, W. was dispatched back to Sachsenhausen. Whether or not he survived his tribulations is unknown.[78] Leopoldine K. was twenty years old at the time of her deportation from Duisburg. She managed to get back to Duisburg but was arrested on October 15, 1940, and sent to Ravensbrück. Her file does not record what happened to her after that date.[79]

The authorities in the General Government, on the other hand, appear not to have been overly concerned about such unauthorized movements. When eighteen Gypsies, who had been in the camp of Krychow, were caught on February 25, 1941, near the German border, the district office in Lublin ordered that they be released from custody and be given new identity cards for living in the General Government.[80] In August 1944, amid the advances of the Red Army, the General Government was evacuated. The authorities there treated German Gypsies like other Germans and issued them papers certifying their right to return to Germany. Some Kripo offices in Germany were clearly upset about the reappearance of the Gypsies, but eventually they accepted this unwelcome development.

On August 4, 1944, twelve Gypsies who had been deported from Duisburg in 1940 showed up in the city and were promptly taken into custody. In a letter to the Kripo office in Essen, the local branch office justified the arrest with the argument that the Gypsies had begun to roam around the area and that "their conduct had created unrest in the population."[81] In a deposition, Gypsy Friedrich M. explained how the group had come back to Duisburg. Together with about forty families (about 140 persons), M. related, he had been able to join a military transport from Radom to Kattowitz in Upper Silesia. Before leaving Radom, he had informed the local German officials of his departure and had complied with all the requisite formalities. From Kattowitz he had taken the regularly scheduled express train to Duisburg.[82]

On August 15 and on instructions of the Essen Kripo, the newly arrived Gypsies were released. Those of working age were assigned to a pipe manufacturing factory in which the entire group was provided with shelter and food. They also were reminded that they were forbidden to leave Duisburg without police permission.[83] Another family of five that had arrived on August 7 was also sent to this factory. In a deposition Ferdinand A. acknowledged that he had come back to Germany in violation of the order not to return issued in 1940. However, he added, "my return took place under the pressure of circumstances. All further details were handled by the police at the border and I cannot be held responsible for them." He too had to promise not to leave Duisburg.[84]

A group of nine Gypsies arrived in Cologne from Lowitsch (Warsaw district) on August 17. The Cologne Kripo informed the municipal office of nutrition a day later that Zigeunermischling Biri W. and his family had returned from the General Government "in accordance with regular procedures" and that they should be issued food ration cards.[85] In Berlin, a group of fourteen returning Gypsies who had worked for the German railroad in Lublin were assigned to the same employer in Berlin. They were confined in the Gypsy camp at Marzahn and were again made subject to the decree of October 17, 1939, which prohibited any unauthorized move from their place of residence.[86] By February 1945, a total of 105 Gypsies (out of a population of about 465 prior to the deportation) had returned to Hamburg.[87]

The number of Gypsies who survived the deportation to the General Government is not known. Living conditions in numerous instances were very harsh and many are known to have died as a result of severe deprivation or mistreatment. They were sent East as part of a plan to rid Germany of its Gypsies; their return, as the RKPA informed the Nazi party's Office for Racial Policy on September 4, 1940, was "not expected."[88]

Yet deportation was not tantamount to a sentence of death. Then as later there existed no plan for the physical annihilation of the German Gypsies. About 2,500 of them were sent East without much regard for what would become of them there. At first many were subjected to forced labor, but most of the deportees soon gained freedom of movement, and a considerable number used this freedom to try to get back to Germany. After one of these Gypsies had been arrested in August 1940, the Cologne Kripo complained to the RKPA that "the supervision of the Gypsies in the General Government appears to be insufficient."[89] In November 1941 a Gypsy from Duisburg applied to the RKPA for permission to join his children in the General Government, but his application was rejected on the grounds that the authorities there had enough problems with their Gypsies. "According to experience until now," the RKPA told the Kripo of Duisburg on December 16, "the Gypsies and Zigeunermischlinge who have been resettled in the General Government are not tied down to a specific place. Hence their roaming around without target and plan causes the authorities there considerable difficulties."[90]

Although the authorities in the General Government were less than happy with the German Gypsies in their territory, no orders were issued to arrest them or kill them. On December 22, 1942, while the systematic murder of the Jews was fully under way, the administration of the General Government noted in a memo that there were no guidelines for the treatment of the German Gypsies in the General Government, "especially with regard to whether they are to be treated like the Jews."[91] Ten months later, in October 1943, the district government of Lublin queried the commander of the SD and the Lublin Kripo about policy toward the German Gypsies and was told again that there existed no "instructions or orders in this regard."[92] Word was received from the RKPA in March 1944 that a decree about the treatment of the Gypsies in the General Government was in preparation, but the approach of the Red Army and the consequent retreat West quickly made this entire issue moot.[93] The German Gypsies' stay in the General Government ended in the same chaos in which it had begun.

"Cleansing" Alsace-Lorraine

On May 10, 1940, the German armies invaded the Low Countries, and the war of maneuver that followed ended in the quick defeat of France. On June 22, the French laid down their arms; the reannexation of Alsace and Lorraine followed almost immediately. By early July, the Germans began the job of what they called "cleansing" the new territories of undesirable elements.

On July 2, the commander of the security police and SD in Alsace ordered that all Jews, Gypsies, members of foreign races, professional criminals and asocials such as beggars, vagabonds and the work-shy be expelled into the unoccupied zone of France.[94] A letter of August 14 that informed the Strassburg Kripo of the forthcoming operation pointed out that "Gypsy-like itinerants are to be treated like Gypsies."[95] Until the end of the year, a total of 105,000 persons were expelled from Alsace; the number of Gypsies among them is not known.[96]

On July 9, 1941, the Preventive Crime Fighting by the Police decree of December 14, 1937, was made applicable to Alsace, and more arrests of "asocials" followed. By the end of July 1942, the security police reported to Berlin, 2,115 additional persons had been expelled into unoccupied France.[97] In the area under the jurisdiction of the Mühlhausen Kripo, between June 27, 1940, and April 27, 1942, a total of 284 Gypsies were seized.[98] The Strassburg Kripo reported that in the period May 10–19, 1942, 125 Gypsies, Zigeunermischlinge and Gypsy-like itinerants had been expelled.[99]

For the Gauleiter of the Alsace, Robert Wagner, all this was not enough. He pleaded with Himmler for permission to conduct a "final cleansing" *(Schlussbereinigung)* to clear the Alsace "of all that is useless and racially inferior."[100] On August 4, 1942, a conference took place in the RSHA at which the second and "final cleansing" of the Alsace was discussed. Gauleiter Wagner, it was reported, had obtained the consent of the Führer and Himmler for this expulsion which would involve about 20,000 "asocials and criminals," including Gypsies. The "inferior" and "alien" elements were to be replaced by Germans from Baden.[101] The results of this measure are not documented, though there is no reason to assume that it did not proceed as planned.

In Lorraine anti-Gypsy measures got started later. In March 1942, the Lorraine Kripo complained about the large number of Gypsies, who had become a veritable "scourge," and ordered preventive custody for any Gypsy "who does not have a regular job and roams about the countryside" as well as for Gypsy fortune-tellers.[102] We have no figures on the total number of Gypsies affected by the arrests and expulsions that took place in 1942. Some of those arrested as asocial were taken to concentration camps in Germany. The Gypsies expelled into unoccupied France eventually were confined to internment camps in Southern France.[103]

The Expulsion of the East Prussian Gypsies

About 2,000–2,500 Gypsies lived in East Prussia. They were generally more sedentary than Gypsies in other parts of Germany and some of them owned substantial tracts of land.[104] In early 1942, about 2,000 of the East Prussian Gypsies were moved to Bialystok, a city located in a section of Poland that on August 1, 1941, had been annexed to Germany, becoming part of East Prussia. The reasons for this expulsion are not at all clear. Some have surmised that the move was carried out for security reasons at the request of the OKW,[105] but this explanation is less than persuasive. The area of Bialystok was hardly more "secure" than East Prussia itself. In the fall of 1939, as I noted earlier, plans had been made to expel all the German Gypsies to the newly seized territories in the East, but by the summer of 1940 these plans had been shelved. Himmler was said to have decided that the solution of the Gypsy question would have to await the end of the war. The German Gypsies in early 1942 were subject to various restrictions, but there was no talk of further expulsions.

Whatever the reasons, in January and February 1942 some 2,000 East Prussian Gypsies were loaded onto cattle cars and shipped to Bialystok. Some of them, it appears, had been told that they would receive large farms in the formerly Polish area.[106] In Bialystok the Gypsies were put into a big prison. At first, men and women were separated; later entire families were squeezed into the cells of the prison. There were not enough blankets or food, and many children and older people in particular succumbed to diseases that spread rapidly. The men were put to work outside the prison under the guard of Polish SS. Some managed to escape; a few were released as "socially well adjusted."[107]

The number of deaths in Bialystok is not known. In the fall of 1942, the East German Gypsies were moved again and put into a former camp for Russian prisoners of war in Brest-Litowsk. A report of the German police, dated December 10, gives their number as 800.[108] Early in 1943, after the Jews of the city had been killed, the Gypsies were put into the former Jewish ghetto. The men worked under guard for the German railroad. On December 31, 1942, the German administrator of the district reported that the Gypsies from Bialystok had brought typhus to Brest, but that the spread of the disease had been halted.[109] Half a year later, on June 24, 1943, his complaints about the Gypsies had become more ominous. The presence of the Gypsies sent here from Bialystok, he wrote, is a disaster. "Begging and stealing is the main occupation of this scourge. I consider it urgently necessary that these idlers be treated like the Jews and request the appropriate authorization."[110] Less than a year later, the German administrator's wish was granted. On April 16, 1944, an entry in the official camp register of the Auschwitz Gypsy camp notes the arrival of 852 Gypsies from East Prussia.[111] By that time, it should be noted, thousands of other Gypsies from Germany had also been deported to Auschwitz, a subject to which I shall return in a later chapter.

6

Creating Social Outcasts

The plan to send the German Gypsies to the General Government had ended with the expulsion of a mere 2,500. The remaining 30,000 Gypsies in the Reich[1] were subject to a freeze on mobility and were gradually put under various other restrictive measures. Most of these decrees were the result of decisions taken in Berlin; others, it appears, were enacted in response to pressure from local authorities.

A Clamor for More Aggressive Action

From about 1936 on there was a sharp increase in anti-Gypsy agitation. The onset of the war and the enforced residence of the Gypsies brought another wave of demands for more radical measures against this hapless minority. Thus, for example, on November 9, 1939, the mayor of Heinsheim in Baden complained to the *Landrat* (chief magistrate) in Mosbach that a group of twenty-five Gypsies the police had settled in his town had become a terrible nuisance. "If there is work, they shirk it. If there is no work, they come to city hall and ask for work or for financial support. They beg, supports for trees are stolen and used for firewood, etc."[2]

Another complaint reached the Landrat from the mayor of Rittersbach on December 8. In previous years, the official wrote, the town had never had to put up with the presence of Gypsies. However, on October 27 the police had ordered a Gypsy family with eight children who were passing through not to leave the town, and their presence now caused constant annoyance for him and the town's citizens. He requested the Landrat to see to it "that the Gypsies be put into some internment camp."[3]

The Landrat must have received similar communications from other towns for on July 9, 1940, he turned for relief to the Kripo in Karlsruhe. The Gypsies living in enforced residence, he wrote, had become an "unbearable plague" for whom no work could be found. No employer was willing to hire them, since it was unreasonable to expect other employees to work with Gypsies.[4] The RKPA in Berlin responded to this and similar complaints about a month later in a tone of obvious annoyance: Gypsies in other places worked well alongside others, no further resettlements to the General Government were planned for the time being, and "the establishment of special concentration camps for Gypsies is not possible for practical and financial reasons."[5]

The Landrat of Mosbach was not easily silenced. On March 11, 1941, he once again complained to the Karlsruhe Kripo, pointing out that as the result of their enforced residence Gypsies had become a special burden for the rural communities. Many male Gypsies were away for military service and the women were essentially unsupervised, since (due to war conditions) not enough rural police were available. Hence, from the perspective of security as well as in the interest of the small communities, "a final solution of the Gypsy question was urgently required." Because of their lack of discipline, he added, Gypsies were of no use in farm work without the closest supervision.[6]

There followed a meeting with the Karlsruhe Kripo official in charge of Gypsy matters on July 28, 1941, at which the rural administrators were told that there was hope for a final resolution of the Gypsy question in the near future. However, at this point, the official pointed out, it was impossible to remove the entire Gypsy population. Individual Gypsies who conducted themselves in an asocial manner could be put into a concentration camp, but not entire families. The official recommended that Gypsies be assigned to work on roads and similar projects. Those who refused to work, engaged in begging or abused alcohol could then be sent away as asocials.[7] Some of the mayors of larger towns, in turn, had their own complaints. Thus the mayor of Ludwigsburg claimed that Gypsies who were harassed in the countryside were seeking refuge in the cities and he asked his chief of police for "urgent action against the Gypsy plague." The population, he said, is "very angry."[8]

There also were demands for more forthright measures against the Gypsies in the Dortmund area. On April 21, 1941, the chief of police in the small community of Beverungen requested a new domicile for two Gypsy families who had been put there in implementation of the 1939 freeze on mobility. The women in particular, he wrote in his letter to the Dortmund Kripo, engage in begging and stealing and continue these practices despite repeated warnings. Complaints from the population were becoming more and more numerous while adequate supervision of the Gypsies remained impossible.[9]

Both an important citizen of the community, who described himself as a longtime party member, and the mayor supported the request to remove the Gypsies, but the Dortmund Kripo rejected it. The decree of October 10, 1939, they explained, required that Gypsies stay in the locations in which they were found in 1939. The purpose of this decree was to end the Gypsies' aimless roaming, an undertaking especially important in time of war. The enforced residence of the Gypsies was felt to be a burden and an annoyance by affected communities everywhere and efforts were under way to free the population from this "plague." However, these plans could not be implemented immediately. Hence the only recourse at the present time was to take into preventive police custody those Gypsies who behaved asocially and violated specific ordinances. The local police had been remiss in not enforcing the law and in not providing concrete and detailed information about various kinds of wrongdoing.[10]

There followed more exchanges of letters, with each side blaming the other for not acting more forcefully against the "Gypsy nuisance." The RKPA in Berlin too entered the dispute and finally proposed sending the Gypsies of Beverungen to the Gypsy concentration camp in Lodz (Litzmannstadt). However, that camp was liquidated in early 1942 when its inmates were killed in gas vans, and the Dortmund Kripo therefore informed the province president on April 16, 1942, that this "resettlement" could not be carried out. As soon as a move to another location was possible, it would take place without further delay.[11] Half a year later, on October 14, the Dortmund Kripo advised the *Regierungspräsident* (senior government official) in Minden that Himmler had forbidden any further resettlements of Gypsies "for the duration of the war."[12] That was two months before Himmler ordered the deportation of thousands of *Zigeunermischlinge* (Gypsies of mixed ancestry) to Auschwitz. It is not clear whether the Dortmund Kripo had misinterpreted a communication from Berlin or Himmler had indeed changed his mind about deporting Gypsies to the East.

Annoyance arising from the freeze on mobility was exacerbated by the harsh denigration of the Gypsies as an alien and asocial element, which had been under way for several years and continued unabated. For example, an article appearing in a paper published in Bavaria in March 1940 called the Gypsies "parasites belonging to a foreign race" and demanded that they be treated like Jews.[13] Attempts to rid communities of Gypsies were often led by local party organizations. Thus the executive officer of the NSDAP in Vaihingen near Stuttgart in May 1940 noted that his office was receiving constant complaints from the local population about the "Gypsy plague" and demanded that something be done about this "riffraff."[14] Another source of pressure was the Kripo itself. Together with other elements in the state bureaucracy, it urged the adoption of legislation dealing with the Gypsy problem in order to make possible a more uniform course of action. However, the much talked about Gypsy law (*Zigeunergesetz*) was never enacted. Rather than resorting to a law that would have tied their hands, the regime's leaders eventually decided that they preferred handling the Gypsies through ad hoc decrees.

Plans for a Gypsy Law and a Law on Aliens to the Community

A Gypsy law was first mentioned in March 1936. An official in the Ministry of the Interior, Karl Zindel, had been ordered to work up a draft of such a law, and in a memo to State Secretary Pfundtner he put forth some ideas about the content of this planned legislation. Zindel proposed that only genuine Gypsies be allowed to itinerate and that all other travelers be forced to become sedentary. Foreign Gypsies were to be expelled; all unreliable elements were to be put into workhouses or concentration camps. There was to be "no weakness or mildness," and all Gypsies were to be carefully supervised.[15]

Work on a Gypsy law continued. In March 1938, Heydrich's deputy, Werner Best, sent a draft to the Bavarian Ministry of the Interior. The law in preparation, he stressed, would bring about "the final solution of the Gypsy question on the basis of racial principles."[16] A letter to Himmler by the chief of the SS Main Office of Race and Resettlement, Günther Pancke, written in December of that year, gave further details of the law that was being drafted by the RKPA. The legislation would ban any mixing between Gypsies and those of German blood, pure Gypsies would be separated from the Mischlinge, and the latter group would be made subject to "sterilization and isolation."[17]

Early in 1939 the Gypsy law under preparation was mentioned in a lecture by the Karlsruhe Kripo official in charge of Gypsy questions who stressed the importance of dealing with the Gypsies on the basis of a measure that would encompass the entire country. The main target of the proposed legislation, he stated, would be Mischlinge and Gypsy-like itinerants. "In the future it will probably become necessary to establish concentration camps and resort to sterilization in order to achieve in this way a gradual extinction [*Aussterben*] of these asocial elements."[18]

As I noted in an earlier chapter, Heydrich's regulations implementing the decree of December 8, 1938, issued in March 1939, made reference to the Gypsy law. Such a law, he maintained, would be necessary in order to create "the necessary legal foundation" for the measures to be taken against the Gypsy race.[19] And yet it was precisely the fear of making anti-Gypsy measures dependent on such a "legal foundation" that ultimately doomed the planned legislation. Although state bureaucrats pressed for orderly and uniform procedures, the Nazi leadership was far more interested in maintaining its freedom of action. Hence, just as in the case of the Nazi "euthanasia" program, anti-Gypsy measures continued to be handled by way of decrees and police actions rather than legislation. A Gypsy law, no matter how stringent, would have circumscribed what could be done, for a legal limit on Gypsy rights established at the same time a legal guarantee of the rights remaining intact. Anything that was not explicitly forbidden would be allowed. Hence Himmler and his underlings preferred to make use of the police apparatus. In this way they could pursue the most radical measures without fear of colliding with the law and the state authorities enforcing such law.[20]

Ritter's institute too was involved in work on the proposed Gypsy law. A draft, probably from late 1940 or early 1941, speaks of excluding Gypsies from military service and limiting Gypsy marriages.[21] However, Ritter appears to have realized that a Gypsy law would not come to pass, and he began to consider a law dealing with aliens to the community *(Gemeinschaftsfremde)* a suitable substitute for it. Ritter had a long-standing interest in all issues concerning asocials, and the enactment of an aliens to the community law *(Gemeinschaftsfremdengesetz)*, he probably surmised, would provide his institute with a welcome new mandate and would bring new financial support as well. Discussions about this legislation began in 1939, but this law too never saw the light of day. It floundered on irreconcilable differences between several involved ministries, for the proposed law on aliens to the community was far broader in scope than the Gypsy law. The category "aliens to the community" was vague in the extreme and its impact on public morale therefore inestimable.

The Nazis' desire for a homogeneous and harmonious society—a true *Volksgemeinschaft*—led them to seek to eliminate not only those of "foreign blood" but also all unstable and allegedly asocial elements. As I have already noted, this plan targeted not only Gypsies but also a wide array of beggars, prostitutes, vagabonds and other nonconforming segments of the population. Persecution began with sterilization and preventive police custody, but, as in other areas of the Nazi program, a gradual process of radicalization soon took hold. Different party organizations and state bureaus sought to outdo each other in their zeal for the new utopian society of perfection. Hence there soon arose a demand for more comprehensive and more radical measures.

The first reference to an aliens to the community law occurs in a communication between Heydrich and Himmler on April 13, 1939.[22] During the same year the RKPA prepared a draft of such a law that included among aliens to the community the following types of individuals:

1. Nonsedentary persons who could not prove a regular source of income
2. Sedentary individuals who defrayed their living in an illegal manner
3. The work-shy
4. Persons whose way of life endangered the moral life of other members of society
5. Those released from prisons or camps who could not prove a return to an orderly life
6. Minors who had been discharged from institutions because of incorrigibility

The draft law proposed that such "aliens to the community" be interned in concentration camps. Those who might create "undesirable offspring" could be sterilized.[23]

The proposed law went through many additional drafts. The main obstacle to enactment was the conflict of jurisdiction between the RKPA and the Ministry of Justice, which feared that the proposed legislation would seriously weaken the position of the judiciary. Under the drafts proposed by the Ministry of the Interior, the police were to decide who was to come under the reach of the new law. Moreover, the Ministry of Justice regarded the definition of who was to be regarded as an alien to the community as far too vague; it wanted to keep decisions on compulsory sterilization in the hands of the genetic health courts, and it sought a veto power for public prosecutors over dispatches to a concentration camp.[24]

When Minister of Justice Franz Gürtner died on January 29, 1941, the RKPA was encouraged to believe that an important obstacle had been cleared. However, his successor, Otto Thierack, though an ardent Nazi, proved equally obstinate in protecting his turf. Other ministers too voiced their objections. The governor of the General Government, Hans Frank, who carried the title of Reichsminister and had been feuding with Himmler for a long time, argued that it was unacceptable to grant the police such far-reaching powers. Göring maintained similarly that the police should be able to get by with the authority granted it so far, though he later withdrew this comment.[25]

There followed more exchanges of correspondence and meetings of the principals designed to iron out differences of views that had arisen. By the middle of 1944 a compromise had finally been worked out. The aliens to the community law was to take effect on April 1, 1945. However, the war situation, which had become desperate, caught up with the law. On August 1, 1944, the RKPA forbade any further work on matters that did not promote most directly the inner security of the Reich. Similarly, on August 8, 1944, Thierack, "in the interest of the total war effort," ordered a halt to all endeavors dealing with legal reform.[26] In the final days of the war, even Gypsies held in concentration camps were needed for Hitler's depleted armies.

In the absence of legislation dealing with the Gypsy issue, the escalating pressure seeking to make the Gypsies outcasts of society took the form of decrees and local initiatives without much regard for consistency. Confusion over the issue of school attendance by Gypsy children is an example of such administrative disorder.

Expulsions from the Schools

Demands to remove Gypsy children from contact with other youngsters usually came from local officials or party functionaries. I discussed attempts by Austrian officials to expel Gypsy children from the schools in early 1939 in chapter 4. In February 1939, the mayor of Cologne, at the suggestion of the Nazi party's Office of Racial Policy, ordered that Gypsy children in the primary schools be put into a special class. In this way, the *Völkischer Beobachter* reported on March 9, 1939, "Gypsy children, similar to Jewish children, are now kept from living together with German youth." Eventually, a teacher recalls, all Gypsy children in Cologne were taught in a special school.[27]

Taking note of the action of the mayor of Cologne, the administrators of the Hamburg school system in May of the same year suggested that Hamburg should consider a similar measure.[28] Ultimately, all Gypsy children there had to withdraw from the schools. An order issued in May 1942 justified this decision with the argument that Gypsy children constituted "a danger to children of German blood."[29]

The ruling of the minister of education, issued on June 15, 1939, has been mentioned in connection with the situation in Austria. According to this decree, the children of German Gypsies in principle had the right to attend schools. However, "insofar as such children constitute a moral or other threat to their classmates of German blood, they can be expelled from the school."[30] On November 21, 1941, this decree was publicized by the RKPA as valid not only for the Austrian schools but for the rest of Germany as well.[31] Cities such as Hamburg used this ruling in order to get rid of their Gypsy children. No special proof was needed in order to establish the proposition that Gypsy children were indeed a threat to their German schoolmates.

A similar pattern repeated itself in Frankfurt/Main. On May 6, 1940, a member of the municipal council and an official in the party's Office of Racial Policy demanded from the mayor that Gypsy children, "afflicted with lice, neglected and entirely incapable of being educated," be removed from the schools. The mayor at first was unwilling to comply with this demand. According to the law, he replied to the councillor, Gypsy children were required to attend school; in several Frankfurt schools they already sat in a special section, separate from other children. However, a year later the Nazi official prevailed. The publication of the decree of the minister of education, which authorized expulsion for cause, undoubtedly had strengthened his hand. All Gypsy children in Frankfurt were now expelled.[32]

In Düsseldorf and Berleburg (Westfalen) too Gypsy children were removed from the schools.[33] On the other hand, in Munich and Wiesbaden Gypsy children were allowed to stay enrolled until their deportation in 1943.[34] A lack of uniform regulation thus could occasionally be a benefit.

Compulsory Labor

Wartime mobilization involved the increased regimentation of the German workforce. Leaving one's place of employment became a violation of law, and "idling" at work could be considered sabotage. However, Gypsies were subject to special tribulations. Held in enforced residence, many of them were put to work as low-paid laborers in construction or road building. In other instances no suitable work was available at the location in which Gypsies had been told to reside or no jobs could be found for them because German workers refused to work next to Gypsies.[35] This in turn led to begging or other illegal activities. In Magdeburg, for example, eighteen-year-old Elisabeth F. was arrested on February 1, 1941, for unauthorized peddling. In a statement given to the police she explained that she was the only support of her family. Her father was in a concentration camp and her mother was sick. Not wanting to go begging, she had resorted to selling buttons. In a rather unusual show of sympathy, the police showed some understanding for her plight. An inquiry at the local labor exchange confirmed that it was extremely difficult to find work for female Gypsies, since other women did not want to work with them in the same place. The arrest ended with a warning. To impose a fine, the police report concluded, was futile since the young woman would be unable to pay it.[36]

Employers often complained about the work habits of their Gypsy workers, and such complaints could bring about unpleasant consequences. Seventeen-year-old Kurt A. of Magdeburg had been arrested during Operation Work-Shy in 1938 but was released a few months later and put to work at a construction company. In June 1940 the firm complained to the Nazi labor organization about A.'s irregular attendance. "It should be unacceptable that German youth bleeds on the field of battle while non-Aryans gad about in their chosen homeland and work whenever it pleases them." A. was arrested on November 8 and admitted that he had repeatedly failed to show up for work. In July he had stopped working at the construction company altogether because his remuneration was inadequate. His mother was being held in a concentration camp and he had to support three younger siblings. Between July and November he had therefore found temporary work at several other places. A. now promised to go back to the construction company and to work conscientiously, but in May 1942 he was arrested again for repeated absences. Released after a severe warning, A., together with other Gypsies, was eventually deported to Auschwitz.[37]

Thirty-one-year old Walter L. was employed by the same construction company and was arrested in November 1940 because he had stayed away from work. He admitted that he had put an ointment on his leg to create an infection and thus be excused from work because of sickness. L. signed a statement in which he promised to mend his ways. "I have been told that if I do not immediately resume work at Rennwanz [the construction company] I have to expect to be taken into preventive police custody." Several months later, L. was again in custody for having repeatedly missed work and was sent for an indefinite term to a work camp.[38] According to a decree of Himmler, the purpose of such "work education camps" was education and training, not punishment. "Detainees are to be made to do arduous work, so that they can forcibly be brought to realize that their behavior is detrimental to the nation, so that they can be trained to work in an orderly and regulated fashion and so that they may serve as a warning and deterrent to others."[39] If a stay of several weeks in a work education camp failed to achieve its purpose and the former inmates resumed an irregular work habit, they could count on being sent to a concentration camp. L.'s subsequent fate is not known. Two Gypsy women in Magdeburg, arrested for repeatedly having been late for work or not showing up at all, in August 1942 were sent for four weeks to an "education camp for women."[40]

Detention in work camps involved not only Gypsies; foreign as well as German workers were also subject to this "educational" tool. However, Gypsies were particularly vulnerable. Not only did they have little experience with work discipline, but they were subject to another handicap: in many locations they were no longer allowed to use public transportation and it was therefore difficult for them to get to work. It was not unusual for Gypsies to have to walk several kilometers in order to reach their place of employment.[41]

Sometimes they were issued special permits allowing them to use a particular bus or tram and marked "valid only for going to work." Ernst K. was arrested in Magdeburg on February 24, 1943, for having used a tram with a permit that had expired on December 31, 1942. His eleven-year-old son, who was with him, had no permit at all. Before the two could be punished for this offense, the family was caught up in the general deportation to Auschwitz that began a month later. K. died there on December 18, 1943.[42]

Despite the freeze on mobility and the strict mobilization for a war economy reaffirmed in March 1941, Gypsies too old or too sick for work in construction could sometimes receive a license to practice an itinerant trade. A ruling issued by the Munich Kripo on November 26, 1941, provided that such persons, if they exercised a roving occupation important to the war effort such as making baskets or sharpening saws, could receive a license for this trade. It is noteworthy that even though the decree of October 1939 ordering a freeze on mobility did not include Gypsy-like itinerants, this November 1941 ruling of the Munich Kripo was valid not only for Gypsies and Zigeunermischlinge but also for "all other persons who itinerate in the manner of Gypsies."[43] The Munich police had always insisted that the "white Gypsies" were at least as bad as the Gypsies by race, and they continued to enforce some restrictive measures against this group even in the absence of explicit authorization from Berlin. Lack of uniformity had also cropped up in relation to issuing permits for change of residence. This led to a decree of the RKPA, promulgated on July 13, 1942, that asked for strict enforcement of the duty to work at one's assigned place of residence. Permits to move were to be issued only in exceptional cases, for, the decree noted, Gypsies used every conceivable excuse to try to resume their previous itinerating lifestyle.[44]

During these years of compulsory labor, conditions in the municipal Gypsy camps worsened considerably. No money was allocated to maintain or repair the caravans or huts in these camps, and the hygienic situation, never very good, deteriorated further. In some cases, Gypsies still residing in their own apartments were forced to move into the camps, leading to further crowding. The Gypsy camp in Frankfurt at Dieselstrasse in July 1939 held twenty-four families for a total of 119 persons. By October 1940 the number had increased to 146, including sixteen Gypsies who had been moved there from Mainz, and by May 1941 the camp held 160 individuals. On May 15, 1941, the Frankfurt welfare office noted with satisfaction that practically all the Gypsies had been channeled into productive labor. Of the 160 camp inmates only seven were old or sick enough to receive support.[45]

The father of Herbert Adler had a good job at the Frankfurt post office, and his family lived in a five-room apartment. In 1940 the Adler family had to move to the Gypsy camp and were put in a moving van that had been converted into a dwelling. The primitive hut had neither electricity nor running water. The camp was moved to Kruppstrasse 14 in 1942, and then even the children were put to work. Herbert Adler recalls how he and his little brother, then nine years old, had to load trucks with bricks and stones for road construction. Of the twenty-nine-member Adler family only three sur-vived the deportation to Auschwitz.[46]

The Gypsy camp in Berlin-Marzahn held almost eight hundred persons in July 1939. After the outbreak of the war special efforts got under way to put everyone to work. Gypsies worked in factories, in construction and in a nearby gravel pit. On the other hand, plans to move every Gypsy in Berlin to the camp were not realized and some families continued to live in their apartments in various parts of the city.[47]

The Gypsy camp in Cologne was closed down after the deportation to the General Government in May of 1940. The few remaining Gypsies lived dis-persed over the city and, as the authorities noted, "are almost completely inte-grated into the work process."[48] In nearby Düsseldorf, on the other hand, the Gypsy camp was kept open and held about seventy persons after May 1940. The occupants of the camp, including the older children, were made to work in armaments factories, in construction and in a woolen mill near the camp. The largest number worked in a glass-blowing factory also close to the camp. They were counted every morning and evening and were warned to return from work without delay. The camp remained open until the end of the war.[49]

Similar conditions prevailed in the Gypsy camp in Königsberg (East Prussia), "Am Continer-Weg," which had been set up as early as 1928. After the start of the war, all able-bodied persons had to work at regular jobs, and this requirement was tightened as a result of an instruction from the RKPA issued on July 22, 1941. It appears that the local Kripo had inquired about the possibility of expelling the Gypsies into the newly seized Eastern territo-ries, but Berlin replied that "a general and final solution of the Gypsy ques-tion is not possible at this time." Instead, the RKPA proposed establishing or enlarging an existing camp. All those able to work should be forced to work in the city of Königsberg or the surrounding area. "Refusal to work or sloppy performance is to result in dispatch to a concentration camp." In the interest of making productive use of everybody, Gypsies not suited for regu-lar employment and older children were to be given work in the camp.[50] The average number of Gypsies in this camp during the war years was about two hundred persons. It continued to operate until the end of the war.[51]

As I have already noted, not all German cities had camps for "their" Gyp-sies. In Munich, for example, in 1941 about two hundred Gypsies lived in their own apartments or caravans in various parts of the city, but they were not forced into a camp. The Gypsies, a memo by the local Kripo dated October 29, 1941, explained, were controlled by the police and almost all of them worked.[52] Compulsory labor, it appears, was thus the general pattern everywhere, whether Gypsies lived in a camp or resided in their own homes.

Dismissal from Military Service

Official commentaries on the Nuremberg Laws (1935) had identified Gyp-sies as being of "alien blood" and barred them, just like Jews, from becoming

German citizens. Nevertheless, and typical of the confusion that attended the legal status of the Gypsies, most of those residing in the country were still considered German citizens and therefore subject to military service. The law regulating military conscription, announced on May 21, 1935, had laid down "Aryan descent" as a requirement for active military service, but a new version of this law, issued on June 26, 1936, substituted the word "Jew" for "non-Aryan." This change was made at the urging of the Ministry of Foreign Affairs and in response to expressions of unease among German allies such as Japan that resented the vilification of "non-Aryans." Unlike Jews, Gypsies thus were expected to serve in the military.[53]

The German army had long looked upon Gypsies as unreliable. They were said to seek to avoid military service and to become deserters once conscripted.[54] Hence it is not surprising that after the ascent of the Nazi regime the military command sought to restrict the military service of Gypsies. A confidential decree dealing with the induction of non-Jewish German citizens of alien blood issued on November 22, 1937, provided for the exclusion of "full-blooded Gypsies" and of persons who strongly resembled Gypsies. These individuals, on account of their alien blood, did not fulfill those demands of "appearance and conduct, character and demeanor" expected from a German soldier. They were to be transferred to the inactive reserves.[55] On July 21, 1939, this decree was extended to Gypsies who had served in the Austrian army.[56]

It appears that despite this order not a few Gypsies continued to serve in the armed forces. Many were protected by their commanding officers, probably more as a matter of soldierly solidarity than because of a conscious rejection of racism.[57] Philomena Franz recalls that her brother Johann, who had been inducted into the cavalry, was for a time shielded by the commander of his unit. Johann knew a lot about horses and was well liked by his comrades. Johann fought in Poland, France and Russia before he was finally discharged and sent home.[58] Until well into 1942, Gypsies who had not yet been classified by the Ritter institute and whose appearance did not match the stereotype were conscripted into the armed forces.

On February 11, 1941, the High Command of the Armed Forces (OKW) noted the disregard of the 1937 guidelines and called for its strict enforcement. The induction of Gypsies and Zigeunermischlinge, even of volunteers, was to cease. Those already serving in the armed forces were to be discharged on account of "lacking suitability for active service" and were to be assigned to the inactive reserves. On orders of Himmler, the instruction noted, the RKPA would provide the military with information about the racial status of affected individuals.[59] On April 24, the RKPA conveyed this order to regional and local Kripo offices and asked them to furnish this information for the cohort of 1923, which had just been called up for military service.[60] During the following years, the Kripo, making use of the assessments compiled by the Ritter institute, continued to supply information about the racial makeup of young men facing induction.

Pressure to purge the Gypsies from the armed forces also came from the Nazi party. In a letter addressed to the party chancellery, an official of the

Propaganda Ministry raised this issue on September 26, 1941. The population, he noted, "often cannot understand that alien individuals [*Fremdvölkische*] can also be German soldiers." He had received the names of several Gypsies who were still on active service and inquired about what was to be done. The party chancellery replied several days later that such information was being collected in its office and then sent on to the OKW.[61]

Hitler too was upset about the presence of Gypsies in the armed forces. We know of only two occasions on which Hitler briefly expressed himself on the "Gypsy question." Both comments were prompted by his concern about their military service. His aide-de-camp, Major Gerhard Engel, who served as liaison between Hitler and the High Command of the Army (OKH), kept a diary. On May 2, 1940, he made the following entry:

> Once again great excitement and trouble. F. [Führer] has received documents from either Bormann or the Reichsführer [Himmler] according to which Gypsies fulfill their military service in the army. They are said to be so-called "sedentary" Gypsies from near Nürnberg. In this connection, F. points out to me and Schm. [Rudolf Schmundt, Engel's superior] with great agitation that Gypsies are aliens [*artfremd*] and, in regard to the laws laying down special status, are to be treated like Jews. Reichsführer SS had issued perfectly clear instructions on the treatment of this group of people, and his office kept tabs on them. Most likely one dealt here again with one of the usual cases of cheating that sought—as with many Jews—to let these individuals disappear in the army and cover them with the mantle of Christian love for one's neighbor. He was fed up with this defense of Mischlinge and other such characters, and he would speak about this with Keitel [chief of OKW].[62]

On the following day, Engel recorded in his diary, the matter had been cleared up. The "Gypsies" in question, it turned out, were in possession of perfectly good German passports and therefore had been inducted properly. "The whole affair apparently has been started by denunciations from the population to party offices. The background, as always in such cases, involves economic matters, for these formerly Gypsy families are rich and own successful businesses." In the evening Hitler was informed of the facts of the case. "F. did not like it but remained silent and told me that he would cause further measures to be taken."[63]

The subject of Gypsies in the military came up again on February 10, 1941, at a dinner conversation between Hitler and Heydrich at which Hitler's aide-de-camp, Werner Koeppen, was present. Heydrich related that "some Gypsies who have our citizenship have been inducted into military service. Field Marshal Keitel will put an end to this immediately." Heydrich went on to say that Mischlinge, the descendants of marriages between Gypsies and Germans, were the most asocial elements, and Hitler voiced the view "that the Gypsies are the greatest plague for the rural population."[64] One day later, on February 11 and as mentioned above, the OKW indeed once again published its 1937 guidelines according to which no Gypsies or Zigeunermischlinge were to be inducted.

In some instances, Gypsies sought to get out of military service by voluntarily reporting their Gypsy origins. Hermann P. from Berlin had been in the Wehrmacht since 1938. His racial status had been rated "Zigeunermischling with predominantly German blood." In 1941 P., invoking his Gypsy status, attempted to obtain a discharge, but his application was refused on the grounds that the quantity of his Gypsy blood was minimal.[65] In another such case, Peter L. noted in his application that his seven children were not receiving any state assistance on account of his Gypsy status. He had served in World War I and had even been a prisoner of war in France for several years. L. was discharged on December 30, 1941; he was deported to Auschwitz in March 1943.[66]

The effort to eliminate all Gypsies from the armed forces continued into 1942. On February 7, Göring, in his capacity as minister of aviation and commander in chief of the German air force, prohibited Gypsies and Zigeunermischlinge from serving as auxiliaries or members of the air raid warning system.[67] On July 10, the OKW once again barred Gypsies from the military, even as volunteers. As before, Zigeunermischlinge were to be transferred to the inactive reserve. New was the provision that "full-blooded" Gypsies be given a dishonorable discharge.[68] Again, the Kripo was enlisted in determining which Gypsies still served in the armed forces. On August 28, the RKPA informed Kripo offices of the OKW order and emphasized that even those who did not have the stereotypical Gypsy appearance should now be discharged. Cases in which the required discharge was not implemented were to be reported to the RKPA. In cooperation with the labor exchanges, those discharged were to be assigned to productive labor.[69]

Some Gypsies attempted to stay in the military, probably as a means of protecting themselves and their families. Gustav F. had volunteered for the Wehrmacht in October 1938. After he had been discharged on May 5, 1942, on account of being a Gypsy, he applied for reinstatement, but his application was denied. A memo from the Cologne Kripo noted that no exceptions to the general policy could be made.[70] Julius H. in 1941 had been assessed as Zigeunermischling ("with predominantly German blood"), but he remained a member of the Nazi Party. It is likely that he was fully assimilated and probably no longer considered himself a Gypsy. In March 1942, the district office of the NSDAP for Franken (*Gauleitung Franken*) wrote to the party's Office of Racial Policy and inquired whether H. would be allowed to serve in the military. His induction was expected in several weeks. H. had repeatedly expressed his interest in entering military service. "I am of the opinion," the party official wrote, "that since H. has been a volunteer in the fight against Bolshevism already in 1919 his request should be approved."[71] The outcome of this case is not known.

Julius H. apparently was not the only person of Gypsy descent who wanted to be regarded as a German, for on September 22, 1943, the OKW issued yet another order that sought to accommodate individuals with similar background and political outlook. Zigeunermischlinge in the armed forces who "according to their total behavior, character, personality as well as ideological outlook can be considered fully reliable" and had proven their readiness for sacrifice by their conduct in the face of the enemy could be kept on active service. Their units were to submit appropriate applications, but exceptions to the general policy of exclusion were to be approved only in very special circumstances. This order, enacted probably to accommodate the large number of requests from commanding officers who wanted to keep Gypsy personnel, remained in force for less than a year. It was canceled on July 12, 1944. Added now was a provision barring Germans married to Gypsies or Zigeunermischlinge from military service.[72]

Tightening the exclusionary policy in the face of great shortages in military personnel indicates the degree to which racialist thinking pervaded the top military leadership. Excluding Gypsies from the armed forces was parallel to expelling them from the Labor Corps (*Arbeitsdienst*). The duty of young people to serve in this organization was introduced on July 26, 1935. Jews were excluded from the very beginning, but the exclusion of Gypsies came only in 1942, when regulations for their military service were tightened also.[73]

Regulation of Marriages and Sexual Relations

Legislation enacted in 1935 had forbidden both marriage and extramarital relations between Germans and persons of "alien blood," and various regulatory procedures were put into place to enforce these laws and protect the "purity of the German blood." Decrees adopted in 1935 and early 1936 had made it clear that these provisions covered not only Jews but also Gypsies. But enforcement for Gypsies appears to have been lax until about 1941.

Some couples sought to circumvent the law by getting married before strangers. Not a few Gypsies inducted into military service made use of the institution of war marriage, in which the qualifications of the marriage partners were less important. Commanding officers, interested in the well-being and good morale of their unit, often supported such marriages.[74] In response to this practice, the Regierungspräsident in Arnsberg (Westfalen) on June 18, 1941, reminded his marriage registrars that even in cases of war marriages, when one of the marriage partners was a Gypsy, Zigeunermischling or Gypsy-like itinerant they were required to demand proof of fitness to marry.[75]

A decree issued by the minister of the interior on June 20, 1941, noted that, according to experience, "Gypsy blood endangered the purity of the German blood to a marked degree." He therefore ordered marriage registrars to exercise special care when one of the prospective marriage partners had "Gypsy blood" or when there were reasons to suspect such a blood tie. The decree also annulled the provision adopted on January 3, 1936, that had allowed marriages between Germans and Gypsies with a quarter or less "alien blood."[76]

The Nuremberg Laws covered marriages between Germans and those of "alien blood." It did not deal with marriages *among* Gypsies. Yet despite the lack of a legal warrant, officials desirous of halting the propagation of the Gypsies soon began to prevent such marriages as well. Thus, for example, the Landrat in Hechingen (Baden) on August 11, 1941, advised the marriage registrar in Burladingen that marriage between two named Gypsies should not take place. Both of these individuals were Zigeunermischlinge, and they therefore fell under the June 20 order of the minister of interior.[77] On December 24, 1942, the Ministry of Interior issued a formal notice that "marriages between Zigeunermischlinge are undesirable and are to be prevented."[78]

When two such individuals decided to live together anyway they faced the danger of being sent to a concentration camp. On October 25, 1941, the RKPA issued an instruction on "concubinage" that invoked as legal authority the December 1937 Preventive Crime Fighting by the Police decree. Persons who practiced cohabitation when their marriage faced legal obstacles, the instruction noted, were guilty of trying to thwart the purpose of the law and therefore "acted asocially." The guilty parties were to be warned that if they did not separate and cease any sexual intercourse they would be sent to a concentration camp for an indefinite period. If they persisted in their extramarital relationship despite this warning they were to be taken into preventive police custody, that is, sent to a concentration camp.[79]

Gypsies who wanted to get married thus faced a catch-22 situation. Gypsies had their own marriage ceremonies and many of them never entered a civil marriage. German authorities had always looked askance at the institution of Gypsy marriage, which they regarded as little better than concubinage. Yet Gypsies were now being prevented from formalizing their marital ties and getting married according to German law. If, having been denied the right to enter a civil marriage, they lived together according to Gypsy custom, they faced being sent to a concentration camp.

We do not know how often the decree against concubinage was invoked. Cases that were prosecuted involved relationships between Gypsies and persons of "German blood." Wilhelm H. was a Gypsy musician in Cologne who lived with a German woman called Anna S. in what the Kripo called a "Gypsy marriage" *(Zigeunerehe)*. He was arrested on July 23, 1941, and made to sign a declaration in which he promised to stop living with S. and to stop having sexual relations with her or any other person of "German blood." Anna S. too agreed to end the relationship with H. and to forego sexual contact with any other Gypsy or Zigeunermischling. Thereafter both of them disappeared. The police believed that they had moved to Danzig, and the authorities there were asked to look for them. The German woman was arrested on January 29, 1942, in Oldenburg; H. was seized in Cologne on April 16 and on June 10 was sent to concentration camp Buchenwald. His life ended there on March 6, 1945, a few weeks before U.S. troops liberated the camp.[80]

In the case of trader Josef P., also of Cologne, the outcome was more fortunate. He was arrested on August 12, 1941, and was made to promise to end his relationship with Katharina P., a German divorcée, and with any other woman of "German blood." Yet he soon found himself in custody again, accused of having taken up with another German woman. Once more P. made a commitment to stop all such relationships, only to get into trouble over various delicts involving his trading practices. On February 15, 1944, P. was found to be an "asocial" and sent to concentration camp Natzweiler. He survived the ordeal of the camp.[81]

Most of the relationships between Gypsies and Germans involved Gypsy men and German women. However, there were exceptions. Karl H., "of German blood," was arrested on January 9, 1942, and admitted that he had lived with a Gypsy woman, Christine L., for four years. A child was born to them in 1939; another was born shortly after his arrest on March 24, 1942. H. got away with the promise to end this relationship, but the Gypsy woman was sent as an "asocial" to Auschwitz and died there on March 28, 1944. Her two children were likewise sent to the camp; the youngest was not yet two years old. Their subsequent fate is not recorded.[82]

The German partners in these kinds of relationships did not always escape unscathed. On September 11, 1942, Arono F. of Cologne, a Gypsy, had been ordered to stop all sexual relations with Anna R., who was German. In a memo to the local Gestapo office, the Cologne Kripo suggested that R. be punished. The law, their letter of November 23 admitted, did not provide penalties for the German partner in such cases. However, R. by her conduct had besmirched the honor of German women and therefore should be given two weeks protective custody. The Gestapo obliged. F., in turn, was sent to Auschwitz; he survived.[83]

Wartime conditions provided yet another excuse for limiting Gypsies' marriage rights. On March 3, 1942, the minister of the interior ruled that in view of the "war-imposed need to limit administrative work" it would accept no more applications for exemption from the Law for the Protection of the German Blood allowing marriage to a person of "alien blood."[84] On September 25 of the same year this order was extended to cover applications for marriages between Gypsies and Zigeunermischlinge as well.[85] Gypsies who consented to be sterilized occasionally would be given permission to marry or remain married. I shall discuss the situation of the sterilized in detail in a later chapter.

Personnel shortages were invoked to justify discontinuation of administrative procedures that were no longer desired; however, it did not stop the Kripo from keeping tabs on Gypsies' sexual conduct. According to existing police files, there must have been plenty of snooping in order to find out who was living with whom and to prevent "pollution of the German blood." These intrusions into private lives continued throughout the war years and are recorded even during the closing months of the war. The obsession with racial purity had priority over most other considerations.

Labor Law and Social Legislation: On an Equal Footing with Jews

The year 1942 saw the imposition of further restrictions and liabilities on the Gypsy population, especially with regard to employment. According to

German racial legislation, a textbook on the subject pointed out, "Gypsies are of alien blood [*Fremdblütige*]" and therefore must be separated from the German people just as the Jews are, "even though many special measures taken against the Jews are not necessary for them."[86]

On March 13, 1942, labor minister Seldte gave the order that, as of April 1, Gypsies were to be subject to the same special provisions of the labor law that had been decreed for Jews.[87] This meant that, as a rule, they were to be employed in special groups or separated from other workers. They could no longer be apprentices, the provisions protecting children 14–18 years old were not applicable to them, they did not receive supplements for large families, they could be dismissed without notice, and they were not entitled to pay for work missed because of sickness. On March 26, the minister of finance decreed that Gypsies, like Poles and Jews, had to pay a 15 percent surtax on their income tax known as *Sozialausgleichsabgabe*. This special tax was justified on the grounds that, unlike Germans, they were not required to pay dues to the German Labor Front (*Deutsche Arbeitsfront*), the Nazi labor organization.[88] These decrees applied to Gypsies and Mischlinge except those with only one Gypsy grandparent. The Kripo was instructed to supply the employment offices with the names of the persons who were affected by these provisions.[89]

Until 1942 and except in Austria, the families of Gypsies sent to a concentration camp were supposed to receive help from the Nazi Party's welfare agency (*Nationalsozialistische Volkswohlfahrt*, or NSV). This help at times had been extended only grudgingly or not at all, but theoretically it was available. The NSV, which handled state functions such as the annual winter support program (*Winterhilfswerk*), in June 1942 was relieved of the obligation to support Gypsies. On June 8, 1942, the RKPA notified all regional and local Kripo offices that from now on the next of kin of Gypsies and Zigeunermischlinge (except those who were only one quarter Gypsy) would no longer receive support from the NSV.[90] Asocial families, another RKPA circular issued several months later explained, should not be helped because they constituted a great danger for the German people. The fact that the head of the family was incarcerated did not change this fact.[91]

Local authorities reacted to the new pariah status of the Gypsies in different ways. The mayor of Berlin, taking note of the changed position of Gypsies under the labor law, gave orders on May 13, 1942, that henceforth Gypsies no longer be given extra rations for heavy labor or night work.[92] Authorities in Vienna, on the other hand, pointed out that Gypsies performing strenuous agricultural labor could not adequately do this work if given rations like those allotted to the Jews.[93] At a meeting in Berlin between officials of the Ministry of Nutrition and Agriculture and the RKPA on November 4, the issue of food rations for Gypsies was discussed. The results of this discussion were communicated to Vienna and to the Office of Nutrition for the city of Berlin. Himmler, Kripo officials pointed out, had given orders that the treatment of the Gypsies be put on a new basis. This would most likely lead to the expulsion of about 20,000 Gypsies; the remaining 5,000–

8,000 Gypsies would not require special administrative regulations. Moreover, it was difficult to separate the reliable from the unreliable Gypsies, and it made no sense to subject prominent Gypsies such as well-known violin players to a reduced food ration. For all these reasons, the nutrition office in Berlin was asked to annul the measure it had taken.[94]

Himmler's expulsion plans led to the deportation of thousands of Gypsies to a special Gypsy camp in Auschwitz in March 1943. During the months preceding this expulsion, Gypsies continued to be subject to various disabilities though, as we have seen, not all local initiatives in this regard were approved by decision makers in Berlin. We know of another such instance from the town of Minden in Westphalia. On July 30, 1942, a party official drew the attention of the chief of police to the fact that ninety-five Gypsies still lived in Minden. Repeated complaints, he wrote, had been received from housewives because they had to stand in the same queue with Gypsies in order to buy groceries and other products. In order to end this "intolerable situation," he proposed that special shopping hours and stores be set aside for Gypsies. Similar arrangements, he pointed out, had been made in other cities. The association of retail stores also supported the idea.[95] This proposal failed to be adopted. Gypsies and Jews, the chief of police replied, were indeed on an equal footing with regard to the labor law. However, in all other areas of life the government had not yet issued relevant regulations. "At this time," he concluded, "I therefore cannot approve your request because a legal basis for such an edict does not exist."[96]

By 1942, the Nazi regime had largely abandoned any pretense of conducting the affairs of state on the basis of the rule of law, yet local authorities, as in the case just mentioned, occasionally still adhered to regular administrative procedures. Presumably, local officials invoked such legalistic reservations when it was convenient. Nevertheless, such episodes point up the curious coexistence of Nazi arbitrariness with remnants of a legal order that prohibited the state from acting against an individual unless the law explicitly authorized it. In an interesting discussion of the Nazi dictatorship published in 1941, exiled German political scientist Ernst Fraenkel coined the term "dual state" for a state that combined vast power unlimited by any law with certain limited protections based on legal rights and privileges.[97] As I noted earlier, the regime preferred to deal with the "Gypsy problem" on the basis of ad hoc decrees rather than legislation precisely in order to overcome the presumption provided by the principle of the rule of law that what was not forbidden was allowed.

The enactment of measures that deprived the Gypsies of equal legal status continued right up to the deportation of 1943. On December 24, 1942, the minister of finance gave the order that effective April 1, 1943, Gypsies would no longer be entitled to the regular deductibles when paying their taxes.[98] This decree, like all other regulations denying Gypsies various rights and privileges extended to the German population, applied to pure Gypsies and Zigeunermischlinge with two or three Gypsy grandparents. Determinations of racial status in each specific case were to be made by the RKPA, which used for this purpose the assessments created by the Ritter institute.

Racial Categorizations

As I explained in chapter 3, in the spring of 1936 the Ministry of the Interior had ordered the establishment of a research institute to ascertain the racial makeup of the Gypsy population in Germany. The need to determine who counted as a Gypsy assumed special urgency after the enactment of the Nuremberg Laws, which were based on racial criteria. The Research Institute for Racial Hygiene and Population Biology (*Rassenhygienische und bevölkerungs-biologische Forschungsstelle*) was headed by Robert Ritter. Its main purpose, as Ritter put it in early 1940, was to "provide scientific and practical data for the measures taken by the state in the areas of eugenics and racial hygiene."[99]

On August 7, 1941, the RKPA issued detailed instructions on the compilation and utilization of racial assessments. On the basis of these expert assessments (*Sachverständigen-Gutachten*), the instruction pointed out, the RKPA identified a person as a Gypsy, a Zigeunermischling or a Gypsy-like itinerant (i.e., a non-Gypsy). The assessments then were transmitted to the regional Kripo offices. They included a racial diagnosis and remarks about the tribe to which the person in question belonged. Since it was impossible to determine the exact degree of mixed-race status, the assessments were to make use of the following simplified schema:

1. Z   pure Gypsy (*Vollzigeuner* or *stammechter Zigeuner*)
2. ZM+ *Zigeunermischling* with predominantly Gypsy blood
3. ZM   *Zigeunermischling* with equal parts German and Gypsy blood
       (a.) a ZM degree I is a person who has one German and one pure Gypsy parent
       (b.) a ZM degree II is a person who has one German and one ZM degree I parent
4. ZM- *Zigeunermischling* with predominantly German blood
5. NZ   non-Gypsy

The assessments also were to include an indication of the tribe to which a Gypsy belonged, since tribal membership in most cases made it possible to determine whether the person in question was German or foreign. Members of the following tribes were to be regarded as foreign Gypsies: "Rom" from Hungary ("who share certain racial characteristics with the Jews"), Gelder-ari, Lowari, Lalleri and certain clans from the Balkans. Many of these foreign Gypsies, the instruction noted, now carried German names and German identity papers to which they were not entitled. Such papers were to be confiscated and the Gypsies in question treated like foreigners. Members of the Sinti tribe were Germans; many of them had lived in Germany for several generations.[100]

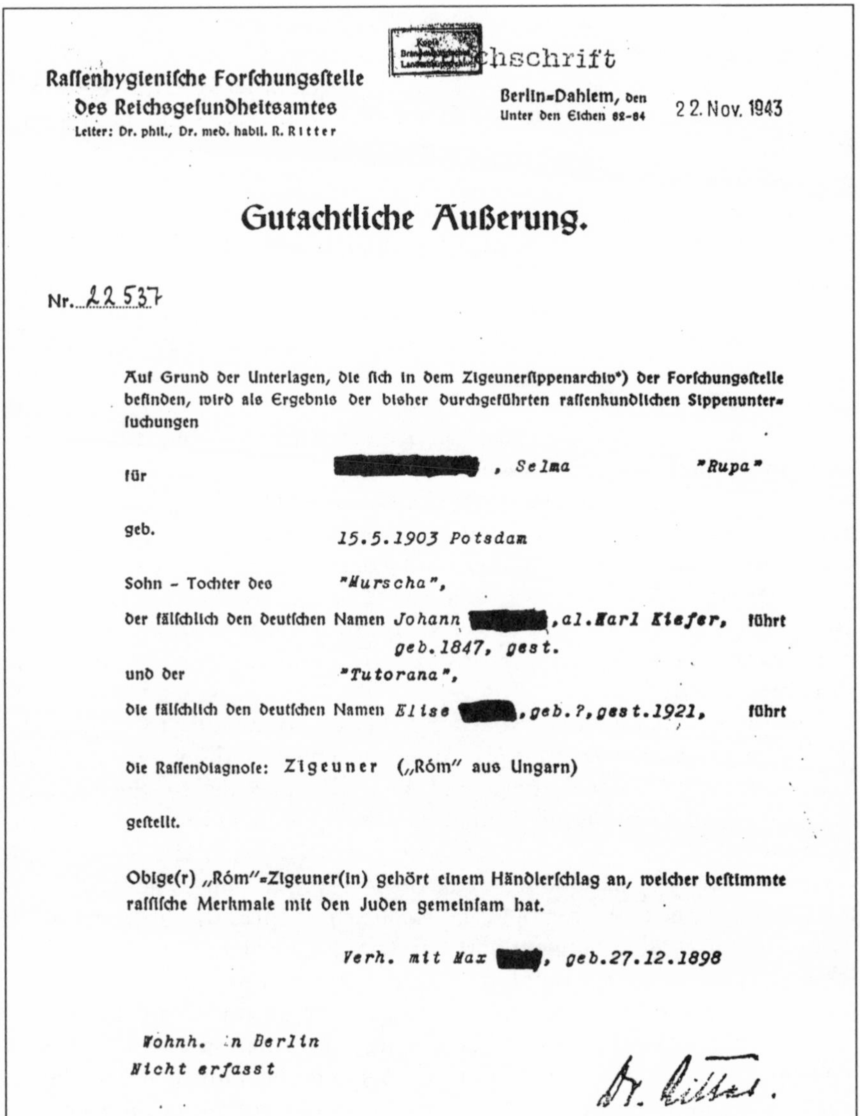

Abschrift

Rassenhygienische Forschungsstelle
des Reichsgesundheitsamtes
Leiter: Dr. phil., Dr. med. habil. R. Ritter

Berlin-Dahlem, den
Unter den Eichen 82-84 22. Nov. 1943

Gutachtliche Äußerung.

Nr. 22 537

Auf Grund der Unterlagen, die sich in dem Zigeunersippenarchiv*) der Forschungsstelle befinden, wird als Ergebnis der bisher durchgeführten rassenkundlichen Sippenuntersuchungen

für [redacted], Selma "Rupa"

geb. 15.5.1903 Potsdam

Sohn – Tochter des "Murscha",

der fälschlich den deutschen Namen Johann [redacted], al. Karl Kiefer, führt
geb. 1847, gest.

und der "Tutorana",

die fälschlich den deutschen Namen Elise [redacted], geb. ?, gest. 1921, führt

die Rassendiagnose: Zigeuner („Róm" aus Ungarn)

gestellt.

Obige(r) „Róm"-Zigeuner(in) gehört einem Händlerschlag an, welcher bestimmte rassische Merkmale mit den Juden gemeinsam hat.

Verh. mit Max [redacted], geb. 27.12.1898

Wohnh. in Berlin
Nicht erfasst

Dr. Ritter.

Racial assessment of a Rom Gypsy, belonging to a group that "shares certain characteristics with the Jews," prepared by Robert Ritter on November 22, 1943. COURTESY OF BRANDENBURGISCHES LANDESHAUPTARCHIV, POTSDAM, REP. 30 BERLIN C, TIT. 198, NR. 32.

The assessments were to be forwarded by the Kripo to the local registries that kept records of inhabitants (*Einwohnermeldeämter* and *Volkskarteien*). In this way local and other authorities could determine whether a Gypsy should be allowed to marry, should be dismissed from the armed forces, and so on. More detailed instructions on how the assessments were to be treated followed on

September 20. Of note in this circular is a provision concerning the Jenische. In October 1939, it appears, some of these "white Gypsies" erroneously had been thought to be real Gypsies and therefore had been ordered not to leave their place of residence. If they were now found to be non-Gypsies and thus released from this regulation, the Kripo was instructed to consider treating them as asocials in accordance with relevant decrees.[101]

The door to the use of nonracial criteria was also left open with regard to "Mischlinge with predominantly German blood" married to Germans. In these cases, as practice before and after the 1941 decrees shows, the RKPA's assessment and the decision depended on whether the person had shed his or her Gypsy way of life and was considered "socially adjusted."[102] Thus, for example, in January 1940 the Ritter institute inquired from the authorities in Dillenburg (Hesse-Nassau) whether certain Gypsies there were sedentary and had a regular job or needed public support.[103] In some cases, individuals were summoned to the Kripo and grilled about their way of life.[104] Those passing muster could be exempted from the punitive regulations affecting Gypsies, such as the freeze on mobility. The same exemption was available to second-degree Zigeunermischlinge (those with only one Gypsy grandparent). According to a decree of the RKPA issued on July 16, 1940, such persons could be released from the Gypsy regulations if they were married to sedentary persons of German blood and were generally socially adjusted.[105]

The same principle was invoked with regard to the duty to serve in the Youth Corps (*Jugenddienstpflicht*). An order issued by the youth leader on May 15, 1942, drafted with the help of the RKPA, provided for the exclusion of Gypsies and Zigeunermischlinge. However, an exception was made for youngsters whose parents had been rated by the RKPA as Mischlinge "with predominantly German blood" and as "socially adjusted." The RKPA forwarded this order to the regional and local Kripo offices with instructions to report on the social adjustment of the parents affected by this provision. The report was to include the opinion of the police and the local party organization, references from employers, and information on any criminal record.[106]

The Ritter institute had been collecting information about the racial makeup of the German Gypsies since 1936, but doing individual assessments was a slow and laborious process. The racial categorization in each case depended on the racial status of a person's four grandparents. A "pure Gypsy," for example, had to have at least three "pure Gypsy" grandparents[107]—and this information was not easily obtainable. Many Gypsies, in addition to their real name in Romani, used several non-Gypsy names, acquired in various difficult situations such as arrest or military desertion. Others possessed several baptismal certificates, each with a different name.[108] The difficult work of his institute, Ritter noted in an article published in February 1941, had been helped by the fact that after October 1939 Gypsies had been kept in a fixed residence and that all of them had been counted and reported to the authorities in Berlin. The total number of Gypsies in the Reich was about 30,000, but so far only slightly more than 10,000 assessments had been completed. It would take another year and a half, he estimated, to finish the job.[109] Thirteen months later, in March 1942, the count of assessments had only increased to 13,000, and assessing every Gypsy in the country was projected to require "about another year."[110]

The deportation of the Gypsies from the western border area in May 1940 had been slowed by the nonavailability of the racial assessments, and the same problem continued to plague the enforcement of the various restrictive measures against Gypsies enacted during the following two years. In response to an inquiry from Munich, in July 1942 the RKPA therefore ordered that persons not yet evaluated were to be treated as Gypsies until the racial assessment in hand proved otherwise.[111]

By November 1942, the number of completed assessments had risen to 18,922,[112] and in March 1943 Ritter reported that practically all of the Gypsies in Germany and Austria (the so-called Altreich and the Ostmark[113]) had been evaluated. The count now stood at 21,498. "After completion of the work," Ritter noted, "more than 9,000 Zigeunermischlinge could be concentrated by the police in a special Gypsy camp in the Sudetenland."[114] Ritter was referring to the Gypsy camp in Auschwitz, which of course was located in the Warthegau (the annexed part of Poland) and not in the Sudetenland. In March 1944 Ritter could announce the completion of the work—23,822 Gypsies and Zigeunermischlinge had been evaluated.[115] By then, many of the originally 30,000 Gypsies in the Reich were no longer alive. Thousands had died of disease or maltreatment in Auschwitz. More than 5,000 Gypsies from the Burgenland had been murdered in the gas vans of Kulmhof. The approaching Allied victory finally put an end to the conscientious effort of Ritter and his associates to establish the racial status of each and every Gypsy in Greater Germany and thus render their contribution toward the solution of the "Gypsy problem." A memo of the Berlin Kripo, dated November 24, 1944, noted that "because of the war no further assessments can be issued."[116]

Ritter's work on Gypsies was part of his larger interest in the biology of criminality, and this interest led him to undertake research on what he called "other asocial and criminal groups."[117] This came to include the Jenische (Gypsy-like itinerants) and families with especially large numbers of lawbreakers. The broadened scope of Ritter's work is reflected in several name changes for his institute, which eventually came to be called Research Institute for Criminal Biology. From December 1941 on, Ritter also headed the Institute for Criminal Biology of the Security Police, which had been established at Himmler's instigation. The aim of this institute was to ascertain the hereditary roots of crime and thus make a contribution toward "the prevention of crime on the basis of racial hygiene."[118] Special attention was devoted to youthful offenders. Ritter's work was financed by several agencies, including the Reich Health Office, the RKPA and the Ministry of the Interior. Still, Ritter never had enough money and his far-flung research depended on support from nongovernmental sources such as the German Research Foundation (*Deutsche Forschungsgemeinschaft*). He apparently was fascinated by Gypsies and even spent time trying to learn the rudiments of the Romani language.[119] The assertion of Gypsy affairs scholar Döring that from about 1941 on Ritter and Nebe (the director of the RKPA) lost interest in research on Gypsies because they disagreed with Himmler's approach to the Gypsy problem remains unsubstantiated.[120]

Conclusion

The pariah status created for the German Gypsies in 1939–1942 was based on a racist approach that made little allowance for nonracial factors. The Ritter institute had always considered Zigeunermischlinge the most depraved and criminal element and recommended various repressive measures; "pure Gypsies" were held to be less dangerous. However, in conflict with this view of the "Gypsy problem," many of the decrees enacted in these years penalized the "pure Gypsies" most severely while an exception was occasionally made for Mischlinge who had little "Gypsy blood" and were considered "socially adjusted." Needless to say, both approaches relied on pseudoscientific categories and dubious reasoning, and in terms of morality there was little to choose between them. By the end of 1942, as we shall see later, the priorities were again reversed, and Himmler granted special privileges, including exception from deportation, to "pure Gypsies." Obviously, after confronting the issue of the Gypsies for almost ten years, the regime still had not evolved a clear policy, though an unmistakable process of radicalization was under way that boded ill for the future.

7

Detention and Deportation from the Ostmark (Austria)

When Austria was annexed in 1938, about 11,000 Gypsies resided in what came to be called the Ostmark. Some 8,000 lived a sedentary existence in the Burgenland; many of the other 3,000 Gypsies spent the winter months in permanent dwellings but roamed about in their caravans during the summer. The freeze on mobility decreed in October 1939 put an end to this practice, but it did not satisfy those who demanded more stringent measures in the struggle against the "Gypsy plague."

Demands for Radical Solutions

In a report dated October 9, 1939, the SS domestic intelligence service (*Sicherheitsdienst*, or SD) informed the authorities in Berlin that the population of Austria demanded energetic action against the Gypsies. What was needed was the detention of "these asocial elements," badly infected with various contagious diseases, in closed camps. Moreover, the SD noted, the Gypsies had always been smugglers in the border regions and represented a danger as potential spies for foreign powers.[1]

Some officials in Austria regarded the establishment of Gypsy camps as an inadequate remedy. According to the chief public prosecutor, Dr. Meissner, reporting to his superior in Berlin on February 5, 1940, the Gypsies represented a serious racial and economic danger, especially in the district of Oberwart in the Burgenland, where some 4,000 of them lived almost exclusively from begging and stealing. To put the Gypsies into work camps would not solve anything. They represented a racially inferior element that multiplied at a very high rate and threatened to contaminate the surrounding population. The only effective way of freeing the people of the Burgenland from "this plague" was "to sterilize all Gypsies *without exception.*"[2]

Local officials too urged tough remedial measures. On February 3, the mayor of Schwarzach complained to the *Gauleiter* (Nazi party official) in Salzburg about Gypsies' begging and stealing and urged that something be done "to free the community from this scourge."[3] Referring to the "Gypsy nuisance in the community of Schwarzach," the Kripo of Salzburg requested the governor of the district of Salzburg to contact the RKPA in Berlin and urge "an early solution of the Gypsy question."[4] Similar appeals are preserved from officials in Pongau and Zell am See.[5]

Following the freeze on mobility, many Gypsies in the Burgenland had been forced into camps. The Vienna office of the SD, reporting in February 1940, noted that the initial effect had been good. However, the Gypsies continued to be a burden. "What the Gypsy women do not get through support of the communities they steal. In some communities of the Burgenland the farmers know ahead of time that a third of their harvest will be stolen by the Gypsies." The people of the Burgenland, the report continued, who had been suffering for years from "the Gypsy plague," waited impatiently "for a final solution [*eine endgültige Lösung*] of the Gypsy question." One report asks whether it might not be possible to find a place for these asocial elements outside of Germany.[6]

Two months later, on April 15, the Vienna SD reported that word had been received about a resettlement of the Gypsies of the Ostmark to Poland that would take place "in the near future." This reference to a deportation to the East came less than two weeks before Heydrich issued his order for the deportation of 2,500 German Gypsies to the General Government. The problem with Gypsies in Vienna, the SD noted, had become more acute with the arrival of warmer weather. Many of them were now begging and engaging in black market sales in the streets of the city. Due to the war, not enough police were available to make arrests and halt these practices. It was especially difficult to keep Gypsy women in custody because most of them were either pregnant or had babies. The police had proposed establishing a Gypsy camp, but this plan had floundered over disagreement about who would shoulder the cost of feeding the Gypsies. A real solution to the problem, the report ended, was possible only through zero population growth or resettlement.[7]

The Gypsies of the Ostmark, it turned out, were not included in the deportation to the General Government that took place in May 1940. But in early July the Kripo of Salzburg could report that "the majority" of the Austrian Gypsies would be "resettled" to Poland in the second half of August. Meanwhile the Gypsies of the area were to be concentrated in an already existing camp in Salzburg in which they could undergo the necessary medical examination. The camp was to be under police guard to prevent the Gypsies from trying to escape resettlement.[8] Also in preparation for this deportation, local police offices were asked to report the number of Gypsies in their area of jurisdiction and to list the names of those who had regular employment or owned substantial property such as houses, farm animals and implements and so on.[9]

The plan to deport Austrian Gypsies to the East fell victim to the same logistical problems that had brought an end to the further expulsion of German Gypsies. On August 23, three days before the first transport was to leave, word was received from Vienna that "due to suddenly encountered transport difficulties the expulsion cannot be carried out and the Gypsies have to stay at their previous locations for the time being and until the end of the war."[10] The "transport difficulties" mentioned here referred of course to the logjam created by the forced movement into the General Government of over 300,000 Poles. The Poles were being expelled to make room for the large influx of ethnic Germans from the Baltic states. This transfer of population, very dear to Hitler and Himmler, had priority over all other resettlement schemes, and for the time being it created a respite for the Gypsies of both the Altreich and the Ostmark.

Gypsy Camps

A decree issued by the RKPA on October 31 provided instructions on how the Gypsies of the Ostmark were to be handled in the immediate future. The planned resettlement to the General Government had been canceled "because after the war a different solution of the entire Gypsy question is anticipated." However, the existing situation needed urgent attention. Tolerable living conditions had to be created for the approaching winter, and local communities had to be relieved of the welfare burden posed by the Gypsies. The instruction prescribed slightly different measures for the approximately 6,000 Gypsies of the Burgenland, two thirds of them women and children, and for the seven hundred Gypsies in the rest of the Ostmark.[11] That added up to a total of 6,700 Gypsies, whereas at the time of the Anschluss the number was estimated to be 11,000. We know that close to a thousand male and female Gypsies from the Burgenland had been seized as work-shy and asocial in July 1938 and sent to concentration camps. There were undoubtedly many more such arrests in the following two years. Still, the discrepancy between these two sets of figures is substantial and remains unexplained.

The Gypsies of the Burgenland were to be concentrated in what the instruction called "settlements." They were to be under guard and allowed to leave the encampment only under supervision. In order to minimize the cost of public welfare, all male Gypsies, except those who had special skills and were already gainfully employed, were to be put to work in special work camps near Linz and Eisenerz. These camps were to be under the supervision of a member of the criminal police; a Gypsy released for this purpose from a concentration camp was to be responsible for each barrack. Their wages were to be used for paying for the common meals; the surplus, after giving each worker pocket money worth 10 percent of the wage, was to be handed over to the public relief offices to defray the cost of supporting the families of the workers. Women and older children were to be employed in cottage trades. The Gypsies in the other parts of the Ostmark too were to be channeled into productive labor. Those employed were to support those unable to work; public funds were to be tapped only when "a bare minimum of existence" could not otherwise be guaranteed. Women able to work were to be used for cleaning the streets and removing snow. Intentional violation of the rules was to be punished with preventive police custody.[12]

We know of several camps operating more or less according to the guidelines provided in the decree of October 31. In a part of Salzburg called Leopoldskron a Gypsy camp had been in existence since May or June 1939. The setup was similar to other municipal camps created in the Altreich, (described in chapter 1). Initially this camp held about 130 persons. In late August 1940, it was enlarged to accommodate Gypsies who had been concentrated at the Salzburg racetrack for deportation to the General Government. From this point on, the inhabitants numbered between three hundred and four hundred. The camp was surrounded by a fence and was run by the Salzburg Kripo. Permission was required to leave the camp, mail was censored, and the lights were turned off at 8 P.M. At night the camp was watched by armed guards. The men were put to work at road construction, flood control and other such projects; the women wove baskets, cleaned the camp, cooked and took care of the sick. In October 1940, twenty-three Gypsies were ordered to serve as extras in Leni Riefenstahl's film *Tiefland*. Pay for the various outside jobs went to the authorities to defray the cost of operating the camp; the Gypsies received pocket money.[13]

Overall, conditions in the Salzburg camp apparently were not terribly bad. A policeman who served in the camp recalled the occasional administration of corporal punishment and detention in a penal bunker for those violating the rules of the camp, but there were no abnormal deaths.[14] In March–April 1943, a majority of the inhabitants were deported to the Gypsy camp in Auschwitz. A smaller group was transferred to Gypsy camp Lackenbach in the Burgenland.

On November 23, 1940, the administrators of several counties in the Burgenland, acting on the RKPA decree of October 31, established Gypsy camp Lackenbach. Located in the district of Oberpullendorf on the grounds of a rundown former estate of Count Esterhazy, the camp at first had no barracks and many of the Gypsies had to live in stables with leaky roofs. Those who came with their caravans were somewhat better off. There was a shortage of water, and sanitary conditions were extremely poor. By April 1941, the camp had 591 inhabitants; the highest enrollment was reached in November of that year, when there were 2,335 Gypsies in the camp. Eventually barracks were built and the lot of the inhabitants improved somewhat. Still, there were many deaths as a result of insufficient nutrition and inadequate medical care. In late 1941, a typhus epidemic broke out that led to between 250–300 deaths. The first commandant of the camp, Hans Kollross, also died of typhus.[15]

The camp was run by the Vienna Kripo. In February 1941, SS–Obersturmführer Franz Langmüller became head of the camp, a position he occupied until September 1942. Under his rule inhabitants suffered the kind of brutalities associated with Nazi concentration camps. In October 1948, Langmüller was tried for crimes of "torture and violations of human dignity," and witnesses related the outrages to which they had been exposed during his tenure. Langmüller himself was accused of having caused the death of 287 inmates. Mothers were made to walk barefoot in the snow if their children relieved themselves in the open, men had to clean toilets with bare hands, and grown-ups and children had to carry heavy stones for construction in the camp. Those who were caught shirking work were brutally beaten and denied food. If someone escaped, collective punishment was imposed and the inmates had to stand hours in the open for roll call. Two Gypsies released for this purpose from a concentration camp served as prisoner functionaries (*Kapos*) and often were as brutal as the guards.[16]

Conditions improved somewhat in late summer of 1943 under a new commandant, Julius Brunner. A larger number of Gypsies now were sent to work outside the camp and were fed a better diet. Some worked on road construction; others were employed on farms. The wages of these workers went to the camp administration, and the Gypsies received merely pocket money. An order issued by the Kripo post of the camp on February 1, 1943, prohibited Gypsies' lingering on their way to and from work or visiting restaurants, coffee houses, theaters or movies.[17]

Camp Lackenbach originally had been set up for Gypsies in the Burgenland, but it soon received Gypsies from other locations as well. The camp diary that is preserved records the arrival of over one hundred Gypsies from Vienna on July 4, 1941.[18] Others were sent there because they were said to have refused work or after serving a prison sentence.[19] When the camp was liberated in March 1945, it still held between three hundred and four hundred inmates. The others had been deported East or had died in the camp.

Very little is known about the life of other Gypsies in the Ostmark during these years. Several orders are preserved from the district of Oberwart in the Burgenland, which imposed various restrictions on the Gypsies living there. In early July 1941, male Gypsies were limited to three cigarettes daily; in view of the prevailing scarcity, no tobacco products at all were to be sold to Gypsy women or children. Other items not rationed but in short supply such as lemons and citrus fruits were forbidden to Gypsies. "I consider it the obvious duty of every shopkeeper," wrote the *Landrat* (chief magistrate), "to give German people [*deutsche Volksgenossen*] preferential treatment over Gypsies."[20] In September the same official complained about frequent absenteeism among Gypsies and gave orders that such offenders be locked up for a weekend and be put on a diet of bread and water.[21] On November 7, 1941, Gypsies were forbidden to use public transportation except railroads.[22]

Deportation to Lodz (Litzmannstadt)

Plans to deport Austrian Gypsies to the East had come to naught in the summer of 1940, but in late 1941 a massive deportation finally took place that was to have deadly consequences. The first mention of sending Gypsies to the Jewish ghetto in Litzmannstadt comes in a letter from the mayor of that city in September 1941. Initially, it appears, the intention had been to move 60,000 more Jews from Germany and the Protectorate (the former Czechoslovakia) into the already crowded ghetto. However, after objections from Reichsstatthalter Greiser, the governor of the Warthegau (the annexed part of Poland), that number had been reduced to 20,000 Jews and 5,000 Gypsies. Still, the authorities in Litzmannstadt were strongly opposed to this plan.

On September 24, Mayor Werner Ventzki of Litzmannstadt explained his great concern about the expected influx in a letter to the administrator of the area, *Regierungspräsident* (senior government official) Friedrich Übelhör. The planned transfer of 20,000 Jews and 5,000 Gypsies, Ventzki wrote, would create serious problems. Population density would increase dramatically, an outbreak of typhus could be expected that would endanger the rest of the city, and the factories in the ghetto that produced vital goods for the German armed forces would no longer be able to fulfill their targets. Also, order and security in the ghetto would be threatened especially by bringing in Gypsies, who are agitators, given to crime and are "arsonists of the worst sort." It was questionable whether the Gypsies would be able to appoint someone who could function as chief spokesman for them in the way the Jews had been able to do. Preparing a place for the Gypsies would require a minimum of two to three months.[23] On October 4, Übelhör forwarded this letter to Himmler and added his own fears. All around the ghetto, he pointed out, lived 120,000 Germans who would be in grave danger if an epidemic broke out, which was practically inevitable. Even if it were possible to continue to produce important goods for the armed forces, there was the danger of arson by the Gypsies. These Gypsies would be "a permanent danger for the security and order of the ghetto." In case the transfer took place against his advice, Übelhör warned, he had to decline responsibility for the consequences.[24]

In his reply on October 10 Himmler rejected Übelhör's objections to the planned move. The danger of an epidemic was exaggerated; the demands of war production had become the favorite reason for opposing any new venture. As to the Gypsies, the danger of arson could easily be handled by telling them that in case of a fire, irrespective of its origin, ten Gypsies would be shot. With such an approach, Himmler argued, the Gypsies would become the best firemen.[25] More exchanges followed. In another teletyped communication to Himmler, Übelhör complained that Eichmann, following a visit to the ghetto, had intentionally misrepresented the true state of affairs to Himmler. Such tactics amounted to Gypsy-like horse-trading tricks. Himmler, in turn, accused Übelhör of adopting the wrong tone and ignoring the fact that Himmler was his superior. You should remember, he wrote, "that Litzmannstadt is part of the German Reich and that the interests of the Reich have first claim before those of your area of jurisdiction."[26]

Himmler also brushed aside objections from the War Economy and Armaments Office of the OKW,[27] and beginning on October 16 transports of Jews began to arrive in Litzmannstadt. On November 5 the first trainload of Gypsies from the Ostmark reached the same destination, and by November 9 a total of 4,996 Gypsies had been deposited in the ghetto. Of these, 1,130 were men, 1,188 were women and 2,689 (more than half of the total) were children; eleven died during the journey.[28] Most of the Gypsies were from the Burgenland. Two transports were made up of inmates from the Lackenbach Gypsy camp. The criterion of selection there as elsewhere, it appears, had been inability to work; hence the large number of old people and children included in the five transports.[29]

A chronicle composed by inmates of the Lodz ghetto that has been preserved provides some information about events that followed. The Austrian Gypsies were squeezed into several houses in the ghetto, separated from the Jewish inhabitants by a barbed wire fence. The houses had no furniture or even beds, and sanitary conditions were catastrophic.[30] It is not clear whether the Germans ever had any clear plans in regard to the Gypsies. On November 22, the employment office in Posen requested the dispatch of 120 workers for a weapons and munitions factory there,[31] but it is not known whether any Gypsies were in fact sent there. Very soon a deadly epidemic of typhus broke out in the camp, which made any scheme of putting the Gypsies to work academic.

The Jewish administration of the ghetto was ordered to supply the Gypsy camp with food and medical care, and during the first six days after their arrival the Gypsies were sent soup and coffee. Then two kitchens were set up in the encampment, though the Jewish ghetto continued to provide the provisions. The Jewish undertakers were made to remove and bury the deceased, and by November 12, after only a few days in the camp, the count of the dead stood at 213. The bodies, usually clothed only in underwear, were interred in a special section of the Jewish cemetery. The local Kripo, in charge of the camp, was sent a daily report on the number buried.[32]

German authorities in Litzmannstadt had predicted that the influx of so many new people confined in a limited space and provided with sparse nourishment would lead to epidemics, and the atrocious conditions in the Gypsy camp soon made this a self-fulfilling prophecy. Among the victims of the typhus epidemic that devastated the camp was the German commandant of the camp, a Kripo officer by the name of Eugenius Jansen, who died of typhus in late December, and at least one Jewish doctor who had been ordered to work there. On December 29, the chronicle records that Dr. Karol Boehm from Prague, fifty years old, died in the hospital for infectious diseases from typhus, which he had contracted while providing medical care in the Gypsy camp. Four other Jewish physicians also caught the disease there and had to be hospitalized. One of them subsequently died. One of the Jewish undertakers was also infected.[33]

Typhus is a highly contagious disease that is transmitted by lice. In untreated cases, the mortality rate ranges between 10 and 40 percent; people over forty are especially vulnerable. The spread of the disease is facilitated by hunger and exhaustion and by crowded and primitive accommodations that lack facilities for washing, including towels and soap. These, of course, were precisely the conditions that the Germans imposed on many of their captives, including the Gypsies, and the rapid spread of typhus among them was hardly surprising. Moreover, the second quarter of 1941 had seen a large outbreak of typhus among the civilian population in the General Government, and during the course of the year large numbers of German soldiers too became infected with the disease. In December 1941 alone, there were some 90,000 cases.[34] In these circumstances, the Germans were all too ready to adopt radical remedies to cope with any outbreak of typhus.

By the end of December, the typhus epidemic raging uncontrolled in the Gypsy camp had led to 613 deaths. Medical care for the sick apparently consisted of little more than separating the infected from those still healthy. The fact that not only Jews but a high-ranking German official had died of the disease probably led to the decision to liquidate the camp and kill all those still alive. The chronicle of the Jewish ghetto for the first week of January 1942 records that for the past ten days Gypsies were taken away in trucks. "The camp, which is practically deserted now, will no doubt be entirely eliminated by the end of this week. Apparently, its elimination was dictated by necessity, since there was a danger that the typhus would spread."[35]

This was not the first time that the Nazis had used murder as a way of combating an epidemic among non-Germans that threatened to get out of control, nor was it to be the last time. Jews, Gypsies and other "alien races" were seen as natural carriers of lethal parasites such as lice,[36] and the resort to draconian measures for ending epidemics among them was almost standard operating procedure. "The Nazi methods of 'fighting' infectious diseases," writes Isaiah Trunk, "were well known and were feared not less than the epidemics themselves."[37] One of the mobile killing units operating behind the German troops advancing into Russia, *Einsatzkommando* 9 of *Einsatzgruppe* (special task force) B, reported on September 23, 1941, that a contagious disease with fever had broken out in the Jewish ghetto of Janowitschi. "Since there was reason to fear that the disease would spread into the city and to the rural population, the inmates of the ghetto numbering 1,025 Jews were subjected to special treatment [*sonderbehandelt*],"[38] which was the euphemism for killing Jews or other victims. Another such report from White Russia noted that "between January 23 to 29, 1942, on account of the spread of the typhus epidemic, [the unit] has shot 311 persons in Minsk in order to clean up the prisons."[39] Einsatzgruppe A reported on April 24, 1942, that it had executed 1,272 persons, "among them 983 Jews who were afflicted with contagious diseases or were so old and decrepit that they were no longer suitable for work."[40]

The German administration of Litzmannstadt had accepted the Gypsies only under protest. The typhus outbreak eliminated any chance of recovering the cost of their upkeep from forced labor and thus in effect doomed even those not yet infected by the disease. The decision to stop the typhus epidemic by liquidating the Gypsy camp and killing all the inhabitants was probably taken in late December 1941. By early January 1942, the Gypsies were being taken to the village of Chelmno (Kulmhof) about thirty-five miles northwest of Litzmannstadt, where a killing center for Jews using gas vans had started to operate on December 8, 1941. The practice was to kill a certain number of Jews whenever the ghetto of Litzmannstadt became over-crowded,[41] and this same facility was now used to "solve" the problem of the typhus epidemic among the Gypsies.

The killing center of Chelmno, which ultimately was responsible for the murder of over 300,000 Jews, initially was run by a *Sonderkommando* (special detachment) under one Herbert Lange. It employed gas vans that had previ-ously been used in East Prussia and the incorporated Eastern territories for Nazi-style "euthanasia" operations. Six members of the SS unit that oper-ated the extermination camp were tried by a German court that rendered its verdict in 1963, and the proceedings of this trial brought out various details about the killings. The victims were taken by truck to a small castle in the village of Chelmno that had been renovated and fenced in. Here they were told to undress in preparation for a bath prior to being moved to Germany for work, and then they were herded into another truck that was said to be a bath. When the truck was full (the usual load was fifty persons), the door of the truck was closed and exhaust was fed into it. After no more noise could be heard from inside the truck, it would be driven into a wood where the bodies were buried. In the spring of 1942 a crematorium was built to burn the bodies. Three gas vans were in operation, and the average rate of killing was 1,000 victims a day. The SS unit was assisted by a detachment of over a hundred Order Police; seventy Jewish workers were employed in disposing of the bodies.[42]

In January of 1942, about 4,400 Gypsies from Litzmannstadt were killed in the gas vans of Chelmno, but there are few witnesses. Several Poles living nearby report seeing Gypsies on the trucks transporting victims to the killing center.[43] A member of the Sonderkommando Lange, who substituted for the regular drivers of the gas vans about ten times, recalls that most of the "transports" were Jews, "but once there were Gypsies." Another mem-ber of the SS unit also remembered Gypsies being taken out of the gas vans.[44] There are no other details about the last days of the murdered Gyp-sies. There were no survivors.

Much connected with the deportation and death of the Burgenland Gyp-sies remains unclear. Next to nothing is known about the decision-making process that led to the deportation of the Gypsies and to their ultimate death in the gas vans. The decision to deport 5,000 Austrian Gypsies to the East came at a time when no other large-scale deportations of Gypsies were being planned or carried out. It is likely that the Gypsies from the Burgen-land were singled out and deported in response to pressure coming from the authorities and the Nazi party in the Ostmark, who for a long time had demanded to make *"das Burgenland zigeunerfrei!"* It is improbable that the decision to deport the Gypsies also included the idea of killing them. There had been frequent calls for sterilization and confinement in camps but no demands for physical annihilation. The authorities in Berlin who ordered the deportation probably sought no more than getting rid of a long-standing annoyance without giving much thought to the ultimate fate of the deported Gypsies. The decision to liquidate the camp and murder all of the still living inmates most likely was made locally and in response to the spreading typhus epidemic; it certainly was not part of some overall plan to annihilate all Gypsies. Needless to say, such a "medical" motive does not make the murders any less criminal and reprehensible.

The administrator of the district of Oberwart in the Burgenland, address-ing his mayors and police posts on November 11, 1941, expressed the view that the deportation of 2,000 Gypsies in the preceding week had marked "great progress in the solution of the Gypsy question." He ordered the con-solidation of several Gypsy camps that were left with very few inhabitants; the proceeds from any property left behind for the time being were to be put into trust funds administered by the local communities. Further deporta-tions were expected.[45] In early 1942, the Landrat, drawing attention to expected further measures toward a solution of the Gypsy question, recom-mended that those owning landed property be encouraged to sell it. "This has to be done in such a way that no alarm is created and Gypsies not be made to think that an expulsion is expected today or tomorrow."[46]

Many Gypsies, according to the memo of November 11, had volun-teered to accompany their next of kin who had been arrested, but these requests were rejected. All questions about Gypsies resettled to the ghetto of Litzmannstadt, the Landrat announced on March 19, 1942, were to be directed to the Graz Kripo which would forward them to the RKPA in Berlin.[47] By that date none of the deported Gypsies was still alive: they had either died of typhus or had been asphyxiated in the gas vans of Chelmno. On December 28, 1942, the RKPA noted in a memo to local Kripo offices that some Gypsies sought to find out for themselves what had happened to those deported to the East in May 1940 and November 1941. Such travel was strictly forbidden.[48]

At the time of the Anschluss, close to 8,000 Gypsies lived in the Burgen-land. A census held in 1952 revealed that several years after the end of the war and the downfall of the Nazi regime there were only 870 Gypsies left in the Burgenland—281 men, 372 women and 217 children. The great major-ity of the survivors—636 of them—had spent some time in a concentration camp.[49] There can be no doubt that the Gypsies of the Burgenland suffered far more than any other group of German or Austrian Gypsies.

8

The Killing of "Spies" and Hostages in German-Occupied Europe

On June 22, 1941, Hitler's armies invaded the Soviet Union, and in the course of this long war large numbers of Gypsies were murdered by the Nazis. Most of these killings were carried out by special units known as *Einsatzgruppen* (special task forces) that followed the advancing German armies. Their initial assignment was to protect the rear of the fighting troops, mainly by shooting all actual or potential enemies. In Russia the Gypsies were explicitly targeted for death for the first time. German Gypsies were being subjected to various discriminatory measures and were generally made social outcasts, but their lives were not in danger. What accounts for this difference in treatment?

Soviet Gypsies as Spies and Partisans

The Einsatzgruppen made their first appearance during the annexation of Austria and Czechoslovakia. They took on a more extensive role during the Polish campaign in 1939. They were assigned to eliminate the Polish intelligentsia, which was the mainstay of Polish national identity and a potential threat to German rule over the Slavic *Untermenschen* (subhumans). By May 1941, Heydrich had organized four Einsatzgruppen, each between 500 and 990 men strong and divided into several *Einsatzkommandos* and *Sonderkommandos* (special detachments), for a total strength of 3,000 men.

Prior to the invasion of the Soviet Union the commanders of the Einsatzgruppen were assembled for a series of orientation meetings at which they listened to exhortations defining their forthcoming mission. The speeches were given by Reinhard Heydrich and Bruno Streckenbach, the chief of personnel in the RSHA. According to the recollection of several participants, the RSHA officials informed the Einsatzgruppen officers that the Führer had ordered the liquidation of Jews, Communist functionaries and Gypsies on the grounds that they endangered the security of the troops.[1] A written order issued by Heydrich on July 2, known as the shooting order (*Erschiessungsbefehl*), recapitulated the oral instructions.[2] At his trial for war crimes in 1948, Otto Ohlendorf, the head of Einsatzgruppe D, interpreted Heydrich's shooting order as providing for the killing of "Jews, Gypsies, communist functionaries, active communists, and all persons who could endanger security."[3] The Gypsies, Ohlendorf explained under cross-examination, being people without a permanent home, had been given to espionage as far back as the Thirty Years' War. In his area of operation, Ohlendorf added, they also had been involved in partisan warfare.[4] The Führer's order, according to Einsatzkommando leader Bradfisch, provided for the liquidation of Jews "and other racially inferior elements."[5] If remembered correctly, this language would furnish an additional motive, a racial one, for the killing of the Gypsies.

The orders given to the mobile killing units regarding the murder of Jews have been the subject of some contention,[6] but as concerns the targeting of Gypsies there is little ambiguity. Roving Gypsies, once again, were regarded as spies and as such they were included in the list of enemies to be eliminated. The difference from other such persecutions was the severity of the measures adopted against them. In earlier crises or wars Gypsies had been expelled or forbidden to itinerate. However, the war against the Soviet Union was seen by Hitler and his henchmen as an ideological struggle against two mortal enemies of Germany—Jews and Bolsheviks. As orders issued to the troops affirmed with regularity, it was to be fought as a war of extermination against all political and racial opponents, and no chances could be taken. Gypsies, regarded as spies, were killed without mercy— men, women and children.

The steadily growing number of attacks by partisans made the Germans nervous and trigger-happy and further increased the ruthlessness with which the war had been fought from the very beginning. Soon anyone encountered outside of his or her regular place of residence became a suspect and risked being shot. During the first two months of the war, the 18th Panzer Division gave orders that all civilians found "wandering about" in the combat zone were to the "treated" by the troops and handed over to the Einsatzgruppen if found in the rear areas. When "the term 'partisan' seemed insufficient to legitimize brutality, especially where obviously helpless civilians were concerned," writes Bartov, "the army sometimes resorted to the euphemism 'spy' or 'agent,' a uniquely useful term precisely because it was based on the assumption that innocence was the best indication of guilt."[7] Indiscriminate shootings "for suspected espionage" became so frequent that eventually orders had to be issued to bring "suspects" before an appropriate officer for interrogation rather than simply kill them on the spot. The Einsatzgruppen, on the other hand, continued to treat any roving Gypsies as partisans or spies and those encountered were shot. In a meeting held in November 1941 with army officers and military police on the subject of vagabonds, the head of Einsatzkommando 8, attached to Army Group Center, argued that men of military age who were stopped at a checkpoint, had no adequate proof of identity and had been itinerating since the beginning of the war should be assumed to be partisans and therefore should be liquidated as asocials and a threat to public safety.[8]

One of the principal sources of information for the murder of Soviet Gypsies are the periodically issued activity reports of the Einsatzgruppen that were sent to Berlin. Sometimes the Gypsies were said to have been shot for specific crimes, though such allegations may also have been included as a cover in case the reports fell into the wrong hands. On August 30, 1941, six Gypsies were shot for looting.[9] A report dated September 23 noted that thirteen male and ten female Gypsies had been shot because "they had carried out numerous thefts and had terrorized the rural population."[10] Six Gypsies, according to another report dated a few days later, had been shot as "asocial elements."[11]

In many other cases the shooting of Gypsies was recorded simply as a separate category next to other victims such as Jews and Communists. For example, a report by Einsatzgruppe B for March 1942 listed such charges as provocative remarks, attempted murder by poison, sabotage and membership in a partisan band as the reasons for subjecting Russians to "special treatment." For Jews and Gypsies, on the other hand, no special reasons were given.[12] Obviously the instructions given to the Einsatzgruppen must have branded both of these groups per se a threat that had to be eliminated (although each posed a threat of a different sort), and no further justification for their killing was required.

The Einsatzgruppen, assisted by police units, methodically swept towns and villages to seize and kill all the Jews they could find. At times they staged elaborate hunts for Jews who were hiding in the woods or in other places of refuge. In the case of the Gypsies, on the other hand, few search operations specifically targeting Gypsies appear to have taken place, for Gypsies were not considered a high priority enemy.[13] Gypsies were killed when handed over by other military units or when encountered, either in a village or town or in the countryside. For example, Einsatzkommando 4a, moving from one location to another in October 1941, came upon a Gypsy band of thirty-two persons. Since they had no identity cards and could not explain the origin of German equipment found in their wagons, the activity report noted, "they were executed."[14] Some army units too had standing orders to kill them. "Gypsies," read an instruction issued October 10, 1941, by the military commander in Weissruthenien (part of Byelorussia), "are to be shot immediately on the spot wherever they are seized."[15]

Other killing units preying upon the Gypsies were under the command of senior SS and police leaders (*Höhere SS- und Polizeiführer*, or HSSPF). Three such officers had been appointed by Himmler for the newly occupied Soviet territories, thus combining SS and police functions. A report issued by the senior SS and police leader for Russia Center recorded the execution of fifty-three Gypsies between October 12 and 14, 1941 (along with sixty-two Russian soldiers, four Communists and ten Jews).[16] Rural police units too supplied special task forces (*Gendarmeriezüge*) that participated in the pacification of the countryside. A letter written by a rural police officer stationed near Lemberg (Ukraine) in June 1942 tells of frequent such expeditions: "Three to four actions a week. Sometimes Gypsies and at other times Jews, partisans and other rabble." Cooperation with the SD was excellent.[17] On the other hand, the 281st Security Division in October 1943 took the position that "the participation of military units in the liquidation of Gypsies and Jews, a political measure assigned to the SD, is nowhere prescribed and is to be refused." The jurisdiction of the military was limited to handing over Gypsies and Jews to the SD, who took care of them according to their own regulations.[18] That was also the role assumed by the army's Secret Field Police (*Geheime Feldpolizei*, or GFP). A GFP activity report for the month of March 1942 noted that fifty-five persons, among them fifty-one Gypsies, had been taken to a Sonderkommando of the SD "for follow-up."[19]

On November 21, 1941, the commanding general of Army Group Rear Area North issued an order that exempted from execution sedentary Gypsies with a fixed residence of at least two years who were not suspected of any political or criminal wrongdoing.[20] Whether this order was promulgated on the commander's own initiative or came about as a result of orders from above is not known. According to postwar testimony by the leader of one of the Einsatzkommandos, Himmler had a special interest in the Gypsies and "Gypsy tribes [therefore] were not to be eliminated."[21] A member of Einsatzgruppe D recalled that in November or December 1941 Himmler is supposed to have issued an order ending the execution of Gypsies in the Soviet Union.[22] It is possible that both of these recollections confuse the partial exemption issued on November 21, 1941, with a complete ban on further executions. In the Baltic states too, as we shall see later, orders were given that sedentary Gypsies who did not constitute a danger on political or criminal grounds were not to be killed. The extent to which the order exempting reliable sedentary Gypsies was observed is not clear. In many instances there is not enough information to determine whether executed Gypsies were sedentary or not.

In at least one case the order of November 21, 1941, protecting sedentary Gypsies, was invoked and used for a mild rebuke. In May 1942, at the instigation of the army's Secret Field Police, 128 Gypsies were shot by the local military commander of Norwoshew (281st Security Division, Army Group Rear Area North) for suspected aid to the partisans. For reasons that remain obscure, an investigation was started during the course of which an order issued by Field Commander 822 (*Feldkommandantur* 822) on May 12 came to light. That order provided that "Gypsies are always to be treated like partisans." The deputy commander of the 281st Security Division, who conducted the investigation of the shooting, thereupon informed the field commander that his order was in conflict with the order issued by the commander of Army Group Rear Area North on November 21, 1941. The order of May 12 was to be canceled; the field commander was reminded to conduct himself in accordance with the November 21 order. In reporting the incident to the commanding officer of Army Group Rear Area North, the 281st Security Division took the position that while the shooting of the Gypsy suspects could not be considered authorized by valid regulations, it nevertheless had to be seen as warranted. Past experience had shown that "Gypsies in almost all cases are connected with the partisans and such a link had to be assumed in this case as well," even though it had not been possible to establish complete proof. The punishment imposed, the report ended, had also been justified by the results. Since the shooting of the Gypsies no further surprise attacks had taken place.[23]

Given the prevalence of such attitudes, it is not surprising that the killing of Gypsies in the occupied Soviet Union continued unabated. Exposed to a continuous stream of propaganda and indoctrination, German troops in the East increasingly came to believe that they defended their homes and families against the menace of Jewish-Asiatic-Bolshevik Untermenschen. There was also the pressure of combat and especially the fear created by the ever-increasing number of attacks and ambushes staged by partisans. As a result, writes Bartov, the "orders to confine the murders to certain categories of people and then further to limit them due to changing circumstances were widely ignored by the troops." Fine distinctions between categories of victims were disregarded and there resulted a general barbarization that led to indiscriminate shootings on a wide scale.[24]

Many of the Gypsies on the Crimean peninsula lived a settled life, but this did not save them. Einsatzgruppe D reached the Crimea in November 1941 and soon reported the liquidation of large numbers of Gypsies. Between November 16 and December 15, the unit managed to murder a total of 824 Gypsies.[25] From February 16 to 28, 1942, the Einsatzgruppe killed "421 Gypsies, asocials and saboteurs."[26] During the second half of March, the group executed 1,501 persons, among them "261 asocials including Gypsies." Apart from a few remnants in the north, the same report noted with satisfaction, there now are no more Gypsies to be found on the peninsula.[27] Altogether, Einsatzgruppe D by April 8, 1942, had slaughtered a total of 92,000 Jews, Krimchaks (a Crimean tribe classified as Jewish) and Gypsies.[28] Several weeks later, on May 22, 1942, another report advised that the inclusion of the Krimchaks and Gypsies in the fate of the Jews had attracted no particular attention among the population.[29]

In other parts of the occupied Soviet Union too the killing of Gypsies continued at an undiminished pace. On May 6, 1942, all the Gypsies in the village of Siwaschi in Ukraine—about thirty men, women and children— were shot by unknown men in SS uniforms.[30] An activity report by Einsatzgruppe B records that between September 1 and September 14, a total of 301 Gypsies were "subjected to special treatment [*sonderbehandelt*]."[31] In December 1942, a special police unit, led by Brigadeführer von Gottberg and also referred to as Einsatzgruppe Gottberg, carried out a series of operations characterized as "antipartisan." The marching orders for Operation

Hamburg in the area of Slonim in White Russia declared that "every bandit, Jew, Gypsy and suspected partisan is to be regarded as an enemy" and therefore is to be destroyed. The operation yielded 2,658 Jews and 30 Gypsies. During Operation Altona in the area of Kossow-Byten the unit killed 126 Jews and 24 Gypsies.[32] Undoubtedly many more Gypsies were killed than was documented.

The extreme cruelty with which these killings were carried out is brought out by an incident involving Einsatzgruppe B. Operating in the area of Smolensk, the unit reported in April 1942 that between March 6 and March 30 it had shot forty-five Gypsies.[33] In 1965, Albert Rapp, the head of Sonderkommando 7a, which had done these killings, was tried for war crimes before a German court. Rapp, testimony revealed, had carried out his murderous task with zeal. He had branded Jews and Gypsies as "depraved and asocial people, dirty and infested with disease, who had to be exterminated." A shooting of Gypsies in March 1942 involved mostly women and children. Despite the cold weather, the victims had to take off their outer garments before being shot. Mothers had to carry their babies to the ditch prepared as a mass grave. There the executioners snatched them from the arms of the mothers, held them at arm's length, shot them in the neck and then tossed them into the ditch. According to witnesses, the shooting was carried out with such haste that many of the victims fell or were thrown into the ditch when they were still alive. "The tangled pile of bodies in the ditch kept on moving and rose and fell." Rapp was found guilty of murder and was given ten life sentences.[34]

The killing of Gypsy women and children was standard practice. A report on the work of the army's Secret Field Police in late July 1942 justified this mode of operation on the grounds that "if only those who are suspected or convicted of helping the partisans were to be punished, the remainder would become still more hostile toward the German forces and would put themselves even more at the disposal of the partisans. Hence it is necessary that such bands be exterminated *mercilessly*."[35] At his trial after the war, Otto Ohlendorf, head of Einsatzgruppe D, put forth a similar justification for killing the children. Our orders, Ohlendorf testified, "did not only try to achieve security, but also permanent security, because the children would grow up and surely, being the children of parents who had been killed, they would constitute a danger no smaller than that of the parents."[36] On December 16, 1942, OKW head Keitel relayed a Führer order according to which the struggle against partisan "bands" was to be conducted "with the most brutal methods," not sparing women and children if destroying them promised success.[37] Some Soviet Gypsies did support or fight with the partisans, but this fact hardly justified the wholesale killing of women and children.

The Situation under Civilian Administration

As the German armies continued to advance into Soviet territory, a civilian administration took over control from the military. It was headed by Alfred

Rosenberg, the newly appointed minister for the occupied eastern territories (*Reichsminister für die besetzten Ostgebiete*). His domain was divided into two parts—the *Reichskommissariat Ostland* (Reich territory East), comprising the Baltic states Lithuania, Latvia and Estonia, and the *Reichskommissariat Ukraine*, each having at its head a *Reichskommissar* (Reich commissioner). Each Reichskommissariat was divided into districts (*Generalbezirke*) led by a *Generalkommissar* (district commissioner). The SS and police apparatus formally operated alongside but in fact was not subordinated to this civilian administration. Hitler's decree of July 17, 1941, which made Rosenberg responsible for the eastern territories, had at the same time reserved all security issues to Himmler, who was authorized to give direct orders to the Reichskommissars.[38] The decree provided that the senior SS and police leaders attached to each Reichskommissar were to be subordinate to him, but they also took orders from Himmler. The heads of Einsatzgruppe A and C were at the same time in charge of the Security Police and SD in their area of operation. They took orders from the senior SS and police leaders as well as from the RSHA in Berlin.[39] Needless to say, this complicated table of organization was bound to create problems of jurisdiction, though the supremacy of Himmler and his Security Police was carefully preserved.

The lot of the Gypsies did not change for the better when they formally came under civilian rule. Most of the information that has been preserved concerns Latvia, which with 3,839 Gypsies in 1935 had the largest number of Gypsies in the Baltic states. Many of them led a settled life, owning or renting land or engaging in occupations such as horse transport.[40] The Einsatzgruppen had been instructed to enlist the help of local sympathizers, and in Latvia a special unit commanded by Viktor Arajs, known as the Latvian Auxiliary Security Police, is said to have killed many Gypsies during the months of July through September 1941.[41] The German authorities forbade Gypsies to reside along the coastline, and this order may have been the reason for the first large-scale killing of Latvian Gypsies by the Germans. On December 5, the Latvian police of the coastal town of Libau seized the 103 Gypsies living in the town—24 men, 31 women and 48 children—and handed 100 of them over to the German Order Police, commanded by SS and Police Leader Fritz Dietrich. The Latvian police had a German liaison officer and generally followed German orders. In this case they undoubtedly knew the purpose of the arrests. The memo recording the transfer speaks of giving the Gypsies to the German police unit "for follow-up [*zur weiteren Veranlassung*]," a phrase regularly used as a synonym for killing. On December 5, as Dietrich reported on December 13 to his superior, "the Gypsies of Libau, a total of 100 persons, were evacuated and executed in the vicinity of Frauenburg."[42]

On December 4, 1941, the Reichskommissar for the Baltic states, Hinrich Lohse, a party member since 1924, issued a decree that defined Gypsy policy:

Gypsies who wander about in the countryside represent a twofold danger:

   1. as carriers of contagious diseases, especially typhus

2. as unreliable elements who neither obey the regulations issued by
   German authorities nor are willing to do useful work

There exists well-founded suspicion that they provide intelligence to the
enemy and thus damage the German cause. I therefore order that they are
to be treated like the Jews.[43]

Lohse's order was written on the letterhead of his Department of Health
and People's Welfare, but we know from subsequent correspondence that
the decree was issued at the instigation of Bruno Jedicke, the commander of
the Order Police in the Baltic states. Jedicke was a subordinate of Friedrich
Jeckeln, the senior SS and police leader for the Ostland. It has been suggested that Lohse's order was predated in order to provide an after-the-fact
justification for the killing of the Libau Gypsies.[44] On January 12, 1942,
Jedicke distributed Lohse's order and instructed "in each case to cause the
necessary follow-up."[45]

Lohse had spoken of "Gypsies who wander about in the countryside [*im
Lande umherirrende Zigeuner*]," but he had failed to discuss how sedentary
Gypsies were to be treated. An instruction, probably authored by the head of
the Security Police for Latvia on January 27, addressed this issue. It ordered
the arrest of all Gypsies and the confiscation of their property; exempt from
this order were "sedentary Gypsies who are engaged in regular work and
who do not constitute a danger to the community in political or criminal
respects." The choice of words in this order bears a striking resemblance to
the November 21, 1941, order of the commander of Army Group Rear Area
North, mentioned earlier in this chapter, and it may indicate that both of
these decrees, exempting sedentary Gypsies from execution, resulted from
orders received from Berlin. A clarification of the instruction of January 27,
issued on April 3, reiterated that the arrest order was meant "only for itinerating Gypsies [*vagabundierende Zigeuner*] who are encountered."[46]

A report by the SS and police leader of Libau, dated May 18, records the
execution of 173 "nonsedentary Gypsies from the districts of Libau and
Goldingen" during an unspecified reporting period.[47] The diary by the same
officer mentions the execution of "sixteen itinerating Gypsies" from the district of Hasenputh on May 21, 1942.[48] In many other instances it is impossible to know whether the killed Gypsies were itinerating or sedentary. On
April 24, 1942, Einsatzgruppe A reported the execution of 1,272 persons,
among them seventy-one Gypsies.[49] According to a former prison guard,
Alberts Karlowitsche, in April of that year about fifty Gypsies were taken
from the prison of Wolmar (Walmiera) to a wood and shot. Most of the victims were women and small children.[50] There are reports of other killings in
the towns of Bauska and Tukums.[51]

The fate of the Latvian Gypsies at times depended on the whim of local
authorities. In the Kurland part of Latvia existed two Gypsy settlements. A
large group of Gypsies, who had previously been itinerating, were employed
in a sawmill near Talssen. They lived in a camp they had built before the

onset of the winter of 1941 and were left unmolested.[52] Another group of sedentary Gypsies lived in the town of Frauenburg. In March 1942, eleven of them who made their living by hauling wood appealed for help to the Reichskommissar. They were decent people, the signed petition stated, owned little houses and their children attended the local primary school and the high school. Yet they were now in dire straits, for they had lost their livelihood when their horses were confiscated. The petitioners indicated their willingness to do any kind of work that was available in Frauenburg or its vicinity.[53]

The Political Department of the Reichskommissariat Ostland, which had received the petition, thereupon turned to the senior SS and police leader of the Ostland in order to find out on what principles the treatment of the Gypsies was based. The reply took some time in coming. It stated that the Gypsy question, according to a personal agreement between the Reichskommissar and the senior SS and police leader, was being solved by the police in the exercise of its own jurisdiction. Details could not be put into writing. When officials sought further information directly from the Reichskommissar, they were sent Lohse's order of December 4, 1941. The same response went to the Generalkommissar for Latvia who had posed similar questions. The Reichskommissar, it was said, did not want to change the arrangement agreed upon.[54]

The civilian administration of Latvia and the Ostland were not the only ones left out of the formulation of Gypsy policy. The Ministry for the Occupied Eastern Territories, the superiors of the Reichskommissariat Ostland, also had been kept in the dark. On June 11, 1942, Otto Bräutigam notified the Reichskommissar Ostland that the ministry now planned to take up "the future treatment of the Gypsies in the occupied eastern territories." In order to have a factual basis for policy, he asked for information about the status of the Gypsy question. "In particular, I request your opinion on whether the Gypsies are to be treated like the Jews. Also of interest is information on how the Gypsies there [in the Baltic states] live, whether the Gypsies are sedentary or itinerating, whether and which occupations they hold and whether the number of Zigeunermischlinge is substantial."[55] An identical inquiry went to the Reichskommissariat Ukraine.

In its reply, dispatched on July 2, the Reichskommissariat Ostland did not specifically address the question of whether the Gypsies should be treated like the Jews, although it referred to Lohse's order of December 4, 1941. The letter described the nuisance posed by the remaining Gypsies in the Baltic states, especially in the Kurland section of Latvia. It can be read as a plea that sedentary Gypsies be shot as well.[56]

During the month of July, the Ministry for the Occupied Eastern Territories drafted a decree that accepted this position, affirming that the Gypsies of the territories, unless citizens of another country, "are to be treated like Jews. No distinction is to be made between sedentary and itinerating Gypsies. Zigeunermischlinge, as a rule, are to be assigned the same status as Jews, especially if they live like Gypsies or otherwise are not socially adjusted." The identification of a person as a Gypsy was to be made on the basis of self-acknowledgment, the identification by other members of the clan, or lifestyle and social circumstances. In some cases, inquiries about descent were appropriate; consideration was then given to the appearance of the individual and of other clan members as well.[57] In this and similar memos Nazi bureaucrats used ordinary phrases such as "to be treated like the Jews" to hide the reality of cold-blooded murder—perhaps from themselves as much as from others.

For reasons that remain unclear, work on this draft continued until May 1943. The next draft that is preserved, in a drastic about-face, abandoned the idea of shooting all Gypsies in favor of "concentrating [them] in special camps and settlements where they are to be kept under supervision. The treatment of Gypsies is not to be on the same basis as that of the Jews. No distinction is to be made between sedentary and itinerating Gypsies. Zigeunermischlinge, as a rule, are to be treated like Gypsies, especially if they live like Gypsies or otherwise are not socially adjusted." The implementation of the decree and especially the identification of a person as a Gypsy was to be made by the Generalkommissars. The drafting of the necessary measures was to be in the hands of the commander of the Security Police and the SD.[58]

The reasons behind this radical change in the draft decree are unknown. By May 1943, the majority of the German Gypsies had been sent to the special Gypsy camp in Auschwitz, and it is possible that the Ministry for the Occupied Eastern Territories, by making its proposed policy similar to that of the RSHA, sought in this way to make it more acceptable to Himmler. The rivalry between Rosenberg and Himmler was acute, but Rosenberg knew that in matters of security Himmler would always have the last word.

The ministry had indicated that it planned to implement the decree unless objections had been received by June 14. On June 11, the Latvian Generalkommissar informed the Reichskommissar Ostland that he had no objections to the proposed measure. "To put all Gypsies into work camps can only be welcomed, especially since the Gypsies in Latvia are not only a work-shy but also a criminal and politically tainted element."[59] The Security Police, on the other hand, probably on instructions from Berlin, simply ignored the invitation to comment. The commander of the Security Police in Latvia wrote the Generalkommissar in Riga on June 12 that since the Security Police were to be in charge of implementing the decree there was no need for him to comment on it at this time. "Instructions on the question of the treatment of the Gypsies in the occupied eastern territories will come shortly from the Reichssicherheitshauptamt."[60] The contempt that Himmler's men felt for the Rosenberg ministry could not have been expressed more clearly.

On October 19, the commander of the Security Police and SD for the Ostland informed the Reichskommissar that in response to his inquiry the RKPA had informed him of Himmler's plans for the Gypsies. Sedentary Gypsies and Zigeunermischlinge were to be treated like all other inhabitants of the occupied territories. All itinerating Gypsies and *Mischlinge* (persons of mixed ancestry), however, were to be assigned the same status as the Jews and to be put into concentration camps. These principles, the RKPA had advised, would be embodied in the forthcoming decree of the Ministry for the Occupied Eastern Territories. Upon its promulgation, the RSHA would issue the necessary implementing regulations. Until then, nothing further was to be done.[61]

On November 15, 1943, the long-delayed decree of the Ministry for the Occupied Eastern Territories finally appeared, and it did indeed follow Himmler's decision practically verbatim:

> Gypsies and Zigeuner-Mischlinge who reside or have their usual abode in the occupied eastern territories and are sedentary are to be treated like regular inhabitants. All itinerating Gypsies and Zigeuner-Mischlinge in the occupied eastern territories are to be assigned the same status as the Jews [*sind den Juden gleichzustellen*] and are to be put into concentration camps.

The implementation of the decree, including decisions about who was to be considered a Gypsy, was placed into the hands of the Security Police in consultation with the political department of the Generalkommissar. "The regulations necessary for implementation will be issued by the Reichssicherheitshauptamt."[62]

The decree of the Ministry for the Occupied Eastern Territories, for all the delay accompanying its promulgation, did not really establish anything new. The decree put into formal language the actually existing situation: Itinerating Gypsies were regularly shot when apprehended; sedentary Gypsies had a chance to survive. The decree also established a somewhat more elaborate procedure for determining who was to be considered a Gypsy and treated as one, though the kind of painstaking genealogical research undertaken by the Ritter institute in Germany obviously was not practical. In a meeting between the political department of the Generalkommissar for Latvia and a representative of the Security Police, held on March 29, 1944, it was agreed that the Security Police would inform the political department about each individual case of a Gypsy seized (e.g., his descent, whether itinerating, etc.) and that "the dispatch to a concentration camp or other treatment" would take place only after the political department had had a chance to comment.[63]

Whether or not this provision was really implemented is not known. In any case, the changing fortunes of war soon made all of these regulations academic. The Russian summer offensive, which began on June 10, within several weeks brought the Red Army to the border of East Prussia and bottled up fifty German divisions in the Baltic states. Nazi Germany's colonial empire in the East was rapidly disintegrating, and the long ordeal of the Gypsies of the Soviet Union under German occupation was finally coming to an end.

No firm figures are available about the total number of Gypsies killed by the Einsatzgruppen and other German military units in the East.[64] In addition to those who were shot, an undeterminable number of Gypsies were murdered in a "euthanasia" center in Minsk, where members of "inferior races" were put to death by the administration of lethal doses of morphine.[65] It is estimated that somewhat less than half the Gypsies of Latvia survived the Nazi onslaught.[66] In 1926, the Soviet Union is said to have had a Gypsy population of about 60,000, and half of them are supposed to have perished under the Nazis.[67] However, it is not at all clear on what basis these estimates are made, and it is therefore impossible to know how close they come to the actual number of victims. Gypsies were initially targeted as a blanket category (like Jews and Communist functionaries) and were to be destroyed. But the main reason for including them among potential enemies was their alleged tendency to spy, and in actual practice a distinction, referred to in various regulations, evolved in the treatment accorded to itinerating and sedentary Gypsies; in many cases sedentary and "socially adjusted" Gypsies did survive. The fact that Gypsies were seen as members of an alien, inferior and despised race undoubtedly helped create a willingness on the part of German soldiers to kill Gypsies, but the racial element appears to have been relatively unimportant. "Pure" Gypsies and Zigeunermischlinge were generally treated the same way. It is clear that the killing of the Gypsies of the Soviet Union was not part of any overall plan to exterminate all Gypsies.

The Killing of Hostages in Serbia

On April 6, 1941, German divisions, reinforced by Italian and Hungarian forces, attacked Yugoslavia, and on April 17 Yugoslavia surrendered unconditionally. In Croatia a quisling government was formed even before the formal end of hostilities; Serbia came under military occupation. Many German units were withdrawn from Yugoslavia in preparation for the attack on the Soviet Union, and this weakening of the German presence prompted the Communist-led resistance movement to step up its activities. On July 12, about three weeks after Germany had invaded the Soviet Union, the Serbian resistance issued a call for a general uprising. The German occupation authorities reacted with reprisal executions, and, as the partisan movement grew in strength and aggressiveness, they began a policy of shooting an ever increasing number of hostages, especially Communists, Jews and Gypsies.

Unlike those in the Soviet Union, large-scale killings in Serbia were not based on orders issued by central authorities in Berlin but were primarily the responsibility of local military commanders. The complex German occupation structure was headed by the military commander in Serbia, who was assisted by two staffs. The administrative staff was under State Councillor and SS-Gruppenführer Harald Turner who, among other tasks, supervised the activities of an Einsatzgruppe commanded by SS-Standartenführer Wilhelm Fuchs; the command staff was headed by Lt. Col. Gravenhorst. Also present were a plenipotentiary for the economy and a representative of the Foreign Office. Several of these men, as we shall soon see, were involved in one way or the other in devising the harsh reprisal policies that took the lives of many Gypsies.[68]

Soon after the start of the occupation, on May 31, the military commander announced a regulation that imposed various restrictions on both Gypsies and Jews. Some of these provisions, for example the dismissal of lawyers, doctors, dentists and pharmacists as well as all public office holders, probably did not affect many Gypsies; several other rules did. Gypsies had to wear a yellow armband with the imprint "Gypsy"; members of both sexes between the ages of fourteen and sixty were made subject to compulsory labor; all Gypsies were barred from theaters, cinemas, swimming pools, restaurants and public markets; they were subject to a curfew between 8 P.M. and 6 A.M., and they were not allowed to leave their place of residence without permission of the district military command. Anyone descended from at least three Gypsy grandparents was considered a Gypsy; Zigeunermischlinge (those with one or two Gypsy grandparents or married to a Gypsy) were to be treated like Gypsies.[69]

As a result of an intervention by the Serbian government and "in order to eliminate certain harshnesses," on July 11 this racial definition of Gypsies was changed to one emphasizing social standing. From then on, Gypsies who were Serbian citizens, could prove that they had been sedentary since 1850, and "had a respected occupation and led a regular lifestyle" were exempted from the restrictions imposed by the decree of May 31. Local mayors had to certify that the Gypsies were indeed sedentary.[70] Those who could not obtain this certification were made subject to compulsory labor or were taken to concentration camps. By the middle of September two such camps had been set up in Belgrade and Sabac, where Gypsies and Jews were being collected. Apparently the military had begun to think of shooting large numbers of hostages.[71]

On September 16, amid growing partisan activity, General Franz Böhme was appointed military commander of Serbia. In his first report to Böhme, dated September 21, Turner recommended to step up the tempo in the arrest of Jews and Gypsies.[72] By now draconian reprisal measures were becoming the rule and the pool of hostages to be shot had to be increased. On October 2, a German unit was ambushed near the town of Topola and twenty-one soldiers were killed. Causing particular fury was the fact that those who had surrendered had been executed by machine-gun fire at close range.[73] Two days later, "in retaliation for the brutal killing of twenty-one German soldiers," Böhme ordered the shooting of 2,100 inmates from the concentration camps in Belgrade and Sabac.[74] The great majority of the victims were Jews; two hundred were Gypsies. On October 9, the Security Police reported to Berlin that it was building a new camp for 50,000 inmates.[75]

Böhme's order to shoot 2,100 persons relied on a directive issued on September 16 by General Keitel, the head of the OKW, which implemented Hitler's demand for the "harshest measures" against Communist insurgencies in the occupied territories. The directive authorized the execution of fifty to one hundred Communists as atonement for the death of one German soldier.[76] On October 10, Böhme ordered the distribution of a general reprisal policy to all units. It provided for the arrest of all Communists, actual or suspected, of all Jews, and of a certain number of democratically inclined inhabitants. One hundred hostages were to be shot for each German soldier killed and fifty hostages for each soldier wounded. If possible, the executions were to be carried out by the units that had suffered the casualties.[77]

During the next two weeks, an estimated 9,000 Jews, Gypsies and other civilian hostages were executed.[78] We have a report on a shooting carried out on October 30 by a unit of the 704th Infantry Division, commanded by 1st Lt. Hans-Dietrich Walther. After picking up "the selected Jews and Gypsies from the prison camp Belgrade," they drove the hostages by truck to the place of execution. Most of the time consumed by the operation was spent digging ditches that were to serve as graves; "the actual shooting went forth very quickly (100 men in 40 minutes)."

> The shooting of the Jews is simpler than that of the Gypsies. One has to admit that the Jews go to their death composed—they stand very calmly whereas the Gypsies cry, scream and move constantly while they already stand at the place of the shooting. Several even jump into the ditch and pretend to be dead.

At first, the lieutenant reported, his soldiers appeared to be unaffected by the mass executions. However, on the second day it became clear that one or the other did not have the nerve to engage in such shootings for a prolonged time.[79] Walther himself asked to be relieved from further shootings after presiding over the third execution in a little over a week in which his men killed about six hundred Jews and Gypsies.[80]

There can be no doubt that these mass shootings were illegal under the international law of war. In certain circumstances, the law of war recognizes the need for reprisals or hostage taking. As the military tribunal trying the Hostage Case after the end of World War II acknowledged, even the killing of hostages or reprisal prisoners may be justified as a last resort in procuring peace and tranquility in an occupied territory.[81] However, such executions must be proportionate to the wrong for which they are to retaliate, and, as article 50 of the Hague regulations states unequivocally: "No general penalty . . . shall be inflicted upon the population on account of the acts of individuals for which they cannot be regarded jointly and severally responsible."[82]

In the case of Serbia, no evidence was ever adduced that the Jews and Gypsies shot had anything to do with the armed struggle against the German occupation forces. Although some Jews and Gypsies undoubtedly did serve with the partisans, the mass executions inflicted upon these two groups of people were clearly disproportionate. Jews and Gypsies were singled out on account of deep-seated hostility and therefore subjected to collective punishment in flagrant violation of the laws and customs of war. In the eyes of the German military commanders it was considered axiomatic that Jews were Communists and therefore Germany's enemies; Gypsies were regarded as spies. They therefore had no qualms about imposing draconian reprisal measures on Jews and Gypsies. Lastly, it is highly doubtful that these mass shootings had a deterrent effect upon the population; they probably only increased the willingness of Serbs to join the partisans. Thus even on grounds of utility for the German war effort these mass killings lacked rationality. As Telford Taylor, arguing the prosecution's case in the Hostage Case stated, "The law must be spared the torrent of senseless death which these men let loose in southeastern Europe."[83]

Some of the men who played a leading role in ordering these killings had ambivalent feelings, which did not, however, prevent them from continuing their deadly mission. On October 17, exaggerating his own part, Turner wrote in a letter to a friend:

> In the last eight days I had 2,000 Jews and gypsies shot in accordance with the ratio 1:100 for bestially murdered German soldiers, and a further 2,200, likewise almost all Jews, will be shot in the next eight days. This is not a pretty business. At any rate, it has to be, if only to make clear what it means even to attack a German soldier, and for the rest, the Jewish question solves itself most quickly in this way.[84]

Turner also was aware that the shooting of innocent people could further damage the attitude of the Serbian population toward the German occupation. On October 25 the German command, after two large massacres of Serbian inhabitants seized at random, ordered a new reprisal policy that forbade killing Serbians who had not participated in the insurrection.[85] However, Jews and Gypsies were not seen as innocents. In a memo dated October 26 Turner wrote:

> As a matter of principle it must be said that the Jews and Gypsies in general represent an element of insecurity and thus a danger to public order and safety. It is the Jewish intellect that has brought on this war and that has to be destroyed. Gypsies, on account of their inner and outer disposition, cannot be useful members of the family of nations. It has been established that the Jewish element plays an important part in the leadership of the bands and that Gypsies in particular are responsible for special atrocities and intelligence. That is why it is a matter of principle in each case to put all Jewish men and all male Gypsies at the disposal of the troops as hostages.[86]

The hostage pool expanded on October 29, when 250 more Gypsies were arrested in Belgrade, and yet the supply of available victims was rapidly being depleted. A statistical study of the reprisal program prepared for the German command revealed that as of December 5, 1941, there had been at least 11,164 reprisal shootings. But given the number of German casualties at the hands of the partisans, that still left a shortfall of 20,174 reprisals.[87] With random reprisals excluded and the supply of Jews and Gypsies exhausted, the quotas could no longer be met. Hence on December 22 the reprisal ratio was set at fifty to one and twenty-five to one and for killed and wounded respectively. Yet for the groups targeted hitherto there was to be no change. The order continued the mandate to take as reprisal prisoners "communists captured without weapons, gypsies, Jews, criminals, and so forth."[88]

By the end of October, most male Jews and a large number of male Gypsies had been killed. On November 3, Turner gave orders to prepare the transport of women and children—the families of the dead hostages—to a camp near Belgrade,[89] and by early December concentration camp Sajmiste (the Germans called it Semlin) held several thousand Jews and 292 Gypsy women and children. Living conditions in the camp were atrocious, with inadequate food and heating. In February 1942, a gas van arrived and in March the Germans began to kill the Jewish women and children in the camp. The Gypsies were released a few days before the gassing of the Jewish inmates got under way.[90]

In August 1942, Turner prepared notes for a report to the newly arrived German military commander in which he listed the unique accomplishment of the previous administration: "Serbia only country in which *Jewish question* and *Gypsy question* solved."[91] Before the war, Serbia is said to have had 150,000 Gypsies; estimates of the number killed by the Nazis range between 1,000[92] and 10,000–20,000.[93] Many were taken for forced labor to Germany or to German concentration camps. It is clear that a considerable number of male Gypsies were shot as hostages, but beyond that there remain many uncertainties. How many Gypsies were certified to be sedentary and did they continue to be treated differently than those itinerating? Why were the Gypsy women and children in the Sajmiste camp spared the fate of the Jews? We do not know the answers to these questions.

Christopher Browning has argued convincingly that the shootings of male Jews in Serbia in the fall of 1941 "were carried out within the framework of a reprisal policy developed in response to the partisan uprising and were not part of the European-wide genocide program which in any case was still in the planning stage, [though] the Wehrmacht in fact dealt with Jewish hostages differently than Serbs solely because they were Jews."[94] The same holds true for the Serbian Gypsies. They were singled out to become hostages and to be shot because they were Gypsies and because German military commanders considered Gypsies as given to espionage and support of the enemy. Yet it should be noted again that, however criminal and morally indefensible, these killings were the result of a policy developed in response to very specific local conditions and were not part of a general plan to annihilate all Gypsies.

Part III

A COMMUNITY DESTROYED

(1943–1945)

9

Deportation to Auschwitz

In 1939, and again in 1940, attempts to deport all Gypsies in the Reich to the East had come to naught. Some 2,500 German and 5,000 Austrian Gypsies had been sent to the General Government and the Warthegau in 1940 and 1941 respectively, but most Gypsies continued to live in the places to which they had been assigned at the outbreak of the war. On December 16, 1942, Himmler issued his so-called Auschwitz decree that led to the deportation of more than 13,000 German Gypsies, considered to be inferior *Mischlinge* (persons of mixed ancestry), to a special Gypsy camp in Auschwitz. This mass deportation began in March 1943, and for most of the deported it turned out to be a one-way journey. All the details of the decision-making process that led to this deportation are not known, but the key departments and persons involved in these fateful events can be identified.

Preservation of "Racially Pure" Gypsies

The Combating the Gypsy Plague decree, issued on December 8, 1938, had insisted that in seeking to solve the Gypsy question racially pure Gypsies and Mischlinge had to be treated differently. The distinction between the two kinds of Gypsies had been stressed by Ritter. As I noted in chapter 3, Ritter rejected the view that because the Gypsies originally came from India and because their language was related to Sanskrit they were to be considered "Aryan." For Himmler, on the other hand, who had a lively interest in the Aryan origins of the Germanic people, "pure" Gypsies apparently held a special fascination, and in 1942 he gave orders to undertake new research into their way of life.

In 1935 Himmler had created a research institute, *Ahnenerbe* (Ancestral Heritage), for the purpose of studying the spirit and heritage of the Nordic Indo-Germanic race. The institute aimed at legitimating SS ideological assumptions through scientific study. The executive secretary of the institute became SS-Standartenführer Wolfram Sievers, later to achieve notoriety on account of the involvement of Ahnenerbe in medical experiments on concentration camp inmates. On May 12, 1939, renowned scholar of Indo-Germanic languages Walther Wüst at the University of Munich, newly appointed curator of Ahnenerbe, gave a lecture at a special meeting of the German Academy. In this lecture, "Early German Times and Aryan Intellectual History," Wüst argued that Gypsy fairy tales are told in an idiom that is "Indo-Aryan" and thus manifest "unadulterated Aryan thinking."[1] For Himmler, who had an insatiable curiosity about everything Aryan, these remarks appear to have become one of the sources of his belief that pure Gypsies were descendants of the primordial Indo-Germanic people or at least were closely related to them.

By 1942 Ahnenerbe had 197 employees and had become part of Himmler's personal staff.[2] On April 20, 1942, Himmler noted in a diary after a telephone conversation with Heydrich: "No annihilation of the Gypsies."[3] The context of this cryptic remark is unknown, but it is in keeping with Himmler's general attitude toward the German Gypsies. On September 16, 1942, Himmler gave orders that Ahnenerbe, in cooperation with Kripo head Nebe, "establish a closer and very positive contact with the Gypsies still living in Germany in order to study the Gypsy language and, beyond that, learn about Gypsy customs." Also at this time, the RKPA let it be known that Himmler had "forbidden any further resettlements of Gypsies for the duration of the war."[4] The original text of Himmler's order of September 16 is not preserved; it is mentioned in a letter addressed by Sievers to the Vienna Kripo on January 14, 1943. Carrying out Himmler's mandate, Sievers wrote, Johann Knobloch, an assistant to the dean of the Faculty of Philosophy at the University of Vienna SS-Hauptsturmführer Prof. Dr. Christian, had chosen as his dissertation topic the language of the Gypsies of the Burgenland. Sievers requested that the Kripo facilitate Knobloch's research and, if appropriate, allow him access to the Lackenbach concentration camp to interview Gypsies held there.[5] Knobloch, warned that his subjects might soon be "resettled," worked with dispatch; his dissertation "Romani-Texte aus dem Burgenland" was completed in 1943.[6]

On October 13, 1942, less than a month after Himmler had called for closer contact with the Gypsies, the RKPA informed regional and local Kripo offices of a new policy for "pure" Gypsies. Coming after years of harassment and discrimination that often had inflicted the worst disabilities and penalties upon the "pure" Gypsies, whereas Zigeunermischlinge at times had received somewhat better treatment, the new regulation, signed by Nebe, marked a significant about-face:

The Reichsführer-SS [Himmler] intends that in the future racially pure Gypsies be allowed a certain freedom of movement, so that they can itinerate in a fixed area, live according to their customs and mores, and follow an appropriate traditional occupation. The Reichsführer-SS assumes at the same time that the Gypsies encompassed by this order will conduct themselves irreproachably and not give rise to any complaints.

Zigeunermischlinge, who from the point of view of the Gypsies are good Mischlinge, shall be returned to specific racially pure Sinti Gypsy clans. If they apply for membership in a racially pure clan and the latter has no objections, they shall be assigned the same status as racially pure Gypsies.

The treatment of the remaining Zigeunermischlinge and of the Rom-Gypsies is not affected by this intended new regulation.[7]

The instruction went on to list the names of nine head men or spokesmen (*Zigeunerobmänner* or *Sprecher*) who had been appointed, one each for the various parts of the country. One spokesman was to serve the Lalleri Gypsies, a closely knit tribe originally from the German-speaking part of Bohemia and Moravia that in 1939 had become a German protectorate. The spokesmen were to inform the "racially pure" Gypsies in their area about the intended measures and encourage them to lead an orderly life. They were to report criminal acts by any Gypsy (not only the racially pure) to the nearest Kripo office. They were to make lists of "racially pure" Gypsies and send the names to the RKPA in Berlin. The nine spokesmen were granted freedom of movement in the area assigned to them and were given the right to resume their traditional occupations, but the Gypsies under their care had to stay at their respective places of residence and continue the work to which they had been assigned until further notice. The instruction also included a sample identification card to be issued to the spokesmen that described them as liaison persons between the "pure" Gypsies of their tribe and the police. The card stated that their task was to make sure that the Sinti Gypsies for which they were responsible obeyed their own racial laws and refrained from any sexual intercourse with those of German blood or with Zigeunermischlinge.[8]

Himmler's instruction establishing a special status for "racially pure" Gypsies incorporated some key ideas first proposed by Ritter. The veteran Gypsy researcher had always considered the few relatively "pure" Gypsies (estimated at no more than 10 percent of the total) as the better element. He had favored granting them the right to carry on an itinerating way of life (albeit under careful supervision) that would keep them separate from the German population, and he had suggested selecting spokesmen from their ranks who would provide liaison to the authorities.[9] On the other hand, as Ritter's assistant Eva Justin recalled after 1945, many of these proposals, made in a time of peace, were no longer very practical during a war situation. Most of the Gypsies no longer owned caravans, and at a time when even the farmers had to give up their animals it would have been quite a problem to provide them with horses. Given the rationing of food, how would the itinerating Gypsies be fed? How would they make a living? Research into the Gypsy problem for many years had been the preserve of

Ritter's institute, and Ritter probably was less than happy about the intrusion of Himmler's Ahnenerbe into his privileged domain. Justin reflected this rivalry when she questioned the need for another person (Knobloch) to research Gypsy language and customs. She mused that Himmler had been influenced by amateurs—people other than Ritter and the RKPA, who had what she considered a more realistic approach to the Gypsy problem.[10]

According to Justin, Nebe said that he had no choice but to announce Himmler's fanciful plan, but that nothing much would come of it. He turned out to be right in as much as the Gypsies were never allowed to itinerate. The October 13 instruction did not specify the area in which "pure" Gypsies would exercise their newly granted freedom of movement. Auschwitz commandant Rudolf Höss in his postwar memoirs named the area of Lake Neusiedler on the border between Austria and Hungary as the place assigned to the pure Gypsies,[11] but this recollection cannot be corroborated. The RKPA is supposed to have thought of a reservation in the General Government and even to have proposed allowing the pure Gypsies to join an "Indian legion" recruited from Indian prisoners of war. These schemes too lack supporting detail.[12] On February 10, 1943, the issue of the "settlement of the pure Gypsies" was discussed in a thirty-five-minute meeting between Sievers and Nebe.[13] There is no further reference to this subject in any documentary source.

The nine spokesmen were given their assignments at a meeting held in Berlin. A communication from the RKPA to regional Kripo offices sent out on January 11, 1943, noted that so far only five of the nine spokesmen had submitted the lists of those to be accepted into the ranks of the "racially pure" Gypsies. Lists that were received would be sent out to the regional offices and checked carefully in order to eliminate any Zigeunermischlinge with a criminal record. After making a decision, the Kripo was to summon the spokesmen and explain the reasons for accepting or rejecting a particular individual. In those instances where no lists had been put forth the Kripo was to compile their own list on the basis of available files and make a decision after hearing the opinion of the spokesman in question. No person was to be accepted into the ranks of the "racially pure" Gypsies over the objection of the spokesman.[14]

The January 11 memo informed the Kripo of Frankfurt/Main, Cologne and Düsseldorf that the list submitted by their spokesman, Johann Lehmann, had been found to be "unsuitable." Lehmann had been dismissed and Jakob Reinhardt had been appointed as his successor. Apparently Lehmann had taken money from persons who wanted to be put on his list.[15] There were other such cases of alleged wrongdoing. Gregor Lehmann, spokesman for the Lalleri tribe, was denounced to the Russians by survivors after the war for taking bribes and subsequently disappeared into the Gulag.[16] Konrad Reinhardt, spokesman for the Stuttgart area, was also accused of extorting money. He was interrogated by war crimes investigators, but the disposition of his case is not recorded.[17] On the other hand, the spokesman for Berlin and Breslau, Heinrich Steinbach, was honored after the war for his integrity.[18] The Gypsies may not have fully realized the consequences of not being included on the lists of the "racially pure" Gypsies, but, given their experience in the preceding years, they clearly had reason to be fearful. The absence of any definition of what constituted a "good Mischling" gave the spokesmen tremendous power. Hence it is not surprising that the process of selection at times was beset by corruption; the stakes were very high.

In one known case a German official sought to protect a Gypsy family by suggesting their inclusion in the exempt category. On November 18, 1942, the *Landrat* (chief magistrate) of Wolmirstedt near Magdeburg inquired at the RKPA in Berlin whether it might be possible to attach the Mischling family Oskar B. to a "racially pure" family. The reply must have been negative, for several months later the entire family—husband, wife and their eight children—was deported to Auschwitz. One of the daughters, sixteen-year-old Marie B., died in the Ravensbrück concentration camp in October 1944; the fate of the others is not known.[19]

It is likely that Himmler really believed the pseudoscientific tale of the Aryan origin of the Gypsies and therefore wanted those considered "racially pure" preserved as a potentially valuable addition to the stock of Aryan blood. In Poland Himmler pursued a policy of *Wiedereindeutschung*—the removal of every "valuable trace of German blood" from Poland[20]—and it appears that he aimed at a similar goal in regard to the Gypsies. Initially the pure Gypsies were not to be allowed to mix with Germans, but Ahnenerbe was told to explore their language and customs. In case this research confirmed Aryan roots, the pure Gypsies, presumably, could then be absorbed into the pool of German blood or at least be kept protected as a people closely related to the Aryans. The research of Johann Knobloch (referred to above) was to throw light on this question as was the work of another researcher, Georg Wagner, originally a staff member of Ritter's Institute for Criminal Biology.

In 1942, Wagner had done research on Gypsy twins in several concentration camps, including Mauthausen,[21] and received his Ph.D. in 1943 with a dissertation entitled "Rassenbiologische Beobachtungen an Zigeunern und Zigeunermischlingen."[22] In September 1943, Wagner joined Ahnenerbe to investigate the Indo-Germanic roots of the Gypsies. His base was Königsberg in East Prussia and from there he traveled to Lithuania, Latvia, Estonia and Finland. Wagner was equipped with a pass that identified him as a racial biologist "who, on orders of the Reichsführer-SS, carries out research of a special and urgent nature about which details may not be divulged." All civilian, police, SS and military authorities were asked to render him every possible assistance.[23] On account of Germany's worsening fortunes in the war and the tightening of its manpower pool, Ahnenerbe had come under pressure to cut back its work, but Wagner's assignment was not affected by this new stringency. "Whatever men and departments are now still active in Ahnenerbe," its chief, Sievers, had asserted in May of 1943, "originates in the personal decision of the Reichsführer-SS." All purely scientific work had been limited and only policy-oriented work related to the war effort was still being pursued.[24] Even if these assurances represented hyperbole and were the result of a bureaucrat seeking to protect his turf, Wagner's hiring and retention during these years of cutbacks indicate the importance that Himmler attributed to this research. Wagner continued his work until the collapse of Nazi Germany. Another pass issued to him on January 9, 1945, stated that he carried out an "urgent cultural task" which on account of its importance deserves the "special support of all authorities."[25] Himmler himself by that time undoubtedly had other more important things on his mind. He never got the answer to the question of the Aryan roots of the Gypsies he had sought for so long. Meanwhile, however, a large number of Gypsies had escaped deportation and likely death.

The Auschwitz Decree

In a letter dated December 3, 1942, Martin Bormann, head of the party chancellery and also carrying the title "secretary to the Führer," complained to Himmler about the new arrangements for "racially pure" Gypsies. He had heard about the plan from his own expert on these matters, who had met with Nebe. It was envisaged, he wrote, to let these Gypsies cultivate their "language, rites and customs" and even itinerate freely and join special units of the armed forces. This exceptional treatment was said to be justified because these Gypsies had generally not conducted themselves in an asocial manner and because "their system of belief preserved valuable Germanic customs."

> I consider this view of your expert as overblown. Such a special treatment for the racially pure Gypsies would represent a fundamental departure from presently applied measures for fighting the Gypsy plague and would not be understood by the population and the lower ranks of the party leadership. The Führer too would not approve of it if a segment of the Gypsies is given back their old freedoms.

Bormann ended by saying that these proposals appeared to him to be "improbable" and asking for clarification.[26]

In the bureaucratic chaos that was Nazi Germany, Bormann was a rising star. His complaint to Himmler about the new Gypsy policy was an example of the power he claimed and exercised. After Hess disappeared in May 1941, Bormann increasingly controlled access to the Führer. He was in charge of Hitler's dwindling contacts with the outside world, while he himself was well informed about the mood of the country. His assertion that the lower ranks of the party leadership and the population as a whole would have little sympathy for Himmler's new plan for the Gypsies was probably correct. For many years many individuals inside and outside the party and government had demanded tough measures against the "Gypsy plague." To grant special privileges to even a part of this despised group of social outcasts was not a popular idea.

Himmler met with Hitler on the afternoon of December 6 and with Bormann the same evening.[27] No record of the content of these conversations has been preserved, though we have a handwritten notation by Himmler on Bormann's letter that reads "Führer. Aufstellung wer sind Zigeuner" (Führer. Tabulation who are Gypsies). This was probably to remind Himmler that he needed data on the Gypsies when meeting with Hitler. It appears that Himmler was able to overcome Bormann's objections and any reservations Hitler may have had, for the decree of October 13 was never retracted and "racially pure" Gypsies were exempted from deportation to Auschwitz. A memo prepared in the Ministry of Justice on February 27, 1943, took note of information received from Bormann's party chancellery: "New research has shown that among the Gypsies are racially valuable elements."[28] There is no evidence for the assertion that Himmler issued the Auschwitz decree "in response to Bormann's pressure and probably Hitler's order" or that he was forced to act "to prove his anti-Gypsy commitment."[29] As we know, the plan to deport the Zigeunermischlinge had been in preparation for some time. Its timing may have been influenced by the fact that by March 1943 Ritter had completed the racial assessments for practically all of the Gypsies in Germany and the former Austria.

No copy of what generally is referred to as the Auschwitz decree of December 16 has been found. It would appear that this decree consisted merely of a short order by Himmler for the deportation of the Zigeunermischlinge that never left the premises of the RuSHA in Berlin and that many of the details were worked out on subsequent days. We know of one such meeting, held on January 15, 1943, which dealt with the question of what to do with Gypsies exempted from deportation. In addition to four RKPA officials, this meeting was attended also by Ritter and his assistant Justin and by one representative each of the SD and the SS Main Office of Race and Resettlement. Most of the discussion concerned particulars of the issue of sterilization, a subject I discuss fully in chapter 12.[30]

Full details about the planned deportation were distributed on January 29. In implementation of the order of the Reichsführer-SS of December 16, 1942, an instruction sent out by the RKPA stated, Zigeunermischlinge, Rom-Gypsies and members of Gypsy clans from the Balkans were to be selected for "preventive custody" and dispatched to a concentration camp. "The dispatch takes place to the concentration camp (Gypsy camp) Auschwitz for entire families without regard for the degree of mixed blood." The following categories of persons were exempt from deportation:

1. Racially pure Sinti and Lalleri Gypsies
2. Zigeunermischlinge who were part of the racially pure group in accordance with the decree of October 13, 1942
3. Gypsies who were legally married to persons of German blood
4. Socially adjusted Gypsies who had a regular job and a permanent residence before the count of Gypsies (in 1939; the decision about who belonged to this group was to be made by the local Kripo in consul-

tation with party and welfare officials and taking into account the reports of employers)

5. Gypsies who had been exempted by the RKPA from the regulations for Gypsies
6. Gypsies who were still in military service or had been discharged after being wounded or with decorations (in World War II)
7. Gypsies engaged in work important for the war effort
8. The spouse and minor children of Gypsies enumerated in categories 3–7
9. Gypsies for whom a suspension seemed indicated for special reasons as decided by the local Kripo
10. Gypsies who could prove foreign citizenship[31]

The RKPA, it appears, had little confidence in the ability of the spokesmen to come up with the information that was needed to implement the Auschwitz decree, for the determination of racial status was to be based not on the lists prepared by the spokesmen appointed on October 13 but on the racial assessments prepared by the Ritter institute. In cases in which such assessments were not available, the Kripo was to arrive at a judgment on the basis of what was known of the person's origins, lifestyle and use of the Gypsy language. The exemptions were not to be applied to Gypsies with a criminal record or to those who were caught itinerating. All doubtful cases were to be resolved by the RKPA.[32]

Except for the "racially pure" Gypsies, all those exempted from deportation above the age of twelve were to be urged to consent to sterilization. In a meeting held on January 15 it had been agreed that in cases of refusal the dispatch of such persons to a concentration camp was to be considered. The deportation was to get under way on March 1 and be completed by the end of that month. To prevent flight, the entire plan was to be kept secret; after the operation was completed, secrecy no longer had to be observed. Those sent to Auschwitz were to take along personal clothing and food for the journey; all other property had to be left behind.[33]

It appears that the RKPA, once having received the go-ahead order from Himmler, was able to draft the implementing regulations of January 29 largely according to its own views. The terminology and content of the instruction both reflected the thinking of Nebe and Ritter, who are known to have cooperated closely.[34] The idea of putting the Zigeunermischlinge (who were regarded as the most harmful element among the Gypsies) into camps had been favored by Ritter in particular for some time. He had also been a longtime advocate of compulsory sterilization.[35] As I have noted, Ritter participated in the January 15 meeting devoted to drafting details for the planned sterilization measures. Judged as a whole, the implementing regulations for the Auschwitz decree provided the Kripo with a great deal of flexibility in selecting the Gypsies to be deported or exempted. Its officials were free to apply racial criteria, but there was also the possibility of using the category "socially adjusted [*sozial angepasst lebende Zigeunerische Personen*]." In

Staatliche Kriminalpolizei
Kriminalpolizei(leit)stelle

Essen , am 10.3.1943

Nr. 22/43 (g)

1. Auf Grund des Befehls des Reichsführers-SS vom 16. 12. 1942 wird der nachstehend genannte Zigeunermischling in das Zigeunerlager (KL Auschwitz) überführt:

Zuname: ▇▇▇▇▇ (bei Frauen Geburtsname): ▇▇▇▇

Vorname: Selma Zigeunername: Tauba

Geburtszeit: 23.10.1910 Geburtsort: Bischofswerder

Letzter Aufenthaltsort: Duisburg, ▇▇▇▇

Bei Minderjährigen Personalien

des Vaters:

der Mutter:

2 Mit 2 Anlagen
an die Kommandantur des Konzentrationslagers
Auschwitz
I. A.

Abdruck des rechten Zeige-
fingers des Häftlings:

Order of March 10, 1943 for the deportation of a Zigeunermischling to the Gypsy camp in Auschwitz. COURTESY OF NORDRHEIN-WESTFÄLISCHES HAUPTSTAATARCHIV, DÜSSELDORF, BR 1111/51.

cases in which no racial assessment was available, social criteria such as lifestyle could be used to determine racial status. In each instance, and in contrast to the centralized practice of previous years, local Kripo officials could determine whether a person was to be deported or deserved exemption. A provision of the instruction stated explicitly that "applications to the RKPA for the confirmation of arrests are not necessary."[36]

The Deportations

Preparations for the large-scale deportation began right after the receipt of the decree of January 29. Thus, for example, on February 5 the Karlsruhe Kripo sent out instructions to all local police authorities in the state of Baden to compile the requisite lists and informed them of the criteria to be used in their preparation. The letter was marked "Secret! Urgent!" Replies were due ten days later, on February 15.[37] A report submitted by the policemen accompanying one of the transports from Baden after their return from Auschwitz noted that everything had proceeded "in an orderly fashion" but that the journey of three days and two nights had been difficult, not only in regard to the need for constant watching but because "during the trip we had to live with these people and their bad smell."[38] The guards felt sorry for themselves but not for their victims.

The proportion of persons exempted from deportation varied. In some locations, as in the Magdeburg area, practically all Gypsies were selected for deportation. In April 1941, Kurt L. had been released from jail after serving a five-year prison term for killing another Gypsy in a fight. A police report compiled about a month later noted that L. was legally married and lived in an apartment that was "very clean." Both he and his wife had regular jobs. "She is described as hardworking. Both make a clean impression. . . . The prison term served by L. has had an obvious effect and also mellowed him. There is no reason to expect that L. will again run afoul of the law. . . ." Given this positive assessment, Kurt L. and his wife seemingly could have been exempted from deportation as socially adjusted Gypsies. But they were both deported on March 1. Kurt L. died in Auschwitz on March 13, 1944; he was thirty-seven years old.[39] Meliza L. claimed Turkish citizenship, but since she was unable to provide proof she and her six children were deported; their subsequent fate is not recorded.[40] A memo of the Magdeburg Kripo dated March 11, 1943, noted that the deportation of the Magdeburg Gypsies to Auschwitz had taken place on March 2 and added that "a return to Magdeburg is not likely."[41]

In general, the information we have on the selection process is sporadic. The city of Giessen in Hesse had twenty-five Zigeunermischlinge, of whom fourteen were deported to Auschwitz; the other Mischlinge were exempted.[42] In Munich the majority of the about two hundred Gypsies living in the city were sedentary and relatively well-to-do. Most of them lived in houses or apartments. On March 8 and on the following days, 141 were arrested and on March 13 put on a train to Auschwitz. Among the deportees was a five-month-old baby and a woman of seventy-nine years.[43] In Oldenburg, on the other hand, the Catholic population sought to protect the Gypsies; of eighty-four registered only four were deported.[44]

As in Magdeburg, local authorities often tried to get rid of as many Gypsies as possible. The mayor of the small community of Breitscheid, under the jurisdiction of the *Kripo* of Frankfurt/Main, had tried to have the thirty-eight Gypsies of Breitscheid sent to the Gypsy camp in Frankfurt since at least March 1941. But that camp, he had been told, was full and could not take any more people.[45] In early March 1943, much to the satisfaction of the mayor and the Landrat, twenty-one Gypsies were deported to Auschwitz. The local officials had wanted all of the Breitscheid Gypsies sent away, but the Frankfurt Kripo sent word that three families (a total of fifteen persons) were racially pure and therefore were exempt from deportation.[46] The Landrat was unwilling to accept this decision and asked for reconsideration. The Gypsies of Breitscheid, he wrote the Kripo, were a great burden to the community and could not be adequately supervised. None of them were engaged in work essential to the war effort, and the local employment office had no objection to their expulsion. Now that they were to be deported they all of a sudden wanted to be racially pure. "That the named families are racially pure was not known until now. Their conduct certainly does not support this assumption."[47] Two months later, on

May 10, the three families were moved to the Gypsy camp in Frankfurt. "As a result of this measure," noted the Landrat with satisfaction, "the district is thus free of Gypsies."[48]

Among the few Germans who objected to the deportation of the Jews were employers who, at a time of scarce manpower, did not want to lose workers vital for war production. "The industrialists," writes David Bankier, "wanted to keep their Jewish workers, who were paid the lowest salaries and stripped of labor rights."[49] The same happened in Breitscheid in regard to the Gypsies. The firm of Eduard Pfaff, engaged in construction for the nearby dynamite factory Würgendorf, protested to the Landrat that the sudden loss of five Gypsy workers jeopardized their production schedule and thus the war effort. Despite promises, no substitutes had been made available. Eventually three of the workers, who as "racially pure" Gypsies had been sent to the Gypsy camp in Frankfurt, were provided housing by the employer and resumed their work. The two Mischlinge had been deported to Auschwitz.[50]

In Berlin the large electric company AEG sent one of its executives to the local Kripo in order to plead on behalf of Hugo R., who had been classified as a "Zigeunermischling with predominantly Gypsy blood." In a follow-up letter dispatched on March 13, 1943, the company described R. as an "industrious and punctual" worker who had never been the subject of complaints. "In view of the shortage of younger, healthy German-speaking transport workers we are most anxious that R., who as he has told us is to be evacuated, be kept by us." On April 6, the Kripo ruled that R. should be regarded as "socially adjusted" and be exempted from deportation.[51]

In many instances, the deportation of 1943 was characterized by considerable ruthlessness. The order for the expulsion of May 1940 had provided for the possible exemption of frail persons over the age of seventy and women seven or more months pregnant, yet no such consideration was shown this time. In late 1942, Mathilde K. had been sentenced to a prison term of one year for speaking ill of Hitler. Released on February 5, 1943, because she was pregnant, K. was sent to Auschwitz on March 26. She died there on October 16.[52] In 1939, Gypsy artist Richard F. had rescued a child who had fallen into the Rhine. For this courageous deed he had received a commendation from the mayor of Cologne presented "in the name of the Führer." In June 1940, F. was drafted into the armed forces, but on March 11, 1943, he was deported to Auschwitz. His subsequent fate is not known.[53]

The instruction of January 29 had ordered the police to seize all Gypsy children in institutions or in foster care, and the Kripo implemented this order without hesitation. Some children were sent to Auschwitz as part of the large transports in March 1943; in other cases children were found and deported only after considerable delay. On March 6, 1943, the Catholic bishop of Hildesheim, Joseph Godehard Machens, drew the attention of Cardinal Bertram, the primate of Germany, to the wave of arrests from Catholic homes. During the last few days, Machens wrote, Catholic Gypsy children had been seized in four places in his diocese.

There is fear that their lives are endangered. . . . I ask myself with heavy heart what can be done in order to protect our brethren in the faith and at the same time make clear to our faithful that we distance ourselves from such measures. These acts not only represent disdain for divine and human rights but undermine the moral convictions of our people and taint Germany's name. . . . The poor victims should not have to complain that not everything was done. The German public should not get the impression that we dare not speak loudly the "Non licet tibi [this is not allowed]."[54]

Bertram ignored this plea for a protest on behalf of the Gypsy children, perhaps in part because he knew how little the German people cared about the fate of the Gypsies. Two weeks later, the Catholic Bishops' Conference meeting at Paderborn decided not to comply with a request from the Ministry of Interior to submit lists of admissions to Catholic institutions because it was feared that these lists could be used in a renewal of euthanasia for mental patients.[55] Of course, the mental patients were Germans, and in the matter of the killing of the insane the bishops had public opinion on their side. The Gypsies, on the other hand, were a widely despised group of outcasts, and a protest on their behalf was apparently seen as not worth the risk.

In January 1944, the RKPA sent instructions to all children's homes to ascertain the presence of Gypsy children. The names of those reported were then sent to the local Kripo offices for action. In May 1944, the Nürnberg-Fürth Kripo ordered the arrest of ten children, ranging in age from nine to sixteen, from the Eltmann children's home and had them sent to Auschwitz. The order, written in cold, bureaucratic language, spoke of dispatching "Gypsy persons [*zigeunerische Personen*]."[56] An even larger group of children was seized from the Catholic St. Josephspflege in Mulfingen (Württemberg). Eva Justin, an assistant of Ritter, had spent six weeks at this institution in the spring of 1942 and had received her Ph.D. degree for research conducted on these children.[57] On May 9, 1944, thirty-nine Gypsy children between the ages of nine and nineteen, twenty boys and nineteen girls, were taken from this home and sent to Auschwitz. Only four survived.[58]

The Kripo pursued the deportation of Gypsy children with zeal. Fifteen-year-old Karoline L. had been in the care of a family in Cologne since the age of four weeks. Her foster father was German and her foster mother was a Gypsy, but, as the local Kripo noted in an inquiry to the RKPA in April 1943, "they are legally married and are socially adjusted [*sozial angepasst*]." Karoline had graduated from elementary school with good grades—conduct: very good; diligence: good; attendance: regular. However, Karoline looked "like a typical Gypsy," and after the RKPA had sent word that L. was a Rom Gypsy, the Cologne Kripo decided that she should be deported: "In the interest of solving the Gypsy problem, I consider it appropriate that L. be sent to the Auschwitz camp if her parents are already in this concentration camp." Karoline's original parents, it turned out, had been deported from Leipzig on March 1. Their daughter followed them to Auschwitz on December 13. Her subsequent fate and the reaction of the foster parents are not recorded.[59]

In February 1944, Helene K. was arrested in Cologne and sent to Auschwitz. By June the Kripo had finally learned the address of her two children, ages twelve and thirteen, who were in foster care on a farm near Paderborn, and sought their arrest. The legal guardian thereupon turned to a juvenile court judge for instructions, who in turn queried the Essen Kripo: Was the order for deportation final? Was an appeal possible, or could a further examination of the facts of the case lead to a change in the order? The children, the judge pointed out, had been in foster care for more than four years and had not displayed any criminal or other bad tendencies. The older child had turned into a good worker and the farmer was well satisfied with both of them. On July 25, 1944, the Essen Kripo replied in a tone of annoyance that the two Zigeunermischlinge were being sent to Auschwitz on the basis of an order by the Reichsführer-SS and "that the order is final and a police measure against which there is no appeal. I now request emphatically to implement the order."[60] The outcome of this case is not known. The children probably escaped being sent to Auschwitz, for the Gypsy camp was closed down a few days after the dispatch of this letter. We do not know whether the Kripo managed to find another place of incarceration for them.

Even infants were not spared. Gertrud H. was not yet one year old when the Cologne Kripo decided on her deportation in December 1943. A Gypsy woman who had been accepted into the ranks of the "racially pure" Sinti was chosen to take the infant to Auschwitz and was given a special travel permit for the trip. The infant's background and her subsequent fate in Auschwitz are not recorded.[61]

As in the case of the deportation to the General Government in 1940, the property of the deported Gypsies was ordered confiscated. Even before the deportation got under way, a decree issued on January 26, 1943, by the minister of the interior stated that the Gypsies in question had been "hostile to the [German] people and state" and that their property therefore was forfeited. The RKPA distributed this finding to the Kripo and instructed them to ask the local Stapo offices (the executive arm of the Gestapo) for appropriate action.[62] The Stapo, in turn, notified the finance authorities of the names of the deported Gypsies. In Berlin the Stapo reported the "evacuation" of 252 Gypsies and the confiscation of RM 12,951.39. This list was also published in the official gazette.[63]

The actual liquidation of the property left behind took considerable time. In Berlin, the finance offices used forms prepared for the confiscation of the property of deported Jews and substituted the word "Gypsy" for "Jew." In some cases, by force of habit, they even added the name "Sara" to the names of several Gypsy women. (According to a decree of August 17, 1938, the first names Sara and Israel had to be added to the names of Jews whose names were not considered sufficiently Jewish.) Among the forms that has been preserved is one that refers to the same person as both Jew and Gypsy.[64] The officials either were in a great hurry or they viewed Jews and Gypsies as one interchangeable category.

During the following months, several Berlin landlords pressed for the payment of rent owed by deported Gypsies and the removal of furniture from sealed apartments so that they could rent them to other parties. The gas utility demanded payment for a damaged gas meter. One woman inquired from the police about a dress she had lent to a Gypsy colleague at work "who has suddenly not returned. I am afraid that I cannot do without it since I have very little to wear."[65] All were eager to receive what was owed them. The abrupt disappearance of many of the Gypsies was noticed, but there are no reports of any expressions of concern about their fate. "Socially adjusted Gypsies" assimilated into the German population may have been exempted from deportation in part in order to prevent any adverse reaction.[66]

The Impact of the Auschwitz Decree on the Gypsies of the Reich

Ever since the late 1930s an ever more vociferous chorus of voices had demanded a solution of the "Gypsy problem" by putting the Gypsies into camps and by sterilizing those able to propagate. In March 1943, after several false starts, a significant attempt to realize this program finally got under way when more than 13,000 German and Austrian Gypsies were deported to a special Gypsy camp in Auschwitz. Many of those exempt from deportation were made subject to compulsory sterilization. Unlike 1940, the Gypsies by now were sufficiently marginalized that no lawyer is known to have challenged the deportation order. How many German Gypsies were affected by the Auschwitz decree and its follow-up provisions?

In November 1942 the RKPA had given the number of "racially pure" Gypsies as 1,097; it was estimated that some 3,000 "good Mischlinge" would be added, thus bringing the total number of those falling under the protective provisions of the October 13 decree to more than 4,000.[67] This surely was not a handful, as has often been asserted. Himmler, it has been said, wanted to keep alive just a few pure Gypsies as a kind of live museum or as "rare animals," an insignificant and meaningless exception to his plan to destroy the Gypsy people.[68] But if Himmler indeed sought to save only a handful, why did he authorize the elaborate scheme of taking "good Zigeunermischlinge" into the ranks of the "racially pure" Gypsies? According to two highly placed RKPA officials in early November 1942 (discussed in a different context in chapter 6), Himmler had given orders to the RSHA "to regulate the treatment of the Gypsies in Germany in a new manner." According to this plan, about 20,000 Gypsies would be expelled and "about 5,000–8,000" would be left in the Reich for whom no special administrative measures would be necessary.[69] These figures jibe with other estimates.[70]

Deducting the number of Gypsies deported to Auschwitz from the number of Gypsies living in the Reich at the time of the Auschwitz decree gives an indication of how many Gypsies were actually exempted. In November 1942, the RKPA reported that there were 28,627 Gypsies in the Reich (Germany and Austria).[71] According to the official registry (*Hauptbücher*) of the Auschwitz Gypsy camp (which was buried by prisoners who were office clerks and salvaged after the war), 13,080 Gypsies from Germany and Austria arrived in Auschwitz in several transports.[72] This would mean that about 15,000 Gypsies remained in the Reich after the mass deportation of March 1943, but this figure is not totally reliable. In many instances, the nationality of the inmates listed in the registry was based on nothing but the name. When the Auschwitz registries were dug up in 1949, the books were very wet and some pages were severely damaged and illegible.[73] The number deported to Auschwitz may therefore have been higher and the number left behind correspondingly smaller. Still, whether we accept the estimate of about 6,500 Gypsies exempted according to the plans of the RKPA or the figure of 15,000 based on the number of arrivals in Auschwitz, there can be little doubt that the number of Gypsies left in Germany was substantial; it was not a handful.

Most of the literature on the subject maintains that the exemptions provided in the Auschwitz decree were essentially ignored and that practically all the Gypsies of Germany and Austria were deported to Auschwitz in March 1943.[74] That has also been the quasi-official view propounded by contemporary spokesmen of the German government. In an address on December 16, 1994, to a special session of the upper house of the German parliament commemorating the anniversary of the Auschwitz decree, Bundesrat President Johannes Rau declared that on the basis of this decree "the SS carried off all the Sinti and Roma they could get hold of."[75] In the light of available evidence, this view is unsustainable. It should go without saying that whether the deportation of 1943 encompassed practically all or *only* about half of the Gypsy population has no bearing whatsoever on the criminality and utter depravity of the Nazis' actions that led to the uprooting and death of thousands of Gypsies.

Deportations from the Protectorate of Bohemia and Moravia

After Germany annexed Austria and the Sudetenland in 1938, many Gypsies took refuge in Czechoslovakia, and by 1939 it had a population of about 6,500 Gypsies. Following the occupation of Czechoslovakia in March 1939, Hitler proclaimed the Protectorate of Bohemia and Moravia. Slovakia was made "independent" under a quisling government; Ruthenia, the easternmost part of Czechoslovakia, was handed over to Hungary. In the Protectorate the German overlords gradually introduced the same measures of control and persecution of the Gypsy population that had been instituted in Germany and Austria, culminating in deportation to Auschwitz.

A decree of the government of the Protectorate issued on April 28, 1939, set up compulsory labor camps for those shirking work and not having a regular source of income. These camps were for "asocials" and did not target Gypsies specifically. From 70 to 80 percent of the Gypsies in the Protectorate were sedentary; the first anti-Gypsy measures were directed against those leading a nomadic life. On May 9, 1939, Gypsies were forbidden to travel in hordes; a decree of November 30, 1939, forbade any itinerating at all and ordered all Gypsies to settle within two months. Those caught without a firm abode were arrested and sent to labor camps set up in accordance with the decree of April 28. Two camps in particular, established in August 1940, began to hold significant numbers of Gypsies as well as Gypsy-like itinerants. They were Lety near Pisek in Bohemia and Hodonin near Kunstat in Moravia.[76]

In their mode of operation, the Lety and Hodonin camps resembled the Lackenbach Gypsy camp in Austria. The men were put to work without pay in quarries, road construction, farm labor and similar jobs. Discipline was harsh and any violation of the camp rules was punished severely. In Lety and Hodonin, however, the guards were not Germans but Czech policemen.[77] Conditions in the camps worsened after the government of the Protectorate issued a decree on "preventive crime fighting" on March 9, 1942. Until the two camps were closed down in 1943, between 2,600 and 2,800 inmates spent various amounts of time in these camps—beggars and other "asocials," Gypsies and Zigeunermischlinge as well as Gypsy-like itinerants (known as "white Gypsies"). They were allowed only two letters, which were subject to censorship, a month. It was forbidden to play cards or speak the Romani language. There was not enough food, the barracks became overcrowded, and contagious diseases such as typhus spread. There were 327 deaths in Lety and 197 in Hodonin.[78]

"Asocial elements" convicted of a crime were sent to Auschwitz. Records kept by the police of Brno (Brünn) indicate that between April 29, 1942, and February 24, 1944, there were fourteen transports taking such persons to Auschwitz, among them 177 Gypsies. After the establishment of the special Gypsy family camp in Auschwitz, these Gypsies were transferred from the general camp to the Gypsy camp.[79]

A census of the Gypsy population in the Protectorate held on August 2, 1942, showed that there were 5,830 Gypsies and Zigeunermischlinge in the Protectorate. About 4,000 of these were sedentary. Like Gypsies in the Reich, they had to sign a declaration that they would not leave their place of residence and that they would face arrest if they abandoned their jobs or if their children did not attend school regularly. At a meeting convened to discuss the Jewish question on October 10, 1941, Heydrich had talked of sending the Czech Gypsies to Franz Stahlecker in Riga, the commander of Einsatzgruppe A,[80] but nothing came of this suggestion. After the issuance of Himmler's Auschwitz decree of December 16, 1942, the sedentary Gypsies too became subject to deportation.

According to the register of the Auschwitz Gypsy camp, beginning on March 7, 1943, six large and several smaller transports left the Protectorate for Auschwitz. The first phase, which ended on March 19, included 2,679 men, women and children. By early May, as the police in Brno reported, almost all Gypsies who had been living freely had been deported. The transport that arrived in Auschwitz on May 7 included 417 inmates of the Lety camp; 767 Gypsies from the Hodonin camp were in a transport that reached Auschwitz on August 22. By October 19, 1943, a total of 4,386 Gypsies from the Protectorate had been deported. Following these large deportations, the two Czech Gypsy camps were no longer needed. Lety was closed on May 21, 1943, Hodonin on December 1, 1943.[81]

The last phase of the deportations was concluded in early 1944 and involved Gypsies who had been in hospitals or prisons or had been captured after escaping. This involved a total of 175 persons. Altogether, the names of 4,493 Czech Gypsies are listed in the register of the Auschwitz Gypsy camp. Among the children born in the camp, 342 bore Czech names. The Gypsies from the Protectorate thus constituted the largest national group after those from the Reich proper.[82]

10

Life and Death in the Gypsy Family Camp
of Auschwitz

On February 26, 1943, the first large transport of Gypsies arrived in Auschwitz. It contained about two hundred Gypsies from the Buchenwald concentration camp who were put into Birkenau II e, a new and as yet uncompleted section of the Birkenau part of Auschwitz (B II e). A second transport reached the camp on March 1, and from this date on the pace of arrivals quickened. By the end of 1943, a total of 18,738 Gypsies had been registered by name, the largest part having been delivered by the end of May. Eventually about 23,000 men, women and children were to be incarcerated for varying lengths of time in the Gypsy family camp.[1]

The Camp Ordeal

Unlike the Jews and other victims of the Auschwitz death camp, the arriving Gypsies were not subjected to selection—they were not chosen for either slave labor or the gas chambers. Instead they were put into the newly built Gypsy family camp, so called because entire families were allowed to stay together. The only other family camp in Auschwitz was established in September 1943 for about 18,000 Jews from Theresienstadt. At that time the Nazis were apparently concerned about a visit to Auschwitz by the Red Cross, and the new arrivals therefore were forced to write letters stating that they were being well treated. Most of these Jews were eventually killed in the gas chambers, and the Jewish family camp was liquidated in July 1944.[2] In the case of the Gypsies, no such consideration was involved. As Yehuda Bauer has commented, "That the Germans kept the Gypsies alive in family groups for almost a year and a half without separating men from women indicates that

View of the Auschwitz-Birkenau camp with the Gypsy camp in the right background. COUR-TESY OF DR. LUDWIG EIBER.

no decision as to their fate had been made when they were sent to the camp. If there had been a plan to murder them, it would not have taken the SS that long to do so."[3] I shall return to this issue at the end of the chapter.

The Gypsy family camp was located close to the ramp on which the selection for the gas chambers took place. The smoke from the crematoria, less than four hundred feet away, was ever present. When the first Gypsies arrived in Auschwitz, the camp was not yet ready. The administrative barracks were still under construction, and the barbed wire fence had not yet been erected around the camp. The prisoners were housed in wooden barracks that were originally meant to serve as stalls for horses; the barracks had no windows, only ventilation slits in the roof. Thirty-two such barracks were used to sleep about five hundred persons each on three tiers of bunks. Each family was assigned to one bunk bed; by draping the bed with cloth they sought to create a minimum of privacy. Gradually the barracks became over-crowded and at times held as many as 1,000 prisoners. Initially the barracks had only an earthen floor; some barracks gradually were able to get bricks or cement to create a more solid foundation. Each barrack had a stove but lacked fuel, and during the winter months the cold easily penetrated the wooden walls. Several barracks were set aside for washing, but the water supply was unreliable and the water was often contaminated. The latrines were thirty-six-foot-long concrete benches with holes. Hygienic conditions

Inside of a Gypsy barrack in Auschwitz. COURTESY OF DR. LUDWIG EIBER.

in the camp quickly deteriorated and led to the outbreak of disease.[4] Rudolf Höss, the longtime commandant of the Auschwitz death factory, wrote after the war, "Conditions in Birkenau were utterly unsuitable for a family camp. Every prerequisite was lacking, even if it was intended that the Gypsies be kept there only for the duration of the war."[5]

Upon arriving, the Gypsies were tattooed with a number carrying the prefix Z (*Zigeuner*). They were shorn and subjected to disinfection but were allowed to regrow their hair. They also kept their own clothing, to which a black triangle signifying "asocial" status was attached. The Gypsies were not given regular work, though in the camp's early days groups of men, women and children above the age of ten labored at constructing a road in the camp and moving stones and other building materials for this purpose. Some men also built a railroad spur. Tadeusz Szymanski, a Polish doctor who served in the Gypsy camp, recalls that "there was no compulsory labor for the Gypsies, as was the case with other Auschwitz prisoners. If they did some work, it was only cleaning up their own camp, collecting herbs for the camp soup, and they also performed certain administrative functions."[6] As in other camps, inmates served in various posts in the system of self-administration organized by the SS. Most of these functionaries, especially those with a criminal background, fulfilled this assignment with cruelty and viciousness; a few tried to help as well as they could.[7] There are reports of SS guards who protected Gypsy inmates against the cruelty of the Kapos.[8]

The camp food was utterly inadequate in both quantity and quality. The prisoners were supposed to receive 1,600 calories, barely enough to sustain nonworking persons.[9] However, this amount of nourishment was never provided and the inmates almost always suffered from hunger. Some of the food, as in other camps, was apparently stolen by the SS. For a time, inmates were allowed to receive food parcels, but this practice was eventually stopped. German doctor Ernst B., whom Robert Lifton describes as "a human being in SS uniform," claims that "sufficient rations . . . were delivered to the camp for all of them to survive" but that certain highly placed Gypsies kept a lot of the food for themselves, thus denying it to all others, including hungry children. Dr. B. described scenes of fathers and mothers eating while their children starved. As a result of these experiences, Dr. B. told Lifton, he had "developed the worst possible opinion of Gypsies."[10] There is no corroboration for these reports, though at least one former inmate of another Auschwitz camp also reports the phenomenon of starved and desperate fathers stealing food from their sons.[11] Given the extreme deprivation experienced by inmates of all of the camps, such disregard of traditional moral norms is, of course, hardly surprising.

In early April 1943, shortly after the establishment of the family camp, Höss requested a special ration for pregnant women, babies and small children from Oswald Pohl, the head of the SS Economic-Administrative Main Office (*SS-Wirtschafts-Verwaltungshauptamt*), which administered the Nazi camp system. Pohl thereupon inquired from Rudolf Brandt, Himmler's personal secretary, what he should do. The administration of the Auschwitz camp, he wrote, had asked for this special ration on the grounds that "the Reichsführer-SS desires it because he has in mind something special for the Gypsies [*weil er etwas Besonderes mit den Zigeunern vorhabe*]." Pohl outlined various types of rations that could be provided and asked Brandt to let him know of Himmler's wishes. On April 15, Brandt informed Pohl of Himmler's decision. Pregnant Gypsy women were to receive a ration equivalent to that provided for women from the East engaged in forced labor; children were to be given a ration midway between that for these women laborers and the amount of food provided to German children.[12] According to Höss, these special rations soon stopped, "for the Food Ministry laid down that no special children's food might be issued to the concentration camps."[13]

As a result of inadequate nourishment and poor sanitary conditions, diseases spread rapidly. Robert Lifton's source, Dr. B., described the Gypsy family camp as "extraordinarily filthy and unhygienic even for Auschwitz, a place of starving babies, children and adults."[14] At first, two regular barracks served as a hospital, but by July there were five hospital barracks and eventually a sixth was added. Each of these barracks held from four hundred to six hundred patients under the most primitive conditions. There were no bedpans or urinals, and the unconscious or very sick who could not make their way to the toilet lay in their excrement. At times, there were as many as 2,000 patients in the hospital barracks attended by about thirty physicians and over sixty auxiliary personnel. However, as Dr. Tadeusz Szymanski recalls, "there was neither the proper equipment, nor food or medicine in sufficient quantities nor the proper assortment. Finally even when there was the proper choice of medicines not much could be done for the state of health of the Gypsy community, since any prophylactic campaign in camp was out of the question."[15]

The highest mortality was caused by typhus. The spread of this disease was facilitated by the atrocious hygienic conditions and the poor nourishment in the camp. By May 1943, an epidemic of typhus had broken out. The Gypsy family camp was put under quarantine with no additional inmates being admitted for several months. Once a month the inmates of the camp were deloused in the so-called sauna, but this did not stop typhus outbreaks. About 30–40 percent of the Gypsies who contracted typhus died. Other diseases that caused a high mortality were diarrhea and scabies leading to secondary infections. All of these people, Dr. Szymanski writes, "could regain their health, provided they received the proper food and good, individual care and that was, of course, out of the question."[16] Lucie Adelsberger, a Jewish doctor employed in the Gypsy camp hospital, described the frustration caused by having to take care of hundreds of patients without an adequate supply of medications. Many of them had become walking skeletons; the bodies of others were swollen due to food deprivation. Often all that doctors could do for their suffering patients was console them. "This did not improve their lot; they died like flies."[17]

In addition to hunger and disease, the inmates suffered from deliberate cruelty at the hands of Kapos and SS guards. Some of these mistreatments were described by survivors at the Auschwitz trial held in Frankfurt from December 1963 to August 1965. Additional details emerged during the proceedings against SS-Rottenführer Ernst-August König, a block leader in the Gypsy camp. On September 18, 1991, eight months after he had been sentenced to life imprisonment, König committed suicide in his jail cell. Camp inmates, the testimony of numerous witnesses revealed, were subjected to a variety of degrading and often deadly brutalities. There was the practice of making prisoners do "sport," which consisted of exercises accompanied by beatings that often resulted in death. Drunken guards would reach for Gypsy women, including those who were married, and strike and kick those who refused to sleep with them. Small infractions of the rules could lead to severe punishment.[18]

And yet, bad as all this was, prisoners from the other parts of the Auschwitz camp, who came in contact with the Gypsies, often envied life in the Gypsy family camp. The Gypsies, writes Olga Lengyel in her memoir of Auschwitz, "enjoyed various liberties that were forbidden to the other internees."[19] Many of the Gypsies had brought along their musical instruments and were allowed to form small bands to which the SS guards listened with pleasure. Polish Auschwitz survivor Wieslaw Kielar noted in his book *Anus Mundi*:

The children . . . were hungry little waifs, unbelievably dirty and ragged, as were their parents, who would sit for hours outside their huts looking for lice in their tattered clothes. But there were also well-dressed gypsies, especially the young and beautiful girls. There was no need for them to come to the wires begging for a piece of bread or a cigarette. They sat in the block seniors' rooms, in private quarters where the music played, the girls danced, intoxicating liquor flowed and sex was freely available. The matter of racial inferiority tended to become blurred in the course of orgies and drinking bouts, in which the entire high society took part including SS men, led by Rapportführer Plagge, who was almost unrecognizably changed, benign almost amicable. He too had a mistress here; besides which he drank hard and filled his pockets with easily grabbed jewelry. I knew what went on with the gypsies because I was so close a neighbor.[20]

Two inmates, who had their locksmith workshop immediately adjacent to the Gypsy camp, also wrote of "the lovely Gypsy girls [who] turned the heads of several SS men."[21] None of this, of course, was unique to the Gypsy family camp. The desperate condition of the inmates in all Nazi concentration camps led to the occurrence of prostitution and other types of previously unacceptable behavior.

Reports by non-Gypsy survivors of Auschwitz about conditions in the Gypsy camp are not always fully reliable, and there is no denying the life of extreme deprivation from which the great majority of the Gypsies suffered and to which thousands succumbed. However, in the scale of misery that characterized life in the death factory of Auschwitz, the Gypsy family camp did not represent the worst that was possible, and it is therefore not surprising that some fellow inmates came to envy what Kielar called the "free life" of the Gypsies.[22] The very fact that families were able to stay together provided a boost to morale.

Gypsies from Germany and Austria constituted by far the largest group of inmates—nearly 14,000 and thus almost two thirds of the camp population. Gypsies from the Protectorate of Bohemia and Moravia numbered about 4,500. Polish Gypsies, with about 1,300, were the third largest group. The remainder came from various other German-occupied countries in Europe.[23] In general, survivors relate, Czech Gypsies found it easier to adjust to camp life than their German counterparts. The Gypsies from the Protectorate considered themselves Czech patriots and felt that they shared the suffering of the entire Czech people. Many of the German Gypsies, on the other hand, did not understand why they had ended up in Auschwitz. There are numerous reports of Gypsies arriving in military uniform and proudly exhibiting their medals. One was an officer who had earned the Iron Cross, First Class, and who gave the Nazi salute upon arrival.[24] Höss recalled:

Many men were arrested while on leave from the front, despite high decorations and several wounds, simply because their father or mother or grandfather had been a gypsy or a gypsy half-caste. Even a very senior Party member, whose gypsy grandfather had settled in Leipzig, was among them. He himself had a large business in Leipzig, and had been decorated more than once during the First World War. Another was a girl student who had been a leader in the Berlin League of German Girls. There were many more such cases.[25]

Many Gypsies attempted to flee Auschwitz though few succeeded. According to camp records, thirty-two Gypsy prisoners were shot while trying to escape. From early July 1943 on, the barbed wire fence surrounding the Gypsy camp was charged with high voltage, but even this obstacle did not end all efforts to escape. Those who were caught were either shot or put into a penal company in which all work had to be done at the double. There were few survivors among the inmates suffering this punishment.[26]

Medical Experiments

One of the more notorious figures of the Auschwitz death camp was SS-Hauptsturmführer Josef Mengele. According to survivors, when doing duty on the selection ramp, Mengele was particularly zealous in choosing victims for the gas chambers. Mengele also was actively involved in conducting medical experiments on inmates, many of them Gypsies.

Born in 1911, Mengele received a doctorate in anthropology in Munich at the age of twenty-four. In 1938 he got a second doctorate in medicine with a dissertation on the genetics of cleft palates, working under the renowned geneticist Otmar von Verschuer at the Frankfurt Institute for Hereditary Biology and Racial Hygiene. In 1942 Verschuer became head of the Kaiser Wilhelm Institute for Anthropology in Berlin, and Mengele went with him as an assistant and continued work on twin data. Nazi racial hygienists were convinced of the ultimate genetic origins of racial and social differences. Studies of how identical twins behaved in different environments were expected to prove the crucial importance of nature over nurture. In May 1943, Mengele was posted to Auschwitz and became chief physician of the Gypsy family camp.[27]

In addition to his duties in the hospital of the Gypsy camp and on the ramp, Mengele found time to engage in research on identical twins. His subjects were chosen from the entire Auschwitz camp. Mengele's assistant, Polish prisoner and anthropologist Martyna Puzyna, recalls conducting measurements of about 250 pairs of twins, though the total number of twins involved was far higher. Mengele was also interested in the physiology and pathology of dwarfism and children born with other abnormalities. During measurements, which could last hours, subjects had to stand naked in an unheated room. Mengele often took photographs of these children. He also had a Czech-Jewish prisoner, painter Dina Gottlieb (now Babbitt), make drawings of body parts and individual subjects. Among the paintings that have survived are eight portraits of Gypsies.[28]

After the examinations (anthropometric, morphological, X ray and psychiatric) were completed, many of the subjects were killed by injections of

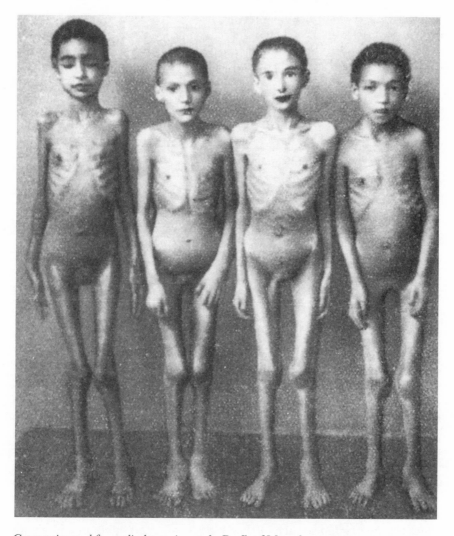

Gypsy twins used for medical experiments by Dr. Josef Mengele. COURTESY OF PANSTWOWE MUZEUM OSWIECIM BRZEZINKA.

phenol into the heart given by Mengele himself or his assistants and their bodies were dissected. The analysis of the body parts during dissections was done by several prisoners who were doctors, among them Miklos Nyiszli, a Hungarian-Jewish pathologist, who survived and wrote about his grisly experiences. Nyiszli's laboratory and dissecting room was located in the compound of crematorium II and was outfitted with the most modern equipment. In the "cause of death column" Nyiszli was instructed to list various diseases.[29]

Mengele sent reports on the findings of these dissections to Verschuer's institute in Berlin. He also dispatched organs of special scientific interest that were preserved in alcohol; these packages were marked "war material—urgent" and received priority in transit. One of Mengele's research projects involved the study of hereditary factors in eye color, especially a condition called heterochromia of the iris, in which a person's eyes are of different colors. Dr. Nyiszli recalls finding heterochromia (one blue eye and one brown eye) in six Gypsy twins he was ordered to dissect on one occasion. In another instance an entire family of eight was killed so that their heterochromatic eyes could be sent to Berlin.[30]

Mengele showed special interest in Gypsy children, and in the summer of 1943 he ordered the establishment of a kindergarten for children below the age of six in barracks 29 and 31 of the Gypsy camp. The walls of these barracks were whitewashed and decorated with colored paintings of scenes from fairy tales. Outside of barrack 31 was a playground with a sandbox, swings and other equipment. Several hundred children stayed in this facility from 8 A.M. until 2 P.M., cared for by several women prisoners. For a short time, the children in this facility received milk, butter, white bread, meat broth and even jam and chocolate. Mengele himself was gentle with these children. He brought them toys and sweets, and the children trusted him and called him "uncle" and "daddy."[31]

The kindergarten became a propaganda showcase and was often visited by top-ranking SS and civilian officials who took photographs and films of the children at play. More importantly, the kindergarten served as a pool of guinea pigs for Mengele's experiments. From this group of children Mengele selected living experimental material for his twin studies and his investigation of heterochromatic eyes. We have no exact count of the number of Gypsy children who passed through Mengele's laboratory. According to one prisoner clerk, initially there were more than sixty pairs of twins in the Gypsy camp. When the camp was liquidated on August 1, 1944, only seven pairs were still alive.[32]

The registries of the Gypsy camp show that the camp held nearly 6,000 children under the age of fourteen, including 363 babies who were born there. In the summer of 1943 the ordinarily rare disease of noma, or water cancer, made its appearance in the Gypsy camp, and children and young people were hit hardest by this affliction. The disease manifests itself in a gangrenous condition of the face and mouth that leaves gaping holes in the cheeks. The primary cause of noma is severe debilitation resulting from malnutrition; many Gypsy children by then were all skin and bone. In the fall of 1943, Mengele decided to study the causes of noma and to find methods of treatment. Patients suffering from noma were placed in barrack 22, and a well-known pediatrician, Bertold Epstein from the University of Prague, was transferred from the Buna section of Auschwitz to take charge of this research. Noma patients were given medications and special food rations, and their condition improved. Then the special ration was withdrawn, and the patients deteriorated rapidly. Even Mengele, who had wanted to look into the genetic or racial sources of noma, eventually came close to conceding that it was the inadequacy of the normal camp diet and the impossible hygienic conditions that caused noma. To the prisoner physicians this, of course, had been clear from the start. Anatomical material from this research too was sent out for analysis. The head of a twelve-year-old Gypsy child was sent to an SS laboratory with instructions, signed by Mengele, to prepare histologic slides. It is not known whether this child was killed or died of noma.[33]

Another subject of research was malaria. The physician in charge of this research was Dr. Heinz Thielo who in the fall of 1943 injected twenty Gypsies from Lublin with blood taken from malaria patients at the time of their highest temperature. Mengele apparently participated in this research as well, for it was mentioned that he had caught both typhus and malaria when in February 1944 he was proposed for a medal in recognition of his work on the "racial origins of the Gypsies."[34]

Mengele's research in Auschwitz was an odd mixture of science and ideologically motivated pseudoscience. He was the typical Nazi scientist who suffered from no moral scruples whatever and took full advantage of the availability of human guinea pigs. Mengele's willingness to kill subjects in order to gain access to their organs is in line with his reputation as one of the most fanatical and ruthless SS doctors doing duty on the selection ramp. At times Mengele is said to have personally killed twins simply to resolve a dispute over diagnosis and then to have dissected the bodies while still warm.[35] Survivors speak of his extraordinary indifference and even fascination with human pain.[36]

And yet Mengele also appears to have had another side, which manifested itself in occasional acts of kindness toward Gypsy inmates in particular. Mengele's displays of affection for the children in the kindergarten he established has been mentioned earlier. Berta R., a German Gypsy who worked as a helper in the Gypsy hospital, testified in a legal proceeding held in 1973 that Mengele had arranged special rations for some patients with diphtheria and thus had saved their lives.[37] Several other former inmates gave similar testimony at the Auschwitz trial.[38] Dr. Iancu Vexler, a French-Jewish doctor in the same hospital, has stated: "It is incontestable that Doctor Mengele made efforts to make the life of the Gypsies more bearable."[39] Mengele is supposed to have had a favorite Gypsy boy, about four years old and always dressed in white, with whom he is said to have paraded around the camp for an entire summer.[40] The fact that Mengele let this little boy too be killed in the gas chambers in August 1944 indicates that the two sides of Mengele's character could coexist with each other. He could be both kind and relentlessly cruel to his victims, though, when subjected to an overall evaluation, his character emerges very clearly as utterly depraved.

Another Nazi doctor engaged in medical experiments on Gypsy inmates in Auschwitz was Carl Clauberg, a gynecologist from Königshütte in Upper Silesia. Himmler had expressed a strong interest in finding a cheap and quick method of sterilization. In this way, he believed, it would be possible to exploit to the fullest the work of slave laborers recruited from inferior races such as Slavs and Jews and at the same time prevent their propagation.

Clauberg came to Auschwitz in December 1942 and in April 1943 began his experiments, which consisted in injecting a corrosive liquid into the uterus of women inmates. This was done without the use of anesthesia. In a letter to Himmler addressed June 7, Clauberg boasted that one doctor with ten assistants could sterilize 1,000 women a day using this method. The experiments were conducted on Jewish and Gypsy women. According to Telford Taylor's opening statement at the Doctors' Trial in 1946: "Several thousand Jews and Gypsies were sterilized at Auschwitz by this method."[41] As late as July 1944, Clauberg was able to get permission to enlarge the facility in which this research was being conducted.[42] Released by the Russians in 1955, Clauberg died two years later while awaiting trial in Kiel.

The Liquidation of the Gypsy Family Camp

The first mass murder of Gypsies in Auschwitz took place on March 23, 1943. On that day, a group of about 1,700 Gypsies—men, women and children—from the Bialystok region, alleged to have among them cases of typhus, were taken to the gas chambers and killed. These Gypsies had arrived just a few days earlier and had been isolated in barracks 20 and 22. Their fate must have been decided upon arrival, for they were not registered and given numbers. Another such killing took place on May 25, when 1,035 Gypsies either sick with typhus or suspected of having it were gassed. Among the killed were camp inmates who had arrived from Bialystok and Austria on May 12. Polish camp physician Tadeusz Szymanski recalls that, following instructions, "the camp office crossed off the gassed Gypsies from the number of prisoners on the camp list, as having died a natural death, due to sickness, spreading out the dates of the death over the following few weeks." While desperate camp doctors tried to stem the spread of typhus as well as they could, the SS proceeded to solve the problem by extermination—a simple and tested method of fighting an epidemic among Jews, Gypsies and other "inferior people."[43]

Among those sent to their death in May 1943 were a group of patients with tuberculosis. One evening in the late fall of that year, Mengele picked out sixty or so Gypsies afflicted with this disease. The sick were told to undress to their shirts, given blankets to cover themselves and loaded on trucks that took them to the gas chambers. From this time on, Dr. Szymanski writes, no Gypsies with chest pains ever again appeared before the physicians in the hospital.[44]

By the spring of 1943, the shortage of labor in Germany had become acute, and in the following months an increasing number of concentration camp inmates were put to work in various enterprises producing weapons and other equipment for the war effort. The Gypsies of Auschwitz too were included in this policy, and between April and July 1944 about 3,500 considered fit to work were transferred from the Gypsy camp in Auschwitz to various concentration camps in Germany. On April 15, 884 men were taken to

Buchenwald and 473 women were transported to Ravensbrück.[45] Hundreds more Gypsies were sent out during the following three months.

On May 16 an attempt was made to liquidate the Gypsy camp, but it ended in failure. The camp at this point still held about 6,000 inmates. At 7 P.M. on that day a curfew was announced and SS troopers, armed with automatic weapons, surrounded the camp. However, it appears that the commander of the camp, ethnic German Georg Bonigut, had told one of his prisoner clerks, Tadeusz Joachimowski, of the planned gassing. Joachimowski, in turn, warned the Gypsies, who decided to resist and armed themselves with knives, spades, crowbars and stones. When ordered to leave the barracks, they refused. There can be no doubt that the heavily armed SS could have overcome this show of defiance, but they decided not to cause a confrontation and to reach their goal by a different route.[46]

There followed more selections of able-bodied Gypsies for work in Germany. In addition to finding much-needed laborers, this action also reduced the number of younger Gypsies able to put up resistance to the planned liquidation of the camp. According to Joachimowski, he was told to compile a list of those German and Austrian Gypsies who had served in the military and had received decorations; the list also included the families of these veterans. It was said that those who agreed to be sterilized would be released. On May 23, more than 1,500 Gypsies were moved to the main camp, Auschwitz I. A day later, on May 24, a transport of 144 women left for Ravensbrück and 82 men were dispatched to Flossenbürg. Their ages ranged from seventeen to twenty-five years.[47]

The inclusion of decorated veterans in this transfer and the requirement of sterilization were similar to the exemptions provided in the original rules for the deportations issued by the RKPA in January 1943. It is therefore possible that the RKPA had a hand in the decisions leading up to the final liquidation of the Gypsy camp. From a letter addressed by Reichsarzt Grawitz to Himmler on June 28 we know that Nebe had suggested to Himmler that healthy Gypsies from Auschwitz, not suitable for work, be used for medical experiments, adding that: "with regard to these Gypsies [presumably he meant here those not used for medical experiments] I shall soon submit to the Reichsführer a special proposal."[48] The content of this proposal is not preserved, but it may have included suggestions for selecting out Gypsies according to the criteria of exemption used at the time of the deportations in March 1943. Gypsies such as the decorated veterans should not have been sent to Auschwitz in the first place.[49]

During the last days of July, more Gypsy veterans and their families and other able-bodied Gypsies were taken to Auschwitz I. Those left behind were told that this group would be sent ahead to construct a new and better Gypsy camp. On July 31, a train loaded with over 1,600 Gypsies stood for several hours on the ramp of Birkenau. A survivor of this transport recalls that the inmates of the Gypsy camp were close enough to the ramp to be able to communicate with those on the train by way of shouts and signs.[50] The sight of the Gypsies on the train lent plausibility to what those not selected had been told about their own expected transfer to another camp. The train with the Gypsies bound for Germany left at 4 P.M. The final hours of the Gypsy family camp had arrived.

On August 2, after the evening roll call, a curfew was imposed on the Gypsy camp. It still held 2,898 inmates, most of them the sick, older men and women and children. Armed SS men surrounded the barracks. The events that followed are described by Dr. Nyiszli, Mengele's Hungarian assistant:

SS guards, leading their police dogs, invaded the Gypsy quarters and chased the inhabitants outside, where they were made to line up. Rations of bread and salami were distributed. The gypsies were made to believe that they were being shipped to another camp, and they swallowed the story. A very easy and efficacious way of calming their fears. No one thought of the crematoriums, for then why would rations of food have been distributed? . . . The strategy worked to perfection. Everything went off as planned. Throughout the night the chimneys of numbers one and two of the crematoriums sent flames roaring skyward, so that the entire camp was lighted with a sinister glow.[51]

Other witnesses report beatings. Some Gypsies protested that they were Germans and had fought for Germany. Several children who had hidden were found the next day and promptly sent to their death. On instructions of Mengele, the bodies of twelve sets of twins were not burned but given to Dr. Nyiszli to be dissected.[52]

There is no conclusive information as to when and by whom the decision to liquidate the Gypsy family camp was made. However, strong circumstantial evidence points to Höss. On May 8, after an absence of several months, he resumed command of Auschwitz with the special mission of preparing facilities for the murder of the Hungarian Jews. The first transport of Hungarian Jews arrived in Auschwitz on May 16, and by May 24 more than 100,000 Jews had been gassed. Yet the capacity of the gas chambers and crematoria soon proved insufficient for this huge influx, and temporary housing had to be found for those who could not be killed immediately. It appears that the Gypsy camp was liquidated in order to make room for these Hungarian Jews. That Hungarian Jews were housed in the former Gypsy camp is confirmed by several witnesses.[53]

In his postwar memoir, Höss tried to deflect attention from his own role in this murderous episode. He wrote that the Gypsies, though "a source of great trouble," were his "best-beloved prisoners." According to Höss, Himmler visited Auschwitz in July 1942, "and I took him all over the gypsy camp. He made a most thorough inspection of everything, noting the overcrowded barrack huts, the unhygienic conditions, the crammed hospital building . . . . He saw it all, in detail, and as it really was—and he ordered me to destroy them. Those capable of work were first to be separated from the others, as with the Jews."[54]

Pery Broad, an SS officer in the Political Department of the camp and a defendant in the Frankfurt Auschwitz trial, has also implicated Himmler in the decision to murder the Gypsies.[55] Yet even if this information is correct, Höss's account of Himmler's involvement is implausible. Himmler's visit to Auschwitz took place in July 1943; in 1942 the Gypsy camp did not yet exist. More importantly, the first attempt to liquidate the Gypsy camp did not take place until May 16, 1944, almost a year after Himmler's visit and the alleged order to destroy the Gypsies. If Himmler was involved at all in the decision to kill the Gypsies, it may have taken the form of oral instructions given to Höss before his departure for Auschwitz in early May 1944. Himmler, according to a member of his personal staff, often issued important orders regarding the camps in this form.[56]

About 23,000 Gypsies, alleged to be asocial *Mischlinge* (persons of mixed ancestry), were put into the family camp in Auschwitz without much aforethought of their ultimate fate. Their stay there was of unlimited duration and, as a rule, no release was possible. In April 1944 the mother-in-law of a Gypsy woman who had died in the camp applied for the release of her daughter-in-law's children. The Essen Kripo replied that "releases of Gypsies from the Gypsy camp do not take place as a matter of principle."[57] Although conditions in the camp were atrocious, causing an extremely high rate of mortality, incarceration was not tantamount to a sentence of death nor was it meant to be such a sentence. The purpose of sending the Gypsies to Auschwitz was to get rid of them, not to kill them. If a program of annihilation had been in effect, why wait over one year to murder them? Why provide special rations, even for a short time, to pregnant women and children? Keeping the Gypsies alive for seventeen months cost precious and scarce wartime resources as well as manpower. Even Kenrick and Puxon, who generally stress the similarity between the treatment of the Jews and Gypsies, acknowledged in the 1972 edition of their book *The Destiny of Europe's Gypsies* that

> [it cannot be said] for certain on the basis of existing knowledge that the Gypsies were sent to Auschwitz to be killed. Those unfit for labor were not gassed on arrival and only a few Gypsies worked during the first months, so there was no general policy of "Annihilation through Work". Also the Gypsies in other camps were not transferred to Auschwitz.[58]

No evidence has come to light since 1972 to force a change in this appraisal. Deportation to Auschwitz was not part of a plan to annihilate all Gypsies; instead, it probably represented the lowest common denominator among various Nazi officials concerned with policy toward the Gypsies. Responding in part to steadily increasing hostility toward the Gypsies among all parts of the population, these officials had gradually adopted more radical views and had come to agree on taking decisive measures in confronting the "Gypsy problem."

Höss has written that the Gypsies were to be kept in Auschwitz until the end of the war and then released,[59] and such a scenario is not inconceivable. We know that some of those involved with making Gypsy policy had contemplated putting the Gypsies into areas of the East not needed for German settlers. In 1942, when the deportation to Auschwitz was decided, a German victory in the East and the consequent availability of vast new territories still seemed a real possibility. The expulsion of about 2,500 German Gypsies into the General Government in 1940 had resulted in disruptions, since most of the deported eventually regained their freedom of movement. These kinds of problems were prevented by putting the deported Gypsies into a camp, as Ritter and others had long proposed. The question of how many could survive the rigors of such a camp was of no interest to anyone, for the individuals involved were considered asocial and racially inferior elements to whose death everyone was supremely indifferent.

The official registries of the Gypsy camp were hidden and preserved. Still, it is impossible to determine the exact number of victims; we do not have a complete count of those who escaped, were released or were transferred to other camps. The registries list 20,943 inmate names, to which must be added the 1,700 Gypsies from Bialystok who were gassed without being registered. This amounts to a total of 22, 643—almost 23,000—Gypsies who were put into the Gypsy camp. Of these more than 5,600 were killed in the gas chambers, and about 3,500 were moved to other camps. That leaves close to 14,000 who died in the Gypsy camp from disease, medical experiments, maltreatment or killing by the guards. Altogether, at least 85 percent of the Gypsies sent to Auschwitz died there owing to their incarceration.[60]

The total number of Gypsies who perished as a result of the deportations to Auschwitz is even higher. We know that many of the 3,500 sent to other concentration camps in 1943 and 1944 did not survive these camps. One transport of eight hundred Gypsies was sent back from Buchenwald and arrived in Auschwitz on October 5, 1944. Most of these Gypsies were young people and children who apparently had been found unsuitable for work. They were gassed on October 10.[61] This raises the total death toll in the Auschwitz Gypsy camp to over 20,000 victims. There is no way to determine with any exactitude how many of these were from Germany and Austria, the focus of this study. Of the about 13,000 Gypsies from the Reich sent to Auschwitz, perhaps as few as 2,000 survived. From among the 4,493 Gypsies registered as deported from the Protectorate of Bohemia and Moravia only 583 are reported to have been alive at the time of liberation.[62]

11

Gypsies in Other Concentration Camps

The first large-scale arrests of Gypsies destined for the concentration camps took place in 1938 during Operation Work-Shy. Other individual Gypsies were sent to the camps during the war years for various offenses grouped under the name "asocial conduct." Camp inmates were used for slave labor as well as for medical experiments. The total number of Gypsies incarcerated in the camps is not known. About 1,500–2,000 were arrested as asocials in 1938–1939, and around 3,500 were transferred to German concentration camps from Auschwitz. This means that at least 5,000 Gypsies were imprisoned for varying amounts of time in concentration camps other than Auschwitz.

Despite the proclaimed intent to "reform" inmates, as well as pressure from above to use them as a labor force, mortality in the camps, the result of systematic mistreatment, malnutrition and disease, was always extremely high. Long-term survival depended on finding a special position such as work in the kitchen, in a repair shop or as a clerk. For those not fortunate enough to find a niche of this sort, the average lifespan between 1934 and 1944 was one or two years, and for some years it was shorter. Records recovered after the war show that during the second half of the year 1942 no less than 60 percent of the total number of inmates—57,503 out of about 95,000—died within six months.[1] An undeterminable number of camp inmates were killed in a "euthanasia" program known as 14 f 13, which targeted those no longer able to work.[2] Overall, Wolfgang Sofsky estimates that "approximately two-thirds of the prisoners in the concentration camps did not survive."[3] In a letter to Himmler written on April 30, 1942, the chief administrator of the camps, Oswald Pohl, claimed that in meeting the needs of the war economy he had transformed "the concentration camps from their previously one-sided political form into an organization responding to economic endeavors."[4] Yet in reality this transformation was never achieved. The system of the concentration camps, writes Hermann Kaienburg, "was based not on the primacy of economics but on the primacy of politics."[5] With a plentiful supply of new prisoners being available, terrorization continued to take precedence over considerations of economic rationality. Inmates of the camps at all times were treated by the SS as enemies of the state, ensuring a maximum of suffering and death.

"Extermination by Work"

On August 20, 1942, Hitler appointed Otto Thierack, an ardent Nazi, as his new minister of justice and authorized him "to take all necessary measures to create a National-Socialist system of justice. In doing so he can depart from existing law."[6] Among the first measures taken by Thierack in fulfillment of this assignment was a more radical attack upon asocial elements. In his view, it made no sense that criminals sat safely in prisons while decent Germans risked and lost their lives fighting at the front. On September 14 Thierack met with Goebbels, who proposed killing all Jews and Gypsies as well as Poles sentenced to prison terms of three to four years and Czechs and Germans sentenced to death or life imprisonment. "The idea of extermination by work [*Vernichtung durch Arbeit*] is the best."[7] Thierack concurred with this proposal and took it to Himmler for his consideration.

In a meeting held on September 18, Thierack and Himmler agreed that certain imprisoned "asocial elements would be handed over to the Reichsführer SS for extermination by work." To be included were all Jews, Gypsies, Russians, Ukrainians and Poles confined to penal institutions and sentenced to prison terms over three years and Czechs and Germans sentenced to terms over eight years. It was also agreed that in the future Jews, Poles, Gypsies, Russians and Ukrainians residing in the incorporated eastern territories who violated the criminal code would not be tried in ordinary courts but dealt with directly by Himmler's police apparatus, that is, sent to the concentration camps.[8]

On September 29 Thierack addressed a meeting of public prosecutors in Berlin on this subject. Some 7,600 prisoners who represented "unworthy life to the highest degree," Thierack declared, would be put to work in places in which they would perish. From this point on, Poles, Jews, Russians, Ukrainians and Gypsies would no longer be a burden on German courts. They would be handled by the police.[9]

In a letter to Bormann dispatched on October 13, Thierack asked the head of the party chancellery to obtain Hitler's approval for this plan, which he explained in the following words:

> With a view to freeing the German people of Poles, Russians, Jews, and
> gypsies, and with a view to making the eastern territories incorporated

into the Reich available for settlements of German nationals, I intend to turn over criminal proceedings against Poles, Russians, Jews, and gypsies to the Reich Leader SS. In so doing I work on the principle that the administration of justice can only make a small contribution to the extermination of members of these peoples [*dass die Justiz nur in kleinem Umfange dazu beitragen kann, Angehörige dieses Volkstums auszurotten*]. Undoubtedly the administration of justice pronounces severe sentences on such persons, but that is not enough to constitute a material contribution toward the realization of the above-mentioned aim. Nor is any useful purpose served by keeping such persons in German prisons and penitentiaries for years, even if they are utilized as labor for war purposes as is done today on a large scale.

I am, on the other hand, of the opinion that considerably better results can be accomplished by surrendering such persons to the police, who can then take the necessary measures unhampered by any legal criminal evidence.

Thierack proposed certain conditions for the inclusion of Poles and Russians in this arrangement. On the other hand, he added, "the police may prosecute Jews and gypsies irrespective of these conditions."[10]

Thierack's assertion that the courts meted out especially severe sentences to Gypsies was correct. We know of several cases in which Gypsies received the death sentence for relatively minor offenses. In November 1942, a court in Stuttgart condemned to death four Gypsies for having stolen food items and a bicycle. Three of them had no prior criminal record and two of them were minors.[11] Eduard H. from Ingolstadt, nineteen years old, was executed in Munich on March 26, 1943, because he had committed several break-ins. In its sentence the court noted that because of the "racial inferiority" of the offender and the consequent danger to the community, an especially severe sentence was indicated.[12] Yet, according to Thierack, not all courts could be relied upon to hand down such draconian sentences. Hence more drastic measures were needed.

On November 5, the RSHA notified the Kripo and the SD of the agreement that had been reached between Himmler and Thierack. The Führer was said to have given his approval.[13] However, as Thierack informed Bormann and Himmler on November 16, the *Gauleiter* (Nazi party officials) of the eastern provinces now expressed strong reservations. Subjecting the Poles to summary extrajudicial treatment, they argued, would cause unrest and would impair their willingness to volunteer for work in Germany. On the other hand, Thierack added, no objections had been voiced to the surrender of Jews and Gypsies, which could proceed forthwith.[14]

Yet Thierack apparently knew nothing of Himmler's special plans for the Gypsies, which were taking shape during the very time when the ever zealous minister of justice talked of exterminating the Gypsies by working them to death. As noted in a previous chapter, on December 6 Himmler had separate meetings with Hitler and Bormann in which he outlined his scheme for preserving the racially pure Gypsies and overcame the objections Bormann had voiced to this new policy. It is very likely that Himmler also told them of the planned deportation of the *Zigeunermischlinge* (Gypsies of mixed ancestry) to Auschwitz, which was announced on December 16. Hence on December 14, Bormann informed Thierack that, although the surrender of the Jewish prison inmates could go forth, certain questions still had to be cleared up with regard to the Gypsies. "I therefore request to postpone action on this matter until you receive from me further information."[15] This information, clarifying the status of the Gypsies, was never issued and the matter of the surrender of the Gypsies remained on hold.[16]

During the winter of 1942–1943, a total of 12,658 inmates were transferred from the prisons to Himmler's concentration camps. By April 1, 1943, almost half of these—5,953 inmates—were no longer alive. As a postwar court proceeding established, many of these prisoners were killed immediately upon arrival in the camps; others were worked to death in accordance with Thierack's plan for "extermination by work." Most of them were sent to Mauthausen, a concentration camp of category III that was subject to a particularly severe regime and from which inmates as a rule were not expected to emerge alive. The fate of prisoners can be followed in 3,337 cases. Of these, it was found, 645 were dead within one month of transfer. Altogether, about 75 percent of those handed over either were killed outright or died during their stay in the camps. A breakdown into different categories of prisoners is available for 3,139 inmates. Of these, thirteen were Gypsies who were transferred even though no official authorization existed for this action.[17]

Details about several such cases are preserved in the Magdeburg police files. Peter M., a thirty-year-old basket weaver, was sentenced on July 3, 1939, to a prison term of five years and one month as "a dangerous career criminal." His criminal record consisted of several thefts as well as one instance each of vagrancy and illegal fishing. M.'s prison term was supposed to run until April 6, 1944, but on June 10, 1943, he was sent to the Neuengamme concentration camp. A printed form in his file noted that this transfer had taken place as a result of "an agreement between the minister of justice and the Reichsführer-SS und Chef der Deutschen Polizei." His subsequent fate is not known.[18] Another Gypsy, Peter M., sentenced to a four-year prison term on May 2, 1939, was transferred to Neuengamme on February 13, 1943. He is recorded to have died there on April 2, 1943, of "circulatory weakness and pneumonia," less than two months after his arrival in the camp. He was not yet thirty-three years old.[19]

The total number of Gypsies caught up in Thierack's purging of the prisons is not known. Information is available on Gypsies who were subjected to "preventive police custody" in concentration camps *after* completing their term of imprisonment. Such incarceration had first been authorized by the Law against Dangerous Career Criminals of November 24, 1933; a decree issued by Interior Minister Frick on December 14, 1937, had extended it to persons labeled "asocial." On July 15, 1940, Gypsy Friedrich L. was sen-

Inmates of the concentration camp Neuengamme at work. COURTESY OF KZ-GEDENKSTÄTTE NEUENGAMME AND RIJSINSTITUUT VOOR OORLOGSDOCUMENTATIE.

tenced to eighteen months imprisonment for several break-ins and thefts. Upon completion of his sentence, the Frankfurt Kripo ordered him sent to Dachau "on account of his criminal and asocial way of life . . . . The stay [in Dachau] is unlimited."[20] Other cases involved petty offenses. Ludwig L. from Giessen in 1940 had quit his job without permission and had been sentenced to a prison term of six months. On April 24, 1941, after he had served his time in prison, L. was ordered into "preventive police custody" and dispatched to Dachau.[21] On January 16, 1940, Alois W. from Nürnberg was caught on a train to Würzburg without permission to leave Nürnberg and without a train ticket. He was given a prison term of six weeks and after his release on May 3 was sent as an "asocial" to Dachau. On August 16 he was transferred to Mauthausen.[22] Whether these three men survived their stay in the camps is not recorded. To judge from the large number of Kripo files that refer to preventive police custody, the practice of sending Gypsies who had completed a prison sentence to a concentration camp for an unlimited stay there must have been widespread.

The end of the war found Gypsies in practically all German concentration camps. Information about their fate there is preserved from some of the larger camps, though we have only estimates of the number of Gypsies held there. In some cases no records are preserved; in others, Gypsies were registered as asocials rather than as Gypsies. In a few instances Gypsies were marked with a brown triangle, but most Gypsies were given the black triangle used for asocials.[23]

Dachau

Between 1933 and 1945, more than 200,000 men were incarcerated in Dachau, the first German concentration camp, which was located just outside Munich. Of these, 31,591 inmates are known to have died.[24] Several thousand more who were never registered were killed by shooting. In June 1939 several hundred Gypsies from the Burgenland were sent to Dachau, and additional individual Gypsies were dispatched there during the war years. In 1945, Munich-Riem, one of Dachau's many external subcamps, is known to have held a group of about two hundred Gypsies. Conditions in these subcamps were often worse than in the main camp. In Munich-Riem food was insufficient, there was no hospital, and inmates who collapsed from weakness on the two-kilometer march to work were shot by the guards.[25]

Gypsies were used in medical experiments conducted in Dachau. In 1942 and 1943, Dr. Sigmund Rascher carried out experiments on reviving half-frozen persons by exposing them to human warmth. This information had been requested by the air force, which was interested in such therapy for pilots shot down over the Atlantic and recovered after spending considerable time in the icy waters. On October 3, 1942, Rascher requested four Gypsy women for these chilling and warming experiments.[26] Dr. Schilling conducted experiments on malaria that also utilized Gypsies.[27]

More detailed information is preserved about experiments with the potability of sea water conducted in Dachau in 1944 for which the air force requested forty healthy inmates. Nebe proposed the use of "asocial Zigeuner-mischlinge" and Himmler approved this suggestion, even though Reichsarzt Grawitz was concerned that the foreign racial characteristics of the Gypsies might invalidate the significance of the experiments for German men.[28] In early August, forty-four Gypsies in Buchenwald, recently transferred from Auschwitz, were selected for these experiments from a larger group of volunteers. The Gypsies had been told that they would be sent to a "better work detail," and it was only upon their arrival in Dachau that they were informed of the real nature of the "work." Once again, they are said to have given their consent to participate in the experiments, but in the view of the repressive conditions of the concentration camp it is doubtful that this consent had much meaning.[29]

The testimony of survivors, fellow inmates and inmate doctors in Dachau gives us a fairly good picture of the course of the experiment. The human guinea pigs were put on air force emergency rations and then divided into several groups. One group was deprived of food and drink, a second was given only seawater, a third, seawater with an additive that eliminated the salty taste of the water, and a fourth, seawater in which the salt content had been neutralized by the addition of silver nitrate. The experiment, which

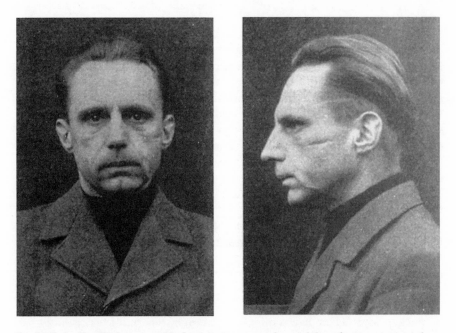

Dr. Wilhelm Beiglböck, responsible for experiments on the potability of sea water carried out on Gypsy inmates of the concentration camp Dachau. COURTESY OF DR. LUDWIG EIBER.

was scheduled to run twelve days, lasted between six and ten days. During this time, the subjects underwent blood probes and liver punctures. According to Ignaz Bauer, a French inmate employed in the infirmary, the victims soon manifested symptoms of starvation and severe thirst. They rapidly lost weight and became increasingly agitated; those who started to scream and rave were tied to the beds. When they were close to death, they were injected with a preparation that was supposed to prevent their demise. Only the fact that fellow inmates were able to smuggle in food and drink is said to have saved the lives of the persons involved in this torturous experiment.[30] Hermann Becker-Freyseng and Wilhelm Beiglböck, the German doctors who ordered and ran the experiment, were sentenced by an allied military court to twenty and fifteen years imprisonment respectively.[31]

After the liberation of the camps, a group of Gypsy survivors of Dachau charged that privileged political inmates of the camp, especially Communists, mistreated the Gypsies in order to gain an advantage for themselves. In their function as block and barrack Kapos, they were said to have handed over Gypsies for medical experiments.[32] No corroboration is available for this particular accusation, though the dominant role of the political inmates, often exercised at the expense of other prisoners, is well attested to by many camp survivors.

Buchenwald

The Buchenwald concentration camp near Weimar, established in 1937, had the third-largest number of inmates. A total of 238,979 prisoners were held there; 56,545 died.[33] From the beginning, Buchenwald had a high percentage of so-called asocial prisoners, though the number of Gypsies is not known with any precision. Buchenwald was one of the camps to which those seized during Operation Work-Shy were sent in 1938. That same year, a camp band was formed that was made up mainly of Gypsies. The band had to play when the exhausted prisoners returned to the camp after work and during the so-called counting-out loud when prisoners were whipped.[34] When Dachau was temporarily vacated in October 1939, several hundred Gypsies were among those transferred to Buchenwald.

The treatment of the asocials, and the Gypsies among them, is said to have been particularly harsh. In the spring of 1938, a Gypsy made an escape attempt. He was caught and subjected to exemplary punishment that is described by Eugen Kogon in his recollections of Buchenwald:

> Commandant Koch had him placed in a wooden box, one side covered by chicken wire. The box was only large enough to permit the prisoner to crouch. Koch then had large nails driven through the boards, piercing the victim's flesh at the slightest movement. The Gypsy was exhibited to the whole camp in this cage. He was kept in the roll call area for two days and three nights without food. His dreadful screams had long lost any semblance of humanity. On the morning of the third day he was finally relieved of his suffering by an injection of poison.[35]

Many other prisoners were killed by injections administered by two SS second lieutenants without medical degrees who functioned as camp doctors. Most of the victims were Gypsies from the Burgenland.[36]

During the following years the number of Gypsies in Buchenwald dwindled rapidly. The winter of 1939, remembered by inmates as the famine winter, was particularly bad. Gypsies are said to have died of typhus and dysentery "like flies."[37] In February 1943, about two hundred Gypsy inmates were transferred to the new family camp in Auschwitz. A year later, only sixty-four Gypsies were left in Buchenwald, at which time thirty of them were selected for a medical experiment with a new antityphus vaccine from Denmark. The memo authorizing this test ordered that "the experiments be limited to Gypsies."[38]

In April and early August 1944, well over one thousand able-bodied Gypsy men were transferred from the Gypsy family camp in Auschwitz to Buchenwald and from there to Dora-Mittelbau, initially a subcamp of Buchenwald and eventually an independent complex through which passed more than 60,000 prisoners. The inmates of Dora-Mittlebau were used to construct an underground factory carved out of a mountain and later were employed in building V-1 and V-2 rockets in this secret facility. The food rations were insufficient for the heavy work performed, accommodations were overcrowded, and medical care was highly inadequate. By the time Dora-Mittlebau was closed down in April 1945, a total of 20,000 inmates had died.[39] The number of Gypsies among these victims is not known. A trainload of eight hundred Gypsy children, brought to Buchenwald from Auschwitz but found unsuitable for work, was returned to Auschwitz in October 1944 to be gassed. Even "hard-boiled prisoners," Kogon recalls, were deeply moved by the "screaming, sobbing children, frantically trying to get to their fathers or protectors among the prisoners."[40]

During the year 1944, a student of forced labor in the concentration camps has written, mortality in the camp system reached an all-time high. "The last year of the war saw a general break-down in supply and communications, which in turn stimulated a higher than usual rate of corruption among SS personnel and prisoner functionaries in the distribution of the minimal food supplies among the prisoners. . . . Untreated illness and infection, coupled with exhaustion, caused thousands of prisoners to perish. Allied bombing of armaments plants, both inside and outside the camps, resulted in further deaths."[41] When American troops reached Buchenwald on April 11, 1945, they found mountains of unburied dead and more than 20,000 starving and sick survivors. Over 56,000 inmates had died during the eight years the camp had been in existence. The number of Gypsies among them is not known.

Ravensbrück

Located about thirty miles north of Berlin, the Ravensbrück concentration camp was used primarily for the incarceration of women. The first Gypsy women to be admitted were 440 women from the Burgenland who were arrested as part of an operation against allegedly work-shy and asocial Gypsies in the Burgenland in June 1939. A fellow inmate recalls that the Gypsy women and their children arriving in the camp on June 29 were left sitting outdoors for two days and two nights until they were registered, given clothing and put in a special block. None of the children are said to have survived.[42] More Gypsy women arrived in the following two years from Poland, Yugoslavia and other German-occupied countries. By January 1941, there were 550 Gypsies in the camp.[43]

Given the poverty and general backwardness of the Burgenland Gypsies, it is not surprising that some of their fellow inmates had a low opinion of them. The clash of lifestyles was just too pronounced. Germaine Tillion, a French ethnologist who was incarcerated in Ravensbrück as a member of the resistance, writes in her memoir of the camp that the Gypsy women, with few exceptions, "were astonishingly barbaric." Two Belgian Gypsies and an old French Gypsy, who had a basic education and came from a higher social stratum, complained to her that "living with the German Gypsies [was] unbearable for them."[44] Isa Vermehren, imprisoned because of family members' involvement in the German resistance, writes that the Gypsies "stole like magpies and taught their children the same skill."[45] It is impossible to know to what extent these reports reflect common anti-Gypsy prejudices or observed reality.

The liquidation of the Gypsy family camp in Auschwitz in the spring and summer of 1944 brought several hundred new Gypsy women and children to Ravensbrück. A survivor recalls that she was put to work in a munitions factory in which she labored twelve to fourteen hours a day.[46] Another woman, twenty-five-year-old Charlotte P., died within three months of arriving at Ravensbrück.[47]

Some of these women and children in early 1945 became the subjects of sterilization experiments by Dr. Clauberg, who had moved his activities from Auschwitz to Ravensbrück. Even girls as young as eight and ten years were victims of these procedures. Dr. Zdonka Nedvedova-Nejedla, a Czech inmate physician who worked in the camp hospital, testified after the war that most of these sterilizations were performed without anesthesia. "I nursed these children all night after the operation. All these girls were bleeding from the genital and were suffering such pain that I had to give them sedative secretly."[48] Dr. P. W. Solobjewa, a Soviet woman physician held captive in the camp, reported that about a hundred Gypsy women were sterilized in February 1945, among them twelve-year-old girls. Two of these died two days after the operation.[49] Twelve-year-old Else F., after undergoing sterilization, was sent to Bergen-Belsen and survived. The physical and psychic damage incurred, she noted in a recollection authored in 1987, is inestimable.[50]

There are also reports of men being sterilized in Ravensbrück. Former soldiers, sent to Ravensbrück from Auschwitz in 1944, were promised release if they agreed to be sterilized. Forty such Gypsy veterans are said to have been sterilized by Dr. Franz Lucas in early 1945. At the Auschwitz trial Lucas admitted to have performed three such operations; the others, he claimed, had been faked. After sterilization, instead of being given their freedom, several of these men were transferred to Sachsenhausen.[51]

Natzweiler-Struthof

The Natzweiler concentration camp, located in the Alsace on the site of a winter sport resort, was established in 1941. It is estimated that between 1941 and 1943 about 6,000 inmates died there as a result of severe mistreatment.[52] Natzweiler was also the site of medical experiments performed on prisoners, including Gypsies. The victims for these experiments were procured by the Institute for Military-Scientific Applied Research (*Institut für Wehrwissenschaftliche Zweckforschung*, or IWZ), established by Himmler's Ahnenerbe in 1942.

On November 12, 1943, a transport of one hundred Gypsies arrived in Natzweiler from Auschwitz. The prisoners were to be used in experiments conducted by Prof. Eugen Haagen with a new vaccine against typhus; however, the "experimental material" turned out to be unsuitable. Eighteen of the Gypsies upon arrival were dead. Others, as Haagen complained bitterly to his superiors, were in such bad shape as to be unusable. He therefore had the Gypsies sent back to Auschwitz and requested a second contingent of one hundred Gypsies who were between twenty and forty years old, and in good physical condition. This second transport reached Natzweiler on December 12.[53]

The experiment began in January 1944. The Gypsies were divided into two groups of forty each. One group was vaccinated, the other was not, and both groups then were injected with the typhus bacillus. Dr. Poulson, a Norwegian inmate doctor who was assigned to watch the development of symptoms among the human guinea pigs, described the conditions as "terrible." Both groups were kept inadequately clothed in small rooms without blankets and under horrible hygienic conditions. Some patients developed high temperatures, but miraculously none died.[54]

Sixteen of these same Gypsies were used in June 1944 in experiments run by Prof. Otto Bickenbach of the Medical Faculty at the University of Strasburg with exposure to phosgene gas. Some of the victims received varying amounts of a protective injection, and others were sent into a gas chamber unprotected. Four Gypsies in the control group died as a result of the experiment. In his testimony before a French military court after the war, Bickenbach claimed that the experiments had been ordered by Himmler and that he had participated in them under duress and in order to prevent worse.[55] When Natzweiler was closed down in early 1945 in the face of the Allied advance, the inmates of the camp were sent to Dachau. Several of the Gypsies who survived the medical experiments have made depositions describing their experiences which were later published.[56]

Mauthausen

The Mauthausen concentration camp was situated among lovely rolling hills some fourteen miles from Linz in Austria, but its beautiful location was deceptive. Mauthausen was considered the harshest of the Nazi concentration camps. "Inmates sent to Mauthausen," writes Gordon J. Horwitz in his study of the camp's relationship to the town of Mauthausen, "were deemed incapable of being rehabilitated and hence not qualified for eventual release. In practical terms, the issuance of an order to Mauthausen represented a life term or death sentence for the inmates. They were sent there never to return."[57] Death rates in Mauthausen bear out this characterization. Of a total of 197,464 prisoners who were admitted to the camp, 102,795 perished.[58]

In September 1939, Mauthausen held 1,087 Gypsies, most of them from the Burgenland. Additional Gypsies were sent there during the following years. In June and July 1941, two transports arrived in Mauthausen from Buchenwald holding a total of 122 Gypsies. Several hundred Gypsy women and their children were sent to Mauthausen from Ravensbrück in early March 1945. Those still alive two weeks later were moved on to Bergen-Belsen.[59]

Inmates carrying heavy stones on the "staircase of death" in the concentration camp Mauthausen. COURTESY OF KZ-GEDENKSTÄTTE NEUENGAMME AND RIJSINSTITUUT VOOR OORLOGSDOCUMENTATIE.

Adolf G., an Austrian Gypsy from Stegersbach in the Burgenland, survived his stay in Mauthausen to tell of his experiences in the notorious camp. G. lost his wife in Ravensbrück and his son in Auschwitz. Arrested in June 1938 and sent to Dachau, G. was transferred to Mauthausen on March 21, 1939. His account of life there is corroborated by others who, against all odds, survived the ordeal. Inmates were given light clothing and wooden slippers and put to work in the stone quarry. This involved carrying heavy stones up 180 steps, known as the "staircase of death" because of the beatings, shootings and fatal accidents to which the crowded mass of inmates was exposed there. The food was totally inadequate for the heavy labor performed, and a stay in Mauthausen was indeed synonymous with "extermination by work." There were other tribulations that could lead to death. SS guards amused themselves by kicking the prisoners' caps from their heads. When the victims sought to retrieve their caps (it was forbidden to be without a cap), the guards opened fire and reported the deaths as "shot while trying to escape." When a prisoner did actually succeed in getting outside the camp, the other inmates had to stand for long hours at roll call without food. Few prisoners were able to make good on attempts to escape. Punishment for violating the camp rules such as failing to make beds with the required precision consisted of beatings or several hours of a cold shower. At first Gypsies were the worst treated inmates. Later Poles and Russians achieved this dubious distinction.[60]

Slightly over 4,000 women were incarcerated in Mauthausen, but only for a relatively short time. An analysis of the cause of death for 271 female inmates, which included Gypsies and asocials (with some overlap between these two categories), showed that 154 (or 57 percent) of these women were killed in the camp's gas chamber; others died as a result of air attacks or being "shot while trying to escape."[61] In March 1945, Mauthausen, its subsidiary camp Gusen, and Mauthausen's forty-nine satellite camps held 84,500 inmates.[62] Many of them did not live to see the day of liberation.

Sachsenhausen

Many Gypsies arrested in northern Germany during Operation Work-Shy in 1938 were sent to the Sachsenhausen concentration camp, located north of Berlin, yet little information about their stay there is preserved. In August 1940, the camp is known to have held 2,069 prisoners labeled "asocial," but the number of Gypsies is unknown.[63] Documentation is available about medical experiments performed on Gypsies in Sachsenhausen in 1942.

On May 15, 1942, Reichsarzt Grawitz requested Himmler's permission for Prof. Werner Fischer to conduct serological studies on Gypsies in order to "gain new insights into the nature of racial differences." The experiments, he proposed, could be carried out in the concentration camp Sachsenhausen, "since a sufficient number of Gypsies (about 50) are available there." The experiments involved taking a small amount of blood and administering a vaccination. "The ability to work would not be impaired."[64] On June 5 Himmler's chief of staff Brandt notified Grawitz that the Reichsführer had given his consent. Himmler had requested to be kept informed about the results of the experiments and had suggested that Fischer study Jewish blood as well.[65] Several weeks later, on June 20, Grawitz reported to Himmler that Fischer had started his studies of differences in the blood of human races. "The first examinations are carried out on forty Gypsies. Thereafter, the experiments will be extended to Jews."[66] Nothing more is known about these experiments and their aftermath.

SS Special Unit Dirlewanger

During the last two years of the war, a novel way to get released from the concentration camps developed when prisoners were conscripted or given the opportunity to volunteer for a special military unit, SS Sonderkommando Dirlewanger. Many of them had seen military service prior to being deported to Auschwitz, where they had been promised their freedom if they agreed to be sterilized. Those who agreed to this procedure were sent to Ravensbrück and after sterilization on to Sachsenhausen. From there some of these Gypsies were taken into the Dirlewanger unit as late as April 1945.[67]

In September 1940, Himmler ordered the establishment of a special military unit to be composed of convicted poachers. Commanded by SS–Sturmführer Oskar Dirlewanger, a Ph.D. in political science who had been deprived of his degree for molesting a minor, the unit became known as SS Sonderkommando Dirlewanger. Initially the unit was composed of about 2,000 poachers; in 1943 it was enlarged to regiment size by the inclusion of concentration camp inmates. The Dirlewanger unit saw action in the East and became notorious for its cruel and destructive mode of operation. In February 1945 it was renamed "36. Waffen-Grenadier-Division der SS."[68]

On February 19, 1944, Himmler ordered Dirlewanger to choose up to eight hundred new recruits for his unit from among "the asocials and professional criminals in the concentration camps." These individuals were to be given an opportunity to redeem themselves by serving at the front. It was better, Himmler maintained, that these people die rather than "good German lads in their boyhood."[69] Some prisoners were conscripted, and others volunteered in order to get out of the concentration camps. Another recruitment drive was launched in November 1944. The largest number of new recruits came from Dachau and Sachsenhausen—966 were political inmates in protective custody and 1,064 were prisoners in preventive police custody. They were put into a special battalion and were ordered to be used in the most dangerous places at the front. The Dirlewanger unit at this time was increasingly referred to as a suicide troop *(Himmelfahrtskommando)*. SS officers kept a strict watch over their men, yet many of the former political inmates succeeded in deserting to the advancing Russian troops.[70] To make up for heavy casualties and desertions, the unit began to include SS men and soldiers convicted of various offenses.[71]

The number of Gypsies who served in the Dirlewanger troop is not known, but we have the testimony of several survivors who were members of the special unit. In 1944 Hermann W., a violin builder and musician from Karlsruhe, was sent from Auschwitz to Sachsenhausen. In March 1945, he, together with 168 other Gypsies, was conscripted into what he called a "death squad" and sent to the front without any military training. He was captured by the Russians and returned home after three years in captivity.[72] Julius H. was a Gypsy from the Burgenland who was put into the Dirlewanger unit in April 1945 near Cottbus, where Hitler's generals made a last desperate attempt to stabilize the collapsing front line at the river Oder. Only 700 of the original 4,000 men in the unit are said to have survived. H. himself was taken prisoner by the Russians.[73] Several other such accounts are preserved. A Gypsy from Munich volunteered for the Dirlewanger unit when he was promised the release of his family, a promise that was not kept.[74]

12

Gypsies Exempted from Deportation

The number of Gypsies exempted from deportation to Auschwitz in March 1943 and left living in the Reich can only be estimated. As I noted in chapter 9, it must have been at least 5,000 and may have been as high as 15,000. The latter figure would mean that more Gypsies were exempted than were deported, and a statistic from Württemberg/Hohenzollern suggests that this could indeed have been the case. In September 1943 the Stuttgart Kripo noted that there were still about seven hundred Gypsies in that state (out of a population of about 1,000 before the 1943 deportation).[1] As provided in the implementing regulations for the Auschwitz decree issued in January 1943, some of those allowed to stay in the Reich were "racially pure" Gypsies and *Mischlinge* accepted into the ranks of the "pure Gypsies"; others were exempted from deportation for reasons such as social adjustment or meritorious military service.

During the last two years of the war, cutbacks in administrative personnel became quite drastic, and the intensified bombing of Germany further hampered regular bureaucratic proceedings. Many records were lost in bombings; others were destroyed by Nazi officials at the end of the war or were burned by survivors of the camps or displaced persons who squatted in Nazi offices and used files to warm their temporary living quarters. As a result of these factors, the documentary record for this period is sparse. Fortunately, the preserved Kripo files and especially the inquiries into the social adjustment of Gypsies provide us with some knowledge of the conditions under which the Gypsy community lived at that time, though most of these records concern the tribulations of *Zigeunermischlinge* (Gypsies of mixed ancestry). We know very little about the lot of the "racially pure" Gypsies. These records also throw an interesting light on the thinking of the bureaucrats who made and implemented Gypsy policy.

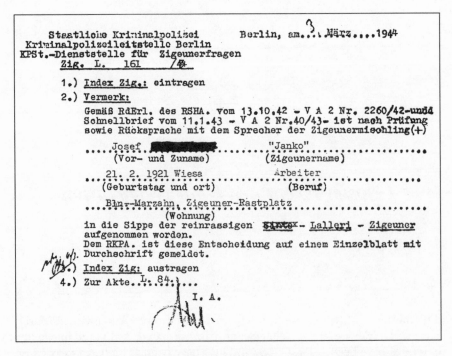

Memo of March 3, 1944 confirming the acceptance of the Zigeunermischling Josef L. into the "racially pure" clan of the Lalleri Gypsies. COURTESY OF BRANDENBURGISCHES LANDES-HAUPTARCHIV, POTSDAM, REP. 30 BERLIN C, TIT. 198, NR. 62.

The Work of the Spokesmen

On October 13, 1942, the RKPA issued new orders regarding the treatment of "racially pure" Gypsies. This decree also empowered nine Gypsy spokesmen to propose "good Mischlinge" for inclusion in the "racially pure" group. The work of these spokesmen did not end with the March 1943 deportation. For many more months, the spokesmen and the Kripo continued to process applications from Zigeunermischlinge who sought to be accepted into the ranks of the protected Gypsies. This status meant not only exemption from deportation but also protection against the threat of sterilization that hung over the Mischlinge.

The regulations for the selection of "good Mischlinge," issued by the RKPA on January 11, 1943, had warned against the acceptance of Gypsies with a criminal record, and this provision for the most part appears to have been observed. Christian S. of Cologne, a "Zigeunermischling with predominantly Gypsy blood," was accepted into the ranks of the pure Sinti on May 5, 1943. His record stated that he had never been in conflict with the law and that he had held regular jobs since the age of fourteen.[2] His brother

Wilhelm, on the other hand, after serving a prison term of one year for having lived off the earnings of a prostitute, was branded a "career criminal" and was sent to Auschwitz on April 30.[3]

There were exceptions. On May 15, 1943, Jakob Reinhardt, the spokesman for Frankfurt/Main, Cologne and Düsseldorf, applied for Zacharias L. to be released from the Orianienburg concentration camp and to be accepted into the "clan of the racially pure Sinti-Gypsies." In March 1934, L. had been sentenced to a prison term of three months and two weeks for the illegal possession of a firearm; in June 1938 he had been sent to a concentration camp as an asocial person. But Reinhardt argued that L. was known to him as "a good Gypsy" and that he was prepared to assume responsibility for him. The Cologne Kripo approved L.'s release.[4]

Once a Gypsy had been accepted into a "racially pure" clan, he was often treated more leniently than other Mischlinge. August W. in Berlin had been picked up by the police for malingering and staying away from work. In a memo signed by him on May 19, 1943, W. promised to mend his ways. "I know that according to the regulations I should have been sent to a Gypsy camp. This has not happened only because I am a racially pure Sinti." Three months later, W. was again in trouble. Riding in the subway, he had failed to yield his seat to a German woman. A policeman who thought him to be a foreigner asked him to do so, but W. refused on the grounds that he was a German. He also failed to show up for work. Once again, W. promised that this kind of behavior would not be repeated. Otherwise, he acknowledged, he would be sent to a concentration camp. W. emerged from these incidents with a mere warning.[5]

Helene W., twenty-two years old and residing in the Berlin Gypsy camp of Marzahn, had been accepted into the Lalleri clan together with other family members. In September 1943 she was sentenced to a prison term of two months for theft. After her release, she promised to become a conscientious worker, but a year later her employer complained that W. was late in the morning or left work early at the end of the day, and sometimes did not show up at all. Summoned to the police, W. admitted that she had no excuse for this behavior and pledged to do better in the future. As a check on her conduct, Gregor Lehmann, the spokesman for the Lalleri, was asked to submit her wage record every two weeks, and that was the end of the affair.[6]

Despite the advantages of being accepted into a "racially pure" clan, not all those eligible agreed to this change of status. Berlin musician Wadosch B. in January 1943 was ordered to stop playing music and accept regular employment. B. had been assessed as a "Zigeunermischling with predominantly Gypsy blood." But when given the opportunity in May 1943, he declined acceptance into the ranks of the "racially pure Gypsies" on the grounds that he had been living in Berlin since 1903, had a regular job and maintained no links to the Gypsies.[7] A similar case is reported from Nuremberg. As Eduard Siebert, the spokesman for the area, explained to the Kripo in July 1943, he had contacted Peter W., who had shown no interest in being accepted into a "racially pure clan." It appears that W. had been exempted from deportation on the grounds that he was "socially adjusted," and he, like B. in Berlin, had no interest in being too closely identified with the Gypsy people.[8]

Not surprisingly, the spokesmen used their position of influence to benefit members of their family, but this endeavor was not always successful. After his appointment as spokesman for the Stuttgart area, Konrad Reinhard requested the release of a nephew, Michael R., from a concentration camp. R. had been imprisoned several times for vagrancy and similar offenses and in 1938 had been sent from Cologne to the Neuengamme concentration camp. In November 1942 he had been transferred to Sachsenhausen. His uncle argued that R. was a decent person who had spent four years in a camp and deserved to be given his freedom. He also suggested that the spokesman for Cologne be asked for his opinion on the case, but the Cologne Kripo did not think much of this suggestion. If R. was to be released from Sachsenhausen, they wrote to the RKPA in May 1943, he should be sent to the Gypsy camp in Auschwitz. Altogether it was not a good idea for the spokesman in one area to plead for persons in the jurisdiction of another spokesman who would find it difficult to reject such a request. Furthermore, releasing R. would encourage Reinhard to seek permission for the return of his brothers and sisters sent to the General Government. The RKPA agreed with this view and suggested that Jakob Reinhardt, the spokesman for Cologne, be instructed to turn down the request of his colleague from Stuttgart. And this is how the affair ended. On May 13, 1943, the spokesman for Cologne stated for the record that Michael R. had no next of kin in Cologne. "For this reason I have no interest in accepting him into the clan of the racially pure Sinti Gypsies in Cologne."[9]

In December 1942, as I noted in chapter 6, the Ministry of the Interior, desirous of halting the propagation of the Gypsies, had issued an order banning marriages between Zigeunermischlinge. Mischlinge accepted into the "racially pure" Gypsy clan, on the other hand, not only were allowed to marry, but those living together according to Gypsy custom (what the officials called a "Gypsy marriage") were encouraged to formalize their ties. Thus, for example, in June 1944, the Berlin Kripo issued permission to marry to two such couples. An entry in their file noted that "in view of their clan membership and [the possibility of] children their marriage is desirable."[10]

Socially Adjusted Gypsies

The regulations implementing the Auschwitz decree had provided that "socially adjusted" Gypsies who had had a regular job and a permanent residence before the Gypsy count in the fall of 1939 be exempt from deportation. Decisions in each case were to be made by the local Kripo after consultation with party and local officials and taking into account reports by employers. Inquiries about the social adjustment of Zigeunermischlinge had been going on ever since the Ritter institute had begun its work on racial categorizations. These kinds of inquiries are also preserved in connection with sterilization proceedings (discussed below) and for applications by individuals who sought exemption from the various restrictive measures imposed upon the Gypsy community, such as the freeze on mobility or the prohibition on marriage. The total number of exemptions granted on grounds of social adjustment is not known. The fact that the RKPA had a printed form confirming release from the punitive Gypsy regulations would indicate that a considerable number of Gypsies benefited from this procedure.[11]

In several instances the initiative for granting such exemptions came from the Ritter institute and took place many months after the deportations of March 1943. Whether Ritter initiated these proceedings in the light of new information that had come into his possession or whether he responded to applications by the individuals involved is not clear. The final decision in these cases was rendered by the RKPA. For example, on February 5, 1944, the Ritter institute informed the Berlin Kripo that it considered exempting Hermann P., assessed as a "Zigeunermischling with predominantly German blood," from the special regulations for Gypsies, including sterilization. For this reason the institute required information about P.'s social status. The Berlin police replied on February 16 that P. had attended school until the age of fourteen, that he had no criminal record and that his employers had similarly reported nothing negative about him. On April 3 the RKPA issued its decision reclassifying P. as a non-Gypsy.[12] In other cases, the RKPA merely exempted individuals from the special Gypsy regulations "on grounds of social adjustment" without declaring these persons to be non-Gypsies.

Some cases involving socially adjusted Gypsies were resolved only after considerable delay. By 1943 manpower of all kinds, including administrators, was getting exceedingly tight, yet these time-consuming inquiries, many of them filling thick files, were allowed to run their course. In August 1943, the Recklinghausen Kripo, after prodding by the RKPA, started an inquiry into the social adjustment of Maria K., born in 1900 and registered as a Gypsy. Information supplied by the Kripo of Duisburg, K.'s current residence, revealed that she was married to an "Aryan" man who served in the military and had been a party member since 1932. Maria K. too belonged to several auxiliary party organizations, and the local party leader confirmed that "K. is fully committed to the National Socialist ideology." Her household was said to be "clean and tastefully run. There is no evidence of a Gypsy way of life." Despite these favorable reports, a decision in this case did not come until many months later. On May 18, 1944, the RKPA notified the Recklinghausen Kripo that K. had been assessed as (ZM-), that is, a "Zigeunermischling with predominantly German blood." However, "on account of her social adjustment" she was to be "treated as a non-Gypsy and no longer subject to the regulations imposed on Gypsies and Zigeunermischlinge."[13]

Other evaluations that have been preserved use similar language. Karl M. of Bonn was reported to be married with five children. He was a member of the German Labor Front (*Deutsche Arbeitsfront*, or DAF) since 1937 and "part of a family that lives in socially adjusted and orderly circumstances."[14] The F. clan in Berlin was said to be composed of "four families, exempted

Reichskriminalpolizeiamt
Reichszentrale zur Bekämpfung
des Zigeunerunwesens

Berlin C 2, am ___2. Januar___ 194**5**
Werderscher Markt 5/6
Tel.: 16 43 11

Tgb Nr. 2314/44=V.[/] / A 2 b 5

–24411–   **Feststellung**

Auf Grund der Unterlagen, die sich in der Reichszentrale zur Bekämpfung des
Zigeunerunwesens befinden, hat nach den bisher durchgeführten rassenkundlichen
Sippenuntersuchungen

████████████ , Ursula

geb.   14. 2. 1931 Berlin-Neukölln

Sohn- Tochter des Kurt ██████, geb. 26.2.1904

und der   Emilie ██████, geb.11.6.1905   "Gulidai"

als   Zigeunermischling (–)

zu gelten, fällt jedoch unter Würdigung ihrer ██ sozialen Anpassung gemäß
Erlaß vom ___2. 1. 1945___ Tgb. Nr. ___2314/1944___ -V-/___ A 2 b 5
nicht mehr unter die für Zigeuner und Zigeunermischlinge geltenden Bestimmungen
und wird künftig als Nichtzigeuner behandelt.

I.A.

Druck: RKPA. 3000 8. 44

Decision of January 2, 1945 confirming the exemption of the Zigeunermischling Ursula R. from the Gypsy regulations on account of her "social adjustment." COURTESY OF BRANDEN-BURGISCHES LANDESHAUPTARCHIV, POTSDAM, REP. 30 BERLIN C, TIT. 198, NR. 133.

from dispatch to the Kl. [concentration camp] Auschwitz because they are Gypsies who have followed a regular occupation for ten years and so far have not given rise to any complaints."[15]

The processing of these kinds of cases continued until practically the end of the war, a period in which the authorities would be expected to have more pressing concerns. A record from Berlin dated December 1, 1944 notes that Christel N., "in recognition of her social adjustment," was no longer subject to the special Gypsy regulations.[16] Ursula R. received the same certification on January 2, 1945. This thirteen-year-old girl had been raised by "Aryan" parents and was said to bear no resemblance to a Gypsy nor to have any contact with Gypsies.[17] Katharina R. and her ten-year-old daughter Christel from Berlin, who were said to be "socially adjusted," were declared "provisionally exempted" on November 21, 1944. Adhering to orderly procedures even in the most difficult circumstances, the Berlin Kripo inserted a notice in the file that the status of the daughter was to be reevaluated on December 10, 1945![18]

Some cases gave rise to conflicting assessments by different officials. The family of the widow Maria P. in Aachen in March 1944 had been certified by the local Kripo to be "sedentary and socially adjusted," but the regional Kripo office in Cologne disagreed. The son Josef P., they noted, who served in the military, had an extensive criminal record that included begging, vagrancy and fraud. In 1941 P. had been sentenced to a prison term of one year for being AWOL. A second child, a daughter, had been taken away from the family. "Under these circumstances," the Cologne Kripo wrote the RKPA on July 10, "I cannot agree to the view that this family is socially adjusted." The final disposition in this case is not recorded.[19]

A similar disagreement arose in Berlin in early 1943. The Ritter institute had recommended that three families of "Zigeunermischlinge with predominantly German blood" be exempted from the regulations for Gypsies. The three Gypsies were said to be married to "persons of German blood" and living a socially adjusted life. However, the Berlin Kripo took a different view. The three families in question, they informed the RKPA on January 9, still maintained contact with the Berlin Gypsies. One of the men, who was in military service, had recently applied for discharge on the grounds that he was a Gypsy and felt like a Gypsy. One of the women now lived with a Gypsy Mischling and her child was being raised as a Gypsy. For these reasons, the Berlin Kripo proposed that the members of this extended family continue to be considered Gypsies.[20] The outcome of this dispute is unknown, though it is unlikely to have been in favor of exemption.

Involuntary Sterilizations

Ever since the late 1930s, an ever widening circle of party officials and ordinary citizens had demanded the sterilization of the Gypsies. Such a measure aimed at halting the propagation of the Zigeunermischlinge had been advocated by Ritter and his associates. It had also been urged by Wilhelm Kranz and Siegfried Koller in their quasi-official study of asocials published in 1941.[21] By 1943 the regime was ready to move ahead with such a program. The implementing regulations for the Auschwitz decree issued in January of that year recommended the sterilization of all Gypsies above the age of twelve exempted from deportation on grounds of social adjustment. Sterilization had also been recommended for those exempted for other reasons such as marriage to a person of "German blood" or meritorious military service. As it turned out, the plan to prevent the procreation of the Zigeunermischlinge was only partially implemented.

There were several reasons for this outcome. First, shortly after the outbreak of the war, in order to save precious medical manpower and hospital facilities, the Ministry of the Interior had given orders to limit sterilizations to the "most urgent" cases in which there was "an especially acute danger of propagation." This policy remained in force throughout the war years; on September 6, 1944, it was tightened further on the grounds that the requirements of the "total war effort" demanded additional restrictions on sterilizations.[22] The question of whether the sterilization of Gypsies represented "urgent" cases was never formally addressed, but of course the restrictions imposed were simply an acknowledgment that wartime conditions did not allow business as usual.

Second, and probably more important, the regulations issued in January 1943 did not order sterilizations but used exhortatory language: "It is desirable to obtain consent to the sterilization of Gypsies above the age of twelve and not yet sterile [*die Einwilligung . . . ist anzustreben*]." Parents were to give consent for the sterilization of minors. In cases of refusal, the RKPA was to decide on what was to be done.[23]

A discussion of whether Jewish Mischlinge exempt from deportation were to be made subject to compulsory or voluntary sterilization had taken place at the Wannsee conference of January 20, 1942, and at two subsequent conferences.[24] Hence the distinction between compulsory and voluntary sterilization undoubtedly was meaningful and was well known to the bureaucracy; to the officials charged with carrying out the implementing regulations of the Auschwitz decree the choice of words indicated that the sterilization of the Gypsies was something to be sought but was not a measure to be carried out at all cost. To be sure, as we shall see, the authorities used both promises and threats to obtain this consent. Yet at least some of those who stood their ground and refused to submit escaped sterilization. They were able to achieve a reevaluation of their case or the doctors and officials involved with the formalities for sterilization did not pursue the matter very aggressively. At the very least, the requirement of consent meant delay, and such delays, occurring during the final two years of the regime, often meant that time simply ran out on the sterilizations. The general disorder resulting from the stepped-up bombing of Germany during the last two years of the war also contributed to the incomplete implementation of the sterilization program.

Instructions sent out by the RKPA stated that the sterilization of the Zigeunermischlinge was to be carried out by the same hospitals and doctors charged with performing sterilizations under the Law for the Prevention of Genetically Diseased Offspring of 1933. Notifications of completed sterilizations were to be sent to the RKPA as well as to public health departments. The costs were to be born by the Ministry of the Interior. Compensation for income lost as a result of the surgery was to be paid only to those "engaged in truly productive labor as, for example, in agriculture or in armaments factories, etc. In view of the human material involved approval [of such payments] will have to be checked especially carefully. . . . The Zigeunermischling is to be encouraged to have the intervention carried out as soon as possible."[25]

Unlike under the sterilization law, orders for sterilization were not issued by the genetic health courts but by the RKPA, which invoked the "permission" of the Reich Committee for the Scientific Processing of Serious Hereditary and Genetic Diseases (*Reichsausschuss zur wissenschaftlichen Erfassung von erb- und anlagebedingten schweren Leiden*). This committee had been established in August 1939 to take charge of the killing of handicapped children. It operated under the direction of the chancellery of the Führer and played an important role in Hitler's "euthanasia" program.[26] The same committee also handled the sterilization of inmates of concentration camps. As the administration of the camps informed the commanders of the camps in

November 1942, "operating under a special grant of authority from the Führer," the committee has the right "to issue permission for sterilizations in special cases that are not covered by law. In these cases a legal decision of the genetic health courts is not required."[27] The same exemption from existing law governed the sterilization of the Zigeunermischlinge that began in the early summer of 1943.

All elements of the bureaucracy cooperated fully. On orders of the RKPA, Kripo offices asked local authorities to obtain consent for the sterilization of Gypsies who were exempt from deportation on grounds other than "racially pure" status. The consent forms were then sent to the RKPA in Berlin, which next produced "permissions" by the Reichsausschuss. With these permissions in hand, the Kripo advised local authorities to proceed with the sterilizations. If the Gypsies in question gave their consent, the entire procedure could be concluded in about three months.[28]

Gypsies who agreed to their sterilization and who were considered "socially adjusted" could be declared exempt from the restrictive Gypsy regulations. We know of several such inquiries aimed at determining the question of social adjustment. On March 27, 1944, the Kripo of Nürnberg-Fürth asked the Nazi Party's regional Office of Racial Policy for its opinion regarding the social status of Jakob R., "a Zigeunermischling with predominantly German blood." After sterilization, the RKPA considered exempting R. from the Gypsy regulations. The Office of Racial Policy, in turn, contacted the local party organization, which gave a favorable assessment. R. "has not given rise to any complaints. He is described as quiet, decent and industrious. Nothing negative is known regarding his political outlook." A personal interview at the Office of Racial Policy to evaluate R.'s appearance followed, and on May 5 the party office rendered its report to the Kripo. A "thorough inquiry" had not produced any indication of asocial conduct. "Still the presence of alien blood (*Zigeunermischling*) in the external appearance of R. is unmistakable. His deportment and appearance, on the other hand, do not leave a bad impression."[29] Whether this ambiguous assessment enabled R. to pass muster is not known.

The same Office of Racial Policy rendered a similarly equivocal evaluation for Johann T., who was described as a good worker but married to a sloppy wife. His external appearance, "judged from a racial point of view," was said to be "not favorable." Even if T. were to be sterilized, the Nazi officials lamented, the sad fact remained that T. had already fathered six children.[30] In this case too the Kripo's final decision is not recorded.

Gypsies who agreed to be sterilized often could obtain permission to get married. Gypsy Anna B. had had four children with August W., a non-Gypsy, but her application to wed the father of her children had been denied several times. After she agreed to be sterilized, the permission to marry was granted. The memo confirming this permission, dated August 28, 1944, noted that since B. had been sterilized, "no progeny that would endanger the purity of the German blood is to be expected." Hence the marriage in question did not violate the provisions of the Law for the Protection of the German Blood and Honor (promulgated in 1935).[31]

The Gypsy violin builder Fridolin K. in the 1930s, subjected to compulsory sterilization on October 3, 1943. COURTESY OF DR. LUDWIG EIBER.

Consent to sterilization did not guarantee permission to marry. Gypsy Maria S. had been living with musician Andreas N., described as of "German blood" but very shortsighted, for some time. In late 1943 she applied for permission to marry him, indicating that she was prepared to be sterilized. On January 17, 1944, the Kripo of Nürnberg-Fürth denied the application. The RKPA, it was noted, had rejected an earlier request by N. and had suggested that the Gypsy woman be sent to Auschwitz "because she has violated the National Socialist principle of the purity of the German blood." For reasons that remain unclear, S. was not deported and in September 1944 she had herself sterilized. The local Kripo surmised that she had taken this step in the hope of being exempted from the Gypsy regulations. In October S. was reported to have spent a night with N. in an out-of-town inn. She was summoned to the police and told that unless she stopped having sexual relations with N. and promised not to leave her place of residence she would be sent to a concentration camp. On November 9, S. acknowledged the warning; the documentary record ends at this point.[32]

When a person refused to be sterilized, the police would often threaten dispatch to a concentration camp, and this threat usually brought about the desired consent. Johann S. had been assessed as a "Zigeunermischling with predominantly German blood" and in September 1942 had been dismissed from the army. He had served in the Wehrmacht since October 1939, had seen action in France as well as in Russia, and had received several medals.

His distinguished military service probably saved him from deportation to Auschwitz, but on May 13, 1943 the Nürnberg-Fürth Kripo ordered that S. be sterilized. A few days later the local Kripo reported to the RKPA that S. had refused to give his consent. Any descendants, he was said to have argued, would have only a minimal amount of Gypsy blood. Moreover, he had done his duty to the fatherland as a soldier and therefore deserved not to be sterilized.[33]

The RKPA rejected this claim and ordered the Nürnberg-Fürth Kripo to step up the pressure. "We suggest to work on S. in an appropriate manner so that he will agree voluntarily to his sterilization. He should be told that if he continues to maintain his refusal the question of dispatch to a concentration camp will be considered, since there are grounds for expecting that he will procreate undesirable mixed-blood descendants." When S. again refused to give his consent, the RKPA gave orders that he be arrested as an asocial and made subject to "preventive police custody." His refusal to be sterilized, the RKPA wrote the local Kripo on September 8, indicated that S. "is not willing to respect the principles of the National Socialist state." On October 10 S. was taken into custody, and on October 31 the RKPA approved the imposition of preventive police custody, to be served in the Auschwitz I concentration camp. One day later, S. finally gave in and agreed to his sterilization. He was released and on May 26, 1944, the RKPA communicated the "permission" of the Reichsausschuss for S.'s sterilization. The sterilization was to be done by September 1 at the latest.[34] The documentary record ends here, and we do not know whether the "voluntary" sterilization of S. was actually carried out.

The same pressure tactics were used in other jurisdictions. Zigeunermischling Ludwig W. of Cologne, thirty-three years old, was married to a German woman with whom he had two children. On June 28, 1943, facing the prospect of being sent to Auschwitz, W. agreed to his sterilization. In a signed memo, W. stated that he had been given an "explanation" and was "now convinced that another generation of Zigeunermischlinge was undesirable for the state of today." He and his wife also agreed to the sterilization of their children—daughter Sonja, age twelve, and son Rigo, age eight. One day later, both children died in an allied bombing attack on Cologne. The parents survived the attack, but their later fate is not recorded.[35] Many survivors report being given the same choice: either sterilization or dispatch to a camp.[36]

Some of those who refused their consent escaped sterilization. Marta Adler, a German woman, recalls that her Gypsy husband, Pitzo, after being discharged from military service, was told to agree to his sterilization or be sent to a concentration camp. He refused and suffered no reprisals.[37] Anton R. had been assessed as a "Zigeunermischling with predominantly Gypsy blood" and ordered sterilized in May 1943. He withheld his consent on the grounds that his father was unknown and that he did not look like a Gypsy. The RKPA eventually agreed that the identity of R.'s father was not fully clear but did not change his racial classification. Still, R. was not sterilized.[38]

There were other such cases. In April 1943, Maria A. of Cologne, a non-Gypsy, refused to agree to the sterilization of her four minor children—Anton, Wilhelm, Josephine and Anna. The father, A. admitted, was Max Z., a "Zigeunermischling with predominantly German blood" and held in Auschwitz. Yet the children, she insisted, "have been raised in socially adjusted circumstances. Their appearance, too, does not indicate a Gypsy origin." She therefore requested an annulment of the sterilization order and exemption from the Gypsy regulations. The Cologne Kripo forwarded the application to the RKPA and endorsed it. A. and her children had no criminal record, the household was orderly, and there was no evidence of asocial behavior. The children looked like the mother and, despite little schooling, promised to become useful members of society. Their employers spoke well of them. In response to this appeal, two of the children were reclassified as "non-Gypsies" and therefore became exempt from the Gypsy regulations. It is likely that the other two children were also spared sterilization.[39]

Some of those ordered to be sterilized appealed their case to the highest levels of the regime. Johannes H. had been conscripted into the army in November 1939 and had been discharged less than a year later on account of a service-induced infection. It appears that his Gypsy origins were not discovered until early 1944, which delayed the order for sterilization. On May 28, 1944, H. protested to Hitler against the treatment he had received. The letter bore the heading "Beloved Führer" and described in great detail how members of his family had served the fatherland for many generations. H. affirmed that he was prepared to lay down his life for the Führer and the new German nation and pleaded that he be treated like a German. Contacted by the RKPA, the Ritter institute affirmed that H. had been rated as "Zigeunermischling with predominantly German blood" and recommended an inquiry into H.'s social status. On October 2 the Duisburg Kripo rendered its report on the affair. H. was said to be a good worker and a person who shared the ideology of the state. He had no contact with Gypsies, did not live like a Gypsy and could be considered socially adjusted. The record does not include the outcome of the case, but H. apparently escaped sterilization.[40]

In some places doctors and local officials, opposed to the sterilization of Gypsies who had lived in the community for a very long time, successfully used delaying tactics. In Siegen a group of well-integrated Gypsies, some of whom owned small houses, were supposed to be sterilized in 1944. A sympathetic official, taking advantage of the bombing of the town, was able to delay enforcement of the order, and all of them escaped sterilization.[41] There were other such cases. In Friesoythe (near Oldenburg) a policeman proved helpful and no Gypsy was either deported or sterilized.[42] In Cloppenburg the end of the war came before intended sterilizations could be carried out.[43] In Schorndorf, under the jurisdiction of the Stuttgart Kripo, the sterilization of Johann G., ordered in August 1944, was still pending in February 1945 and probably was never carried out.[44]

We do not know how many Gypsies were able to avoid sterilization and how many were actually sterilized persuant to the Auschwitz decree. Hansjörg

Riechert, who has done a careful study of Nazi sterilization policy toward the Gypsies, provides the figure of perhaps 2,000–2,500 sterilized between 1943 and 1945 but acknowledges that this is a "rough estimate."[45] In a report dated March 6, 1944, Ritter noted that "a larger part of the asocial Zigeunermischlinge classified have been sterilized," whereas those belonging to socially adjusted clans have been exempted.[46] Since reports of completed sterilizations had to be sent to the RKPA, Ritter may have known how many Gypsies had in fact been sterilized. However, since we do not have the total number of persons classified by Ritter's institute as "asocial Zigeunermischlinge," we are in no position to know what would be a "larger part [*ein grösserer Teil*]" of this group. Whatever the number of victims, there can be no doubt that these sterilizations caused great trauma for the affected persons and their families. For Gypsies, children are of supreme importance and much of the social prestige of both men and women depends on producing offspring. There is also, of course, the larger impact of this sterilization program, which has been called "delayed genocide." I discuss this issue in chapter 14.

Hardships and Discrimination

The daily life of the Gypsies exempt from deportation was closely supervised, and the possibility of being sent to a concentration camp was ever present. On February 24, 1943, Anton M. of Cologne, classified as a Zigeunermischling, was seized in the apartment of Maria L., a divorced German woman, with whom he had been instructed not to have any more contact. Once again he had to promise not to have any sexual relations with L. or any other "persons of German blood. If I fail to obey this order I have to expect to be taken into preventive police custody and be put into a concentration camp." After this encounter, M. disappeared from view and the police surmised that he lived from black market deals. On July 15, 1944, M. was seized in Strasburg. The arrest was accomplished as a result of help from Maria L. His subsequent fate is not known.[47]

At a time of great labor shortages, employers were glad to have Gypsy workers. However, these workers were subject to special scrutiny and the slightest breach of work discipline could trigger complaints to the Kripo and possible dire consequences. On August 30, 1944, the Toran Company in Berlin, a laboratory for radioactive products, notified the police that Rosita P., a seventeen-year-old Gypsy, had been absent from work for several days without excuse. "In today's circumstances, especially at a time of total war, it cannot be tolerated that a young person should incur such a breach of duty. We request punishment." A Kripo investigation revealed that P. had been sick and that no criminal offense had taken place. However, she received a stiff warning to attend work regularly anyway.[48]

A similar affair involved Hermann K., classified as a Zigeunermischling, who was employed on a dairy farm near Berlin. On December 11, 1944, his employer complained to the Kripo that K. stayed out nights or brought German women to his room. His work had started to suffer and several cows had died as a result of K.'s negligence. The employer asked that K. not be sent to a labor camp, for he would be unable to find a replacement for him. "I request a stiff warning." Summoned by the police, K. admitted that he had been out late four times, but he denied having had sexual relations with German women. Three other employees, two of them Poles, he maintained, had started to blame him for everything that went wrong on the farm. K. must have been persuasive for he got off light. He had to promise not to leave the farm at night without his employer's permission and, especially, to avoid any intimate relations with German women. "If I violate these orders I have to expect the harshest police measures." A memo dated January 17, 1945 noted that K. now worked conscientiously and that no further complaints had been received.[49]

A small number of Gypsies sought to avoid deportation to Auschwitz by going underground; the names of such "Gypsy fugitives" were listed in the official gazette of the Kripo.[50] An even smaller number was able to avoid detection. Anna M. was a Gypsy woman with five children ranging in age from four to fifteen years. Expecting to be sent to Auschwitz, M. became a fugitive but was arrested on November 12, 1943. The arrest record stated that she was caught "begging and itinerating in the manner of Gypsies." Three days later she and her children were sent to Auschwitz. The memo in her file recording the dispatch to the Gypsy camp noted "no evidence of criminal conduct." Presumably this meant that she would not be prosecuted for having evaded deportation or for begging. M. died in Auschwitz on January 27, 1944.[51]

Fifty-one-year-old Ferdinand R. was a "racially pure" Gypsy from Berlin living with twenty-three-year-old Elli R., who had been classified as a "Zigeunermischling with predominantly Gypsy blood." When Elli R. was ordered deported to Auschwitz in March 1943, the two left Berlin but were caught on June 29 while trying to cross into Italy. They were returned to Berlin and ordered sent to a concentration camp for leaving Berlin and their jobs without permission. On August 24, Elli R., five months pregnant, was seriously wounded when the prison in which she was being held was hit by a bomb. Because of her injuries and pregnancy her dispatch to a camp was postponed. The child was born on January 21, 1944, and it was noted on June 26 that she was still breast-feeding her infant and had not fully recovered from her wounds. Her subsequent fate is not known. Ferdinand R. presumably was sent to a camp.[52]

Very few Gypsies found refuge with non-Gypsy families. During the last months of the war, Michael H. and his family from Munich were hidden by a farmer near St. Wolfgang.[53] Anna S. from Hannover was given shelter by both Gypsy and non-Gypsy families.[54] On the other hand, we also know of cases in which Gypsies were denounced to the police. On June 8, 1943, Margarete Dickow complained to the Berlin Kripo about two Gypsy families living in a colony of bungalows in Berlin-Karlshorst. A petition signed by her and nine other neighbors alleged that the Gypsies and their children stole fruit, used obscene language and behaved in an indecent manner. The petitioners asked that the Gypsies be taken away, but the police merely warned the two families to conduct themselves above reproach.[55]

Five months later, the organization of garden-cottage dwellers (*Landesbund Berlin-Brandenburg der Kleingärtner*) picked up the cause and lodged another complaint with the police against "intolerable conditions" prevailing in the colony. On the other hand, a second petition, signed by thirty other neighbors, defended the two families. On January 31, 1944, the Berlin Kripo replied to the *Landesbund*. The two families in question were listed as Volga Germans who had escaped Russia after the Bolshevik revolution. They had no contact with the local Gypsies, followed regular occupations and had not previously given rise to complaints. For various reasons, a move to another location was out of the question.[56]

It appears that the angry cottage dwellers thereupon appealed to the next higher police echelon, for on April 7 the RKPA informed the Berlin Kripo that it was considering sending the Gypsy families to Auschwitz. The local Kripo was asked to submit a list of the persons involved, to explain why they had not been deported and to clarify their social status in detail. This information was provided on May 31. The memo noted that no further complaints had been received and that all members of these families, insofar as they were not yet sterile, had agreed to be sterilized.[57] The documentary record ends here and we have no further information about the disposition of this case. We do know that there were other such denunciations, including one in Berlin that called for sending the offending Gypsies to a camp.[58]

The citizens of Berlin involved in these incidents were not the only ones seeking a tougher approach to the "Gypsy problem" during these years. Writing in 1943, a German official noted that Gypsies were "asocial and hereditarily inferior nomadic people" who, like the Jews, represented "alien blood" within the meaning of the existing racial legislation. Since the "Gypsy problem" was biological and social in nature (rather than political and economic as in the case of the Jews), many of the special measures taken against the Jews were not necessary. Still, he concluded, a "further extension of the special legal status of the Jews to the Gypsies is to be expected."[59]

That was also the view of Bormann and Thierack, who considered Himmler's protection of the "racially pure" Gypsies an eccentric idiosyncrasy and did their best to undermine it. The twelfth amendment to the German citizenship law, issued by the Ministry of the Interior on April 25, 1943, can be considered part of this endeavor. The citizenship law of 1935 had not specifically mentioned Gypsies, even though quasi-official commentaries and actual practice in the following years had made it clear that Gypsies had a legal status very similar to that of the Jews. The ordinance issued in the spring of 1943 now clarified any remaining ambiguities: "Jews and Gypsies cannot become German citizens." They also could not acquire the lower status of "revocable citizenship [*Staatsangehörigkeit auf Widerruf*]" or "protected person [*Schutzangehöriger*]."[60] Significantly, the new rule made no distinction between different kinds of Gypsies, as most of Himmler's measures had done, and treated all Gypsies in the same discriminatory manner.

Another decree continued the trend, begun in 1942, of putting Gypsies and Jews on an equal footing in regard to social legislation. On October 3, 1944, it was announced that workers quarantined for typhus would receive financial aid to make up for lost wages. "However, this support is not to be given to Jews and Gypsies."[61] It was probably in opposition to the tendency to treat Jews and Gypsies in the same way that Himmler issued a decree on March 10, 1944, his last known pronouncement on the subject:

> The separately published decrees and rules governing the life of Poles, Jews, and Gypsies within the jurisdiction of the Reich have frequently led to equal treatment for these groups as far as prohibitions of the sale and utilization of certain items, public announcements, and in the press, etc., are concerned. This attitude does not correspond with the differentiated political position to be granted to these groups now, and in the future.

Altogether, Himmler added, "the accomplished evacuation and isolation of these groups" had made the publication of special directives no longer necessary.[62]

By stressing the different treatment to be meted out to Poles, Jews and Gypsies, "now, and in the future," Himmler sought to reaffirm his own approach to the "Gypsy problem," which treated Gypsies and Jews differently and also differentiated between "good" and "bad" Gypsies. As I have noted in this chapter, even the lot of the "good" Gypsies, who were allowed to stay in the Reich but were isolated from the rest of the population, was far from enviable. But it surely was better than the fate of the Jews, which was physical destruction, pure and simple.

During the final year of the war, Gypsies were inducted into the *Organisation Todt*, the agency in charge of construction and fortifications for the defense of the Reich.[63] For service in the *Volkssturm*, the last-ditch militia created by Hitler in September 1944, Gypsies once again were treated like Jews. On December 9, 1944, Bormann gave orders that Jews and Gypsies, as well as Mischlinge of the first degree (those with two grandparents of alien blood), not be drafted into the Volkssturm.[64] This left open the possibility that Mischlinge of the second degree (those with only one alien grandparent) could be inducted. The RKPA, noting a conflict with applicable OKW regulations, on February 16, 1945, informed the Kripo of Munich that no Zigeunermischlinge were to serve in the Volkssturm.[65] It is not clear to what extent these fine distinctions were actually observed during the chaotic last weeks of the Nazi regime. We know of at least one Gypsy, married to a German woman and living in Ingelheim near Mainz, who was drafted into the Volkssturm and killed in the Saar shortly before the end of the war.[66]

Part IV

AFTER THE DISASTER

13

Victims and Perpetrators

The end of the war found the Gypsy community of Germany and Austria in a seriously weakened condition. Of the more than 13,000 persons deported from the Reich to Auschwitz perhaps as many as 90 percent had failed to return alive. All of the 5,000 Austrian Gypsies sent to Litzmannstadt had perished in the ghetto or had been killed in the gas vans of Chelmno. Survivors were traumatized by the ordeal of camp life, which not only had left them destitute but also deeply demoralized. The routine of the concentration camps had violated basic Gypsy customs such as the requirements of ritual purity or the prohibition against being seen naked in public. Many of the elders, who had been models of conduct, were no longer alive. Those who had been sterilized had lost much of their sense of self-worth, for the standing of Gypsy men and women in their families as well as in the larger community depends heavily on fertility. To make things worse, Gypsies often encountered the same treatment at the hands of the new authorities that they had suffered before and during the first years of the Nazi regime.

Harassment Continued

Many liberated Gypsies at first lived in camps for displaced persons or were forced to reside in the same municipal Gypsy camps from which they had been deported. Others were able to obtain horses and resumed an itinerating lifestyle, and very soon the old recriminations were voiced again. On January 26, 1946, the Hannover Kripo complained to the military government about the Gypsies in the region who, together with asocial and work-shy elements, were said to have created a situation of "growing insecurity" in the rural areas. "For Gypsies special measures are required, since according to experience the rate of crime among these people is especially high." Specifically, the police asked for permission to hold Gypsies until their identity could be fully established. To fight this wave of crime, the Kripo averred, was not a matter of race.[1] Some months later, in commenting on the draft of a law dealing with habitual criminals, the police insisted that measures such as special supervision were not an invention of the Nazis but represented merely the realization of demands made by the police for a long time. "New was merely the introduction of preventive custody and its implementation in concentration camps."[2]

On June 7, 1946, the Allied Control Commission for Germany ruled that Gypsies were entitled to the protection of the military government and could not be made subject to special measures of control on account of their race. Relying in part on this ruling, Kripo representatives in the British zone of occupation decided about a year later that holding persons for the purpose of establishing their true identity was unacceptable.[3] However, these decisions did not end the controversy. On February 28, 1948, the Lüneburg Kripo fretted that roving Gypsies, "living primarily from theft, fraud and begging," had created "a great plague" for the countryside. The police were unable to get control of this situation, since many of these Gypsies had identity cards certifying their status as former concentration camp inmates.[4]

Similar reports exist from other parts of Germany. In July 1946, the police of Buchen (Baden) complained to the *Landrat* (chief magistrate) that the number of Gypsies moving through the area was larger than ever. "They live from begging and steal whatever they can get hold of." Neither vegetables nor fruits nor chickens were safe. Moreover, the police alleged, these Gypsies conducted themselves in an arrogant manner and claimed that since they had been persecuted by the Nazis the police were not entitled to give them orders. The Landrat forwarded the complaint to the military government, and eventually the government of Baden addressed the matter. A ruling by the Department of the Interior pointed out that the decree of December 8, 1938, dealing with the "Gypsy plague" could no longer be invoked, since it had aimed at suppressing the Gypsies on racial grounds. On the other hand, measures could be taken against "travelers" *(Landfahrer)* who committed specific offenses such as not registering with the police, begging and vagrancy, fortune-telling and so on.[5]

In Bavaria too the old measures against Gypsies were applied under the new nomenclature of protection against "travelers." On November 28, 1947, the military government had annulled the Bavarian Law for the Combating of Gypsies, Travelers and the Work-Shy of 1926, but on October 14, 1953, the Bavarian legislature approved a new law that dealt with "travelers" *(Landfahrerordnung)*. The word "Gypsy" did not appear in the legislation; travelers were defined sociologically as those who itinerate as a result of a deep-seated inclination or out of a strong aversion to leading a sedentary life. However, in terms of substance the new law for the most part repeated the prohibitions of the 1926 legislation. Travelers needed

permission for itinerating, for having horses and dogs, for camping at specified sites and the like.[6]

Other German states did not adopt formal legislation, but police practice
followed the same principles. In justification it was argued that the Bavarian
law had caused an influx of "travelers" with a criminal record. A draft law
discussed in Niedersachsen in 1954 was promoted with the argument that a
state that did not adopt special measures dealing with this problem would
become a magnet for criminal travelers from all over Germany. Travelers, it
was said, had become "a veritable scourge." They lived from begging, stealing, fraud and fortune-telling, and under existing legislation the police could
not cope with them, especially since some travelers had begun to use motor
cars. The proposed law, it was stressed, did not discriminate against anyone
on account of his national origin or race; it used the racially neutral concept
of Landfahrer, which, of course, could also include Gypsies.[7] A similar discussion took place in Hesse in 1956.

Much of the pressure for new anti-Gypsy legislation came from the ranks
of the criminal police. In Bavaria a special department dealing with "Gypsy
questions" had been set up as early as 1946. Later renamed *Landfahrerzentrale* (Central Office for Travelers), this office was able to use the files of the
former Munich *Zigeunerzentrale* (Central Office for Gypsy Affairs) and also
took over some of its personnel. Josef Eichberger, for example, had worked
in the Munich Gypsy office until 1939, when he was transferred to the
RKPA. There he played a prominent role in organizing Gypsy deportations.[8] Particularly outspoken in drawing attention to the "Gypsy problem"
were two officials with similarly long-running careers during the Nazi
regime— Rudolf Uschold, who had served in the RSHA in Berlin, and
Hans Eller, who had been involved with the deportations from Bavaria.

In an article published by Uschold in a professional police journal in
1951, the Gypsy specialist argued that about 70 percent of the travelers now
living in Germany were *Zigeunermischlinge* (Gypsies of mixed ancestry) and
only about 20 percent were "racially pure Gypsies." All Gypsies were exten-
sively involved with crime and asocial activities. The racially pure Sinti committed petty crimes such as fortune-telling, begging or stealing wood and
chickens; among the Zigeunermischlinge and the *Jenische* (Gypsy-like itinerants) were found habitual and professional criminals. The Nazi regime,
Uschold conceded, had sought a "radical" regulation of the Gypsy question;
some fanatics had sought to exterminate the Gypsies with "inhumane methods." However, these acts of persecution had failed to "make a contribution
toward a solution of the Gypsy problem." This was proven by the criminal
conduct of the Gypsies after the war, when offenses of all sorts had markedly
increased. Many of them continued to travel under false names and, claim-
ing to have been persecuted on racial grounds, avoided work. New Gypsies
were coming into Germany from other European countries. What was
needed, Uschold concluded, was a central office for all of Germany that
would deal with the Gypsy problem, a law against asocials, tougher controls
on travelers, and better international cooperation. His essay, Uschold

insisted, had not aimed at discriminating against the Gypsies but merely had sought to point out that a majority of these people were asocial or given to crime.[9]

Hans Eller, another veteran member of the Bavarian Kripo, took the argument a step further. In an article published in a criminology journal in 1954, Eller maintained that not only had the measures taken against the Gypsies during the Third Reich failed to solve the problem, they had not constituted "racial persecution." Gypsies had been incarcerated in concentration camps on account of their asocial or criminal way of life. In 1943 entire families too had been sent to camps, but it was impossible to know how many and under what circumstances Gypsies had died. It was known that many had succumbed to epidemics and a "personal and innate lack of cleanliness." Eller estimated that about 60 percent of the Gypsies were "given to crime [*kriminell veranlagt*]." Since many of them were now leaving Bavaria on account of the recently enacted Landfahrerordnung, Eller noted, he had written this article in order to draw the attention of his colleagues outside of Bavaria to this "strange group of people."[10]

Not until the changed political climate of the 1960s were many of the special regulations for the treatment of Gypsies and the institutions set up to enforce them abrogated. In March 1965, the Bavarian Landfahrerzentrale was abolished; in July 1970 the Landfahrerordnung was rescinded. In Baden-Württemberg, the special register for combating offenses by travelers (*Zentralkartei zur Bekämpfung von Landfahrerdelikten*) was shut down in October 1971. Since the 1970s the conduct of Gypsies or travelers can no longer be made the subject of special statistical analysis in any German state, though the police do compile data on those referred to as "frequently changing their place of residence" (*häufig wechselnder Aufenthaltsort*, or HWAO). Some feel that these changes are cosmetic and that advanced technological systems have made it possible to do without the earlier crude methods of surveillance and control.[11] On the other hand, certain police complain that itinerating Gypsies and organized bands of Gypsy criminals continue to present special problems and that the new regulations on collecting data hamstring their ability to control crime.[12]

Restitution: Denied and Delayed

During the early postwar years, most Gypsies who applied for restitution were turned down. Some of the arguments used blamed the victims rather than the perpetrators. The courts that became involved in these proceedings at times called as expert witnesses the very same officials who had brought about the deportations. When Rosa M. asked for compensation for her stay in Auschwitz, the Landfahrerzentrale of Munich argued that she had been sent there as "an asocial, not to say, criminal Gypsy" because she had engaged in fortune-telling; she therefore was not entitled to compensation. The position paper was signed by Georg Geyer, who had been an official with the Munich Kripo during the time M. had been sent to Auschwitz. M. finally received a one-time payment of DM 1,500 in 1967 but was not granted a pension until 1987, forty years after her liberation.[13]

The compensation law of the Federal Republic of Germany, enacted in 1953 and issued in a final version in 1965, provided compensation to those who had been persecuted on "grounds of political opposition to National Socialism or for reasons of race, religion or ideology [*Weltanschauung*]."[14] Gypsies were said not to fall under any of these provisions. The asocial behavior of the Gypsies, the highest criminal court of the Federal Republic of Germany (*Bundesgerichtshof*) held in 1956, had given rise to laws and regulations designed to control such conduct already before 1933. The decrees issued by the Nazis during the first years of the regime, even though they included racist ideas, were essentially police measures that aimed at preventing crime and promoting security. Only the Auschwitz decree of December 16, 1942, marked a decisive change in the Gypsy policy of the Third Reich. Hence only those deported as a result of this decree were entitled to compensation.[15]

The assertion that there existed substantial continuities between Gypsy policy practiced before and after 1933 was no doubt correct. Yet the attempt to legitimate decrees proclaimed by the Nazis on the basis of laws and rules enacted before their accession to power was deplorable and reprehensible. Even in the case of an abnormally high crime rate in a certain population it was a clear violation of the rule of law to subject that entire group to discriminatory treatment, as did the Bavarian Gypsy law of 1926 and similar legislation. These laws imputed a dishonest way of life to all Gypsies, a finding based on prejudice rather than fact; their punitive provisions affected everyone regardless of individual conduct. More important, not even hardened criminals, let alone those considered "work-shy" or having convictions for various kinds of petty crime, deserved to be treated without due process of law or subjected to the life of torment that was the lot of concentration camp inmates under the Nazi regime. The argument that the survivors of these camps were not entitled to compensation because they had been sent there as asocials or for the purpose of preventing crime was both factually irrelevant and morally offensive.

Even the deportation to the General Government in 1940 was held to be a measure outside the parameters of the compensation law. A court in Munich concluded as late as 1961 that this resettlement had been based on considerations of military security rather than race and that the stay in various camps there did not constitute confinement in the sense of the compensation law.[16] This decision too was factually flawed. As I noted in chapter 5, the 1940 deportation was part of a larger plan to get rid of all the German Gypsies within one year, and the security rationale was an afterthought. The court adopted uncritically the old canard that Gypsies were given to espionage, although even this accusation hardly justified the uprooting and expulsion of an entire population group.

In December 1963 the Bundesgerichtshof finally revised its decision of 1956. It now conceded that the racial persecution of the Gypsies had begun "at the latest" with the decree of December 1938, which, among other things, had ordered the registration and racial examination of all Gypsies.[17] But even this decision did not end the problems encountered by Gypsies who were seeking restitution. Many of the survivors had great difficulty in talking about their experiences in the camps out of a sense of shame or on account of suspicion that these new inquiries into their lives would lead to further harmful consequences. This resulted in missed application deadlines or incomplete applications. Many of the applicants were illiterate and unaware of the possibility of receiving restitution payments; there was exploitation by the lawyers who represented the Gypsies' interests. The authorities did not recognize "Gypsy marriages," which meant that survivors were unable to receive compensation for the death of a spouse in the camps. The doctors who had to certify damage to health often were less than sympathetic to the cause of the Gypsies, and many of the medical evaluations issued by them were phrased in language that led to the rejection of claims.

Those who sought compensation for compulsory sterilization for a long time received no satisfaction at all. This surgical intervention, it was argued, had not caused any diminution in the ability to earn a living, and those sterilized therefore were not entitled to compensation. Many who had been sterilized experienced serious psychological problems,[18] but they were difficult to prove. It was not until December 1980 that the federal government finally approved a one-time payment of DM 5,000 for those who had been subjected to compulsory sterilization. In March 1988 the government issued new guidelines for handling special hardship cases. Under these rules the sterilized can receive additional assistance if they can show damage to their health and a resulting loss in earning capacity of at least 25 percent.[19] The action of the Bundestag on May 28, 1998, nullifying all Nazi sterilization orders represented a moral victory. For many of the victims, these enactments came too late.

The Role of Arthur Nebe

None of the major figures responsible for the crimes committed against the Gypsies could be put before a court of law. Heydrich died on June 4, 1942, from wounds caused by a bomb that had been thrown by two Czech resistance fighters several days earlier. Himmler escaped judgment by committing suicide on May 23, 1945, two days after his capture; Nebe was hanged on March 3, 1945, for his involvement in the military putsch against Hitler. As head of the RKPA, Nebe played a leading role in the formulation of Gypsy policy. At the same time, his connection to the German resistance has made him one of the more enigmatic figures among the top Nazi leadership.

Born in 1894 to a Berlin schoolteacher, Nebe originally had planned to become a minister, but he failed his high school examination. After serving with distinction in World War I, Nebe was unable to find a job. In 1922 he finally was accepted as a candidate for the criminal police in Berlin. Nebe joined the Nazi party in 1931, and soon thereafter his career took off. In 1935 he became head of the Prussian criminal police and in 1937 chief of the RKPA. By 1941 Nebe had attained the rank of lieutenant-general of the police and SS-Gruppenführer, a position directly below SD chief Heydrich. By that time he had also served as head of an *Einsatzgruppe* (special task force) in Russia that was responsible for killing over 45,000 Jews. Implicated in the 1944 military putsch against Hitler, Nebe went into hiding after its failure. He was betrayed by a jealous woman friend, arrested in November 1944 and hanged on March 3, 1945.[20] Who was the real Nebe?

Since 1945, several of Nebe's colleagues and some students of Nazi Germany have described Nebe as above all a professional police officer, a man who became disillusioned with Hitler and eventually turned into a resolute and principled opponent of the Nazi regime. In his memoirs published in 1947, Hans Gisevius, who was Nebe's colleague in the Prussian police and a close friend, wrote that in 1933 Nebe still believed in Hitler but soon began to develop second thoughts. Nebe's service as the commander of an Einsatzgruppe in Gisevius's book became "a brief command at the front."[21] Some twenty years later, when Nebe's role as the commander of one of Heydrich's mobile killing units had become common knowledge, Gisevius changed his account. In a book of recollections on Nebe published in 1966, *Wo ist Nebe?* (Where Is Nebe?), he argued that his friend had not wanted to take on this assignment. He finally accepted it on the advice of opposition leaders Oster and Beck, who wanted Nebe to retain a key position in the SS apparatus. Altogether, according to Gisevius, Nebe was able to keep his distance from the independently operating units under his command that did the actual killing. As to the 45,000 Jews killed during his tenure of duty, Gisevius alleged that Nebe in his reports to Berlin exaggerated the results by adding a zero to the actual numbers shot.[22]

There are other such accounts. In his book on the military opposition to Hitler, Fabian von Schlabrendorff, who served with Army Group Center to which Einsatzgruppe B was attached, depicted Nebe as a "sheep in wolf's clothing" and as "a determined anti-Nazi in the uniform of an SS officer." Because of Nebe, Schlabrendorff wrote, a large number of Russian lives could be saved. Many of the killings took place without his knowledge.[23] Similar assessments are provided by Peter Hoffmann, Harold C. Deutsch and Allen Dulles.[24]

It has been established that Nebe provided information and other help to the military conspirators, though the dating of his support and his motives remain unclear. On the other hand, there is little evidence to corroborate his friends' testimony about his reticent service with Einsatzgruppe B. Nebe, it turns out, was the only leader of an Einsatzgruppe to volunteer for this job. Heinz Höhne suggests an opportunistic motive: Nebe "thought that by promptly volunteering for duty in the East he would earn himself the clasp to the Iron Cross First Class and curry favor with the unpredictable Heydrich."[25] Even if Nebe may not have fully realized that he had volunteered for one of the greatest mass murders in history, he must have become aware of the true nature of this assignment after the Einsatzgruppen leaders had received their orders shortly before the start of the war against the Soviet Union. Although several of his colleagues in the RSHA managed to avoid being drawn into this machinery of destruction or left after a very short stint of duty, Nebe stayed at his post for four months. One of the men to find a loophole, Franz Six, testified after the war that "one could at any rate *try* to get posted away from an Einsatzgruppe. At least no one was shot for doing so."[26]

And there is more damaging information. The claim that Nebe exaggerated the number of Jews killed is probably false. During the postwar trial of Einsatzgruppen leaders, the defense tried to cast doubt on the reliability of the activity reports sent to Berlin, but was unsuccessful in this endeavor.[27] In spite of occasional inaccuracies, the numbers reported unfortunately tally all too well with the horrendous losses inflicted on the Jews of the Soviet Union, which can be established on the basis of population figures. Freiherr von Gersdorff, who met Nebe during his tour of duty in Russia in 1941 and considered him a decent man, relates with regret that Nebe apparently had been less than honest with him. After the war, while testifying as an expert witness at war crimes trials, Gersdorff found out that Nebe had reported shootings to the RSHA that he had denied at the time in conversations with him and other friends.[28] In an operational report of July 13, 1941, Nebe wrote, "In Grodno and Lida only 96 Jews have been executed so far during the first days. I have given orders that this process must be intensified [*dass hier erheblich zu intensivieren sei*]."[29] According to Bradfisch, head of Einsatzkommando 8, Nebe was always intent on interpreting instructions received from Heydrich and Himmler in the broadest possible way.[30]

On a visit to Minsk on August 15, 1941, Hilberg reports, Himmler asked Nebe "to shoot a batch of a hundred people, so that he could see what one of these 'liquidations' really looked like. Nebe obliged. All except two of the victims were men." After the shooting, which had left Himmler visibly nervous, Himmler was told by SS-Obergruppenführer Erich von dem Bach-Zelewski, one of the three senior SS and police leaders in charge of killing operations in the newly occupied Soviet territories, that such mass executions were a terrible burden on the men doing the shooting. Himmler thereupon gave a speech in which he explained why this "bloody business" was necessary even though everyone found it genuinely repulsive. After the speech, Himmler, Nebe, Bach-Zelewski and the chief of Himmler's personal staff, Wolff, inspected an insane asylum, and Himmler demanded that the insane be killed as soon as possible. He also suggested that Nebe come up with other killing methods that were more humane (i.e. easier on the executioners) than shooting. "Nebe," Hilberg writes, "asked for permission to try out dynamite on the mentally sick people." Bach-Zelewski and Wolff are supposed to have protested that the sick people after all were not guinea pigs, but Himmler decided in favor of the attempt.[31]

In September 1941, according to several witnesses, Nebe ordered Albert Widmann, head of the chemical department in the criminal-technical institute of the RKPA, to come to Minsk with 250 kilograms of explosives and several hoses suitable to convey exhaust gas. Himmler, Nebe explained to Widmann after his arrival, had given orders to apply euthanasia to the incurable mental patients of Russia and to find a method of killing other than shooting. Nebe therefore was going to try out explosives and gas. In the afternoon of the following day, Nebe, Widmann and an expert on explosives drove to a place about 15 kilometers from Minsk where two wooden bunkers had been prepared. One of the bunkers was loaded with explosives and twenty-four mental patients were put into it. Nebe gave the signal to detonate, but the resultant explosion failed to kill the patients. Several of them emerged from the bunker covered with blood and screaming loudly. Thereupon more explosives were brought up, the wounded patients were forced back into the bunker, and a second explosion finally finished the job. The bunker had become quiet and parts of bodies could be seen hanging from nearby trees.[32]

Two days later, Nebe and Widmann conducted an experiment using carbon monoxide gas at the insane asylum of Mogilev. A room on the ground floor of the asylum was bricked up with two openings left for pipes. At first only a passenger car was connected, but it did not produce enough exhaust gas and a truck had to be added. Five patients who had been brought into the room were dead after about fifteen minutes of exposure to the gas from the two motor vehicles. Nebe and Widmann agreed that the killing with explosives was not practical but that the use of exhaust gas held promise. Nebe then apparently reported the results of the two experiments to Himmler.[33]

Also in September 1941, Nebe gave a lecture at a course on how to fight the partisans that was entitled "The Jewish Question with Special Attention to the Partisan Movement." The text of this talk on September 25 is not preserved, but given the connection the Nazis habitually made between Jews and partisans, one can easily guess the deadly nature of the instruction Nebe sought to convey on this occasion. Part of the course involved a live demonstration of a search for suspects in a location south of Mogilev. When no partisans were found, the lesson ended with the killing of thirty-two Jews.[34]

Nebe's name appeared on many orders and communications regarding Gypsies that emanated from the RKPA. In October 1939, it will be recalled, he urged Eichmann to include Berlin Gypsies in the transports of Jews to Nisko. A good indication of what Nebe really thought of the Gypsies can be found in a brief memo cited in a communication between Himmler and Dr. Ernst Grawitz, the chief physician of the SS. In May 1944, Himmler asked SS–Obergruppenführer Grawitz, who carried the title of Reichsarzt SS und Polizei, to give him his views on who would be the best subjects for certain medical experiments to be carried out at the Dachau concentration camp. I discussed these experiments in chapter 11. Grawitz, in turn, solicited the views of three persons, one of them Nebe. In a letter sent out on June 28 Grawitz informed Himmler that Nebe had suggested to use "the asocial Zigeunermischlinge" in Auschwitz. "Among them are persons who are healthy but do not come into consideration for the labor program." Nebe proposed to select the necessary number of human subjects from this group.[35] The suggestion is indicative of how expendable "inferior people" such as the Gypsies were in his eyes.

According to Bernd Wehner, one of his former colleagues at the RKPA, Nebe liked to boast before Heydrich about the accomplishments of his Kripo. He tried to outdo Heinrich Müller, the head of the Gestapo, with whom he is said to have feuded constantly and bitterly. Wehner regarded Nebe as a careerist who joined the ranks of the resistance because of the many crimes in which he had been involved. With a German military defeat becoming a near certainty, Nebe needed protection.[36] Wehner's assessment is probably correct. It is difficult to ignore Nebe's gruesome record as commander of Einsatzgruppe B or his willingness to make human guinea pigs of mental patients or Gypsies. Even if credence is given to the claim that he provided assistance to the resistance during these years, how many crimes is a person entitled to commit in order to camouflage his oppositional activities and stay in the good graces of the leaders of a murderous regime? Nebe's proposal to Himmler to use inmates of the Gypsy camp at Auschwitz for medical experiments came just a few weeks before the July 20, 1944, attempt to overthrow Hitler in which Nebe was implicated. Perhaps the smart SS officer tried to buy insurance for all possible outcomes.

The Fate of Other Perpetrators

Some culprits of lower rank were apprehended and convicted. Ernst-August König, an SS block leader in the Auschwitz gypsy camp, was sentenced to life imprisonment for three killings; he committed suicide in his cell.[37] Franz Langmüller, commandant of the Austrian Gypsy camp Lackenbach, was tried for torturing and killing inmates; he received a prison sentence of one year.[38]

In some other cases, wrongdoing against Gypsies played only a minor part in a larger pattern of criminal conduct. The indictment of the leaders of the Einsatzgruppen mentioned the murder of Gypsies and cited specific instances; the judgment concluded that these "unoffending people" had been "hunted down like wild game."[39] Otto Ohlendorf, commander of Einsatzgruppe D, was questioned about the killing of Gypsies, but we do not know what role this crime played in the guilty verdict against him. General Franz Böhme, military commander in Serbia and responsible for the mass shooting of Gypsy hostages, took his own life after he was indicted by a Nuremberg military tribunal.[40] The head of his administrative staff, Harald Turner, was condemned to death by the Jugoslavs.[41] Hinrich Lohse, the Reichskommissar for the Baltic states, who had ordered the killing of itinerating Gypsies, was sentenced to ten years' imprisonment and the confiscation of property.[42] Friedrich Jeckeln, the senior SS and police leader attached to Lohse, acknowledged the shooting of Gypsies and was executed by the Soviets.[43] Several physicians were convicted of conducting medical experiments on Gypsy concentration camp inmates.[44] Austrian Tobias Portschy, author of a vicious diatribe against the Gypsies and responsible for their persecution in the Styria area, was sentenced to a prison term of fifteen years in 1950 but pardoned in 1957.[45] Adolf Eichmann was found guilty of crimes against humanity for deporting Gypsies,[46] but the evidence for this part of the verdict does not stand up under critical examination.

A large number of Kripo officials involved in Gypsy affairs as well as members of the Ritter institute were investigated, but none were brought to trial. Many of these men and women had had successful careers after 1945; some of them attained responsible positions in the police. The public prosecutor of Cologne investigated forty-six cases of suspected wrongdoing, but nothing came of these investigations: eleven persons had died, in twenty-three cases the statute of limitations had expired, and in twelve cases the evidence was found to be insufficient for an indictment. Hans Maly, who had served in a senior position in the RKPA, was indicted on February 20, 1964, for having ordered the deportation of Gypsies to Auschwitz. Preparations for his trial dragged on but were halted in May 1970 on account of Maly's sickness. He died on October 28, 1971.[47]

Paul Werner, Nebe's deputy in the RKPA, was investigated for the same offense by the public prosecutor of Stuttgart in 1961, but the probe was halted on December 9, 1963. In line with then prevailing legal doctrine, the dispatch of Gypsies to concentration camps until early 1943 was held to have been based on "preventive crime fighting" and not on their racial identity; the death of inmates, it was said, could not have been predicted. Werner's participation in the promulgation of the Auschwitz decree could not be proven.[48] The prosecutors in these proceedings allegedly studied the evidence of the Nuremberg trials, materials compiled by the Munich Institute for Contemporary History and other documentary sources. They also heard a large number of Gypsy witnesses. However, it is questionable that some of them really understood the true nature of the Nazi regime or were willing to open their minds to the inhumanities involved. For example, it was surely absurd to maintain that Werner could not have known about the high likelihood of death that resulted from being sent to a concentration camp.

In October 1948, the public prosecutor of Frankfurt/Main, acting on accusations received from a large number of Gypsy survivors, started an inquiry into the role of Robert Ritter, the head of the Research Institute for Racial Hygiene and Population Biology in the Ministry of Health and of the Institute for Criminal Biology of the Security Police established at the instigation of Himmler in 1941. The importance of the role played by Ritter was evident. His distinction between pure and racially mixed Gypsies and his assertion that the Zigeunermischlinge were a largely asocial element, the propagation of which had to be prevented, had been key elements in Nazi Gypsy policy. By his own account, the racial assessments that he and his associates prepared were designed to "provide scientific and practical data for the measures taken by the state in the areas of eugenics and racial hygiene."[49] The insights gained by his research into the racial origins and characteristics of the Gypsies, Ritter had written in 1941, also formed the basis "for the preventive measures of the police,"[50] that is, incarceration in a concentration camp. The Gypsy problem, he had concluded, could be considered solved only "when the main body of the asocial and useless Zigeunermischlinge are collected in large *labor camps* [*Wanderarbeitslager*] and are made to work, and when the further *propagation of this Mischling population* is prevented once and for all [Ritter's italics]. Only then will future generations of the German people be truly freed from this burden."[51]

After an inquiry that lasted almost two years, the public prosecutor closed the case on the grounds that the evidence was not sufficient to establish the existence of an indictable offense. The Gypsies' testimony, he declared, was notoriously unreliable. Ritter died on April 15, 1951, less than a year after this decision, and much of the documentation of the case is lost. Yet several things are clear. Ritter's claim made after the downfall of the Nazi regime that he never intended the death of the Gypsies and indeed sought to prevent any unfair and inhumane treatment by "fanatics" in the Nazi party[52] is a half-truth at best. Ritter asserted that already back in 1935 he had opposed the plan of certain SS leaders to load all the Gypsies on ships and drown them on the high seas.[53] But even if this story is true, the fate that Ritter had in mind for the majority of the Gypsies can hardly be considered fair and humane.

It is highly probable that, as a close collaborator with Nebe, Ritter had a share in the preparation of the Auschwitz decree. Although this decree did not involve an order to kill the deportees, Ritter surely must have been aware of the fact that a prolonged stay in a Nazi concentration camp meant systematic mistreatment and a high risk of death. We know that Ritter was involved in preparing the provisions about compulsory sterilization issued in January 1943. Both of these key elements of the Auschwitz decree corresponded to Ritter's often articulated view about the necessity of incarcerating and sterilizing the Zigeunermischlinge, who were considered asocial. The claim made by some of Ritter's defenders that the differentiation between "racially pure" Gypsies and Mischlinge made by the racial researcher prevented the deportation and sterilization of a large number of Gypsies[54] is correct but does not absolve Ritter of a share of responsibility for the suffering and death of thousands of less fortunate Gypsies and the involuntary sterilization of many others. Without the racial assessments prepared by Ritter with dogged determination until practically the end of the war, most of the worst measures of persecution against the Gypsies would not have been possible.

Inquiries into the conduct of other members of Ritter's institute also ended without the finding of an indictable offense. In February 1959, the public prosecutor of Frankfurt/Main started an investigation of Ritter's chief assistant, Eva Justin. This action came in response to a charge of criminal conduct received from several Gypsies who accused Justin and several others of having ordered the compulsory sterilization and deportation of Gypsies resulting in many deaths. The probe ended on December 12, 1960, and absolved Justin of the charges leveled against her. The racial assessments compiled by her, the prosecutor acknowledged, "had been the basis of later unlawful measures, which caused the death or sterilization of numerous

Gypsies. However, it is impossible to prove that while preparing the assessments she knew of, or could expect, the promulgation of the unlawful decree of January 29, 1943 [the implementing regulations of the Auschwitz decree]." Justin's claim that she had expected the assessments to be used for the preparation of legislation such as a Gypsy law, the prosecutor stated, was credible, for such laws had indeed been in preparation. The fact that at the time she was "young and inexperienced" and was strongly influenced by Ritter and that she had since repudiated her views on the Gypsy question was also in her favor.[55]

As in the case of Ritter, this finding ignored the fact that the racial assessments prepared by Justin and her colleagues had been used even before 1943 for a variety of discriminatory purposes. Indeed, as a German court held in another case, the very practice of subjecting persons to a compulsory racial examination represented an unlawful exercise of state power based on National Socialist racial teachings, an impermissible invasion of an individual's most basic personal rights.[56] Moreover, there is evidence that Justin was not just an innocent young woman who had been misled by her superior. Many survivors charged that during the examinations she carried out Justin had threatened to cut off their hair if they did not tell the truth and that she had hit them. These charges could not be proven, but we do know of at least one case in which Justin behaved in a more ruthless manner than the Kripo. At the time when this incident, recorded by the Berlin Kripo, took place, Justin was thirty-three years old.

On July 3, 1941, Helene P., a sixty-nine-year-old Gypsy woman, was brought to a district office of the Berlin police so that a racial examination could be carried out. Already in 1939 P. had been found to be hard of hearing and no longer "in full possession of her mental faculties." But Miss W., an examiner from Ritter's institute, insisted that P. be kept in jail until she had provided complete information about the identity of her father. Holding her in jail would also put pressure upon the other members of her clan who, according to W., had given false testimony. When the Kripo officials objected on the grounds that P. was sick and not fit for incarceration (since her arrest she had needed several injections by a physician), Justin entered the case. In a telephone conversation she declared that P. "by all means" had to be kept in jail as a way of pressuring the clan. If this was not done, Justin threatened, she would report the matter to the RKPA. The police officials, not intimidated, had P. examined by the jail physician, who declared her to be unfit for incarceration. P. was released on July 16, thirteen days after the beginning of this ordeal.[57]

Justin's views on the sterilization of the Gypsies were more radical than those of her mentor. Whereas Ritter allowed exemptions for "socially adjusted" Gypsies, Justin insisted that the question of the sterilization of Gypsies be approached exclusively from the point of view of racial hygiene. In early 1943 she completed a dissertation that dealt with 148 young Zigeunermischlinge in Württemberg who had been reared away from their biological families in institutions or by foster parents. These children, she

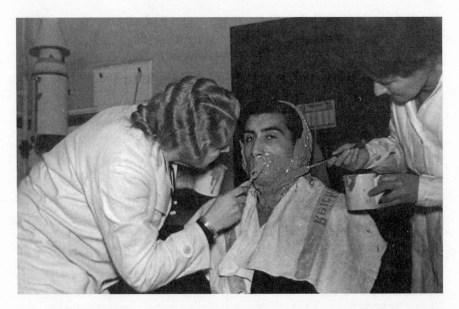

Sophie Ehrhardt preparing a plaster model of the head of a Gypsy. COURTESY OF BUNDES-
ARCHIV KOBLENZ.

concluded, had preserved their inferior racial characteristics. They lived on
the borderline between asocial and social behavior, and their sterilization
therefore was imperative, irrespective of whether they were socially adjusted
or asocial and criminal.[58] Even Gypsy affairs researcher Hermann Arnold,
who generally defended Ritter and his associates, thought that this prescrip-
tion of sterilization for a group defined exclusively in racial terms and the
complete disregard of individual conduct went too far. He called Justin's
position an "inhumane aberration" that was not vindicated by its eugenic
motive.[59] It is not known whether the Frankfurt prosecutor was familiar with
Justin's views when he terminated his inquiry in late 1960. Justin died on
September 11, 1966.

Investigations undertaken in the early 1960s and again in 1981–1982 of
Sophie Ehrhardt and Adolf Würth, two other members of the Ritter institute accused of being accessories to murder, similarly ended without an
indictment. The reasoning was similar to that used in the cases of Ritter and
Justin.[60] In an interview after these proceedings had ended, Würth claimed
that he and Ehrhardt had carried on their investigations "in order to make a
contribution to anthropological knowledge concerning a minority living in
Germany, the Gypsies." Since he and Ritter had not been party members,
Würth stated, "we always had to insert resounding phrases in our writings,
to reflect National Socialist ideas."[61]

The last inquiry into the activities of the Ritter institute involved the case
of Ruth Kellermann and ended on May 3, 1989. Here too no indictable
offense was found, but both the prosecutor and a Hamburg court, which at

one point issued a temporary injunction in the case, displayed a far more critical attitude toward Ritter and his colleagues. For example, the prosecutor rejected the notion that the institute had simply been engaged in scientific research. Rather, he concluded, all the work carried on in the institute was based on the premise that the Zigeunermischlinge represented a potentially criminal element against which something had to be done. The institute had continued to issue assessments even though it was understood that they were used to send Gypsies to concentration camps or bring about compulsory sterilizations. It had been known in the institute, testimony revealed, that Gypsies died in Auschwitz in large numbers because of undernourishment and the horrible hygienic conditions prevailing there. If Kellermann escaped indictment, it was because the statute of limitations had run out on offenses that could be considered the result of her work in the institute. Whatever her culpability, it was not murder or being an accessory to murder.[62]

Demands for Civil Rights and a New Historiography

By the 1970s, the Gypsy community of Germany had undergone important changes. In continuation of a process that had been under way for many decades, a large proportion of Gypsies had become sedentary and only a relatively small minority still traveled during the summer months as peddlers of carpets and similar items, mostly in motorized caravans. A few had become successful businessmen or professionals. Still, Gypsies continued to maintain many of their social customs and habits such as living near each other, being in touch with close relatives and having large families. By the early 1980s it was estimated that German Gypsies numbered between 45,000 and 60,000, roughly double the number that had existed before the Nazi disaster. Most of them now preferred to be called Sinti and Roma. In addition there were another 30,000 or so Gypsy guest workers, mostly from Eastern Europe.[63] Austria was said to have about 19,000 Gypsies.[64] There exists no accurate census of the number of Gypsies living in Germany and Austria today. An estimate published in 1996 puts the number of Gypsies in Germany and Austria at 100,000 and 25,000 respectively.[65]

The German Gypsy community has seen much progress but many problems remain. A report issued by the federal government in December 1982 stated that only about 10 percent of the Gypsies in Germany belonged to the middle class, 15 percent depended on welfare and 25 percent were unemployed. A full 35 percent were illiterate and only 20 percent had completed school.[66] Prejudice and discrimination have not disappeared, being kept alive especially by the large influx of Gypsies from Eastern Europe whose lifestyle often clashes with that of their German hosts. Gypsies continue to be portrayed in the media as lazy, dishonest and given to crime. Crime statistics for 1955–1980 show that, except for a two-year period, Gypsies did have an arrest rate higher than that of the population at large, though most of these offenses were for petty crime such as theft and fraud.[67]

During the last two decades the police have no longer been allowed to keep statistics about the number of Gypsies arrested. The significance of the available statistics may also have been distorted by the fact that they represent arrests rather than convictions. As a frequently harassed group, Gypsies may have a higher rate of arrests without thereby establishing a higher rate of committed crimes.[68]

The collapse of the East European Communist regimes in 1989 led to a large wave of migrants who sought to benefit from the generous provisions for political asylum in the German constitution. By 1994, 7 million foreigners were living in Germany; during that year 127,200 new foreigners bid for political asylum. Among those applying to be accepted as refugees were many Gypsies from Rumania and the former Yugoslavia. In some large cities such as Frankfurt/Main, Stuttgart and Munich the foreign population exceeds 20 percent.[69] Germany sees itself as an ethnically defined nation-state. The view that one can be a German only if one's ancestors were German is widely held and, until 1999, was reflected in the country's citizenship law. Hence, the large influx of foreigners, many of them people of color, gave rise to a wave of xenophobia aimed at preserving the ethnic homogeneity of the German state and occasionally to acts of violence, and Gypsies have been among the victims. In August 1992, East European refugees were the target of a three-day quasi-pogrom in the city of Rostock in the former East Germany. On September 28, 1994, two Gypsy refugees from the former Yugoslavia died in an arson attack in Herford (Westphalia).[70] Austria too has seen a revival of anti-Gypsy sentiment. In the town of Oberwart in the Burgenland only twelve or thirteen of the three hundred Gypsies deported by the Nazis had come back after the war. In February 1995, when the Gypsy settlement had again reached 117 persons, four Gypsies were killed by a pipe bomb concealed in a placard that read "Gypsies go back to India."[71]

Although such attacks are generally committed by neo-Nazis, widespread negative attitudes toward Gypsies play into the hands of extremists. A 1990 survey conducted in Germany that asked people to rank their affinity to members of various ethnic groups showed that Gypsies were by far the most unpopular group—over seven times more unpopular than Poles and Turks.[72] Another survey done by the survey research institute EMNID for the American Jewish Committee in January 1994 revealed that 68 percent of those questioned did not want Gypsies as neighbors and 40 percent judged the behavior of Gypsies as provocative.[73]

The Gypsy civil rights movement was born in the early 1970s. In April 1971, the first World Romani Congress convened in London. In its wake emerged a movement for equal rights for Gypsies on the international level as well as in individual countries, including Germany. In 1971, the Central Committee of Sinti in West Germany was formed; in 1972 it changed its name to Association of German Sinti (*Verband deutscher Sinti*). During the late 1970s, efforts to mobilize support for full civil rights for Gypsies benefited greatly from the assistance of the Society for Endangered People (*Gesellschaft für bedrohte Völker*), especially through the publication of the book *In Auschwitz vergast, bis heute verfolgt* in 1979.[74] In 1982 various local and statewide organizations of Gypsies united under the umbrella of the Central Council of German Sinti and Roma *(Zentralrat deutscher Sinti und Roma)*, sitting in Heidelberg. This committee receives financial support from the federal Ministry for Youth, Women and the Family. Since the middle of the 1980s several local organizations of Rom Gypsies such as the Rom Union in Frankfurt, the Rom e.V. in Cologne, and the Roma National Congress in Hamburg have existed. These organizations were born amidst criticism that the Zentralrat had neglected the interests of the Rom, especially in the area of asylum legislation.[75]

The Association of German Sinti, the Zentralrat and statewide Gypsy organizations have been active in fighting discrimination against Gypsies and in supporting the demand for restitution and the punishment of those responsible for the persecution of the Gypsies under the Nazis. One of the more spectacular activities of the Association of German Sinti concerned the files of the Ritter institute. As bombing attacks upon Berlin became more frequent in 1943, most of these files were moved away from Berlin and stored in several places.[76] Thereafter they disappeared. In 1972, after having been in the custody of former members of the institute, most of the files arrived at the Anthropological Institute of the University of Mainz. From there they were transferred in 1980 to the archive of the University of Tübingen and utilized by Sophie Ehrhardt, who held a position at that university. On September 1, 1981, a group of Gypsies occupied the archive, seized the Ritter files and moved them to the Federal Archive *(Bundesarchiv)* in Koblenz. Their concern was not only that a former member of the institute had continued to work on materials that she had helped compile during her career in the Third Reich; they also sought to protect the privacy of the persons whose physical measurements and genealogical roots are described in these files. Some of the files of the former Ministry of Health in Berlin were transferred to Koblenz after another sit-in held in June 1987. Missing to this day are originals of the almost 24,000 racial assessments compiled by Ritter and his associates, though copies have since turned up in several other locations.[77]

The Gypsy civil rights movement has also been successful in erecting memorials for Gypsies on the sites of several concentration camps, including Buchenwald and Ravensbrück. In April 1989 a group of fourteen Gypsies, including several camp survivors, conducted a hunger strike on the site of the Dachau concentration camp and demanded, among other things, the establishment of a Gypsy cultural center in the town of Dachau. A survey conducted by a Munich newspaper showed that 96 percent of the citizens of Dachau opposed such a center; the town council too turned down the proposal by a large majority.[78]

Since 1987, a Center for Culture and Documentation has been part of the national Gypsy organization, the Zentralrat in Heidelberg. From 1989 on this center has received financial support from the government of the Federal Republic. It has held conferences and has issued publications aimed at educating both Gypsies and non-Gypsies about the history and culture of the

Gypsy community. These publications have made available to a larger public information and documentary materials concerning the persecution of the Gypsies by the Nazi regime, though the quality of the scholarship has generally been low and the analysis at times seriously flawed. Thus, for example, these publications have set forth the view, clearly disproven by numerous incontrovertible sources, that Himmler's Auschwitz decree of December 1942 provided for and led to "the deportation of the last about 10,000 Sinti and Roma still living in the Reich."[79] I return to this matter in chapter 14.

The Zentralrat has promoted a simplified and at times false picture of the fate of the Gypsies under the Nazis. The organization has also displayed a highly hostile attitude toward any person or account likely to call into question the officially sanctioned version of events. A group of researchers at the University of Giessen, organized as the "Projekt Tsiganologie," have been denounced repeatedly for their anthropological approach to the history of the Gypsies. Romani Rose, the head of the Zentralrat, has charged Bernard Streck, a member of this group, with being "caught up in an NS-mode of thinking" no better than that of Robert Ritter.[80]

At times the reaction has bordered on paranoia and has affected writers close to the cause of the Gypsies. For example, Joachim S. Hohmann, author of several studies written with great sympathy for the Gypsy people, in 1984 brought out a book of stories collected by Jenische author Engelbert Wittich (1878–1937). The work was entitled *Bravo Sinto! Lebensspuren deutscher Zigeuner* and was published by the well-known Fischer publishing house. The Zentralrat was apparently displeased by the portrayal of Gypsy daily life in these stories and launched a vigorous protest campaign. Wittich was accused of having been a Nazi informer (an entirely baseless charge), and the publisher was threatened with the occupation of its premises and a suit for damages unless the book was withdrawn. This campaign of intimidation was successful. The publisher recalled the 6,000 printed copies from the bookstores and had them destroyed. In a documentation on this affair published two years later, Hohmann expressed the fear that from now on publications in this field could become "subject to the self-appointed control exercised by a small circle of Gypsy representatives."[81]

Fortunately for the cause of disinterested scholarship, Hohmann's concern turned out to be excessively pessimistic. This is shown by the outcome of another more recent attempt by the Zentralrat to enforce its version of political correctness. The international committee of survivors of the Buchenwald concentration camp had planned a conference on the history of the camp for early October 1996 and had invited historian Michael Zimmermann, author of the first comprehensive scholarly work on Nazi persecution of the Gypsies. Romani Rose, the chairman of the Zentralrat, thereupon protested the invitation to the minister for science, research and culture of the state of Thüringen and asked for its cancellation. Zimmermann, he charged, denied the program of genocide planned against the Gypsies and defamed the survivors by using and accepting as reality Nazi categories such as "asocials" and "preventive crime fighting." These allegations were put forth without any substantiating evidence and indeed were completely unfounded. To his credit, the minister rejected the Zentralrat's request as interfering with the freedom of teaching and research, as did the directors of the Buchenwald memorial, cosponsors of the conference. "History in a democratic society," they declared, "is not the property of individual persons or organized interest groups. . . . The victims of National Socialism deserve our special respect. [However], the associations of victims do not have a special right to determine what is historically true or false."[82] The conference took place as planned; the Zentralrat declined to participate.

The Gypsy community of Germany is better organized than any other such community in Europe, yet the use of questionable tactics has cost the Zentralrat potentially valuable allies.[83] The attempt to prevent the exploration of all aspects of Gypsy history, in particular, is self-defeating in the long run. The examination of the Kripo's role in the persecution of the Gypsies, for example, should not be shunned because Gypsies worry about being stigmatized as criminals, since they were dealt with by the Kripo rather than the Gestapo. Terms employed by the Nazis such as "asocials" and "preventive crime fighting" cannot be ignored; they must be put into their proper context rather than declared tabu. As Michael Zimmermann has correctly stressed, failure to confront the past honestly can only perpetuate the trauma of the victims and their descendants.[84]

14

Conclusion: The Course of
Persecution Assessed

In this concluding chapter I review the overall course of the persecution of
the Gypsies by the Nazi regime in order to discuss three issues: (1) the
development and gradual radicalization of Nazi policy toward the Gypsies,
(2) the question of whether the mass killings that eventually took place
should be considered genocide and (3) the difference between the persecution of the Gypsies and the Jewish Holocaust, with which the Gypsies' experience has often been compared. The three sections of the chapter examine
the same set of historical events but raise different questions of interpretation about these occurrences.

From Harassment to Mass Murder

The numerically small Gypsy population was at first of no particular interest
to the Nazi leadership and Hitler's government. It was in great measure as a
result of pressure from below—local and state officials as well as party rank
and file—that the regime began to address what became known as the "Gypsy
problem." Policy toward the Gypsies evolved through several stages, each following the other more or less consecutively. During the first four years of the
regime, local and state authorities continued and intensified the measures of
control and harassment that they had used since the turn of the century and
during the Weimar Republic. In the second phase, beginning in 1937, Gypsies
were caught up in the program of crime prevention that led to "preventive
police custody" served in concentration camps. The third phase got under way
in late 1938 with Himmler's Fight against the Gypsy Plague decree, which for

the first time made explicit use of racial criteria. Hitler himself played practically no role in the course of persecution, which unfolded in a disorderly manner and without a clear and dominating intent or plan.

Reflecting the preoccupations of the different actors involved, each of these three approaches to the "Gypsy problem" stressed different reasons for imposing punitive measures on the Gypsy population. Local, state and police officials emphasized the alleged asocial conduct of the Gypsies and the prevention of crime. Party stalwarts and many "race scientists" invoked the racial factor and the need to protect the "purity" of "German blood." Much of the incoherence of Nazi policy toward the Gypsies arose from the fact that these different elements were never successfully merged and at times conflicted with each other. Although it was considered axiomatic that the alleged asocial conduct of the Gypsy had roots in the racial inferiority of the *Zigeunermischlinge* (Gypsies of mixed ancestry), socially adjusted Gypsies, including *Mischlinge*, could and often indeed were exempted from various restrictive provisions and punitive measures such as deportation and sterilization. Despite the Nazis' fixation upon racial criteria and characteristics, social adjustment could override racial origin. In fact, in many instances when the racial makeup of an individual could not be ascertained with certitude, social status became normative and was relied upon to determine the degree of racial purity or contamination, thus in effect reversing the causal chain. However arbitrary the labeling of individual Gypsies as "asocial" or "socially adjusted" may have been in many instances, the very use of these criteria shows that social conduct played an important role in Nazi policy toward the Gypsies.

The importance of social conduct, irrespective of racial affiliation is further demonstrated by the treatment of so-called Gypsy-like itinerants, the "white Gypsies" (Jenische). Many of the measures directed against the Gypsies were also applied against the Jenische, even though they were considered of German extraction. For example, in September 1941, the RKPA instructed local Kripo offices to ascertain whether persons initially classified as Gypsies but later found to be Jenische could be subjected to preventive police custody authorized for asocials under the Ministry of Interior decree of December 14, 1937.[1] In some places, notably Bavaria, the Jenische were seen as a bigger problem than the Gypsies. As late as May 19, 1943, the Munich Kripo issued an order regarding identity cards that was directed against "Gypsies, Zigeuner-Mischlinge and Gypsy-like itinerants."[2] We do not know how many Jenische actually ended up in concentration camps, for as a rule neither the police nor the camps listed Jenische as a special subcategory of asocials.[3] Only the Austrian camp Weyer (district Braunau/Inn) did record the incarceration of Gypsy-like itinerants in 1941.[4] An attempt to learn more about the fate of the Jenische under the Nazi regime was recently started in Switzerland, the only European country in which the Jenische have their own organization.[5]

The onset of the war brought a tightening of the net. Gypsies were no longer allowed to itinerate or leave their place of enforced residence without special permission. They were subjected to compulsory labor, dismissed from the armed forces and generally treated as social outcasts. A program to "resettle" all the Gypsies in the newly acquired territories in the East had to be abandoned because of the logistic logjam created by the resettlement of large numbers of ethnic Germans. Still, 2,500 Gypsies were sent to the General Government in May 1940. Five thousand Gypsies from the Ostmark (Austria), considered particularly "asocial," were deported to Lodz (Litzmannstadt) in November 1941. These deportations were part of a plan to rid the Reich of Gypsies by sending them East. An undeterminable number of those "resettled" in the General Government died due to the harsh living conditions. All of the deportees from the Ostmark perished in a typhus epidemic or were murdered in gas vans. Still, these deaths or killings were not part of a general plan for the physical annihilation of the Gypsies. This conclusion is strengthened by actions taken in August 1944. When the General Government was evacuated before the advancing Red Army, many "resettled" Gypsies were treated like other Germans and were given papers certifying their right to return to Germany.

Following the German invasion of the Soviet Union, Gypsies there were targeted as a blanket category (like Jews and Communist functionaries) of people who were to be destroyed. Yet since the main reason for subjecting the Soviet Gypsies to the murderous actions of the roving *Einsatzgruppen* (special task forces) was their alleged tendency to spy, in practice most of the victims were itinerating Gypsies. Sedentary and "socially adjusted" Gypsies in many instances were able to survive; they often benefited from the bureaucratic chaos and struggle between rival offices and organizations that characterized German rule in the occupied Eastern territories. In German-occupied Serbia, local military commanders included male Gypsies among the thousands of Jews shot in reprisals for the uprisings organized by the partisan movement; women and children were spared. In both cases, racial considerations were largely unimportant. "Pure" Gypsies and Mischlinge were treated the same way. Again, these killings were not part of an overall plan to exterminate all Gypsies.

In December 1942, Himmler ordered the deportation of large numbers of allegedly asocial Zigeunermischlinge to a special Gypsy camp in Auschwitz. "Racially pure" Gypsies and "good Mischlinge" were declared exempt as were several other categories such as "socially adjusted" Gypsies and those legally married to "persons of German blood." This mass deportation of more than 13,000 men, women and children was designed finally to get rid of the "bad Mischlinge" by removing them from the Reich, and probably took place at least in part in response to increasing demands from officials and population alike to do something about "the Gypsy problem." The deportees were kept in a family camp until the spring and summer of 1944, when those able to work were sent back to German concentration camps. Children, the elderly and the sick were gassed. Although the number of Gypsies who perished or were killed in Auschwitz is very high, there is no evidence that the deportation was part of a larger plan to destroy the Gypsies. The fact that a substantial percentage of Gypsies, perhaps even a majority, were exempted from deportation and the treatment that the deportees received, spending almost a year and a half in the Gypsy family camp of Auschwitz, suggest that no such a plan existed. It is possible that had it not been for the overcrowding of the gas chambers and the need to find temporary housing for the doomed Hungarian Jews, the killing of Gypsies who were deemed not suitable for work would never have taken place.

Despite the many inconsistencies and stop-and-go phases of Nazi Gypsy policy there were two goals all the decision makers eventually came to agree upon: (1) getting rid of the "bad Zigeunermischlinge" by sending them away or putting them into work camps and (2) sterilizing as many as possible of those allowed to stay in the Reich in order to halt their propagation and prevent the contamination of "pure German blood." The various deportations to the East as well as the sterilization program are best explained by these two aims, which represented the lowest common denominator for actors as diverse in their background and thinking as Ritter, Nebe and Himmler.

The radicalization of Nazi policy toward the Jews has been attributed in part to the brutalizing effect of the war in the East, which gave rise to widespread moral callousness and provided rationalizations for an increasingly murderous policy toward the real and putative enemies of the Reich. There was also a feeling among the Nazi leadership that wartime conditions furnished a cover against unwelcome scrutiny and thus created an opportunity that had to be exploited. Last, rivalry between state and party agencies, as well as between the central leadership in Berlin and the authorities in the occupied territories, has been cited as another factor in the process of radicalization culminating in the Final Solution.[6] All of these factors, and especially the rivalry between different factions in the Nazi state, probably played a role in the development of Nazi policy toward the Gypsies as well. At the same time it is also true that the polycratic character of the Nazi dictatorship and the administrative disorder resulting therefrom at times led to delays in the implementation of policy decisions and therefore worked in favor of the Gypsies. The chaotic administrative situation in Nazi Germany's colonial empire in the East is a case in point.

The Issue of Genocide

No precise count of the number of German and Austrian Gypsies who perished during the reign of the Nazis is possible. Estimates based on the numbers sent to concentration camps, deported to the East and known to have been killed by gas yield figures that range between 15,000 and 22,000 out of a population of about 29,000 in 1942.[7] When it comes to the number of European Gypsies who lost their life as a result of Nazi rule, the situation is even more difficult because for most countries we have no good statistics on the size of the Gypsy population in the pre-Nazi period. In their book published in 1972, Kenrick and Puxon estimated the total number of Gypsy victims in Nazi-occupied Europe in 1939–1945 as 219,000 out of a prewar population of close to 1 million. In 1989, Kenrick lowered this estimate to 196,000 killed out of a population of 831,000.[8] Michael Zimmermann speaks of at least 90,000 killed in the territories controlled by the Nazis.[9] Unfortunately, most of these figures will have to remain more or less firm estimates and no exact count will ever be attainable.

Whatever estimate is accepted, the losses in life experienced by the Gypsy community at the hands of the Nazis are clearly horrendous. The Zentralrat, the main voice of the German Gypsies, has put forth even higher figures. More than 25,000 German and Austrian Gypsies are said to have been killed by the Nazis. "The number of Roma and Sinti murdered in Europe until the end of the war in concentration camps and by the SS-Einsatzgruppen is estimated as one half million."[10] No sources or breakdown by country have been provided for this estimate, which renders it of questionable value. Still, this number has become generally accepted in popular discourse and beyond. Official spokesmen for the government of the Federal Republic regularly speak of a half million Gypsies killed by the Nazis. The assertion of the Zentralrat that Nazi treatment of the Gypsies constituted genocide has also been widely endorsed.[11] In this country too some scholars have argued that "the Gypsies were a target for total genocide."[12]

The Convention on the Prevention and Punishment of the Crime of Genocide was approved by the General Assembly of the United Nations on December 9, 1948. It went into effect on January 12, 1951, and since 1948 has been ratified by 120 countries. In line with the view of the jurist Raphael Lemkin, who coined the term "genocide" from the Greek word *genos* (race or tribe) and the Latin suffix *cide* (to kill), the convention is not limited to the physical destruction of an entire people. It defines as genocide a series of "acts committed with intent to destroy, in whole or in part, a national, ethnical, racial or religious group, as such." These acts include "causing serious bodily or mental harm," inflicting upon a group "conditions of life calculated to bring about its physical destruction in whole or in part," as well as measures "intended to prevent births."[13] The intent was to outlaw as criminal not only a master plan for the extermination of an entire people such as the Final Solution of the Jewish Question. For example, Nazi occupiers treated the Slavs in a way that was designed to turn the Poles and Russians into permanent slaves of the Germanic master race, which would also constitute genocide.

The definition of genocide in the convention involves shortcomings noted by many critics, not the least of which is the failure to spell out the meaning of "in part." What percentage or part of a group must be affected by the various destructive acts enumerated in the convention in order to trigger the crime of genocide?[14] In the absence of an answer to this question the convention has a rather sweeping scope, and at least some measures taken by the Nazis against the Gypsies can be considered genocidal.

In order to establish the commission of the crime of genocide, an "intent" to destroy a group "as such" in whole or in part must be present. Hence, in my view, the various deportations of Gypsies to the East and their deadly consequences do not constitute acts of genocide. These deportations, including the deportation to the Gypsy camp at Auschwitz, were put into effect not out of an intent to destroy the Gypsies as such but in order to expel large numbers of this widely despised minority from Germany. As I have pointed out, neither the mass gassings in Chelmno nor in Auschwitz took place in order to annihilate the Gypsies as a defined group. Based on a vicious utilitarian calculus, these killings were carried out to achieve Nazi-type solutions to specific local situations—preventing the spread of typhus and making room for the doomed Hungarian Jews, respectively. Undoubtedly, the resort to murder presupposed the belief that the Gypsies constituted an inferior group of people whose lives were fully dispensable; remedies other than the cold-blooded murder of perfectly innocent men, women and children would surely have been available. Still, these acts of murder were not part of a plan to destroy the Gypsy people as such. Whatever the moral depravity and criminality of these deeds, they do not constitute genocide within the meaning of the genocide convention. Neither do they represent genocide in terms of other revisionist definitions of genocide, practically all of which affirm that any mass killings, to be considered genocide, must be part of a more encompassing program of extermination directed against an entire group of people.[15]

All German prosecutors investigating these events have come to the same conclusion. In the trial of the Auschwitz SS block leader Ernst-August König, which ended with a sentence of life imprisonment in 1991, the prosecution dropped the charge of participation in a general program of extermination of the Gypsies on the ground that no order for carrying out such a program had been proven.[16] The same finding was reached in the rather forthright probe in the case of Ruth Kellermann, which ended in May 1989. The Auschwitz decree, the Hamburg prosecutor concluded, did not aim at the mass killing of Gypsies. "As regards the Gypsies, there is lacking a clear and traceable chain of orders, analogous to the order for the 'Final Solution of the Jewish Question.' And this conclusion is not contradicted by the occasional statements by important Nazi leaders such as Goebbels to the effect that one should make short shrift of the Gypsies."[17] Although it is possible to question the existence of "a clear and traceable chain of orders" culminating in the Final Solution, it is difficult to gainsay the prosecutor's conclusion that there is no evidence for the existence of a program to annihilate all Gypsies physically. The various measures taken against the Gypsies were discussed openly and left a lengthy paper trail. Hence we can be quite sure that no such plan was ever devised or put into effect.

The involuntary sterilizations of Gypsies carried out pursuant to the Auschwitz decree, on the other hand, can be considered acts of genocide within the meaning of the convention. Not all Gypsies were made subject to what has justifiably been called "biological death,"[18] and the aim was as much to prevent the contamination of "German blood" as to halt the propagation of the Zigeunermischlinge. Still, these actions do fulfill the letter of the convention, which forbids "measures intended to prevent births" within a targeted group. The individuals caught up in this manifestly illegal program were not killed; yet without the prospect of descendants, they were the victims of "delayed genocide."[19]

Michael Zimmermann concludes that it is impossible to demonstrate the existence of an a priori program to destroy the Gypsies but nevertheless calls the brutal persecution of the Gypsies a genocide, a mass murder that was "methodically realized though not planned in advance."[20] Such a use of the term "genocide" would seem to involve a dilution of the concept. The convention, as I have shown, insists that there be present an "intent to destroy [a group], in whole or in part," and it is therefore problematic to speak of genocide without such an intent—or a program or plan for that matter. The planned involuntary sterilization of the Gypsies can be considered an act of genocide within the meaning of the genocide convention, but it is not the same as mass murder.

Some have conflated the terms "holocaust" and "genocide." The Zentralrat has called the genocide of the Gypsies a "holocaust," a "genocide motivated by racism, publicized ideologically, systematically planned, bureaucratically organized and executed as in a factory."[21] The purpose of invoking the concepts "holocaust" and "factory" is, of course, to equate the fate of the Gypsies and the Jews. In a new edition of their book *The Destiny of Europe's Gypsies*, published in 1995, Kenrick and Puxon argue similarly that "the ultimate aim of the Nazis was the elimination of all Gypsies" and that "the Holocaust . . . encompassed Jews and many other people."[22]

The Persecution of Gypsies and Jews Compared

Sybil Milton, a well-known student of Gypsy history under the Nazis, sees a clear parallel between the treatment of Gypsies and Jews. In an exchange with the prominent Holocaust scholar Yehuda Bauer, Milton stated her case in the following way:

> The Nazi genocide, popularly known as the Holocaust, can be defined as the mass murder of human beings because they belonged to a biologically defined group. Heredity determined the selection of the victims. The Nazi regime applied a consistent and inclusive policy of extermination—based on heredity—only against three groups of human beings: the handicapped, Jews, and Gypsies. The Nazis killed multitudes, including political opponents, members of the resistance, elites of conquered nations, but always based these murders on the beliefs, actions, and status of those victims. Different criteria applied only to the murder of the handicapped, Jews and Gypsies. Members of these groups could not escape their fate by changing their behavior or belief. They were selected because they existed, and neither loyalty to the German state, adherence to fascist

ideology, nor contribution to the war effort could alter the determination of the Nazi regime to exterminate them.[23]

At the time of this exchange in 1992, Yehuda Bauer maintained that "one must reserve judgment on the question of parallelism until some basic problems are cleared up. As things stand at the moment, it is clear that the attitude toward the Gypsies was a mixture of traditional anti-Gypsy prejudice and hatred on one hand, and racialist hallucinations on the other hand."[24] I believe that we now have sufficient evidence to resolve the question at issue and to reject the alleged parallelism. Nazi actions toward the Gypsies were not determined by "a consistent and inclusive policy of extermination — based on heredity," as Milton has argued. Although racial criteria certainly were invoked, especially from about 1938 on, they operated in a different way. With regard to the Jews, "pure Jews" were the symbol of eschatological evil that had to be destroyed, whereas Mischlinge were treated somewhat better. In the case of the Gypsies, it was the other way around. Mischlinge were seen as the dangerous and asocial element whereas "pure Gypsies" and "good Mischlinge," under the Auschwitz decree, were exempted from deportation and sterilization. Large numbers of Gypsies from the Reich, perhaps even a majority, escaped deportation to the East. The criterion of social adjustment played an important role in the selection process; Gypsies were not selected for extermination "because they existed."

Most important, no overall plan for the extermination of the Gypsy people was ever formulated, and, as argued above, the evidence shows that none was implemented. The order for the Final Solution too is not embodied in a written record, and there is even a question whether there ever was one specific order.[25] Still, the major elements of the decision-making process leading up to the annihilation of the Jews can be reconstructed from events, documents and testimony. Leading Nazi personalities as well as a host of minor functionaries — from Hitler and Himmler down to Hans Frank and officials in the Ministry for the Occupied Eastern Territories — repeatedly referred to the destruction of the Jews that was under way.[26] No such evidence exists in the case of the Gypsies, despite the fact that their persecution and the proceedings against them were far more public and transparent. In the final analysis, as Steven Katz has correctly concluded, "it was only Jews and the Jews alone who were the victims of a total genocidal onslaught in both intent and practice at the hands of the Nazi murderers."[27] Nazi policy toward the Gypsies lacked the kind of single-minded fanaticism that characterized the murderous assault upon the Jews. Entire categories of Gypsies, such as the "socially adjusted" and the "sedentary," were generally given more lenient treatment. The Gypsies were considered a "nuisance" and a "plague" but not a major threat to the German people, and that is why their treatment differed from that of the Jews.

The purpose of raising these issues is not to engage in what has been called the vulgar exercise of comparative victimization. As Lucy Dawidowicz has pointed out, to affirm the uniqueness of the murder of the 6 million Jews does not represent "an attempt to magnify the catastrophe that befell them nor to beg tears and pity for them. It is not intended to minimize the deaths of the millions of non-Jews that the Germans brought about, or to under-play the immeasurable and unendurable suffering of Russians, Poles, Gyp-sies, and other victims of the German murder machine."[28] The question is not whether the mass murder of the Jews during World War II is more evil than other abominations committed by the Nazis.[29] At stake, rather, is the accuracy of the historical record. What makes the murder of the Jews unique is not the number of victims but the intent of the murderers. Only in the case of the Jews did the Nazis seek to annihilate physically every man, woman and child. This program of total extermination therefore deserves its own appellation—Holocaust or the Hebrew Shoah. Although the term "genocide," as defined by the Genocide Convention, involves various acts designed to destroy a group in whole or in part and is not limited to killing, the term "Holocaust" stands for the attempted physical destruction of an entire people, pursued with relentless determination and, in its most lethal final phase, carried out with the mass-production methods of a modern fac-tory. Only the Jews were caught up in this kind of murderous enterprise. As Elie Wiesel has put it: "While not all victims [of the Nazis] were Jews, *all* Jews were victims, destined for annihilation solely because they were born Jewish."[30] Some Jewish Mischlinge and a limited number of Jews con-scripted for slave labor or released for ransom in the closing months of the war were allowed to escape death, but these were insignificant exceptions to a general policy of total annihilation.

The question of similarities in the Nazi persecution of the Gypsies and the Jews became a divisive issue in the planning of the U.S. Holocaust Memorial Museum in Washington. In the early 1980s, Ian Hancock, a pro-fessor of English and linguistics at the University of Texas and the U.S. rep-resentative of the International Romani Union to the United Nations, pressed for Gypsy representation on the Holocaust Memorial Council as well as for appropriate inclusion of the Nazi genocide against the Gypsies in the exhibits of the museum. According to Hancock, the Gypsies too had been murdered simply because of who they were. It was the survival of old stereotypes that prevented wider knowledge of the Gypsies' suffering. By including the story of what in Romani is called the *Porrajmos*, the "great devouring," in the museum, Hancock argued, it would become possible to broaden historical understanding and draw attention to continuing violence against Gypsies in Eastern Europe and beyond.[31]

In 1985, the Holocaust Memorial Council appointed Hancock to the newly created post of special adviser to the council on Gypsy matters. In 1987, William Duna of St. Thomas University in Minnesota became the first Gypsy representative on the council. The council also commissioned Gabrielle Tyrnauer, a professor of anthropology at the University of Ver-mont and Concordia University in Montreal, to write a report on the Gypsy experience in World War II. Tyrnauer concluded that both Gypsies and Jews had been "targeted for total annihilation."[32]

Tyrnauer's report was marred by poor scholarship. For example, although she reproduced in an appendix parts of the implementing regulations for the Auschwitz decree, including the listing of the groups exempted from deportation, in the body of her report she maintained that the Auschwitz decree of December 1942 sent "all Gypsies, regardless of group or status or degree of assimilation to the death camp."[33] Sybil Milton, whose work has been more careful, was then holding the position of senior historian at the Holocaust Memorial Museum. She proposed that the museum adopt an inclusive definition of the Holocaust and that the exhibition fully integrate the fate of the Gypsies. This was not done. References to Gypsy victims appear in various places in the permanent exhibition, but the exhibits also show that their experience differed from the Jewish experience. Despite criticism from Hancock, Milton and others, the Holocaust Memorial Museum has not adopted parallel persecutions of the Gypsies and the Jews.[34]

The discussion of whether Gypsies and Jews were the victims of the same murderous persecution has been accompanied by much rancor and ad hominem attacks. Some historians, Hancock has alleged, "see only what they want to see" and turn "a blind eye . . . in the direction of Gypsy history."[35] Some Jewish Holocaust scholars, he has written, harbor "anti-Gypsy attitudes."[36] After his appointment to the Holocaust Memorial Council, Duna charged the council with "overt racism" and called it a body that had "willfully downplayed" Romani suffering.[37] Milton has maintained that "Mr. Bauer uses as evidence to support his interpretation the rationalizations and the language used by the Nazis in their drive to exterminate the Gypsies."[38] As I noted in chapter 13, the discussion in Germany has been no less heated. Those who deny that the Nazis sought to destroy both Gypsies and Jews with the same murderous zeal have been accused of seeking "to prevent both legal and moral restitution in the Federal Republic."[39]

This way of discussing a complex historical question is not helpful, and progress in clarifying intricate historical realities is set back when some of the persons making these charges themselves engage in unworthy tactics of persuasion. The assertion that a half million Gypsies died under Nazi rule is put forth regularly without any kind of substantiating evidence, yet those who question the reliability of this figure are accused of minimizing the suffering of the Gypsy people. Hancock has quoted from the Auschwitz decree the sentence that "all Gypsies are to be deported to the Zigeunerlager at Auschwitz concentration camp, with no regard to their degree of racial impurity,"[40] even though no text of this decree has survived. Moreover, the implementing regulations, which we do have, specifically exempted "racially pure Gypsies."

The Gypsy people suffered terribly under the Nazi regime, and there really is no need to exaggerate the horrors they experienced. In order to comprehend fully what happened and why it happened we must pay attention not only to the decisions and decrees issued by the perpetrators but also to the attitudes of the German people to the Gypsy minority. Simplified accounts according to which "Gypsies, like the Jews, were persecuted and annihilated simply and solely on account of their biological existence"[41] are not only a distortion of the historical record but also a hindrance to progress in the relationship between Gypsies and non-Gypsies. Only if we understand why the Gypsies were regarded by all strata of German society with so much distrust and hostility will we be able to confront the sources of such propensities and prevent their recurrence.

Abbreviations and Glossary

Abt.	Abteilung (department)
Ahnenerbe	Ancestral Heritage (an institute created by Himmler for research on the "Germanic race")
Altreich	Germany before the annexation of Austria
Anschluss	Annexation of Austria by Germany in 1938
BA	Bundesarchiv (Federal Archives)
BA-MA	Bundesarchiv-Militärarchiv (Federal Archives-Military Archives)
Bd.	Band (volume)
Bezirk	An administrative unit
Bundesgerichtshof	Federal court of justice
DM	Deutsche Mark
DÖW	Dokumentationsarchiv des österrreichischen Widerstandes (Archive of the Austrian resistance)
EG	Einsatzgruppe (Special task force of the Security Police and SD)
EK	Einsatzkommando (a detachment of an Einsatzgruppe, q.v.)
Feldkommandantur	Field commander (a military post in an occupied territory)
Gau	One of forty-two territorial divisions of the Nazi party
Gauleiter	The Nazi party official heading a Gau (q.v.)
Generalgouvernement	Government General (a part of German-occupied Poland)
Generalkommissar	Official in charge of a German-occupied region (Generalbezirk)

Gestapo	Geheime Staatspolizei (Secret State Police)
GFP	Geheime Feldpolizei (Secret Field Police)
Gruppenführer	SS rank corresponding to major-general
GS	Gedenkstätte (memorial)
Hauptsturmführer	SS rank corresponding to captain
HMM	U.S. Holocaust Memorial Museum
HSSPF	Höherer SS- und Polizeiführer (Senior SS and Police Commander)
HSTA	Hauptstaatsarchiv (Main State Archive)
IfZ	Institut für Zeitgeschichte (Institute of Contemporary History)
IMT	International Military Tribunal
Jenische	Gypsy-like itinerants, a.k.a. "white Gypsies"
Kreis	An administrative district
Kreisleiter	A salaried party official responsible for a Kreis (q.v.)
Kripo	Kriminalpolizei (Criminal Police)—the detective force
Land (pl. Länder)	One of fifteen territorial divisions of Germany until 1945 similar to American states; under the Nazi regime they were effectively run by the government in Berlin.
Landfahrer	Travelers
Landkreis	Rural subdivision of a Regierungsbezirk (q.v.)
Landrat	The chief magistrate of a Landkreis (q.v.)
LHA	Landeshauptarchiv (Main Land Archive)
MInn	Ministerium des Innern (Ministry of the Interior)
Mischlinge	Persons of mixed ancestry
NA	National Archives
Nr.	Nummer (Number)
NSDAP	Nationalsozialistische Deutsche Arbeiter Partei (National Socialist German Workers Party)
NSV	Nationalsozialistische Volkswohlfahrt (National Socialist People's Welfare Organization)
Oberführer	SS rank corresponding to senior colonel
Obergruppenführer	SS rank corresponding to lieutenant-general
Obersturmführer	SS rank corresponding to 1st lieutenant
OKH	Oberkommando des Heeres (High Command of the German Army)
OKW	Oberkommando der Wehrmacht (High Command of the Armed Forces)
Ordnungspolizei	Order Police (regular uniformed police force)
ÖSTA	Österreichisches Staatsarchiv (Austrian State Archive)
Ostland	German name for the occupied Baltic states

Ostmark	The name given to Austria after its annexation in 1938
Regierungsbezirk	Administrative subdivision of a province analogous to a county
Regierungspräsident	The senior government official in a Regierungsbezirk (q.v.)
Reichsarbeitsdienst	Reich Labor Corps
Reichsführer-SS	Himmler's official title as head of the SS
RFSSuChdDPol.	Reichsführer-SS und Chef der Deutschen Polizei (Himmler's title as head of the SS and chief of the German police)
Reichskommissar	Official in charge of a German-occupied territory (Reichskommissariat)
Reichsstatthalter	The governor of a Land (q.v.)
RG	Record Group
RGBl	Reichsgesetzblatt (German Law Gazette)
RKPA	Reichskriminalpolizeiamt (Reich Criminal Police Office)
RM	Reichsmark
Rottenführer	SS rank corresponding to corporal
RSHA	Reichssicherheitshauptamt (Reich Main Security Office)
SA	Sturmabteilung (lit., Storm Detachment—the paramilitary organization of the Nazi party)
SD	Sicherheitsdienst (lit., Security Service—the Nazi party's intelligence service)
Sicherheitspolizei	Security Police (the police force that included the Gestapo and the Kripo)
Sonderkommando	Special detachment
SS	Schutzstaffel (lit., Guard Squadron—the Nazi party's elite force)
STA	Staatsarchiv (State Archive)
StA	Stadtarchiv (Municipal Archive)
Standartenführer	SS rank corresponding to colonel
Untermenschen	Subhumans
Warthegau	The western part of Poland annexed to Germany
Wehrmacht	The armed forces during the Third Reich (army, air force, navy)
Zigeunermischlinge	Gypsies of mixed ancestry
Zigeunerzentrale	Central Office for Gypsy Affairs
ZSL	Zentrale Stelle der Landesjustizverwaltungen (Central Office for the Prosecution of Nazi Crimes)

Notes

Introduction

1. Jean Pierre Liégeois, *Gypsies and Travellers* (Strasbourg, 1987), pp. 13–15; Angus Fraser, *The Gypsies* (Oxford, 1992), pp. 12–14, 39–40.

2. Cf. Ines Köhler-Zülch, "Die verweigerte Herberge: Die Heilige Familie in Ägypten und andere Geschichten von 'Zigeunern'—Selbstäusserungen oder Aussenbilder?" In *Die gesellschaftliche Konstruktion der Zigeuner: Zur Genese eines Vorurteils*, ed. Jacqueline Giere (Frankfurt/Main, 1996), pp. 46–86.

3. For example, Hermann Cornerus, *Chronica novella* (1435), quoted in Fraser, *Gypsies*, p. 67.

4. Liégeois, *Gypsies and Travellers*, p. 130.

5. Reimer Gronemeyer, *Zigeuner im Spiegel früherer Chroniken und Abhandlungen: Quellen vom 15. bis 18. Jahrhundert* (Giessen, 1987), p. 157.

6. Fraser, *Gypsies*, p. 129.

7. Joachim Stephen Hohmann, *Verfolgte ohne Heimat: Geschichte der Zigeuner in Deutschland* (Frankfurt/Main, 1990), p. 14; Fraser, *Gypsies*, p. 154.

8. Fraser, *Gypsies*, pp. 151–54.

9. Ibid., p. 155.

10. Ibid., pp. 248–49; George L. Mosse, *The Crisis of German Ideology: Intellectual Origins of the Third Reich* (New York, 1964), pp. 90–95.

11. Cesare Lombroso, *Die Ursachen und Bekämpfung des Verbrechens* (Berlin, 1902), pp. 34–36.

12. Eva Strauss, "Die Zigeunerverfolgung in Bayern: 1885–1926," *Giessener Hefte zur Tsiganalogie* 3 (1986): 39.

13. Ibid., pp. 40–42.

14. Ibid., pp. 44–46.

15. Ibid., pp. 50–52; Leo Lucassen, *Zigeuner: Die Geschichte eines polizeilichen Ordnungsbegriffes in Deutschland, 1700–1945* (Cologne, 1996), pp. 33–34, 255.

16. STA Ludwigsburg, FL 20/10, Bü. 145.

17. Ibid., F 176/II, Bü. 930.

18. Cf. Hermann Arnold, *Die Zigeuner: Herkunft und Leben der Stämme im deutschen Sprachgebiet* (Olten, 1965). Despite his bias against Gypsies, many of Arnold's observations on the origins and life of the German Gypsies are informative and valuable.

19. HSTA Munich, MInn 72575. See also the discussion by Strauss, "Zigeunerverfolgung," pp. 53–58.

20. HSTA Munich, MA 100438. In a legal dissertation published in 1929, Werner Kurt Höhne argued that despite the inclusion of the travelers the Bavarian law violated the German constitution (*Die Vereinbarkeit der deutschen Zigeunergesetze und -verordnungen mit dem Reichsrecht, insbesondere der Reichsverfassung* [Heidelberg, 1929], p. 14).

21. The full text of the law is printed in Ludwig Eiber, *"Ich wusste es wird schlimm": Die Verfolgung der Sinti und Roma in München, 1933–1945* (Munich, 1993), pp. 43–45.

22. *Ministerial-Entscheidung zur Ausführung des Zigeuner- und Arbeitsscheuengesetz*, STA Munich, LRA 98851.

23. Eiber, *"Ich wusste es wird schlimm,"* pp. 42–43.

24. *Ministerial-Blatt für die Preussische innere Verwaltung-Ausgabe* A 88, no. 45 (November 9, 1927). This decree is part of a collection of measures directed against Gypsies, the Fojn-Felczer Collection, in the archive of the U.S. Holocaust Memorial Museum, Washington, D.C. (RG-07.005*01). The collection was put together by Anton Fojn, a survivor of ten Nazi concentration camps.

25. *Hessisches Regierungsblatt*, May 6, 1929, StA Giessen, L1363–65. For the text of laws and decrees adopted by other German states, see Höhne, *Vereinbarkeit*, pp. 104–206.

26. Fraser, *Gypsies*, p. 253.

27. The long chain of events is documented in the files of the StA Frankfurt, especially Magistratsakten 2203, vol. 1, and R24-no. 8, 1377–78.

28. Yale Strom, *Uncertain Roads: Searching for the Gypsies* (New York, 1993), p. 7; Mariana D. Birnbaum, "On the Language of Prejudice," *Western Folklore* 30 (1971): 262.

29. Introduction by Ian Hancock to David Crowe and John Kolsti, eds., *The Gypsies of Eastern Europe* (New York, 1991), p. 5.

30. Anne Sutherland, *Gypsies: The Hidden Americans* (New York, 1975), pp. 30, 21.

31. Jan Yoors, *The Gypsies* (New York, 1967), p. 51.

32. Martin Block, *Gypsies: Their Life and Their Customs* (London, 1938), p. 21. See also Isabel Fonseca, *Bury Me Standing: The Gypsies and Their Journey* (New York, 1995), who writes: "Gypsies lie. *They lie a lot*—more often and more inventively than other people" (p. 15).

33. Sutherland, *Gypsies*, p. 73.

34. Yoors, *Gypsies*, p. 34.

35. Manfri Frederick Wood, *In the Life of a Romany Gypsy* (London, 1973), pp. 59, 37.

36. Engelbert Wittich, *Blicke in das Leben der Zigeuner* (Hamburg, 1927), pp. 57–58.

37. On the problem of evaluating such tales generally, see Wilhelm Solms, "On the Demonizing of Jews and Gypsies in Fairy Tales," in *Sinti and Roma in German-Speaking Society and Literature*, ed. Susan Tebbutt (Providence, R.I., 1998), pp. 91–106.

38. This trick is described by Marta Adler, who was married to several German Gypsies, in her book *My Life with the Gypsies* (London, 1960), p. 131. See also the account in *Deutsches Kriminalpolizeiblatt*, Nr. 1930, August 16, 1934.

39. Police report on the arrest of Friederike M. on August 18, 1954, HSA Wiesbaden, Abt. 518, Nr. 4899.

40. Rainer Hehemann, *Die "Bekämpfung des Zigeunerunwesens" im Wilhelminischen Deutschland und in der Weimarer Republik, 1871–1933* (Frankfurt/Main, 1987), p. 410.

41. Yoors, *Gypsies*, p. 138; Fonseca, *Bury Me Standing*, p. 35.

42. Cf. Judith Okely, *The Traveller-Gypsies* (Cambridge, 1983), p. 86; Sutherland, *Gypsies*, p. 271; Adler, *My Life with the Gypsies*, p. 58.

43. Fonseca, *Bury Me Standing*, p. 234.

44. Sutherland, *Gypsies*, p. 270.

45. Elisabeth Ferst, *Fertilität und Kriminalität der Zigeuner: Eine statistische Untersuchung* (M.D. diss., Munich, 1943). See also Hugo Herz, *Verbrechen und Verbrechertum in Österreich: Kritische Untersuchungen über Zusammenhänge von Wirtschaft und Verbrechen* (Tübingen, 1908), pp. 160–66.

Chapter 1

1. For the background and the provisions of the Bremen law I have relied on an unpublished manuscript dealing with the persecution of the Gypsies in the jurisdiction of the Bremen Kripo by Hans Hesse, especially pp. 42–44. See also Hans Döring, *Die Zigeuner im Nationalsozialistischen Staat* (Hamburg, 1964), pp. 46–47.

2. Letter of the minister of the interior to all police authorities in Baden, May 17, 1934, GLA Karlsruhe, 338/752, p. 1.

3. Decree of May 17, 1934, *Bekämpfung des Zigeunerunwesens*, sec. 4, GLA Karlsruhe, 357, Nr. 30.981.

4. Karl Siegfried Bader, "Bekämpfung des Zigeunerunwesens," *Kriminalistische Monatshefte* 9 (1935): 265–68.

5. *Ministerialblatt für die Badische Innere Verwaltung*, January 22, 1937, GLA Karlsruhe, 357/30.980.

6. Memo of Gendarmerie Mosbach, February 4, 1937, GLA Karlsruhe, 364 Zug 1975/3 II/25.

7. Döring, *Zigeuner im Nationalsozialistischen Staat*, pp. 47–48; Eiber, "*Ich wusste es wird schlimm*," p. 46.

8. HSA Munich, MInn 72578.

9. Ibid.

10. *Ministerialblatt für die Preussische Innere Verwaltung*, June 17, 1936, 785, reprinted in Wolfgang Wippermann, *Das Leben in Frankfurt zur NS-Zeit*, vol. 2, *Die nationalsozialistische Zigeunerverfolgung* (Frankfurt/Main, 1986), p. 68.

11. Wolfgang Ayass, "*Asoziale*" *im Nationalsozialismus* (Stuttgart, 1995), pp. 20–41.

12. Reichsstatthalter Franz von Epp to the Bavarian prime minister, March 20, 1934, BA Berlin, R 43 II/398.

13. HSA Munich, MInn 72578.

14. STA Ludwigsburg, F164/II, Bü 688.

15. The Polizeipräsident of Dortmund to the Regierungspräsident in Arnsberg, July 16, 1937, STA Münster, Reg. Arnsberg, Nr. 14547.

16. The Polizeipräsident of Bochum to the Regierungspräsident in Arnsberg, July 17, 1937, STA Münster, Reg. Arnsberg, Nr. 14547.

17. The Polizeipräsident of Dortmund to the Regierungspräsident in Arnsberg, August 18, 1938, STA Münster, Reg. Arnsberg, Nr. 14547.

18. Eberhard Jäckel, *Hitler's Weltanschauung: A Blueprint for Power* (Middletown, Conn., 1972), p. 59.

19. The Polizeipräsident of Cologne to the Polizeipräsident of Frankfurt, March 8, 1937, StA Frankfurt, Magistratsakten 2203, Bd. 1. The document is reprinted in Wippermann, *Leben in Frankfurt*, p. 77.

20. Karola Fings and Frank Sparing, "Das Zigeunerlager in Köln-Bickendorf, 1935–1958," *1999: Zeitschrift für Sozialgeschichte des 20. und 21.Jahrhunderts* 6, no. 3 (July 1991): 11–40.

21. The housing office of the welfare department to the mayor, January 17, 1938, StA Frankfurt, Magistratsakten 2203, Bd. 1. The document is reprinted in Wippermann, *Leben in Frankfurt*, pp. 77–78. See also Eva von Hase-Mihalik and Doris Kreuzkamp, "*Du kriegst auch einen schönen Wohnwagen*": *Zwangslager für Sinti und Roma während des Nationalsozialismus in Frankfurt am Main* (Frankfurt/Main, 1990).

22. See Karola Fings and Frank Sparing, "*z.Zt. Zigeunerlager*": *Die Verfolgung der Düsseldorfer Sinti und Roma im Nationalsozialismus* (Cologne, 1992), pp. 25–45.

23. Hohmann, *Verfolgte ohne Heimat*, p. 69.

24. Wolfgang Wippermann and Ute Brucker-Boroujerdi, "Nationalsozialistische Zwangslager in Berlin III: Das 'Zigeunerlager Marzahn,' " *Berliner Forschungen* 2 (1987): 189–94.

25. Ibid.

26. Hohmann, *Verfolgte ohne Heimat*, p. 71 (as in many other instances, Hohmann provides neither source nor precise date for this report).

27. See the sources cited by Michael Zimmermann, *Rassenutopie und Genozid: Die nationalsozialistische "Lösung der Zigeunerfrage"* (Hamburg, 1996), pp. 98–99.

28. The Polizeipräsident to the Oberbürgermeister, April 7, 1936, StA Karlsruhe, 1/H-Reg., Abt. A, Nr. 1391.

Chapter 2

1. Martin Broszat, "Nationalsozialistische Konzentrationslager 1933–1945," in *Anatomie des SS-Staates*, ed. Hans Buchheim, et al. (Munich, 1967), 67–68; George C. Browder, *Hitler's Enforcers: The Gestapo and the SS Security Service in the Nazi Revolution* (New York, 1996), p. 88.

2. Hans Bernd Gisevius, *Wo ist Nebe? Erinnerungen an Hitler's Reichskriminaldirektor* (Zurich, 1966), p. 102; [Bernd Wehner], "Das Spiel ist aus—Arthur Nebe: Glanz und Elend der deutschen Kriminalpolizei," *Der Spiegel*, November 17, 1949, p. 25, and December 1, 1949, p. 25.

3. Browder, *Hitler's Enforcers*, p. 91; Robert Gellately, *The Gestapo and German Society: Enforcing Racial Policy, 1933–1945* (Oxford, 1990), p. 69.

4. The *Grundlegender Erlass über die Vorbeugende Verbrechensbekämpfung durch die Polizei* of December 14, 1937, was not published in the official gazette; it was included in a collection of decrees marked "confidential" that were issued in 1941 by the Reichskriminalpolizeiamt. The collection is entitled *Vorbeugende Verbrechensbekämpfung* and is known as *Erlasssammlung Nr. 15*. A copy can be found at the Institut für Zeitgeschichte in Munich. There is no pagination; the decrees are ordered chronologically.

5. *Richtlinien des Reichskriminalpolizeiamtes über die Durchführung der vorbeugenden Verbrechensbekämpfung*, April 4, 1938, *Erlasssammlung Nr. 15*.

6. Ibid.

7. Addendum to a decree of May 13, 1938 by Himmler, forwarded to all police authorities in Baden in a memo of May 27, 1938, GLA Karlsruhe, 357/30.980.

8. Martin Broszat, *The Hitler State: The Foundation and Development of the Internal Structure of the Third Reich* (London, 1981), pp. 274–75.

9. Speech on the occasion of inaugurating a new building for the RKPA on August 31, 1939, quoted in Bernd Wehner, *Dem Täter auf der Spur: Die Geschichte der deutschen Kriminalpolizei* (Bergisch-Gladbach, 1983), p. 161.

10. Karl Dietrich Bracher, *The German Dictatorship: The Origins, Structure and Effects of National Socialism* (New York, 1970), pp. 352–53; Browder, *Hitler's Enforcers*, pp. 3–4.

11. Arthur Nebe, "Aufbau der deutschen Kriminalpolizei," *Kriminalistik* 12 (1938): 5, 7.

12. This bureau at first was part of Abt. II B 4; from 1939 on, it belonged to Group A, Referat A2 in Amt V (Reichskriminalpolizeiamt) of the Reichssicherheitshauptamt.

13. Its official name was Zigeunerpolizeistelle bei der Polizeidirektion München.

14. *Mitteilungsblatt des Reichskriminalpolizeiamtes* 1, no. 9 (September 1938): 72–73. A complete run of this gazette is available at the National Archives, Washington, D.C., Microfilm Publication T175, roll 433, frames 2963181–2964149.

15. These figures are included in a memo of the Zigeunerzentrale of April 25, 1938, cited by Eiber, *"Ich wusste es wird schlimm,"* p. 51.

16. *Ministerialblatt für die Preussische Innere Verwaltung* 1, no. 27 (June 17, 1936): 783. The decree is reprinted in Wippermann, *Nationalsozialistische Zigeunerverfolgung*, pp. 67–68.

17. *Schutzhaft gegen Arbeitsscheue*, January 26, 1938, *Erlasssammlung Nr. 15*. The decree is reprinted in Hans Buchheim, "Die Aktion 'Arbeitsscheu Reich,' " *Gutachten des Instituts für Zeitgeschichte* (Stuttgart, 1966), 2:189–91.

18. Hans Buchheim, "Die SS—das Herrschaftsinstrument," in *Anatomie des SS-Staates*, 2:77–78.

19. The lecture was given in January 1939 and can be found in Nuremberg documents NO-5591, NA Washington, RG 238, box 96. I have used the translation in Detlev J.K. Peukert, *Inside Nazi Germany: Conformity, Opposition, and Racism in Everyday Life*, trans. Richard Deveson (New Haven, Conn., 1987), p. 213.

20. *Erlasssammlung Nr. 15*.

21. Circular of the Gestapo office Magdeburg, February 26, 1938, LHA Magdeburg, Rep. C30, Wanzleben A, Nr. 106. Similar instructions are preserved from the Gestapo offices of Stuttgart (STA Ludwigsburg, F 164/II Bü 688) and Munich (IfZ, Fa 109).

22. Circular of the RKPA, April 20, 1938, *Erlasssammlung Nr. 15*.

23. Wolfgang Sofsky, *The Order of Terror: The Concentration Camp* (Princeton, N.J., 1997), p. 33.

24. *Vorbeugende Verbrechensbekämpfung durch die Polizei*, June 1, 1938, *Erlasssammlung Nr. 15*. The decree is reprinted in Buchheim, *Gutachten*, pp. 191–92.

25. *Erlasssammlung Nr. 15*.

26. See note 19. The *Jahrbuch Amt V Reichskriminalpolizeiamt des Reichssicherheitshauptamtes SS*, 1939/40, gives the figure of 8,892 asocials in preventive custody as of December 31, 1938 (BA Berlin, RD19/29).

27. Falk Pingel, *Häftlinge unter SS-Herrschaft: Widerstand, Selbstbehauptung und Vernichtung im Konzentrationslager* (Hamburg, 1978), p. 87.

28. The form filled out by the police for each arrested person had a special box in which the official physician had to certify "Lagerhaft- und Arbeitsfähigkeit."

29. Report of the Regierungspräsident, Aachen, to the Oberpräsident, Koblenz, July 29, 1938, HSA Düsseldorf, BR 1050/735.

30. Report of the Polizeipräsident to the Regierungspräsident, Arnsberg, August 18, 1938, STA Münster, Reg. Arnsberg, Nr. 14547.

31. Report of the Landrat of Verden to the Regierungspräsident, Stade, July 7, 1938, Kreisarchiv Verden 3/15b, cited by Hesse, unpublished manuscript, p. 319.

32. Report of the Amtshauptmann of Cloppenburg to the Kripo in Bremen, July 9, 1938, StA Oldenburg, Best. 231–6, Nr. 56, cited by Hesse, pp. 373–74.

33. ZSL Ludwigsburg, 414 AR 540/83, vol. 4.

34. Ayass, *Asoziale im Nationalsozialismus*, p. 166.

35. This figure, given by Zimmermann, *Rassenutopie und Genozid*, p. 118, is taken from the state archive in Weimar. Donald Kenrick and Gratton Puxon in their book, *The Destiny of Europe's Gypsies* (New York, 1972), p. 168, claim, without documentation, that in "June 1938 1,000 Gypsy men and boys from Germany entered Buchenwald." In view of the figures we have on the number of Gypsies arrested in several major German cities, the figure of 1,000 for Buchenwald alone is unlikely to be correct.

36. GS Sachsenhausen, R 201, M 3, p. 252, cited in Ayass, *Asoziale*, p. 197.

37. LHA Magdeburg, C 29 Anh. 2, Nr. 152.

38. Ibid., Nr. 350.

39. Ibid., Nr. 242/1.

40. Ibid., Nr. 43.

41. Ibid., Nr. 156/1.

42. Ibid., Nr. 89.

43. Ibid., Nr. 134.

44. Ibid., Nr. 135/II.

45. Ibid., Nr. 161.

46. Buchheim, "Die SS," p. 78.

47. *Erlasssammlung Nr. 15.*

48. Zimmermann, *Rassenutopie und Genozid*, p. 119.

49. *Erlasssammlung Nr. 15.*

50. LHA Magdeburg, C 29 Anh. 2, Nr. 98, 98/I.

51. HSA Düsseldorf, BR 2034, Nr. 413.

52. LHA Magdeburg, C 29 Anh. 2, Nr. 127.

53. Ibid., Nr. 142.

54. Implementing regulations for decree *Bekämpfung der Zigeunerplage, Erlasssammlung Nr. 15.* The decree and the regulations will be discussed in detail in the next chapter.

55. LHA Magdeburg, C 29 Anh. 2, Nr. 242/1.

56. Ibid., Nr. 245.

57. IfZ, Fa–109.

58. LHA Magdeburg, C 29 Anh. 2, Nr. 231.

59. Ibid., Nr. 258. For a case in which Witte's intervention was not successful, see Nr. 141. In the case of Nr. 350, the outcome is not known.

Chapter 3

1. Sheila Faith Weiss, *Race Hygiene and National Efficiency: The Eugenics of Wilhelm Schallmeyer* (Berkeley, Calif., 1987), p. 148; Michael Burleigh and Wolfgang Wippermann, *The Racial State: Germany, 1933–1945* (Cambridge, 1991), p. 31.

2. Michael H. Kater, *Doctors under Hitler* (Chapel Hill, N.C., 1989), p. 112.

3. George L. Mosse, *Toward the Final Solution: A History of European Racism* (New York, 1978), p. 76.

4. Robert Proctor, *Racial Hygiene: Medicine under the Nazis* (Cambridge, Mass., 1988), p. 38; Benno Müller-Hill, *Murderous Science: Elimination by Scientific Selection of Jews, Gypsies, and Others* (New York, 1988), p. 22.

5. *Grundriss der Menschlichen Erblichkeitslehre und Rassenhygiene*, 2d ed. (Munich, 1923).

6. Benno Müller-Hill, "Human Genetics in Nazi Germany," in *Medicine, Ethics and the Third Reich: Historical and Contemporary Issues*, ed. John J. Michalczyk (Kansas City, Mo., 1994), p. 29. For a discussion of Hitler's eugenic ideas, see Paul Weindling, *Health, Race and German Politics between National Unification and Nazism, 1870–1945* (Cambridge, 1989), pp. 490–92.

7. Robert Gaupp, *Die Unfruchtbarmachung geistig und sittlich Kranker und Minderwertiger* (Berlin, 1925), p. 25, cited by Gisela Bock, *Zwangssterilisation im Nationalsozialismus: Studien zur Rassenpolitik und Frauenpolitik* (Opladen, 1986), p. 361, n. 131.

8. Hans-Walter Schmuhl, *Rassenhygiene, Nationalsozialismus, Euthanasie: Von der Verhütung zur Vernichtung "lebensunwerten Lebens," 1890–1945* (Göttingen, 1987), p. 101.

9. Weiss, *Race Hygiene and National Efficiency*, pp. 152–53;

10. Stefan Kühl, *The Nazi Connection: Eugenics, American Racism and German National Socialism* (New York, 1994), p. 39.

11. *Gesetz zur Verhütung erbkranken Nachwuchses*, Reichsgesetzblatt 1 (1933): 529; the full text of the law is reproduced in Monika Daum and Hans-Ulrich Deppe, *Zwangssterilisation in Frankfurt am Main, 1933–1945* (Frankfurt/Main, 1991), pp. 184–87.

12. Jürgen Simon, "Die Erbgesundheitsgerichtsbarkeit im OLG-Bezirk Hamm: Rechtsprechung zwischen juristischen Vorgaben und ideologischen Anforderungen," in *Juristische Zeitgeschichte*, vol. 1, *Justiz und Nationalsozialismus* (Düsseldorf, 1993), p. 140.

13. Hansjörg Riechert, *Im Schatten von Auschwitz: Die nationalsozialistische Sterilisierungspolitik gegenüber Sinti und Roma* (Münster, 1995), p. 67.

14. Wolfgang Matl, "Ein Albtraum vom reinen Schweden," *Die Zeit*, September 5, 1997, pp. 13–15.

15. Mark H. Haller, *Eugenics: Hereditarian Attitudes in American Thought* (New Brunswick, N.J., 1963), p. 141.

16. Memo of Ministry of Interior, October 5, 1935, BA Berlin, R43 II/720.

17. Bock, *Zwangssterilisation im Nationalsozialismus*, p. 233.

18. Proctor, *Racial Hygiene*, p. 114.

19. *Durchführung des Gesetzes zur Verhütung erbkranken Nachwuchses*, January 7, 1937, STA Münster, Reg. Arnsberg, 13157.

20. Inge Marssolek and René Ott, *Bremen im Dritten Reich: Anpassung, Widerstand, Verfolgung* (Bremen, 1986), pp. 325–26.

21. Fred Dubitscher, "Der moralische Schwachsinn, unter besonderer Berücksichtigung des Gesetzes zur Verhütung erbkranken Nachwuchses," *Zeitschrift für die Gesamte Neurologie und Psychiatrie* 22 (1936): 443–51.

22. Robert Ritter, *Ein Menschenschlag: Erbärtzliche und erbgeschichtliche Untersuchungen über die—durch 10 Geschlechterfolgen erforschten—Nachkommen von "Vagabunden, Jaunern and Räubern"* (Leipzig, 1937), p. 19.

23. Thomas Koch, *Zwangssterilisation im Dritten Reich: Das Beispiel der Universitätsklinik Göttingen* (Frankfurt/Main, 1994), p. 23.

24. Elisabeth Fenner, *Zwangssterilisation im Nationalsozialismus: Zur Rolle der Hamburger Sozialverwaltung* (Ammersbek bei Hamburg, 1990), p. 63.

25. Bock, *Zwangssterilisation im Nationalsozialismus*, pp. 302–3.

26. Riechert, *Im Schatten von Auschwitz*, pp. 93, 135.

27. *Reichsgesetzblatt* (1939), 1:1560.

28. Simon, "Die Erbgesundheitsgerichtsbarkeit," pp. 140–43.

29. Daum and Deppe, *Zwangssterilisation in Frankfurt*, p. 21.

30. Koch, *Zwangssterilisation im Dritten Reich*, p. 24.

31. Marssolek and Ott, *Bremen im Dritten Reich*, p. 319.

32. Saul Friedländer, *Nazi Germany and the Jews* (New York, 1997), 1:142, 152–53.

33. Paragraph 6 of *Erste Verordnung zur Ausführung des Gesetzes zum Schutze des deutschen Blutes und der deutschen Ehre*, in Reichsleiter der NSDAP, ed., *Organisationsbuch der NSDAP*, 4th ed. (Munich, 1937), p. 523.

34. *Ministerialblatt für die Innere Verwaltung* 49 (1935): col. 1429. The text of this decree is reprinted in Wilhelm Stuckart and Hans Globke, *Kommentar zur deutschen Rassengesetzgebung* (Munich, 1936), 1:36–37.

35. A facsimile of this decree is reproduced in Romani Rose, ed., *Der nationalsozialistische Völkermord an den Sinti und Roma*, 2d ed. (Heidelberg, 1995), pp. 25–26.

36. Döring, *Zigeuner im nationalsozialistischen Staat*, p. 57.

37. Reichsleiter der NSDAP, ed., *Organisationsbuch*, p. 520.

38. Wilhelm Frick, "Das Reichsbürgergesetz und das Gesetz zum Schutze des deutschen Blutes und der deutschen Ehre," *Deutsche Juristen-Zeitung*, December, 1, 1935 p. 1391.

39. Stuckart and Globke, *Kommentar zur deutschen Rassengesetzgebung*, 1:55.

40. Several such orders are reproduced in facsimile by Rose, ed., *Der nationalsozialistische Völkermord*, pp. 38–39.

41. Wilhelm Stuckart and Rolf Schiedermair, *Rassen- und Erbpflege in der Gesetzgebung des Reiches* (Leipzig, 1938), p. 10.

42. See Reimar Gilsenbach, "Wie Lolitschai [Eva Justin] zur Doktorwürde kam," in *Feinderklärung und Prävention: Kriminalbiologie, Zigeunerforschung und Asozialenpolitik* (Berlin, 1988), pp. 101–34.

43. Robert Ritter, "Mitteleuropäische Zigeuner: Ein Volksstamm oder eine Mischungspopulation?" in *Congrès International de la Population*, Paris 1937, Extrait 8 (Paris, 1938), p. 53.

44. Robert Ritter, "Untergruppe L3 (Rassenhygienische und bevölkerungsbiologische Forschungsstelle)," in *Das Reichsgesundheitsamt 1933–1939: Sechs Jahre nationalsozialistische Führung*, by Hans Reiter (Berlin, 1939), p. 357.

45. Karl Themel, *Wie verkarte ich Kirchenbücher? Der Aufbau einer alphabetischen Kirchenbuchkartei* (Berlin, 1936), p. 5, cited by Reimar Gilsenbach, *Oh Django, sing deinen Zorn: Sinti und Roma unter den Deutschen* (Berlin, 1993), p. 297. See also Götz Aly and Karl Heinz Roth, *Die restlose Erfassung: Volkszählen, Identifizieren, Aussondern im Nationalsozialismus* (Berlin, 1984), pp. 70–71.

46. Gilsenbach, *Oh Django sing deinen Zorn*, p. 298.

47. Ritter, *Ein Menschenschlag*, p. 34.

48. Katholisches Pfarramt Berleburg to Duisburg Kripo, January 20, 1942, HSTA Düsseldorf, BR 1111, Nr. 36.

49. Robert Ritter, "Zigeuner und Landfahrer," in Bayerischer Landesverband für Wanderdienst, *Der nichtsesshafte Mensch: Ein Beitrag zur Neugestaltung der Raum- und*

Menschenordnung im Grossdeutschen Reich (Munich, 1938), pp. 71–88; Robert Ritter, "Zur Frage der Rassenbiologie und Rassenpsychologie der Zigeuner in Deutschland," *Reichs-Gesundheitsblatt* 13 (1938): 425–26.

50. Ritter, "Zigeuner und Landfahrer," p. 87.

51. J. Lange, *Verbrechen als Schicksal* (Leipzig, 1929).

52. Ritter, "Untergruppe L3," p. 358.

53. James Q. Wilson and Richard J. Herrnstein, *Crime and Human Nature* (New York, 1985), p. 69; Bryan M. Roth, "Crime and Child Rearing," *Society* 34, no. 1 (November–December 1996): 40; Patricia A. Brennan et al., "Biomedical Factors in Crime," in *Crime*, ed. James Q. Wilson and Joan Petersilia, (San Francisco, 1995), p. 75.

54. Wilson and Herrnstein, *Crime and Human Nature*, p. 70.

55. Kater, *Doctors under Hitler*, p. 227.

56. Ritter's position on this issue is best articulated in his essay "Die Bestandaufnahme der Zigeuner und Zigeunermischlinge in Deutschland," *Der Öffentliche Gesundheitsdienst* 6, pt. B (1941): 477.

57. Udo Engbring-Romang, *Fulda-Auschwitz: Zur Verfolgung der Sinti in Fulda* (Darmstadt, 1996), p. 30.

58. Friedländer, *Nazi Germany and the Jews*, p. 324.

59. Adolf Würth, "Bemerkungen zur Zigeunerfrage und Zigeunerforschung in Deutschland," *Anthropologischer Anzeiger: Verhandlungen der Deutschen Gesellschaft für Rassenforschung* 9 (1938): 95–98.

60. Robert Krämer, "Rassische Untersuchungen an den "Zigeuner"-Kolonien Lause und Altengraben bei Berleburg (Westf.)," *Archiv für Rassen- und Gesellschaftsbiologie* 31 (1937–38): 33–55 (the last quotation is from p. 55).

61. Günther, "Die Zigeunerverhältnisse in Berleburg," *Ziel und Weg* 7 (1937): 268.

62. Landjäger Stationskommandant, Esslingen, to Landrat, Esslingen, March 11, 1937, LA Ludwigsburg, F 164/II 688.

63. Heinrich Wilhelm Kranz, "Zigeuner, wie sie wirklich sind," *Neues Volk* 5, no. 9 (September 1937): 27.

64. Otto Finger, *Studien an zwei asozialen Zigeunermischlings-Sippen: Ein Beitrag zur Asozialen- und Zigeunerfrage*, 2d ed. (Giessen, 1937), pp. 53, 64–65.

65. Karlheinz Rüdiger, "Parasiten der Gemeinschaft," *Volk und Rasse* 13 (1938): 88–89.

66. "Die Zigeuner als asoziale Bevölkerungsgruppe," *Deutsches Ärzteblatt* 69 (1939): 246–47.

67. Carl-Heinz Rodenberg, "Die Zigeunerfrage," *Der öffentliche Gesundheitsdienst* 3B (1937): 438, 445.

68. The words are those of an editorial in the *Bauländer Bote* of Adelheim in Baden, September 10, 1938. Similar language can found in other papers, from both large cities and small towns.

69. Memo of Munich Kripo, April 25, 1938, HSA Munich, MInn 72579.

70. Memo of Dr. Mauthe (agency unknown) to minister of interior of Württemberg, July 9, 1938, HSA Stuttgart, E 151/53 Bü 164.

71. *Bekämpfung der Zigeunerplage*, Ministerialblatt des Reichs- und Preussischen Ministeriums des Innern 51 (1938): 2105–10. The decree is also contained in *Erlasssammlung Nr. 15* and is available in the microfilmed copy of *Mitteilungsblatt des Reichskriminalpolizeiamtes* 2, no. 2 (February 1939), National Archives, Washington, D.C, Microfilm Publication T175, roll 433, frames 2963301–2963304.

72. Ibid.

73. Ibid.

74. Ibid.

75. *Ausführungsanweisung*, March 1, 1939, *Mitteilungsblatt des Reichskriminalpolizeiamtes* 2, no. 4 (April 1939): cols. B58–60. The regulations are also to be found in *Erlasssammlung Nr. 15*, and in NA Washington, Microfilm Publication T175, roll 433, frames 2963321–2963322.

76. Ibid.

Chapter 4

1. According to a July 2, 1936, memo for the Bundeskanzleramt (Inneres), the Burgenland had 7,559 Gypsies, DÖW Vienna, Nr. 12543.

2. Erika Thurner, *Kurzgeschiche des Nationalsozialistischen Zigeunerlagers in Lackenbach (1940 bis 1945)* (Eisenstadt, 1984), p. 7. See also Elisabeth Klamper, "Persecution and Annihilation of Roma and Sinti in Austria, 1938–1945," *Journal of the Gypsy Lore Society*, ser. 5, 3, no. 2 (August 1993): 56.

3. "Die Zigeunerfrage in der Ostmark," *Neues Volk* 6, no. 9 (September 1938): 24.

4. "Aus Rassenhygiene und Bevölkerungspolitik," *Volk und Rasse* 13 (1938): 29.

5. *Erlasssammlung Nr. 15*.

6. The order was signed by Landeshauptmann Portschy, DÖW Vienna, Nr. 11151.

7. DÖW Vienna, Nr. 16532; Dokumentationsarchiv des Österreichischen Widerstandes, *Widerstand und Verfolgung im Burgenland, 1934–1945* (Vienna, 1983), p. 259.

8. Tobias Portschy, "Die Zigeunerfrage: Denkschrift des Landeshauptmannes für das Burgenland" (Eisenstadt, August 1938), pp. 6–7, HMM, RG–07.009*01. A memo of the Eisenstadt Kripo of June 24, 1938, gives the figure of two hundred arrested Gypsies. ÖSTA Vienna, 04/Inneres, 102.389–73, 60.

9. DÖW Vienna, Nr. 12543.

10. Portschy, "Die Zigeunerfrage," HMM Washington, RG–07.009*01, pp. 1–9, 23–28.

11. Ibid., pp. 33–36.

12. Ibid., pp. 36–37.

13. Selma Steinmetz, *Österreich's Zigeuner im NS-Staat* (Vienna, 1966), p. 11.

14. *Erlasssammlung Nr. 15*.

15. *Vorbeugende Massnahmen zur Bekämpfung der Zigeunerplage im Burgenland*, June 5, 1939. *Erlassammlung Nr. 15*.

16. *Jahrbuch Amt V Reichskriminalpolizeiamt des Reichssicherheitshauptamtes 1939/40*, BA Berlin, RD 19/29.

17. Dokumentationsarchiv des Österreichischen Widerstandes, *Widerstand und Verfolgung in Niederösterreich, 1934–1945* (Vienna, 1987), 3: 355.

18. *Bekämpfung der Zigeunerplage*, May 13, 1938, *Erlasssammlung Nr. 15*.

19. Circular of Eisenstadt Kripo, May 27, 1938, ÖSTA Vienna, 04/Inneres. 102.389–73, 60.

20. *Eheschliessungsverbot zwischen Zigeunern und Personen deutschen Blutes*, May 23, 1938, Dokumentationsarchiv des Österreichischen Widerstandes, *Widerstand und Verfolgung in Wien, 1934–1945: Eine Dokumentation*, vol. 3, Zigeuner (Vienna, 1973), p. 354.

21. DÖW Vienna, Nr. 12232.

22. Regierungsrat Reischauer to Oberregierungsrat Krüger, March 7, 1939, ÖSTA Vienna, AVA Unterricht, F 4209–313026, a.

23. Krüger to Reischauer, March 11, 1939, ÖSTA Vienna, AVA Unterricht, F 4209–313026, a.

24. Report to Krüger, March 20, 1939, ÖSTA Vienna, AVA Unterricht, F 4209–313026, a.

25. Bezirksschulrat Wilhelm Kasper to Krüger, March 29, 1939, ÖSTA Vienna, AVA Unterricht, F 327994–1939.

26. Der Reichsminister für Wissenschaft, Erziehung und Volksbildung to the Ministry of Education, Vienna, June 15, 1939, ÖSTA Vienna, AVA Unterricht, F 327994–1939.

27. See the facsimile of a letter of November 13, 1939, from the municipal administration to the Reichskommissar für die Wiedervereinigung Oesterreichs mit dem Deutschen Reich reporting on the action of the school administrators in Rose, ed., *Der Nationalsozialistische Völkermord*, pp. 52–53.

28. Gendarmerieposten St. Johann to the Landrat, January 12, 1939, cited by Elisabeth Klamper, "Persecution of the Gypsies," in *Archives of the Holocaust* (New York, 1991), 19: 158–61.

Chapter 5

1. See Reimer Gronemeyer, *Zigeuner im Spiegel früherer Chroniken und Abhandlungen: Quellen vom 15. bis 18. Jahrhundert* (Giessen, 1987), p. 89.

2. Eva Strauss, "Die Zigeunerverfolgung in Bayern: 1885–1926," *Giessener Hefte zur Tsiganalogie* 3 (1986): 59.

3. The Saxonian Ministry of the Interior to local police authorities, April 30, 1916, HSTA Dresden, HMM Washington, RG–14.011M, reel 11.

4. Stellvertr. Generalkommando 8.A.K. to the Landräte, September 13, 1917, LHA Koblenz, 613, Nr. 1647.

5. STA Ludwigsburg, F 209/II, Bü 201.

6. BA Berlin, R 58/273, Kirche 5.

7. Gestapo Düsseldorf to Gestapo Essen, October 17, 1939, HSTA Düsseldorf, RW 58, Nr. 18898.

8. Fürsorgeamt Frankfurt to mayor, August 24, 1938, StA Frankfurt, Stadtkanzlei 2203, vol. 1. The document is reproduced in Wippermann, *Nationalsozialistische Zigeunerverfolgung*, pp. 78–79.

9. Circular of January 26, 1939, HSTA Munich, MInn 72579.

10. Der Beauftragte für die Westbefestigungen to the minister of the interior of Baden, July 13, 1939, HSTA Düsseldorf, BR 1011/155.

11. Grenzzonenverordnung, September 2, 1939, *RGBl* 1:1578.

12. *Bekämpfung der Zigeunerplage*, September 9, 1939, *Erlasssammlung Nr. 15*.

13. See, for example, HSTA Düsseldorf, BR 1111, Nr. 33, 47.

14. *Mitteilungsblatt des Reichskriminalpolizeiamts* 2, no. 12 (December 1939): col. A210.

15. Heinz Boberach, ed., *Meldungen aus dem Reich 1938–1945: Die geheimen Lageberichte des Sicherheitsdienstes der SS* (Herrsching, 1984), 3:475.

16. *Vorbeugende Verbrechensbekämpfung durch die Polizei*, HMM, RG–15.013M, reel 1, frame 286.

17. LHA Magdeburg, C 29 Anh. 2, Nr. 1.

18. Ibid., Nr. 460.

19. Minutes (dated September 27) of Amtschef und Einsatzgruppenleiterbesprechung held on September 21, 1939, IFZ, Eich 983. Another copy can be found at NA Washington, Microfilm Publication T175, roll 239, frames 2728236–40.

20. *Zigeunererfassung*, October 17, 1939, *Erlasssammlung Nr. 15*.

21. NA Washington, Microfilm Publication T175, roll 413. Some additional reports can be found in HSTA Wiesbaden, Abt. 410, Nr. 489.

22. Ibid., frame 2937794.

23. Nebe tried to reach Eichmann on the telephone. His inquiry was relayed in a teletyped message on October 13 that is reproduced in facsimile in Rose, ed., *Der Nationalsozialistische Völkermord*, p. 89.

24. The teletyped message of October 16 too is reproduced in facsimile in *Nationalsozialistische Völkermord*, p. 90.

25. Memo of Zentralstelle für jüdische Auswanderung, Vienna, October 18, 1939, DÖW Vienna, Nr. 2527.

26. Christopher R. Browning, "Nazi Resettlement Policy and the Search for a Solution to the Jewish Question, 1939–1941," *German Studies Review* 9 (1986): 504–5; Jonny Moser, "Nisko: The First Experiment in Deportation," *Simon Wiesenthal Center Annual* 2 (1985): 18. See also Götz Aly, *"Endlösung," Völkerwanderung und der Mord an den europäischen Juden* (Frankfurt/Main, 1995), passim.

27. Each Kripo office drew up its own form of this declaration, but the substantive content is identical. A large number of these forms are preserved in the *Zigeunerpersonenakten* in the LHA Magdeburg and HSTA Düsseldorf.

28. For example, Alexander F. in Berlin received permission to visit his father in Königsberg from January 26 to February 15, 1944, LHA Potsdam, Rep. 30, Berlin C, Nr. 8. The practice was frequent enough that a special form was devised for it.

29. *Erlasssammlung Nr. 15.*

30. *Meldeblatt der Kriminalpolizeileitstelle* München, December 29, 1939, HSTA Munich, MInn 72579.

31. Ibid.

32. *Die Frage der Behandlung der Bevölkerung der ehemaligen polnischen Gebiete nach rassenpolitischen Gesichtspunkten*, NA Washington, Microfilm Publication T-74, roll 9, frame 380600. Another copy can be found in Nuremberg document NO-3732, RG 238, box 70.

33. Cf. Richard Breitmann, *The Architect of Genocide: Himmler and the Final Solution* (New York, 1991), pp. 85–86.

34. The text of this decree is reprinted in Buchheim, *Anatomie des SS-Staates*, 1: 217–19.

35. Bradley F. Smith and Agnes F. Peterson, eds., *Heinrich Himmler Geheimreden 1933 bis 1945 und andere Ansprachen* (Frankfurt, 1974), p. 139.

36. The minutes of this meeting are reproduced in Nuremberg document NO-5322, *Trials of War Criminals before the Nuernberg Military Tribunals under Control Council Law No. 10* (Washington, D.C., 1946–49), 4:855–59.

37. BA Koblenz, R 18, Nr. 5644. A facsimile of Conti's letter is reproduced in Eiber, *"Ich wusste es wird schlimm,"* pp. 68–69.

38. *Arbeitsbericht*, undated, but probably composed in January 1940, BA Koblenz, R 73, Nr. 14005.

39. Raul Hilberg, *The Destruction of the European Jews* (Chicago, 1961), p. 133.

40. The minutes of this meeting are reprinted in International Military Tribunal, *Trial of the Major War Criminals before the International Military Tribunal* (Nuremberg, 1946), 39:438.

41. *Umsiedlung von Zigeunern*, April 27, 1940, *Erlasssammlung Nr. 15.*

42. *Richtlinien für die Umsiedlung von Zigeunern (Erster Transport aus der westlichen und nordwestlichen Grenzzone), Erlasssamlung Nr. 15.*

43. HSTA Wiesbaden, Abt. 407, Nr. 863.

44. Ibid.

45. Polizeipräsident Cologne to mayor of Koblenz, July 23, 1940, facsimile in Rose, ed., *Der Nationalsozialistische Völkermord*, p. 96; Karola Fings and Frank Sparing, *"z.Z. Zigeunerlager:" Die Verfolgung der Düsseldorfer Sinti und Roma im Nationalsozialismus* (Cologne, 1992), pp. 65–67.

46. HSTA Düsseldorf, BR 2034, Nr. 788.

47. Ibid., Nr. 219.

48. Ibid., Nr. 116.

49. Ibid., Nr. 16.

50. Ibid., Nr. 863.

51. Ibid., Nr. 1002.

52. Ibid., Nr. 367, 337.

53. See, e.g., the instructions of RKPA to Frankfurt/Main, Kripo, May 32, 1940, HSTA Wiesbaden, Abt. 407, Nr. 863.

54. The exchange of correspondence is reprinted in Wippermann, *Nationalsozialistische Zigeunerverfolgung*, pp. 92–94.

55. HSTA Düsseldorf, BR 1021, Nr. 441.

56. ZSL Ludwigsburg, 415 AR 93/61, pp. 86–87.

57. *Zigeuner in der Grenzzone*, January 31, 1940, BA Potsdam (now Berlin), 31.01 RWM, Bd. 30, cited by Zimmermann, *Rassenutopie und Genozid*, p. 172.

58. Cf. Hans Buchheim, "Die Zigeunerdeportation vom May 1940," *Gutachten des Instituts für Zeitgeschichte* (Munich, 1958), 1:51–60; Hans-Joachim Döring, "Die Motive der Zigeunerdeportation vom Mai 1940," *Vierteljahrshefte für Zeitgeschichte* 7 (1959): 418–28.

59. This request of the RKPA, dated July 18, 1940, is mentioned in a memo of the Karlsruhe Kripo dated August 21, 1940, sent to local police posts and the Landräte. See STA Freiburg, G 21/3, Nr. 7.

60. ZSL Ludwigsburg, 415 AR 93/61, p. 87.

61. The RKPA memo is mentioned in a letter from the Karlsruhe Kripo to the Landrat of Mosbach, December 20, 1940, STA Freiburg, G 21/3, Nr. 7.

62. NA Washington, Microfilm Publication T175, roll 413, frame 2937931.

63. Ibid., frames 2938116–7.

64. The figure of 2,500 may not be precise. A tabulation found in the files of the Ritter Institute speaks of 2,330 deported Gypsies (BA Berlin, ZSg. 142/22). A summary of evacuations by Heydrich's office gives the figure of 2,800 Gypsies deported to the East between May 11 and November 15, 1940 (Nuremberg document NO-5150, NA Washington, RG 238, box 89).

65. ZSL Ludwigsburg, 414 AR 540/83, 1:120.

66. A police officer who accompanied the train told this to Adolf Würth after the war (Müller-Hill, *Murderous Science*, p. 145). The account is confirmed by a passenger on this train, Josef Klein, the leader of a famous Gypsy band (Michail Krausnick, *Wo sind sie hingekommen? Der unterschlagene Völkermord an den Sinti und Roma* [Gerlingen, 1995], p. 38).

67. IfZ, Fh 28, is a report based on numerous eyewitness accounts. See also IfZ, Gs 05.43; Michail Krausnick, ed., *"Da wollten wir frei sein!" Eine Sinti Familie erzählt* (Weinheim-Basel, 1993), p. 38; Döring, *Zigeuner*, pp. 98–99.

68. Lila Steinberger, "Das Leben des Herrn Steinberger," *Aus Politik und Zeitgeschichte* 31, no. 12 (1981): 22; Michail Krausnick, *Abfahrt Karlsruhe: Die Deportation in den Völkermord, ein unterschlagenes Kapitel aus der Geschichte unserer Stadt* (Karlsruhe, 1991), p. 33.

69. ZSL Ludwigsburg, 208 AR 1906/1966; Michael Zimmermann, "Deportation ins "Generalgouvernement": Zur nationalsozialistischen Verfolgung der Sinti und

Roma aus Hamburg," in *Hamburg in der NS-Zeit: Ergebnisse neuerer Forschungen*, ed. Frank Bajohr and Joachim Szodrzynski (Hamburg, 1995), p. 159.

70. ZSL Ludwigsburg, 414 AR 540/83, 1:114–15.

71. Ibid., pp. 95–96.

72. This description is based on the testimony of a survivor, Robert Weiss, before a court in Kiel on November 11, 1958; the document is filed at STA Detmold, D 1, Nr. 6151, appendix 2. For a report that speaks of conditions similar to a concentration camp, see IfZ, MA 21.

73. HSTA Düsseldorf, BR 1111, Nr. 48.

74. Ibid., BR 2034, Nr. 186.

75. Zimmermann, "Deportation ins 'Generalgouvernement,' " p. 163.

76. HSTA Düsseldorf, BR 1111, Nr. 48.

77. Ibid., Nr. 41.

78. Ibid., BR 2034, Nr. 7.

79. Ibid., BR 1111, Nr. 40.

80. Memo of Innere Verwaltung, Bevölkerungswesen und Fürsorge, Lublin, ZSL Ludwigsburg, 414 AR 540/83, :124.

81. Aussendienststelle Duisburg to Kriminalpolizeistelle Essen, August 8, 1944, HSTA Düsseldorf, BR 1111, Nr. 43.

82. Ibid., Nr. 45.

83. Ibid., Nr. 43.

84. Ibid., Nr. 29.

85. Ibid., BR 2034, Nr. 429.

86. LHA Potsdam, Rep. 30, Berlin C, Tit. 198A, 3, Zigeuner, Nr. 148; Niedersächsischer Verband Deutscher Sinti, *"Es war menschenunmöglich": Sinti aus Niedersachsen erzählen: Verfolgung und Vernichtung im Nationalsozialismus und Diskriminierung bis heute* (Hannover, 1995), p. 80.

87. ZSL Ludwigsburg, 414 AR 540/83, 4:594.

88. Ibid., 415 AR 930/61, p. 86.

89. Cologne Kripo to RKPA, August 21, 1940, HSTA Düsseldorf, BR 2034, Nr. 1115.

90. Ibid., BR 1111, Nr. 48, p. 49.

91. Archiwum Akt Nowych, Reg. GG 433, Bl. 10, cited by Zimmermann, *Rassenutopie und Genozid*, p. 183.

92. Ibid.

93. Ibid.

94. Order by Befehlshaber der Sicherheitspolizei und des SD, July 2, 1940, cited by Lothar Kettenacker, *Nationalsozialistische Volkstumpolitik im Elsass* (Stuttgart, 1973), p. 250.

95. *Säuberung des Elsasses von Zigeunern, Berufsverbrechern und asozialen Elementen,* August 14, 1940, NA Washington, Microfilm Publication T 175, roll 513, frame 9380006.

96. The figure of 105,000 is contained in a report by the Reichskommission für die Festigung des deutschen Volkstums, August 14, 1942, Nuremberg document PS-1470, *Trials of War Criminals*, 4:912–16. The German text can be found in NO-5202, NA Washington, RG 238, box 90.

97. Befehlshaber der Sicherheitspolizei und des SD, Strassburg, to RSHA, April 29, 1942, NA Washington, Microfilm Publication, T 175, roll 432, frames 2962980–88.

98. Memo of Mühlhausen Kripo, April 27, 1942, ibid., frame 2962993.

99. Strassburg Kripo to RSHA, June 20, 1942, ibid., frame 1963003.

100. Gauleiter Robert Wagner to Himmler, March 19, 1942, cited by Ketten-acker, *Nationalsozialistische Volkstumpolitik*, p. 262.

101. The minutes of this meeting are contained in the report of August 14, 1942, cited in n. 94 above.

102. Metz Kripo, "Vorbeugende Verbrechensbekämpfung," March 28, 1942, NA Washington, Microfilm Publication T 175, roll 513, frames 9380068–69.

103. Zimmermann, *Rassenutopie and Genozid*, p. 243.

104. Robert Ritter, "Die Zigeunerfrage und das Zigeunerbastardproblem," *Fortschritte der Erbpathologie, Rassenhygiene und ihrer Grenzgebiete* 3 (1939): 12; Sophie Ehrhardt, "Zigeuner und Zigeunermischlinge in Ostpreussen," *Volk und Rasse* 17 (1942): 53.

105. See the testimony of Geyer before a Munich court on June 24, 1957, IfZ Munich, Ms 410.

106. Cf. Franz Wirbel, "Die Rückkehr von Auschwitz," *Zeitschrift für Kulturaus-tausch* 31 (1981): 468. See also Amanda Dambrowski, "Das Schicksal einer vertriebe-nen ostpreussischen Sinti-Familie im NS-Staat," *Pogrom* 12, no. 80–81 (March–April 1981): 72–73.

107. See the testimony of the survivor Paul Dambrowski, ZSL Ludwigsburg, 415 AR 314/81, Bd. 1, and Zimmermann, *Rassenutopie und Genozid*, p. 229.

108. Schutzpolizei Brest-Litowsk, *Lagebericht*, October 12, 1942, BA Berlin, R94/7.

109. Report of the Gebietskommissar in Brest-Litowsk to the Generalkommissar für Volhynia and Podolia, December 31, 1942, BA Berlin, R94/8.

110. Report of June 24, 1943, BA Berlin, R94/8.

111. Zimmermann, *Rassenutopie und Genozid*, p. 460, n. 434.

Chapter 6

1. A statistical summary of Gypsies living in Germany arranged by states, proba-bly compiled by Ritter's office in Berlin in the spring of 1940, gives the figure of 29,000. BA Berlin, ZSg 142, Anh. 28.

2. GLA Karlsruhe, 364/1975/3II, Nr. 25.

3. Ibid.

4. Ibid., 345, Nr. G2214.

5. RKPA Berlin to Stuttgart Kripo, August 6, 1940, in ibid.

6. Ibid.

7. Ibid.

8. The mayor of Ludwigsburg to his chief of police, July 18, 1940, STA Ludwigs-burg, FL 20/12 II, Bü 381.

9. STA Detmold, M 1 I P, Nr. 1578.

10. Dortmund Kripo to mayor of Beverungen, May 14, 1941, and to Regierungs-präsident in Minden, August 28, 1941, in ibid.

11. Ibid.

12. Ibid.

13. *Volksgemeinschaft*, no. 81, March 24, 1940.

14. Memo of the Kreisgeschäftsführer, April 4, 1940, HSTA Stuttgart, E151/53 Bü 164. For other examples, see Michael Zimmermann, *Verfolgt, vertrieben, ver-nichtet: Die nationalsozialistische Vernichtungspolitik gegen Sinti und Roma*, 2d ed. (Essen, 1993), pp. 53–54.

15. Memo of March 4, 1936, BA Berlin, R18/5644.

16. Letter of March 24, 1938, HSTA Munich, MInn 72579.

17. Letter of December 19, 1938, BA Berlin, Slg. Schumacher, Nr. 399. The letter is also reproduced as Nuremberg document NO-1898, NA Washington, RG 238, box 38.

18. The lecture was probably delivered on February 4, 1939. See GLA Karlsruhe, 345 Zug. 1986, Nr. 12/Nr. 248. The same document can be found in IfZ Munich, Fa 704.

19. *Erlasssammlung Nr. 15.*

20. This position is argued persuasively in a memo by Hans Buchheim dated June 6, 1958, IfZ Munich, Ms 410.

21. *Vorentwurf für Gesetz zur Regelung der Zigeunerverhältnisse in Deutschland,* BA Berlin, ZSg 142, Anh. 28.

22. BA Berlin, NS 19/1300.

23. The draft does not include a date. BA Berlin, R22/943.

24. Files R22/943 and 944 in the BA Berlin contain a close chronological record of the prolonged negotiations. See also Patrick Wagner, "Das Gesetz über die Behandlung Gemeinschaftsfremder," in *Feinderklärung und Prävention: Kriminalbiologie, Zigeunerforschung und Asozialenpolitik* (Berlin, 1988), pp. 75–100.

25. Frank to Chef der Reichskanzlei, April 7, 1942; Göring to Chef des OKW, April 24, 1942, both in BA Berlin, R22/943.

26. BA Berlin, R58/473 and R22/949, cited by Wagner, "Das Gesetz," p. 94.

27. HSTA Düsseldorf, BR 2034, Nr. 173.

28. Memo of May 5, 1939, reproduced in facsimile in Rose, ed., *Der nationalsozialistische Völkermord,* p. 54.

29. Order of May 13, 1942, quoted in *Der nationalsozialistische Völkermord,* p. 50.

30. The Reichsminister für Wissenschaft, Erziehung und Volksbildung to the Ministry of Education, Vienna, June 15, 1939, ÖSTA, AVA Unterricht, F 4209, 327994–1939.

31. *Mitteilungsblatt des Reichskriminalpolizeiamts* 5, no. 4 (April 1942): A538. The decree is reprinted by Wippermann in *Nationalsozialistische Zigeunerverfolgung,* p. 101.

32. For a more detailed description of this episode, see Wippermann, *Nationalsozialistische Zigeunerverfolgung,* pp. 42–46.

33. Zimmermann, *Rassenutopie und Genozid,* p. 190.

34. Eiber, *"Ich wusste es wird schlimm,"* p. 73; Udo Engbring-Romano, *Wiesbaden-Auschwitz: Zur Verfolgung der Sinti in Wiesbaden* (Darmstadt, 1997), p. 52.

35. See, for example, the report of the police of Adelsheim to the Landrat in Buchen of December 14, 1939, GLA Karlsruhe, 345, Nr. G2214.

36. LHA Magdeburg, Rep. C29, Anh. 2, Nr. 461.

37. Ibid., Nr. 192.

38. Ibid., Nr. 479.

39. Decree of May 28, 1941, quoted in Detlev J. K. Peukert, *Inside Nazi Germany: Conformity, Opposition, and Racism in Everyday Life* (New Haven, Conn., 1987), p. 214.

40. LHA Magdeburg, Rep. C29, Anh. 2, Nr. 407.

41. Elvira R. of Braunschweig is one of many survivors to relate this experience. See Niedersächsischer Verband Deutscher Sinti, *"Es war menschenunmöglich": Sinti aus Niedersachsen erzählen* (Hannover, 1995), p. 35.

42. LHA Magdeburg, Rep. C29, Anh. 2, Nr. 404.

43. STA Munich, Pol Dir Mü 7033.

44. *Arbeitseinsatz von Zigeunern und Zigeunermischlingen,* July 13, 1942, *Ministerialblatt des Reichs- und Preussischen Ministerium des Innern,* July 22, 1942, p. 1488. This decree can also be found in NA Washington, Microfilm Publication T 175, roll 433, frame 2963795–98.

45. Hase-Mihalik and Kreuzkamp, *"Du kriegst auch einen schönen Wohnwagen,"* p. 69.

46. Herbert Adler's account is printed in Rose, ed., *Der Nationalsozialistische Völkermord*, p. 47, and in Edgar Bamberger and Annegret Ehmann, eds., *Kinder und Jugendliche als Opfer des Holocaust* (Heidelberg, 1995), pp. 173–78.

47. Wolfgang Wippermann and Ute Brucker-Boroujerdi, "Nationalsozialistische Zwangslager in Berlin III: Das 'Zigeunerlager Marzahn,' " *Berliner Forschungen* 2 (1987): 195–98.

48. Karola Fings and Frank Sparing, "Das Zigeunerlager in Köln-Bockendorf, 1935–1958," *1999: Zeitschrift für Sozialgeschichte des 20. und 21. Jahrhunderts* 6, no. 3 (July 1991): 34.

49. Fings and Sparing, *"z.Zt. Zigeunerlager,"* pp. 43–45, 71.

50. *Abschiebung der ostpreussischen Zigeuner*, July 22, 1941, *Erlasssammlung Nr. 15*.

51. Details about conditions in the camp can be found in testimony by two former policemen given in a restitution proceeding in 1958. STA Detmold, D1, Nr. 6151.

52. STA Munich, Pol Di Mü, Nr. 7033.

53. Döring, *Zigeuner im Nationalsozialistischen Staat*, pp. 39–41; Hansjörg Riechert, "Im Gleichschritt . . . : Sinti und Roma in Feldgrau," *Militärgeschichtliche Mitteilungen* 53 (1994): 383–84.

54. See the informative discussion of this history in Riechert, "Im Gleichschritt," pp. 377–82.

55. *Richtlinien für die Heranziehung von nichtjüdischen fremdblütigen deutschen Staatsangehörigen zum aktiven Wehrdienst*, quoted in Riechert, "Im Gleichschritt," p. 384.

56. Ibid.

57. Ibid., p. 388. Manfred Messerschmidt has noted this phenomenon with regard to Jewish Mischlinge, and it appears to have operated for Gypsies also. See Messerschmidt, *Die Wehrmacht im NS-Staat: Zeit der Indoktrination* (Hamburg, 1969), p. 357.

58. Philomena Franz, *Zwischen Liebe und Hass: Ein Zigeunerleben* (Freiburg i.Br., 1992), p. 46.

59. *Entlassungen von Zigeunern und Zigeunermischlingen aus dem aktiven Wehrdienst*, *Allgemeine Heeresmitteilungen*, February 21, 1941, 82–83. A facsimile of this order is reprinted in Rose, ed., *Der Nationalsozialistische Völkermord*, p. 58.

60. *Bekämpfung der Zigeunerplage (Heranziehung von Zigeunern und Zigeunermischlingen zum Wehrdienst)*, April 24, 1941, HMM Washington, RG-15.013M, reel 1.

61. The two letters, dated September 26 and September 30, 1941, respectively, are reproduced in facsimile in Rose, ed., *Der Nationalsozialistische Völkermord*, pp. 60–61.

62. Hildegard von Kotze, ed., *Heeresadjutant bei Hitler, 1938–1943: Aufzeichnungen des Majors Engel* (Stuttgart, 1974), pp. 79–80.

63. Ibid., p. 80.

64. Report of Werner Koeppen, Nr. 39, p. 2, IfZ Munich, Fa 514.

65. LHA Potsdam, Rep. 30, Berlin C, Nr. 99.

66. The case is described in Riechert, "Im Gleichschritt," p. 397.

67. Ibid., p. 386.

68. *Entlassung von Zigeunern und Zigeunermischlingen aus dem aktiven Wehrdienst*, *Allgemeine Heeresmitteilungen* 9 (1942): 305.

69. *Entlassung von Zigeunern und Zigeunermischlingen aus dem aktiven Wehrdienst und Reichsarbeitsdienst*, August 28, 1942, *Beilage zum Meldeblatt der Kriminalpolizeileitstelle München, Nürnberg, Augsburg, Regensburg und Würzburg*, September 8, 1942, HMM Washington, RG–07.005*01.

70. LHA Düsseldorf, BR 2034, Nr. 14.

71. Gauleitung Franken to Rassenpolitisches Amt, Nürnberg, March 13, 1942, STA Nürnberg, NS-Mischbestand Gauleitung Franken, Nr. 150.

72. Riechert, "Im Gleichschritt," p. 390.

73. Döring, *Zigeuner im Nationalsozialistischen Staat*, pp. 41, 135.

74. For several examples, see Zimmermann, *Rassenutopie und Genozid*, p. 209.

75. The Regierungspräsident in Arnsberg to the Standesbeamten, June 18, 1941, STA Münster, Reg. Arnsberg, Nr. 13155.

76. *Erlasssammlung Nr. 15.*

77. The Landrat of Hechingen to the Standesbeamten in Burladingen, August 11, 1941, facsimile in Rose, ed., *Der Nationalsozialistische Völkermord*, p. 31.

78. Minister of the Interior to Reichsstatthalter im Sudetengau, December 24, 1942 (with copies to all other state governments), HSTA Stuttgart, E 130 b Bü 1098.

79. *Verhängung der polizeilichen Vorbeugungshaft . . . bei Konkubinaten*, October 25, 1941, reproduced in ZSL Ludwigsburg, 415 AR 930/61, p. 20.

80. HSTA Düsseldorf, BR 2034, Nr. 1199. Several documents from this file are reproduced in facsimile in Rose, ed., *Der Nationalsozialistische Völkermord*, pp. 33–35.

81. HSTA Düsseldorf, BR 2034, Nr. 1130.

82. Ibid., BR 1111, Nr. 44.

83. Ibid., BR 2034, Nr. 1123.

84. *Einstellung der Bearbeitung von Ehegenehmigungsanträgen nach dem Blutschutzgesetz*, March 3, 1942, STA Detmold, D 102 Warburg Nr. 38.

85. *Bearbeitung von Ehegenehmigungsanträgen von Zigeunermischlingen*, September 25, 1942, *Erlasssammlung Nr. 15.*

86. Werner Feldscher, *Rassen- und Erbpflege im Deutschen Recht* (Berlin, 1943), pp. 27–28.

87. *Anordnung über die Beschäftigung von Zigeunern*, March 13, 1942, *Reichsgesetzblatt* 1942, pt. 1, p. 138. A facsimile of this decree can be found in Rose, ed., *Der Nationalsozialistische Völkermord*, p. 22.

88. The decree was published in the *Reichsgesetzblatt* 1942, pt. 1, p. 149. For further details about the implications of both of these decrees, see Feldscher, *Rassen- und Erbpflege*, pp. 94–96, and H. Küppers, "Die Beschäftigung von Zigeunern," *Reichsarbeitsblatt* 22 (1942): 176–78.

89. RKPA to the regional and local Kripo offices, *Arbeitsrechtliche Behandlung der Zigeuner*, March 28, 1942, *Erlasssammlung Nr. 15.*

90. *Fürsorgemassnahmen für Zigeuner*, June 8, 1942, *Erlasssammlung Nr. 15.*

91. *Betreuung von Angehörigen polizeilicher Vorbeugungshäftlinge durch die NSV*, November 9, 1942, *Erlasssammlung Nr. 15.*

92. *Verabfolgung von Zusatz- und Zulagekarten an Zigeuner*, May 13, 1942, facsimile in Rose, ed., *Der Nationalsozialistische Völkermord*, p. 23.

93. Reichsstatthalter in Niederdonau, Landesernährungsamt, to minister of nutrition and agriculture, August 28, 1942, BA Berlin, R 14, Nr. 156.

94. Minister of nutrition and agriculture to the Haupternährungsamt der Stadt Berlin, n.d., BA Berlin, R 14, Nr. 156.

95. Kreisgeschäftsführer NSDAP Minden to Polizeiverwaltung Minden, July 30, 1942, STA Detmold, M 1 I P, Nr. 1578.

96. Polizeiverwaltung Minden to Wirtschaftsgruppe Einzelhandel, August 22, 1942, ibid.

97. Ernst Fraenkel, *The Dual State: A Contribution to the Theory of Dictatorship* (New York, 1941), p. xvi.

98. *Verordnung über die einkommensteuerliche und vermögenssteuerliche Sonderbehandlung der Zigeuner,* December 24, 1942, *Reichsgesetzblatt* 1942, pt. 1, no. 131, p. 740, copy in HMM Washington, RG 07.008*01.

99. *Arbeitsbericht,* p. 1, undated, but probably composed in January 1940, BA Koblenz, R 73, Nr. 14005.

100. *Auswertung der rassenbiologischen Gutachten über zigeunerische Personen,* August 7, 1941, *Erlasssammlung Nr. 15.*

101. *Auswertung der rassenbiologischen Gutachten über zigeunerische Personen,* September 20, 1941, *Erlasssammlung Nr. 15.*

102. See, e.g., *Zusätze auf Gutachten über sozial angepasste ostpreussische Zigeuner,* n.d., BA Berlin, R 165, Nr. 181. In several cases, the recommendation here was that the person "no longer fall under the Gypsy regulations."

103. Rassenhygienische Forschungsstelle to Landrat Dillenburg, January 28, 1940, HSTA Wiesbaden, Abt. 410, Nr. 489.

104. See the testimony of Gerhard W. E. Junge, who worked in the Gypsy department of the Hamburg Kripo, ZSL Ludwigsburg, 414 AR 540/83, v. l.

105. *Erfassung der Zigeunermischlinge II.Grades,* July 16, 1940, STA Münster, Reg. Arnsberg, Nr. 14547.

106. RKPA to the regional and local Kripo offices, July 1, 1942, *Erlasssammlung Nr. 15.* The exchange of drafts is found in BA Berlin, R 43II/522b.

107. See the table *Einteilung der Zigeuner nach rassischen Gesichtspunkten,* BA Berlin, R 165, Nr. 181.

108. In a case repeated many times over, a Berlin Gypsy arrested on August 8, 1939, admitted using several different names and was able to tell neither his place of birth nor his original name or that of his parents (LHA Magdeburg, C 29 Anh. 2, Nr. 262). On August 1, 1939, the minister for church affairs admonished Catholic bishops to make sure that only Gypsy children who could produce a birth certificate were baptized. This was to prevent Gypsies from obtaining several certificates of baptism, each with a different name (minister for church affairs to Cardinal Bertram, August 1, 1939, DÖW Vienna, Nr. 16532).

109. Robert Ritter, "Die Bestandaufnahme der Zigeuner und Zigeunermischlinge in Deutschland," *Der Öffentliche Gesundheitsdienst* 6, pt. B (1941): 483–86.

110. The Reichsarbeitsminister to the Reichstreuhänder der Arbeit etc., March 13, 1942, BA Berlin, R 41/288a.

111. RKPA to Munich Kripo, "Beurlaubung von zigeunerischen Personen," July 14, 1942, STA Munich, Pol Dir Mü, 7033.

112. RKPA memo of November 1942, BA Berlin, ZSG 142/21, cited by Zimmermann, *Rassenutopie und Genozid,* p. 151.

113. It is not clear to what extent members of Ritter's institute or others compiled data on the Austrian Gypsies. A letter from the SS Main Office of Race and Resettlement (RuSHA) to Himmler, dated December 19, 1938, discusses an agreement between the RKPA and the RuSHA according to which the latter has the right to collect data on the hereditary-biological status of the Gypsies of the Ostmark (Chef des Rasse- und Siedlungshauptamtes-SS to Himmler, BA Berlin, Slg. Schumacher, Nr. 399).

114. Ritter to the Deutsche Forschungsgemeinschaft, March 23, 1943, BA Koblenz, R 73, Nr. 14005.

115. Ritter to the Präsident des Reichsforschungsrates, March 6, 1944, BA Koblenz, R 73, Nr. 14005.

116. LHA Potsdam, Rep. 30, Berlin C, Nr. 110.

117. Ritter to Deutsche Forschungsgemeinschaft, June 25, 1940, BA Koblenz, R 73, Nr. 14005.

118. Robert Ritter, "Das Kriminalbiologische Institut der Sicherheitspolizei," *Kriminalistik* 16 (1942): 117–19.

119. See the untitled and undated essay describing his effort to learn some Romani in BA Berlin, ZSg 142, Anh. 28, pp. 92–99.

120. Cf. Döring, *Zigeuner im nationalsozialistischen Staat*, p. 69.

Chapter 7

1. *Bericht zur innenpolitischen Lage (Nr. 1)*, October 9, 1939, in *Meldungen aus dem Reich 1938–1945: Die geheimen Lageberichte des Sicherheitsdienstes der SS*, ed. Heinz Boberach (Herrsching, 1984), 2:334.

2. Report of Dr. Meissner to minister of justice, February 9, 1940, Nuremberg document NG-684, reprinted in Elisabeth Klamper, ed. *Archives of the Holocaust* (New York, 1991), 19:171–74 doc. 63.

3. The mayor of Schwarzach to the Gauleiter in Salzburg, February 3, 1940, DÖW Vienna, E 18518/2.

4. Salzburg Kripo to the Landeshauptmann in Salzburg, March 4, 1940, DÖW Vienna, E 18518/1.

5. Ibid., E 18518/2.

6. Report of SD-Leitabschnitt Wien-Niederdonau, February 26, 1940, BA Berlin, R 58/350.

7. Weekly SD report to Gauleiter Bürckel, April 15, 1940, NA Washington, Microfilm Publication T 84, roll 13, frames 40254–56.

8. Salzburg Kripo to the Regierungspräsident in Salzburg, July 5, 1940, doc. 65 in Klamper, ed., *Archives of the Holocaust*, 19:177.

9. Kommandeur der Gendarmerie Niederdonau to Gendarmeriedienststellen, July 4, 1940, ÖSTA Vienna, 04/Inneres, 102.389–73, 60.

10. *Amtsbericht*, Salzburg Kripo, October 10, 1940, DÖW Vienna, E 18518/1.

11. *Bekämpfung der Zigeunerplage in der Ostmark*, October 31, 1940, *Erlasssammlung Nr. 15*.

12. Ibid.

13. See various memos describing the camp in DÖW Vienna, 1851/1–3.

14. Erika Thurner, *Nationalsozialismus und Zigeuner in Österreich* (Vienna, 1983), pp. 41–42.

15. Erika Thurner, *Kurzgeschichte des Nationalsozialistischen Zigeunerlagers in Lackenbach (1940 bis 1945)* (Eisenstadt, 1984), pp. 23–29.

16. Selma Steinmetz, *Österreich's Zigeuner im NS-Staat* (Vienna: Europa, 1966), pp. 18–19.

17. The *Anordnung* is reprinted in Klamper, ed., *Archives of the Holocaust*, 19:191, doc. 78.

18. *Tagebuch des ehemaligen Zigeuneranhaltelagers Lackenbach*, DÖW Vienna, Nr. 11340.

19. Ibid., Nr. 10501c, 12256, 9626.

20. The Landrat in Oberwart to the mayor and police posts, September 9, 1941, reprinted in Klamper, ed., *Archives of the Holocaust*, 19:183, doc. 71.

21. Order of September 25, 1941, in *Archives of the Holocaust*, 19:184, doc. 72.

22. A facsimile of this order is reproduced in Rose, ed., *Der Nationalsozialistische Völkermord*, p. 75.

23. Ventzki to Übelhör, September 24, 1941, NA Washington, Microfilm Publication T 175, roll 54, frames 2568677, 2568682–83.

24. Übelhör to Himmler, October 4, 1941, NA Washington, Microfilm Publication T 175, roll 54, frames 25668–69.

25. Himmler to Übelhör, October 10, 1941, NA Washington, Microfilm Publication T 175, roll 54, frames 2568662–63.

26. Übelhör to Himmler, October 9, 1941, and Himmler to Übelhör, October 9, 1941, NA Washington, Microfilm Publication T 175, roll 54, frames 2568653–55, 2568651. A facsimile of the first page of Übelhör's teletyped message of October 9 is reproduced by Rose, ed. *Der nationalsozialistische Völkermord*, p. 100.

27. Chef des Wehrwirtschaft- und Rüstungsamtes im Oberkommando der Wehrmacht to Himmler, October 11, 1941, NA Washington, Microfilm Publication T 175, roll 54, frames 2568648–49.

28. A detailed statistical report on the arrivals was compiled by the German authorities in Litzmannstadt. A facsimile can be found in Rose, ed., *Der Nationalsozialistische Völkermord*, pp. 101–3.

29. Thurner, *Kurzgeschichte*, p. 24.

30. Lucjan Dobroszycki, ed., *The Chronicle of the Lodz Ghetto, 1941–1944* (New Haven, Conn., 1984), p. 82.

31. Arbeitsamt Litzmannstadt to the Ghettoverwaltung Litzmannstadt, November 22, 1942, reprinted in Klamper, ed., *Archives of the Holocaust*, 19:188, doc. 75.

32. Dobroszycki, ed., *Chronicle*, p. 86.

33. Ibid., pp. 96, 101, 125.

34. Omer Bartov, *Hitler's Army: Soldiers, Nazis and War in the Third Reich* (New York, 1991), p. 24; Christian Streit, *Keine Kameraden: Die Wehrmacht und die sowjetischen Kriegsgefangenen, 1941–1945* (Stuttgart, 1978), p. 177.

35. Dobroszycki, ed., *Chronicle*, p. 108.

36. Cf. Paul Weindling, "Understanding Nazi Racism: Precursors and Perpetrators," in *Confronting the Nazi Past: New Debates in Modern German History*, ed. Michael Burleigh (New York, 1996), p. 79; Christopher Browning, *Path to Genocide: Essays on Launching the Final Solution* (New York, 1972) p. 160.

37. Isaiah Trunk, *Judenrat: The Jewish Councils in Eastern Europe under Nazi Occupation* (New York, 1972), p. 159.

38. *Ereignismeldung UdSSR Nr. 92*, September 23, 1941, Nuremberg document NO-3143, NA Washington, RG 238, box 58.

39. *Ereignismeldung UdSSR Nr. 165*, February 6, 1942, Nuremberg document NO-3401, NA Washington, RG 238, box 65.

40. *Ereignismeldung UdSSR Nr. 195*, April 24, 1942, NA Washington, microfilm publication T 175, roll 235, frame 2724320.

41. Plans for such a remedy for the problem of overcrowding are said to have been discussed as early as July 1941. Cf. Eberhard Jäckel and Jürgen Rohwer, eds., *Der Mord an den Juden im Zweiten Weltkrieg: Entschlussbildung und Verwirklichung* (Stuttgart, 1985), p. 42. See also the confession made on April 15, 1945, to investigators by Dr. Wilhelm Gustav Schübbe, who worked as surgeon in the Erwin Peter hospital of Lizmannstadt, NA Washington, RG 153, box 575.

42. ZSL Ludwigsburg, 203 AR-Z 69/59, vol. 1.

43. Jerzy Ficowski, *Ciganie na polskich drogach* (Gypsies on Polish roads), 2d ed. (Krakow, 1965), pp. 114–15. German excerpts in DÖW Vienna, Nr. 16532.

44. ZLS Ludwigsburg, 203 AR-Z 69/59, 4:626–32, 552.

45. The Landrat des Kreises Oberwart to all mayors and Gendarmerieposten, November 11, 1941, in Klamper, ed., *Archives of the Holocaust*, 19:186–87, doc. 74.

46. *Zigeunerfrage, Lösung,* January 6, 1942, facsimile in Rose, ed., *Der National-sozialistische Völkermord,* p. 76.

47. The Landrat to all mayors, March 19, 1942, in Klamper, ed., *Archives of the Holocaust,* 19:190, doc. 77.

48. *Reisen von zigeunerischen Personen in den Warthegau und in das Generalgouverne-ment,* December 28, 1942, *Erlasssammlung Nr. 15.*

49. Memo of February 7, 1952, ÖSTA Vienna, 04/Inneres, 102.389–73, 60.

Chapter 8

1. See the affidavit of Walter Blume, the head of Einsatzkommando 7a of Einsatzgruppe B, in *Trials of War Criminals before the Nuernberg Military Tribunals under Control Council Law No. 10,* vol. 4, *The Einsatzgruppen Case* (Washington, D.C., 1946–49), p. 140, and the affidavit of Wilhelm Förster, also a member of Einsatzgruppe B, Nuremberg document NO-5520, NA Washington, RG 238, box 95. See also Richard Breitman, *The Architect of Genocide: Himmler and the Final Solution* (New York, 1991), p. 164.

2. Ralf Ogorreck, *Die Einsatzgruppen und die "Genesis der Endlösung"* (Berlin, 1996), pp. 102–3.

3. Quoted in Helmut Krausnick and Hans-Heinrich Wilhelm, *Die Truppe des Weltanschauungskrieges: Die Einsatzgruppen der Sicherheitspolizei und des SD, 1938–1942* (Stuttgart, 1981), p. 158.

4. *Trials of War Criminals,* 4:286–87.

5. Quoted in Helmut Krausnick, "Hitler und die Befehle an die Einsatzgruppen im Sommer 1941," Jäckel and Rohwer, eds., *Der Mord an den Juden,* p. 95.

6. For a good discussion of this controversy, see Christopher R. Browning, *Path to Genocide: Essays on Launching the Final Solution* (New York, 1992), pp. 99–101. As of this writing, the preponderant view appears to be that before the invasion of the Soviet Union the Einsatzgruppen did *not yet* have orders to kill *all* Jews.

7. Bartov, *Hitler's Army,* pp. 93, 125.

8. Streit, *Keine Kameraden,* p. 102.

9. Report of September 1, 1941, Nuremberg document NOKW-1701, NA Washington, Microfilm Publication T 1119, roll 23.

10. *Ereignismeldung UdSSR Nr. 92,* September 23, 1941, Nuremberg document NO-3143, NA Washington, RG 238, box 58.

11. *Ereignismeldung UdSSR Nr. 94,* September 25, 1941, Nuremberg document NO-3146, NA Washington, RG 238, box 59.

12. Nuremberg document NO-3276, NA Washington, RG 238, box 63.

13. Cf. Zimmermann, *Rassenutopie und Genozid,* p. 263.

14. *Ereignismeldung UdSSR Nr. 119,* October 20, 1941, BA Berlin, R 58/218.

15. Order of Der Kommandant in Weissruthenien, October 10, 1941, HMM Washington, RG-53.002M, reel 2, folder 698.

16. Report on executions, October 15, 1941, by the HSSPF Russland Mitte, facsimile in State Museum of Auschwitz-Birkenau, *Memorial Book: The Gypsies at Auschwitz-Birkenau* (Munich, 1993), 2:1566.

17. Letter of Meister der Gendarmerie Fritz Jacob to a friend, June 21, 1942, Nuremberg document NO-5655, NA Washington, RG 238, box 47. On the involvement of the Gendarmerie in such activities generally, see Jürgen Matthäus, "What about the 'Ordinary Men'? The German Order Police and the Holocaust in the Occupied Soviet Union," *Holocaust and Genocide Studies* 10 (1996): 143.

18. 281st Security Division to field commander 822, March 24, 1943, Nuremberg document NOKW-2022, NA Washington, Microfilm Publication T 1119, roll, 26, frame 709–13. An English translation of this document is reprinted in *Trials of War Criminals*, 10:1194–95.

19. Activity report of GFP unit 647, Nuremberg document NOKW-853, NA Washington, Microfilm Publication T 1119, roll 12.

20. This order is not preserved, but it is mentioned in the memo of March 24, 1943, cited in note 18.

21. Interrogation of Ernst Emil Heinrich Biberstein, leader of EK 6 of EG C, June 29, 1947, Nuremberg document NO-4997, NA Washington, RG 238, box 87.

22. Affidavit by Heinz-Hermann Schubert, December 7, 1945, Nuremberg document NO-4816, NA Washington, RG 238, box 85.

23. Deputy commander, 281st Security Division, to Feldkommandantur 822, June 23, 1942, Nuremberg document NOKW-2072, NA Washington, T 1119, roll 56 26, frames 1119–20.

24. Bartov, *Hitler's Army*, p. 82.

25. An excerpt from *Ereignismeldung UdSSR Nr. 150*, January 2, 1942, that includes this figure, is to be found in Nuremberg document NO-2834, in *Trials of War Criminals*, 4:186.

26. *Ereignismeldung UdSSR Nr. 178*, March 9, 1942, Nuremberg document NO-3241, NA Washington, RG 238, box 62.

27. *Ereignismeldung UdSSR Nr. 190*, April 8, 1942, Nuremberg document NO-3359, NA Washington, RG 238, box 64.

28. Hilberg, *Destruction of the European Jews*, p. 256.

29. *Meldungen aus den besetzten Ostgebieten Nr. 4*, May 22, 1942, NA Washington, Microfilm Publication, T 175, roll 235.

30. ZSL Ludwigsburg, 213 AR 422/81, 3:459–60.

31. HMM Washington, RG 53.002M, reel 5, folder 3.

32. *Meldungen aus den besetzten Ostgebieten Nr. 38*, January 22, 1943, Nuremberg document NO-5169, NA Washington, RG 238, box 90; HMM Washington, RG 11.001M.01, reel 10, folder 769.

33. *Ereignismeldung UdSSR Nr. 194*, April 21, 1942, NA Washington, Microfilm Publication T 175, roll 235.

34. IfZ Munich, Ge 01.05, pp. 35, 95–96; ZSL Ludwigsburg, 202 AR-Z 96/60, vol. 15.

35. Report of the *Heeresfeldpolizeichef*, July 31, 1942, Nuremberg document NOKW 2535, NA Washington, Microfilm Publication, T 1119, roll 32.

36. *Trials of War Criminals*, 4:356.

37. *Geheime Kommandosache*, December 16, 1942, reprinted in *Eine Schuld die nicht erlischt: Dokumente über deutsche Kriegsverbrechen in der Sowietunion* (Cologne, 1987), p. 146 doc. 45.

38. The text of this decree is reprinted in *Eine Schuld die nicht erlischt*, pp .65–68, doc 10.

39. Hilberg, *Destruction of the European Jews*, pp. 227–230, 243; Zimmermann, *Rassenutopie und Genozid*, p. 267.

40. Andrew Ezergailis, *The Holocaust in Latvia, 1941–1945: The Missing Center* (Riga, 1996), p. 200; Vanya Kochanowski, "Some Notes on the Gypsies of Latvia by one of the Survivors," *Journal of the Gypsy Lore Society*, 3d ser., 25 (1946): 115.

41. Ezergailis, *Holocaust in Latvia*, p. 185, 188.

42. ZSL Ludwigsburg, II 207 AR-Z 497/1967, 2:132, 135. The prohibition to reside in the coastal area is mentioned in II 207 AR-Z 125/1968, 1:102.

43. BA Dahlwitz-Hoppegarten, R 090, Nr. 147.

44. Zimmermann, *Rassenutopie und Genozid*, p. 270.

45. ZSL Ludwigsburg, II 207 AR-Z 497/1967, 1:9.

46. Ibid., II 207 AR-Z 101/1967, 2: 328–29.

47. Ibid., II 207 AR-Z 125/1968, 1:192.

48. Ibid., 207 AR-Z 125/1968, 1:189.

49. *Ereignismeldung UdSSR Nr. 195*, April 24, 1942, NA Washington, Microfilm Publication T 175, roll 235.

50. ZSL Ludwigsburg, II 207 AR-Z 101/1967, 2:232–33.

51. Ibid., II 207 AR-Z 36/1970, vol. 1, and II 207 AR-Z 85/1970, vol. 1.

52. Ibid., II 207 AR-Z 497/1967, 2:196.

53. The petition was dated March 12, 1942, and bore the signature of eleven persons. BA Dahlwitz-Hoppegarten, R 090, Nr. 147.

54. The letters in this prolonged exchange of correspondence, stretching over several months, can be found in BA Dahlwitz-Hoppegarten, R 090, Nr. 147.

55. Bräutigam to Reichskommissar für das Ostland, June 11, 1942, BA Dahlwitz-Hoppegarten, R 090, Nr. 147.

56. Zimmermann, *Rassenutopie und Genozid*, p. 274.

57. The draft decree is summarized in a letter to the OKH dated July 31, 1942, Nuremberg document PS-1133, NA Washington, RG 238, box 98.

58. *Schnellbrief* of May 21, 1943, to the RSHA, the party chancellery and the OKW, with copies to the two Reichskommissare. BA Dahlwitz-Hoppegarten, R 090, Nr. 147.

59. Generalkommissar in Riga to Reichskommissar Ostland, June 11, 1943, BA Dahlwitz-Hoppegarten, R 090, Nr. 147.

60. Kommandeur der Sicherheitspolizei u. d. SD-Lettland to Generalkommissar in Riga, June 12, 1943, HMM Washington, RG-18.002.M*, reel 1, folder 05.

61. Befehlshaber der Sicherheitspolizei u.d. SD-Ostland to the Reichskommissar für das Ostland, October 19, 1943, BA Dahlwitz-Hoppegarten, R 090, Nr. 147.

62. Reichsminister für die besetzten Ostgebiete to the Reichskommissare for the Ostland and Ukraine and the Generalkommissar for Weissruthenien, November 15, 1943, BA Dahlwitz-Hoppegarten, R 090, Nr. 147.

63. Memo of Abt. I Pol. at the Generalkommissar in Riga, March 29, 1944, ZSL Ludwigsburg, II 207 AR-Z 497/1967, 2:148.

64. The indictment of Einsatzgruppen leaders enumerates various killings of Gypsies with a total number of 1,711 (*Trials of War Criminals*, 4:16–21). However, this is clearly not a complete count of the number of victims.

65. Statement of Dr. Wilhelm Gustav Schuebbe, NA Washington, RG 153, box 575, folder 21-ll; Breitman, *Architect of Genocide*, p. 181.

66. Ezergailis, *Holocaust in Latvia*, p. 200, n. 5; Vanya Kochanowski, "Some Notes on the Gypsies of Latvia by one of the Survivors," *Journal of the Gypsy Lore Society*, 3d ser., 25 (1946): 115.

67. Donald Kenrick and Grattan Puxon, *The Destiny of Europe's Gypsies* (New York, 1972), p. 150.

68. Christopher Browning, "Wehrmacht Reprisal Policy and the Mass Murder of Jews in Serbia," *Militärgeschichtliche Mitteilungen* 33 (1983): 31; Christopher Browning, "Harald Turner und die Militärverwaltung in Serbien 1941–42," in *Verwaltung contra Menschenführung im Staat Hitler: Studien zum politisch-administrativen System*, ed. Dieter Rebenstisch and Karl Teppe (Göttingen, 1986), pp. 351–52; Hilberg, *Destruction of the European Jews*, pp. 433–35.

69. *Verordnung betreffend die Juden und Zigeuner, Verordnungsblatt des Militärbefehlshabers in Serbien*, May 31, 1941, 83–89. A facsimile of this decree can be found in Rose, ed., *Der Nationalsozialistische Völkermord*, pp. 79–80.

70. *Behandlung der Zigeuner*, PA des AA, AZ Pol 3 Nr. 4c, cited by Zimmermann, *Rassenutopie und Genozid*, p. 249.

71. Hilberg, *Destruction of European Jews*, p. 436.

72. Nuremberg document NOKW-892, cited by Walter Manoschek, *"Serbien ist judenfrei": Militärische Besatzungspolitik und Judenvernichtung in Serbien, 1941–42* (Munich, 1993), p. 104.

73. Browning, "Wehrmacht Reprisal Policy," p. 37.

74. Nuremberg document NOKW-192, NA Washington, Microfilm Publication T 1119, roll 3.

75. *Ereignismeldung UdSSR Nr. 108*, October 9, 1941, Nuremberg document NO-3156, NA Washington, RG 238, box 60.

76. Nuremberg document NOKW-2961, *Trials of War Criminals*, 10:1166–69.

77. Nuremberg documents NOKW-891, 557, cited by Browning, "Wehrmacht Reprisal Policy," p. 37.

78. Manoschek, *"Serbien ist judenfrei,"* p. 86.

79. *"Sühnemassnahmen,"* November 4, 1941, Nuremberg document NOKW-905. A facsimile of this report is printed in *Trials of War Criminals*, 11:1139–40.

80. Browning, "Wehrmacht Reprisal Policy," p. 42.

81. *Trials of War Criminals*, 11:1253.

82. Cited in *Trials of War Criminals*, 4:493.

83. Ibid., 11:789.

84. Turner to SS-Gruppenführer Richard Hildebrandt in Danzig, October 17, 1941, Nuremberg document NO-5810, NA Washington, RG 238, box 100 (the English translation is by Browning, "Wehrmacht Reprisal Policy," p. 39).

85. Browning, "Wehrmacht Reprisal Policy," p. 41.

86. Instruction to all Feld- und Kreiskommandanturen, October 26, 1941, Nuremberg document NOKW-802, NA Washington, Microfilm Publication T 1119, roll 12 (part of the translation is again by Browning, "Wehrmacht Reprisal Policy," p. 41).

87. Nuremberg document NOKW-474, NA Washington, Microfilm Publication T 1119, roll 8.

88. BA-MA, RW 40/14, Anlage 29, cited by Browning, "Wehrmacht Reprisal Policy," p. 42; *Grundsätzliche Weisungen für den Winter*, Nuremberg document NOKW-840, NA Washington, Microfilm Publication T 1119, roll 12.

89. Turner to the Feld- und Kreiskommandanturen, November 3, 1941, Nuremberg document NOKW-801, NA Washington, Microfilm Publication 1119, roll 12.

90. Menachem Shelach, "Sajmiste—an Extermination Camp in Serbia," *Holocaust and Genocide Studies* 2 (1987): 251, 258, n. 28; Manoschek, *"Serbien ist judenfrei,"* pp. 173, 178.

91. Lecture notes for presentation before Generaloberst Löhr, August 29, 1942, Nuremberg document NOKW-1486, NA Washington, Microfilm Publication T 1119, roll 20.

92. Zimmermann, *Rassenutopie und Genozid*, p. 258.

93. Kenrick and Puxon, *Destiny of Europe's Gypsies*, p. 119.

94. Browning, "Wehrmacht Reprisal Policy," p. 31.

Chapter 9

1. Walther Wüst, *Indogermanisches Bekenntnis: Sieben Reden* (Berlin, 1943), p. 37. See also Michael H. Kater, *Das "Ahnenerbe" der SS 1935–1945: Ein Beitrag zur Kulturpolitik des Dritten Reiches* (Stuttgart, 1974), p. 414, n. 160.

2. Sabine Schleiermacher, "Die SS-Stiftung 'Ahnenerbe': Menschen as Material für 'exakte' Wissenschaft," in *Menschenversuche: Wahnsinn und Wirklichkeit*, ed. Rainer Osnowski (Cologne, 1988), p. 72.

3. The note is from Himmler's telephone log recently discovered in a Moscow archive. The log is scheduled to be published by Dieter Pohl et al. in 1999 or 2000.

4. Dortmund Kripo to Regierungspräsident in Minden (Westf.), October 14, 1942, STA Detmold, M 1 I P, Nr. 1578.

5. Sievers to Kriminalrat Dr. Zauke, January 14, 1943, Nuremberg document NO-1725, NA Washington, RG 238, box 35.

6. Peter Heuss, "Kulturpolitik im Dritten Reich: Das 'Ahnenerbe' der SS und seine Funktion für Himmlers Rassenpolitik," in *Die Sinti/Roma Erzählungskunst im Kontext Europäischer Märchenkultur*, ed. Daniel Strauss (Heidelberg, 1992), p. 103; Astrid Hemmerlein, "Sinti und Roma im System Heinrich Himmler," (Diplomarbeit, Free University, Berlin, 1994), pp. 56–57.

7. *Zigeunerhäuptlinge*, October 13, 1942, *Beilage zum Meldeblatt der Kriminalpolizeileitstelle München und der Kriminalpolizeistellen Nürnberg, Augsburg, Regensburg und Würzburg*, October 27, 1942, pp. 295–96. The instruction is reprinted in Döring, *Zigeuner im nationalsozialistischen Staat*, pp. 212–14.

8. Ibid.

9. See, e.g., Ritter, "Bestandaufnahme," pp. 477–89, Ritter; "Zigeunerfrage und Zigeunerbastardproblem," pp. 2–20; and Ritter's lecture in Bremen "Das deutsche Zigeunerproblem der Gegenwart," n.d., BA Berlin, Zsg 142, Anh. 28, pp. 211–14

10. Justin's memo *Zigeunerforschung* is quoted in Joachim S. Hohmann, *Robert Ritter und die Erben der Kriminalbiologie: Zigeunerforschung im Nationalsozialismus und in Westdeutschland im Zeichen des Rassismus* (Frankfurt/Main, 1991), pp. 496–97. Hohmann does not provide sources for his material, but there is no reason to question the authenticity of the memo.

11. Rudolf Höss, *Commandant of Auschwitz: The Autobiography of Rudolf Höss* (Cleveland, 1959), p. 138.

12. These ideas are mentioned in a handwritten memo of November 1942 by Eva Justin, BA Berlin, ZSg 142/21, cited by Zimmermann, *Rassenutopie und Genozid*, p. 299.

13. Sievers diary for February 10, 1943, p. 45, NA Washington, Microfilm Publication T 175, roll 665.

14. *Einordnung von Zigeunermischlingen in die Sippen der reinrassigen Sinte- und Lalleri-Zigeuner*, January 11, 1943, *Erlasssammlung Nr. 15*.

15. This information comes from the generally well-informed Hermann Arnold, *Die NS-Zigeunerverfolgung: Ihre Ausdeutung und Ausbeutung* (Aschaffenburg, n.d. [1989]), p. 19.

16. Reimar Gilsenbach, *Oh Django, sing deinen Zorn: Sinti und Roma unter den Deutschen* (Berlin, 1993), p. 158.

17. The accusations by two survivors, made on September 3, 1946, and Reinhardt's response can be found in HMM Washington, RG 06.005.07M, reel 1.

18. Gilsenbach, *Oh Django*, p. 158.

19. LHA Magdeburg, C 29 Anh. 2, Nr. 384.

20. Robert L. Koehl, *RKFDV: German Resettlement and Population Policy, 1939–1945* (Cambridge, Mass., 1957), p. 122. See also Jan Tomasz Gross, *Polish Society under German Occupation: The Generalgouvernement, 1939–1944* (Princeton, N.J., 1979), p. 195.

21. Ritter to commandant of Mauthausen, September 11, 1942, Dokumentationsarchiv des Österreichischen Widerstandes, *Widerstand und Verfolgung im Burgenland, 1934–1945* (Vienna, 1979), pp. 280–81.

22. Heuss, "Kulturpolitik im Dritten Reich," p. 105.

23. NA Washington, Microfilm Publication T 580, roll 156, folder 256.

24. Sievers to Chef des SS-Hauptamtes Berger, May 21, 1943, NA Washington, Microfilm Publication T 175, roll 80, folder 66.

25. Ibid., T 580, roll 156, folder 256.

26. Bormann to Himmler, December 3, 1942, BA Berlin, NS 19/180.

27. Himmler appointment calendar, Sonderarchiv Moscow, 1372/5/23, cited by Zimmermann, *Rassenutopie und Genozid*, p. 300.

28. BA Berlin, R 43 II/1512.

29. Sybil Milton, "Nazi Policies toward Roma and Sinti, 1933–1945," *Journal of the Gypsy Lore Society*, ser. 5, 2, no. 1 (1992): 8; Henry Friedlander, *The Origins of Nazi Genocide: From Euthanasia to the Final Solution* (Chapel Hill, N.C., 1995), p. 293.

30. The minutes of this meeting are printed in Hohmann, *Robert Ritter*, pp. 76–77. As in other instances, Hohmann does not indicate the source of the document, though its authenticity is not in question.

31. *Einweisung von Zigeunermischlingen, Rom-Zigeunern und balkanischen Zigeunern in ein Konzentrationslager*, January 29, 1943, *Erlasssammlung Nr. 15*. The decree is also reprinted in Döring, *Zigeuner im nationalsozialistischen Staat*, pp. 214–18.

32. Ibid.

33. Ibid.

34. See, e.g., the recollection of Adolf Würth in Müller-Hill, *Murderous Science*, p. 144.

35. For example in Ritter, "Zigeunerfrage und Zigeunerbastardproblem," p. 19, and in "Erbärztliche Verbrechensverhütung," *Deutsche Medizinische Wochenschrift* 681 (1942): 539.

36. Sec. 4.3, *Erlasssammlung Nr. 15*.

37. Karlsruhe Kripo to the police and Landräte of Baden, February 5, 1943, GLA Karlsruhe, 364 Zug 1975/3 II, Nr. 24.

38. Ibid., report of March 28, 1943.

39. LHA Magdeburg, C 29 Anh. 2, Nr. 130.

40. Ibid., Nr. 519.

41. Ibid., Nr. 349.

42. Memo of Giessen Kripo, n.d., StA Giessen, L 1363–65; Hans-Günter Lerch, *"Tschü lowi . . ." : Das Manische in Giessen* (Giessen, 1976), p. 98.

43. *Liste über die bei der Aktion am 8.3.1943 in München festgenommenen zigeunerischen Personen*, StA Munich, PDM 581; Eiber, *"Ich wusste es wird schlimm,"* p. 79.

44. Günter Heuzeroth and Karl-Heinz Martinss, "Vom Ziegelhof nach Auschwitz: Verfolgung und Vernichtung der Sinti und Roma im Oldenburger Land und Ostfriesland," in *Unter der Gewaltherrschaft des Nationalsozialismus, 1933–1945:*

Dargestellt an den Ereignissen im Oldenburger Land, ed. Günter Heuzeroth (Oldenburg, 1985), 2:260; Hesse, *Bremen*, p. 421.

45. Mayor Breitscheid to Landrat in Dillenburg, March 13, 1941, HSA Wiesbaden, Abt. 410, Nr. 488; Frankfurt Kripo to Landrat in Dillenburg, May 5, 1941, HSA Wiesbaden, Abt. 410, Nr. 488.

46. Frankfurt Kripo to Landrat in Dillenburg, March 3, 1943, HSA Wiesbaden, Abt. 410, Nr. 488.

47. Landrat in Dillenburg to Frankfurt Kripo, March 5, 1943, HSA Wiesbaden, Abt. 410, Nr. 488.

48. Landrat in Dillenburg to Kreisführer Hampel in Dillenburg, May 5, 1943, HSA Wiesbaden, Abt. 410, Nr. 488.

49. David Bankier, *The Germans and the Final Solution: Public Opinion under Nazism* (Oxford, 1992), p. 135.

50. The lengthy correspondence which, in addition to the employers, involved the Landrat and the Frankfurt Kripo and Dortmund can be found in HSTA Wiesbaden, Abt. 410, Nr. 489.

51. LHA Potsdam, Rep. 30, Berlin C, Nr. 131.

52. GLA Karlsruhe, 507, Nr. 4279.

53. HSA Düsseldorf, BR 2034, Nr. 616.

54. Machens to Bertram, March 6, 1943, Ludwig Volk, ed., *Akten Deutscher Bischöfe über die Lage der Kirche 1933 bis 1945* (Mainz, 1985), 6:39, doc. 823.

55. Ibid., 6:44, doc. 826.

56. *Festnahme zigeunerischer Personen*, Nürnberg-Fürth Kripo to Landrat Uffenheim, May 13, 1944, STA Nürnberg, LRA Uffenheim, Abg. 1956, Nr. 2036.

57. Eva Justin, *Lebensschicksale artfremd erzogener Zigeunerkinder und ihrer Nachkommen* (Berlin, 1944). Justin received her degree on November 5, 1943.

58. Johannes Meister, "Schicksale der 'Zigeunerkinder' aus der St. Josephspflege in Mulfingen," *Jahrbuch des Historischen Vereins Württembergisch-Franken*, May 1984, pp. 197–229. The recollection of one of the surviving children can be in found in Rose, ed., *Der Nationalsozialistische Völkermord*, pp. 171–74.

59. HSTA Düsseldorf, BR 2034, Nr. 1093.

60. Essen Kripo to Duisburg Kripo, July 25, 1944, HSTA Düsseldorf, BR 1111, Nr. 41.

61. Ibid., BR 2034, Nr. 1168.

62. *Zurückbleibendes Vermögen der auf Befehl des Reichsführers-SS vom 16.12.1942 in ein Konzentrationslager einzuweisenden zigeunerischen Personen*, January 30, 1943, IfZ, MA-21.

63. Staatspolizeileitstelle Berlin to Oberfinanzpräsident Berlin-Brandenburg, May 5, 1943, HMM Washington, RG-07008*01.

64. Ibid. This film of documents from the LA Berlin contains many examples of these kinds of confusions.

65. Elfriede G. to Polizei-Präsidium Berlin, March 11, 1943, facsimile in Rose, ed., *Der Nationalsozialistische Völkermord*, p. 133.

66. Buchheim, "Die Zigeunerdeportation vom Mai 1940," p. 59.

67. The figure of 1,097 appears in a memo, *Historisches zur Zigeunerfrage*, composed in the RKPA, probably with the help of Ritter. The estimate of those to be added is in a handwritten memo of Eva Justin. See Zimmermann, *Rassenutopie und Genozid*, pp. 151, 299.

68. Ian Hancock, "Responses to the Porrajmos: The Romani Holocaust," in *Is the Holocaust Unique? Perspectives on Comparative Genocide*, ed. Alan S. Rosenbaum (Boulder, Colo., 1996), p. 47; Wolfgang Wippermann, ed., *Kontroversen um Hitler* (Frankfurt/Main, 1986), p. 48.

69. Memo of the minister of nutrition and agriculture, November 14, 1942, BA Berlin, R 14, Nr. 156. The meeting referred to in this memo took place on November 4.

70. Hans Buchheim of the IfZ in Munich estimated that the decree of October 13, 1942, could have benefited 6,000 Gypsies (ZSL Ludwigsburg, 414 AR 540/83, 4:586).

71. *Historisches zur Zigeunerfrage*, cited by Zimmermann, *Rassenutopie und Genozid*, p. 151. In her 1943 dissertation, Justin wrote that the Gypsy population of the Altreich was "about 20,000 individuals" (*Lebensschicksale*, p. 4). Since the Ostmark, after the deportations to Litzmannstadt, had about 8,000 Gypsies, Justin's number supports the accuracy of the figure of 28,627.

72. Bernhard Streck, "Zigeuner in Auschwitz: Chronik des Lagers B II e," in *Kumpania und Kontrolle: Moderne Behinderungen zigeunerischen Lebens*, ed. Mark Münzel and Bernhard Streck (Giessen, 1981), p. 115.

73. Danuta Czech, *Auschwitz Chronicle: 1939–45* (New York, 1990), p. 339.

74. For example, Martin Gilbert writes in his *Atlas of the Holocaust* (New York, 1993), p. 141: "Following a decree of 16 December 1942, all German Gypsies were deported to Auschwitz." See also Friedlander, *Origins of Nazi Genocide*, p. 293; Wippermann, *Wie die Zigeuner*, p. 167; Steinmetz, *Österreich's Zigeuner*, p. 14; Sybil Milton, "Correspondence on 'Gypsies and the Holocaust,' " *History Teacher* 25 (1992): 519. On the other hand, Yehuda Bauer writes that "only a minority" of German and Austrian Gypsies were sent to Auschwitz. "Gypsies," in *Anatomy of the Auschwitz Death Camp*, ed. Yisrael Gutman and Michael Berenbaum (Bloomington, Ind., 1994), p. 451.

75. Johannes Rau, "Damit es niemals wieder so wird: Der Völkermord an Sinti und Roma," *AVS-Informationsdienst* 16, no. 2 (February 1995): 2–3.

76. Ctibor Necas, "Die tschechischen und slowakischen Roma im Dritten Reich," in *Pogrom* 12, no. 80–81 (March–April 1981): 62; Ctibor Necas, "Das Schicksal und die Vernichtung der Roma im Protektorat Böhmen und Mähren," in *Der 50. Jahrestag der Vernichtung der Roma im KL Auschwitz-Birkenau*, ed. Waclaw Dlugoborski (Oswiecim, 1994), pp. 67–68. See also Josef Mares, "Development of the Gypsy Problem in the Protectorate of Bohemia and Moravia," HMM Washington, RG-07.013*01.

77. This point was stressed by American historian Paul Polanski at the unveiling ceremony for a memorial for murdered Gypsies near Lety on May 13, 1995. See "Havel kennt tschechische Mitschuld an NS-Greueln," *Neue Züricher Zeitung*, May 15, 1995.

78. Necas, "Schicksal und Vernichtung," pp. 69–71. The decree of March 9, 1942, *Vorbeugende Verbrechensbekämpfung*, was published in the *Verordnungsblatt des Reichsprotektors in Böhmen und Mähren* (1942): 582–85, HMM Washington, RG-07.013*01. The same film contains the Lagerordnung of Lety of September 30, 1942.

79. Necas, "Tschechischen und slowakischen Roma," pp. 62–63.

80. The meeting is discussed in Hans Guenter Adler, *Theresienstadt 1941–1945: Das Antlitz einer Zwangsgemeinschaft* (Tübingen, 1960), pp. 720–22.

81. Necas, "Tschechischen und slowakischen Roma," pp. 63–64; the report of May 7 is in HMM Washington, RG-07.013*01.

82. There are slight discrepancies in these numbers. In his 1981 essay, Necas gives the number of those listed in the register as 4,531 (p. 64); in his 1994 publication the number is 4,493 (p. 73).

Chapter 10

1. Czech, *Auschwitz-Chronicle: 1939–1945*, p. 295. For this chronicle, Czech, a staff member of the Auschwitz-Birkenau State Museum, used the official registries of the Gypsy camp.

2. Franciczek Piper, "Die Familienlager in Auschwitz-Birkenau (Genesis, Funktione, Ähnlichkeiten und Unterschiede)," in *Theresienstadt in der Endlösung der Judenfrage*, ed. Miroslav Karny et al. (Prague, 1992), 248–50; Nili Keren, "The Family Camp," in *Anatomy of the Auschwitz Death Camp*, pp. 428–440.

3. Bauer, "Gypsies," in *Anatomy of the Auschwitz Death Camp*, p. 451.

4. Kazimierz Smolen, "Das Schicksal der Sinti und Roma im KL Auschwitz-Birkenau," in *Das Schicksal der Sinti und Roma im KL Auschwitz-Birkenau*, ed. Jan Parcer (Warsaw, 1994), pp. 146–49; Czech, *Auschwitz Chronicle*, p. 341.

5. Höss, *Commandant of Auschwitz*, p. 138.

6. Tadeusz Szsymanski, "The 'Hospital' in the Family Camp for Gypsies in Auschwitz-Birkenau," in International Auschwitz Committee, *Nazi Medicine: Doctors, Victims and Medicine in Auschwitz* (New York, 1986), pt. 3, p. 4; Smolen, "Das Schicksal der Sinti und Roma," p. 140.

7. Smolen, "Das Schicksal der Sinti und Roma," pp. 150–51.

8. Streck, "Zigeuner in Auschwitz," p. 82.

9. Smolen, "Das Schicksal der Sinti und Roma," pp. 150–51. For data on minimum calorie requirements, see Hubert Schmitz, *Die Bewirtschaftung der Nahrungsmittel und Verbrauchsgüter 1939–1950, dargestellt an dem Beispiel der Stadt Essen* (Essen, 1956), p. 471.

10. Robert Lifton, *The Nazi Doctors: Medical Killing and the Psychology of Genocide* (New York, 1986), p. 323.

11. Wladyslaw Fejkiel, "Starvation in Auschwitz," in *From the History of KL Auschwitz*, ed. Kazimierz Smolen et al. (New York, 1982), p. 129.

12. Pohl to Brandt, April 9, 1943; Brandt to Pohl, April 15, 1943, BA Berlin, NS 19/180, pp 3–4.

13. Höss, *Commandant of Auschwitz*, p. 139.

14. Lifton, *Nazi Doctors*, p. 323.

15. Szymanski, "The 'Hospital' in the Family Camp," p. 18.

16. Ibid., p. 23.

17. Lucie Adelsberger, *Auschwitz: Ein Tatsachenbericht* (Berlin, 1956), p. 53.

18. Hermann Langbein, *Menschen in Auschwitz* (Vienna, 1972), pp. 237–38; ZSL Ludwigsburg, 402 AR-Z 47/84, vol. 1.

19. Olga Lengyel, *Five Chimneys: The Story of Auschwitz* (Chicago, 1947), p. 112.

20. Wieslaw Kielar, *Anus Mundi: 1,500 Days in Auschwitz* (New York, 1980), p. 180.

21. Ota Benjamin Kraus and Erich Kulka, *Death Factory: Document on Auschwitz* (Oxford, 1966), p. 203.

22. Kielar, *Anus Mundi*, p. 181.

23. Waclaw Dlugoborski, "On the History of the Gypsy Camp at Auschwitz-Birkenau," in State Museum of Auschwitz-Birkenau, *Memorial Book: The Gypsies at Auschwitz-Birkenau* (Munich, 1993), 1:3.

24. Langbein, *Menschen in Auschwitz*, p. 44; Streck, "Zigeuner in Auschwitz," p. 82.

25. Höss, *Commandant of Auschwitz*, p. 138.

26. Dlugoborski, "On the History of the Gypsy Camp," p. 4; Zimmermann, *Rassenutopie und Genozid*, p. 336.

27. Kater, *Doctors under Hitler*, pp. 233–35; Robert N. Proctor, "Nazi Doctors, Racial Medicine and Human Experimentation," in *The Nazi Doctors and the Nuremberg Code: Human Rights in Human Experimentation*, ed. George J. Annas and Michael A. Grodin (New York, 1992), p. 20.

28. Helena Kubica, "The Crimes of Josef Mengele," in *Anatomy of the Auschwitz Death Camp*, p. 323; Robin Cembalest, "An Artist Seeks to Recover Works from

Auschwitz," *Forward*, May 23, 1997 (a copy of the Cembalest article was provided to me by Harvey Newton). In their book *Children of the Flames: Dr. Josef Mengele and the Untold Story of the Twins of Auschwitz* (New York, 1991), Lucette Matalon Lagnado and Sheila Cohn Dekel speak of about 3,000 pairs of twins involved in Mengele's experiments; about one hundred of them survived (p. 7).

29. Miklos Nyiszli, *Auschwitz: An Eyewitness Account of Mengele's Infamous Death Camp* (New York, 1986), pp. 53–55; Kubica, "Crimes of Josef Mengele," p. 325.

30. Lifton, *Nazi Doctors*, p. 362; Benno Müller-Hill, *Murderous Science: Elimination by Scientific Selection of Jews, Gypsies, and Others* (New York, 1988), p. 71.

31. Szymanski, "The 'Hospital' in the Family Camp," pp. 31–33; Kubica, "Crimes of Josef Mengele," pp. 320–21.

32. Langbein, *Menschen in Auschwitz*, p. 383.

33. Szymanski, "The 'Hospital' in the Family Camp," pp. 30–31; Lifton, *Nazi Doctors*, p. 361; a facsimile of the order for histologic slides, signed by Mengele, can be found in Günter Heuzeroth and Karl-Heinz Martinss, "Vom Ziegelhof nach Auschwitz: Verfolgung und Vernichtung der Sinti und Roma im Oldenburger Land und Ostfriesland," in *Unter der Gewaltherrschaft des Nationalsozialismus 1933–1945: Dargestellt an den Ereignissen im Oldenburger Land*, ed. Günter Heuzeroth (Oldenburg, 1985), 2:255.

34. Streck, "Zigeuner in Auschwitz," p. 94; HMM Washington, RG 06.005M.07, reel 1.

35. Lifton, *Nazi Doctors*, p. 351.

36. Kater, *Doctors under Hitler*, p. 235.

37. HSTA Wiesbaden, Abt. 518, Nr. 4872, Bd. 1.

38. Ernst Klee, *Auschwitz, die NS-Medizin und ihre Opfer* (Frankfurt/Main, 1997), p. 465.

39. Quoted in Christian Bernadac, *L'Holocauste Oublié: Le Massacre de Tsiganes* (Paris, 1979), p. 154.

40. Sara Nomberg-Przytyk, *Auschwitz: True Tales from a Grotesque Land* (Chapel Hill, N.C., 1985), pp. 83–84.

41. Quoted in Annas and Grodin, *Nazi Doctors*, p. 80. See also Czech, *Auschwitz Chronicle*, pp. 414, 809–10; Hilberg, *Destruction of European Jews*, pp. 605–6.

42. Memo of Zentralbauleitung der Waffen-SS und Polizei Auschwitz, July 6, 1944, HMM Washington, RG 11.001M.03, reel 25, folder 95.

43. Szymanski, "The 'Hospital' in the Family Camp," pp. 20–21; Czech, *Auschwitz Chronicle*, pp. 358–59, 405.

44. Szymanski, "The 'Hospital' in the Family Camp," p. 25.

45. Smolen, "Das Schicksal der Sinti und Roma," p. 167.

46. Czech, *Auschwitz Chronicle*, p. 626.

47. Ibid., p. 632.

48. Grawitz to Himmler, June 28, 1944, Nuremberg document NO-179, NA Washington, RG 238, box 4.

49. Zimmermann, *Rassenutopie und Genozid*, p. 341, surmises that Nebe and the RKPA were indifferent to the fate of those not selected for work in Germany, and, at least implicitly, condoned their murder.

50. Wirbel, "Die Rückkehr von Auschwitz," p. 469.

51. Nyiszli, *Auschwitz*, p. 99.

52. Ibid., pp. 101–2; Lifton, *Nazi Doctors*, p. 186; testimony of Konrad Franciszeck Drewa, ZSL Ludwigsburg, 402 AR-Z 47/84, vol. 4.

53. Randolph Braham, "Hungarian Jews," in *Anatomy of the Auschwitz Death Camp*, p. 465; Krystyna Zywulska, *I Came Back* (London, 1951), p. 179; testimony of Erich Bruchwalski, ZSL Ludwigsburg, 402 AR-Z 47/84, vol. 3.

54. Höss, *Commandant of Auschwitz*, pp. 139, 141.

55. "Reminiscences of Pery Broad," in *KL Auschwitz Seen by the SS*, ed. Jadwiga Bezwinska and Danuta Czech (New York, 1984), p. 189.

56. Testimony of Meine, IfZ Munich, Gw 05.02/2.

57. Memo of June 3, 1944, HSTA Düsseldorf, BR 1111, Nr. 44.

58. Kenrick and Puxon, *The Destiny of Europe's Gypsies*, p. 153. These three sentences are omitted from the revised 1995 edition.

59. Höss, *Commandant of Auschwitz*, p. 115.

60. This tabulation is based on figures provided by Dlugoborski, "On the History of the Gypsy Camp," p. 4; Streck, "Zigeuner in Auschwitz," p. 128; Zimmermann, *Rassenutopie und Genozid*, p. 494, n. 212. Slightly different figures are given by Szymanski, "The 'Hospital' in the Family Camp," pp. 41–43. The difficulty of arriving at more precise numbers is stressed by Franciszek Piper, head of historical research at the Auschwitz-Birkenau State Museum, in "The Number of Victims," in *Anatomy of the Auschwitz Death Camp*, p. 70.

61. Czech, *Auschwitz Chronicle*, p. 728; Smolen, "Schicksal der Sinti und Roma," p. 170.

62. Necas, "Das Schicksal und die Vernichtung," p. 73.

Chapter 11

1. Ulrich Herbert, "Arbeit und Vernichtung: Ökonomisches Interesse und Primat der 'Weltanschauung' im Nationalsozialismus," in *Ist der Nationalsozialismus Geschichte? Zu Historisierung und Historikerstreit*, ed. Dan Diner (Frankfurt/Main, 1987), p. 228; Buchheim et al., *Anatomie des SS-Staates*, 2:125.

2. Ernst Klee, *Euthanasie im NS-Staat: Die "Vernichtung lebensunwerten Lebens"* (Frankfurt/Main, 1985), pp. 345–54. See also Walter Grode, *Die "Sonderbehandlung 14 f 13 in den Konzentrationslagern des Dritten Reiches: Ein Beitrag zur Dynamik faschistischer Vernichtungspolitik* (Frankfurt/Main, 1987).

3. Sofsky, *Order of Terror*, p. 43.

4. Quoted in Peter Black, "Forced Labor in the Concentration Camps, 1942–1944," in *A Mosaic of Victims: Non-Jews Persecuted and Murdered by the Nazis*, ed. Michael Berenbaum (New York, 1990), p. 51.

5. Hermann Kaienburg, *"Vernichtung durch Arbeit": Der Fall Neuengamme* (Bonn, 1990), p. 470.

6. *Erlass des Führers über besondere Vollmachten des Reichsministers für Justiz*, August 20, 1942, IfZ Munich, Gw 05.02/2.

7. Notes by Thierack on his meeting with Goebbels on September 14, 1942, Nuremberg document PS-682, NA Washington, RG 238, box 89.

8. Memo on talk between Thierack and Himmler (in the presence of several other officials), September 18, 1942, Nuremberg document PS-654, International Military Tribunal, *Trial of the Major War Criminals before the International Military Tribunal* (Nuremberg, 1947), 26:201–3.

9. BA Berlin, R 22/4199.

10. Thierack to Bormann, October 13, 1942, Nuremberg document NG-558, *Trials of War Criminals*, 3:674–75.

11. Zimmermann, *Rassenutopie und Genozid*, p. 192.

12. The case is described in detail in Eiber, *"Ich wusste es wird schlimm,"* pp. 95–96.

13. RSHA *Schnellbrief*, November 5, 1942, Nuremberg document L-316, IMT, *Trial of the Major War Criminals*, 38:99.

14. Thierack to Himmler and Bormann, November 16, 1942, Nuremberg document NG-1255, NA Washington, Microfilm Publication T 1139, roll 17 (the document can also be found in IfZ Munich, Fa 199/51).

15. Bormann to Thierack, *Betrifft Abgabe der Strafverfolgung gegen Polen, Sovietrussen, Juden und Zigeuner*, December 14, 1942, IfZ Munich, Gya 2/4.

16. Memos compiled in the Ministry of Justice noting a hold on the surrender of Gypsies begin on February 27, 1943, and continue at three-month intervals until as late as October 16, 1944 (IfZ Munich, Fa 199/51).

17. The court proceedings began in Wiesbaden in November 1949 and the record can be found in IfZ Munich, Gw 05.02/1–2. See also Karl-Leo Terhorst, *Polizeiliche planmässige Überwachung und polizeiliche Vorbeugungshaft im Dritten Reich: Ein Beitrag zur Rechtsgeschichte vorbeugender Verbrechungsbekämpfung* (Heidelberg, 1985), p. 168.

18. LHA Magdeburg, Rep. C 29, Anh. 2, Nr. 174.

19. Ibid., Nr. 175.

20. HSTA Wiesbaden, Abt. 409/4, Nr. 4167.

21. Ibid., Nr. 3940.

22. STA Nürnberg, Nürnberg Fürth Kripo, Abg. 1983, Nr. 357.

23. Sofsky, *Order of Terror*, p. 118.

24. Ibid, p. 43.

25. Eiber, *"Ich wusste es wird schlimm,"* p. 89.

26. Rascher to Brandt, October 3, 1942, Nuremberg document NO-285, NA Washington, RG 238, box 6.

27. Eiber, *"Ich wusste es wird schlimm,"* p. 85.

28. Grawitz to Himmler, June 28, 1944, Nuremberg document NO-179, NA Washington, RG 238, box 4; Brandt to Grawitz, July 8, 1944, BA Berlin, N 19/1584.

29. This is the sensible interpretation of available facts by Alexander Mitscherlich and Fred Miele, *Medizin ohne Menschlichkeit: Dokumente des Nürnberger Ärzteprozesses* (Frankfurt/Main, 1960), p. 85.

30. Affidavits by Ignaz Bauer, Fritz Pillwein, Josef Tschofenig, Nuremberg documents NO-910, 911, 912, NA Washington, RG 238, box 21; affidavit by Karl Höllenreiter, Nuremberg document NO-3961, NA Washington, RG 238, box 73; affidavit by Dr. Franz Blaha, Nuremberg document PS-3249, NA Washington, RG 238, box 49.

31. Eiber, *"Ich wusste es wird schlimm,"* p. 88.

32. The charges were made by a committee of German Gypsies headed by K. Jochheim-Armin and Georg Tauber. Details can be found in StA Munich, PDM 581.

33. Sofsky, *Order of Terror*, p. 43.

34. David A. Hackett, ed. and trans., *The Buchenwald Report* (Boulder, Colo., 1995), p. 262.

35. Eugen Kogon, *The Theory and Practice of Hell: The German Concentration Camps and the System behind Them* (New York, n.d.), p. 99.

36. Hackett, *Buchenwald Report*, p. 212.

37. Ibid., p. 138.

38. SS-Wirtschafts-Verwaltungsamt to Reichsarzt SS und Polizei [Grawitz], February 14, 1944, Nuremberg document NO-1188, NA Washington, RG 238, box 26.

39. Sofsky, *Order of Terror*, pp. 43, 179. See also the recollections of Franz Rosenbach in Rose, ed., *Der Nationalsozialistische Völkermord*, pp. 163–64.

40. Kogon, *Theory and Practice of Hell*, p. 45.

41. Black, "Forced Labor in the Concentration Camps," p. 58.

42. Erika Buchmann, *Die Frauen von Ravensbrück* (Berlin [East], 1961), pp. 30–31; Germaine Tillion, *Ravensbrück* (Garden City, N.Y., 1975), p. 240; Heike Krokoswski and Bianca Voigt, "Das Schicksal von Wanda P.—Zur Verfolgung der Sinti und Roma," in *Frauen in Konzentrationslagern: Bergen-Belsen, Ravensbrück*, ed, Claus Füllberg-Stolberg (Bremen, 1994), p. 265; Britta Pawelke, "Als Häftling geboren: Kinder in Ravensbrück," in *Kinder und Jugendliche als Opfer des Holocaust*, pp. 99–100.

43. Tillion, *Ravensbrück*, p. 241.

44. Ibid., p. 31.

45. Isa Vermehren, *Reise durch den letzten Akt: Ein Bericht* (Hamburg, 1948), pp. 94–95.

46. Franz, *Zwischen Liebe und Hass*, p. 67.

47. LHA Magdeburg, C 29 Anh. 2, Nr. 200.

48. Nuremberg document NO-875, NA Washington, RG 238, box 20.

49. Institut für Geschichte der Arbeiterbewegung/Zentrales Parteiarchiv, Berlin, St 63/72, cited by Eiber, *"Ich wusste es wird schlimm,"* p. 93.

50. Cited by Thomas Rahe, "Aus 'rassischen' Gründen verfolgte Kinder im Konzentrationslager Bergen-Belsen: Eine erste Skizze," in *Kinder und Jugendliche als Opfer des Holocausts*, p. 141.

51. Hermann Langbein, *Der Auschwitzprozess: Eine Dokumentation* (Vienna, 1995), 2:613–15.

52. Kettenacker, *Nationalsozialistische Volkstumpolitik im Elsass*, p. 248.

53. This account is based on testimony and documents used by a French military court sitting in Metz, summarized in HSTA Wiesbaden, Abt. 518, Nr. 4654, vol. 1.

54. Ibid. See also the recollection of the French inmate physician Dr. Henri Chretien, Nuremberg document NO-3560, NA Washington, RG 238, box 68.

55. HSTA Wiesbaden, Abt. 518, Nr. 4654, vol. 1. See also Schleiermacher, "Die SS-Stiftung 'Ahnenerbe,' " pp. 80–82.

56. "Ein Sinti berichtet: Ich war ein Versuchskanickel," in, *Mitten unter uns— Natzweiler-Struthof: Spuren eines Konzentrationslagers*, by Jürgen Ziegler (Hamburg, 1986), pp. 96–98; Rose, ed., *Der Nationalsozialistische Völkermord*, p. 154.

57. Gordon J. Horwitz, *In the Shadow of Death: Living outside the Gates of Mauthausen* (New York, 1990), p. 10.

58. Sofsky, *Order of Terror*, p. 43.

59. Horwitz, *In the Shadow of Death*, p. 12; the Buchenwald commandant's order for railroad cars for transport to Mauthausen, June 23, 1941, is included in Klamper, ed., *Archives of the Holocaust*, 19:181, doc. 69; Andreas Baumgartner, *Frauen im Konzentrationslager Mauthausen: Dokumentation, Quellensammlung und Datenbank* (Vienna, 1996), p. 77; Tillion, *Ravensbrück*, p. 105.

60. DÖW Vienna, Nr. 1371.

61. Baumgartner, *Frauen im Konzentrationslager Mauthausen*, p. 86.

62. Horwitz, *In the Shadow of Death*, p. 19.

63. Pingel, *Häftlinge unter SS-Herrschaft*, p. 257, n. 53.

64. Grawitz to Himmler, May 15, 1942, NA Washington, Microfilm Publication T 175, roll 66, frames 2582339–40. A facsimile of this document is found in Rose, ed., *Der Nationalsozialistische Völkermord*, pp. 145–46.

65. Brandt to Grawitz, June 5, 1942, Nuremberg document NO-410, NA Washington, RG 238, box 8.

66. Grawitz to Himmler, June 20, 1942, Nuremberg document NO-411, NA Washington, RG 238, box 8.

67. Hans-Peter Klausch, *Antifaschisten in SS-Uniform: Schicksal und Widerstand der deutschen politischen KZ-Häftlinge, Zuchthaus- und Wehrmachtsstrafgefangene in der SS-Sonderformation Dirlewanger* (Bremen, 1993), pp. 310–11; Wolfgang Günther, *"Ach Schwester, ich kann nicht mehr tanzen": Sinti und Roma im KZ Bergen-Belsen* (Hannover, 1990), p. 95.

68. Klausch, *Antifaschisten in SS-Uniform*, p. 35; Matthew Cooper, *The Phantom War: The German Struggle against Soviet Partisans, 1941–1944* (London, 1979), p. 88; order of SS Führungshauptamt, August 10, 1943, NA Washington, Microfilm Publication T 175, roll 225, frame 2762951; IfZ Munich, Fa 146.

69. Himmler order of February 19, 1944, IfZ Munich, Fa 146.

70. Klausch, *Antifaschisten in SS-Uniform*, pp. 141–42, 262, 295–95.

71. Hellmuth Auerbach, "Konzentrationslagerhäftlinge im Fronteinsatz," in *Miscellanea: Festschrift für Helmut Krausnick zum 75. Geburtstag*, ed. Wolfgang Benz et al. (Stuttgart, 1980), p. 66.

72. Michail Krausnick, *Abfahrt Karlsruhe: Die Deportation in den Völkermord, ein unterschlagenes Kapitel aus der Geschichte unserer Stadt* (Karlsruhe, 1991), p. 15.

73. State Museum of Auschwitz-Birkenau, *Memorial Book*, 2:1505.

74. Eibert, *"Ich wusste es wird schlimm,"* p. 99.

Chapter 12

1. Stuttgart Kripo to Cologne Kripo, September 20, 1943, HSTA Düsseldorf, BR 2034, Nr. 905. The figure of 1,000 Gypsies for Württemberg/Hohenzollern is given in a report by Ritter, probably compiled in the spring of 1940 (BA Berlin, ZSg. 142, Anh. 28). Eva Justin noted in her dissertation completed in late 1942 or early 1943 that "at the present time there are still more than 1,000 Gypsies in Württemberg" (*Lebensschicksale*, p. 11). Additional deportations from southwest Germany after September 1943 may have decreased slightly the number of Gypsies still to be found in the state of Württemberg.

2. HSTA Düsseldorf, BR 2034, Nr. 1180.

3. Ibid., Nr. 1179.

4. Ibid., Nr. 1024.

5. LHA Potsdam, Rep. 30, Berlin C, Nr. 142.

6. Ibid., Nr. 162.

7. Ibid., Nr. 75.

8. STA Nürnberg, Polizeipräs. Abg. 1983, Kripo-Insp. Nürnberg, Nr. 352.

9. HSTA Düsseldorf, BR 2034, Nr. 133.

10. LHA Potsdam, Rep. 30, Berlin C, Nr. 62, 127.

11. See, e.g., LHA Potsdam, Rep. 30, Berlin C, Nr. 93. The printed form read that person X, "unter Würdigung ihrer sozialen Anpassung" no longer falls "unter die für Zigeuner und Zigeunermischlinge geltenden Bestimmungen." Only the date and file number had to be typed in.

12. Ibid., Nr. 99.

13. HSTA Düsseldorf, BR 1111, Nr. 58.

14. Ibid., BR 2034, Nr. 1155.

15. LHA Potsdam, Rep. 30, Berlin C, Nr. 17.

16. Ibid., Nr. 93.

17. Ibid., Nr. 133.

18. Ibid., Nr. 114.

19. HSTA Düsseldorf, BR 2034, Nr. 1047.
20. LHA Potsdam, Rep. 30, Berlin C, Nr. 36.
21. Heinrich Wilhelm Kranz and Siegfried Koller, *Die Gemeinschaftsunfähigen* (Giessen, 1939–41), p. 161.
22. The order of August 31, 1939, has been discussed in chapter 3. The decree of September 9, 1944 can be found in *Reichsministerialblatt für die Innere Verwaltung*, September 15, 1944, p. 895.
23. *Erlasssammlung Nr. 15.*
24. Christian Gerlach, "Die Wannsee-Konferenz, das Schicksal der deutschen Juden und Hitler's Grundsatzentscheidung, alle Juden Europas zu ermorden," *Werkstatt-Geschichte* 18 (1997): 13. See also Hilberg, *Destruction of the European Jews*, pp. 269–73.
25. RKPA to Stuttgart Kripo, May 28, 1943, *Unfruchtbarmachung von Zigeunermischlingen*, HSTA Stuttgart, E 151/53, Bü. 164.
26. Götz Aly et al., *Cleansing the Fatherland: Nazi Medicine and Racial Hygiene* (Baltimore, 1994), pp. 36–39.
27. Wirtschafts- und Verwaltungshauptamt, Amtsgruppe D-Konzentrationslager, to the Lagerkommandanten, November 14, 1942, IfZ Munich, Fa 506/12.
28. A typical case of this sort can be found in STA Ludwigsburg, FL 20/19, Bü. 1277.
29. STA Nürnberg, Rep. 503, NS-Mischbestand Gauleitung Franken, Nr. 150.
30. Ibid.
31. LHA Magdeburg, Rep. C 29, Anh. 2, Nr. 199.
32. STA Nürnberg, LRA Uffenheim, Abg. 1956, Nr. 2036.
33. Ibid., Polizeipräs. Mfr. Abg. 1983, Krip. Insp. Nbg., Nr. 318.
34. Ibid.
35. HSTA Düsseldorf, BR 2034, Nr. 1117.
36. Eiber, *"Ich wusste, es wird schlimm,"* pp. 93–94; Marssolek and Ott, *Bremen im Dritten Reich*, pp. 336–37; Wolfgang Günther, *Die preussische Zigeunerpolitik seit 1871 im Widerspruch zwischen zentraler Planung und lokaler Durchführung* (Hannover, 1985), p. 63.
37. Marta Adler, *My Life with the Gypsies* (London, 1960), p. 175.
38. Eva Justin file, HSTA Wiesbaden, Abt. 461, Nr. 34141.
39. HSTA Düsseldorf, BR 2034, Nr. 1200, 1202.
40. Ibid., BR 1111, Nr. 39.
41. Karin Bott-Bodenhausen and Hubertus Tammen, *Erinnerungen an "Zigeuner:" Menschen aus Ostwestfalen-Lippe erzählen von Sinti und Roma* (Düsseldorf, 1988), p. 46.
42. Heuzeroth, "Vom Ziegelhof nach Auschwitz," p. 250.
43. Ibid., p. 261.
44. STA Ludwigsburg, FL 20/19, Bü. 1277.
45. Riechert, *Im Schatten von Auschwitz*, p. 135, and written communication from Riechert, April 12, 1996.
46. Ritter to the Präsident des Reichsforschungsrates, March 6, 1944, BA Koblenz, R 73, Nr. 14005.
47. HSTA Düsseldorf, BR 2034, Nr. 12.
48. LHA Potsdam, Rep. 30, Berlin C, Nr. 95.
49. Ibid., Nr. 34.
50. For example, the names of ten "flüchtige Zigeuner" appear in the *Deutsches Kriminalpolizeiblatt*, no. 4527, March 8, 1943.

51. STA Magdeburg, C 29 Anh. 2, Nr. 572.

52. LHA Potsdam, Rep. 30, Berlin C, Nr. 121.

53. Eiber, *"Ich wusste es wird schlimm,"* p. 108.

54. Niedersächsischer Verband Deutscher Sinti, *Es war menschenunmöglich*, p. 77.

55. LHA Potsdam, Rep. 30, Berlin C, Nr. 49.

56. Ibid.

57. Ibid.

58. Ibid., Nr. 29.

59. Feldscher, *Rassen- und Erbpflege im Deutschen Recht*, pp. 26, 28.

60. *Zwölfte Verordnung zum Reichsbürgergesetz*, April 25, 1943, RGBi.I, p. 268. A facsimile of the ordinance can be found in Rose, ed., *Der Nationalsozialistische Völkermord*, p. 36.

61. This ruling was issued by Fritz Sauckel, the Generalbevollmächtigte für den Arbeitseinsatz and can be found in NA Washington, Microfilm Publication T 301, roll 22, frame 836.

62. Himmler to the "Obersten Reichsbehörden," March 10, 1944, Nuremberg document NO-3719, NA Washington, RG 238, box 70. A bad English translation is given in PS-664, *Trials of War Criminals before the Nuremberg Military Tribunals under Control Council Law No. 10* (Washington, D.C., 1946–49), 3:713. An announcement, publicized in the *Mitteilungen des Hauptamtes für Volkstumsfragen* on September 9, 1944, similarly explained that there was no need for special identity cards for the Gypsies in the Reich. "The Mischlinge left here are to be regarded as socially adjusted." (The announcement is quoted in ZSL Ludwigsburg, 415 AR 930/61. It also notes that "the greatest part of this group of persons has been transferred to a Gypsy camp." Presumably, this refers to the Zigeunermischlinge.)

63. STA Magdeburg, C 29 Anh. 2, Nr. 469; LHA Potsdam, Rep. 30, Berlin C, Nr. 62, 154. See also Dieter Maier, *Arbeitseinsatz und Deportation: Die Mitwirkung der Arbeitsverwaltung bei der nationalsozialistischen Judenverfolgung in den Jahren 1938–1945* (Berlin, 1994), p. 219.

64. *Behandlung von Sonderfällen bei der Heranziehung zum Deutschen Volkssturm*, December 9, 1944, BA Berlin, N6/98.

65. RKPA to Munich Kripo, February 16, 1945, IfZ, Fa 704.

66. Herbert Heuss, *Die Verfolgung der Sinti in Mainz und Rheinhessen: 1933–1945* (Landau, 1996), p. 41.

Chapter 13

1. Kriminal Polizei-Zentrale, Region Hannover, to the military government, January 26, 1946, HSTA Hannover, Nds. Acc. 46/85, Nr. 408.

2. Landeskriminalpolizeiamt to minister of the interior Niedersachsen, March 13, 1947, HSTA Hannover, Nds. Acc. 46/85, Nr. 408.

3. Memo of Kriminalpolizeiamt Region Hannover, July 8, 1946, report on meeting of April 23, 1947, HSTA Hannover, Nds. Acc. 46/85, Nr. 408.

4. Kriminalpolizeiamt Lüneburg to Landeskriminalpolizeiamt Niedersachsen, February 28, 1948, HSTA Hannover, Nds. Acc. 46/85, Nr. 476.

5. Landespolizeikommissariat to the Landrat Buchen, July 3, 1946; the Landrat to the military government Buchen July 3, 1946; Abt. Innere Verwaltung, Landesbezirk Baden, January 19, 1950, GLA Karlsruhe, 345 Zug. 1986 Nr. 12/Nr. 248.

6. *Bayerisches Gesetz- und Verordnungsblatt*, Nr. 27/1953. The text of the law is reproduced in Eiber, *"Ich wusste es wird schlimm,"* pp. 134–36. See also Gilad Margalit, "Die deutsche Zigeunerpolitik nach 1945," *Vierteljahrshefte für Zeitgeschichte* 45 (1997): 575–79.

7. *Begründung* of *Landfahrerordnung für das Land Niedersachsen*, HSTA Hannover, Nds. 147, Acc. 46/85, Nr. 477 I.

8. Eiber, *"Ich wusste es wird schlimm,"* p. 132; Mathias Winter, "Kontinuitäten in der deutschen Zigeunerforschung und Zigeunerpolitik," in *Feinderklärung und Prävention: Kriminalbiologie, Zigeunerforschung und Asozialenpolitik*, by Wolfgang Ayass et al. (Berlin, 1988), p. 146.

9. Rudolf Uschold, "Das Zigeunerproblem," *Die Neue Polizei*, March 15, 1951, pp. 38–40; April 15, 1951, pp. 60–62.

10. Hans Eller, "Die Zigeuner—ein Problem," *Kriminalistik* 8 (1954): 14–26.

11. Eiber, *"Ich wusste es wird schlimm,"* p. 135.

12. Wolfgang Feuerhelm, *Polizei und "Zigeuner": Strategien, Handlungsmuster und Alltagstheorien im polizeilichen Umgang mit Sinti und Roma* (Stuttgart, 1987), pp. 249–56, 93.

13. Eiber, *"Ich wusste es wird schlimm,"* p. 131.

14. *Bundesentschädigungs-Schlussgesetz*, September 14, 1965, BGBl. I (1965): 1315, cited by Arnold Spitta, "Entschädigung für Zigeuner? Geschichte eines Vorurteils," in *Wiedergutmachung in der Bundesrepublik*, ed. Ludolf Herbst and Constantine Goschler (Munich, 1989), p. 392.

15. Decision of the Bundesgerichtshof of January 7, 1956, IV ZR 211/55. For a good discussion of this decision see Spitta, "Entschädigung für Zigeuner?" pp. 386–87.

16. Decision of the Oberlandesgericht Munich of March 1, 1963, E U 475/59, *Rechtssprechung zur Widergutmachung* 12 (1961): 313–448.

17. Decision of the Bundesgerichtshof of December 18, 1963, IV ZR 108/63, *Rechtssprechung zur Widergutmachung* 15 (1964): 209–211.

18. For a good discussion of these kinds of cases, see P. Petersen and U. Liedtke, "Zur Entschädigung zwangssterilisierter Zigeuner (Sozialpsychologische Einflüsse auf psychische Störungen nationalsozialistisch Verfolgter)," *Der Nervenarzt* 42 (1971): 197–205.

19. Riechert, *Im Schatten von Auschwitz,"* pp. 127–30.

20. Alexander Harder, *Kriminalzentrale Werderscher Markt: Die Geschichte des "Deutschen Scotland Yard"* (Bayreuth, 1963), pp. 11, 336. See also the eight-part series "Das Spiel ist aus—Arthur Nebe: Glanz und Elend der deutschen Kriminalpolizei," that was published in *Der Spiegel* between September 29, 1949 and April 20, 1950. Bernd Wehner acknowledges the authorship of this series in his book *Dem Täter auf der Spur*, pp. 93–94.

21. Hans Bernd Gisevius, *To the Bitter End* (Westport, Conn., 1975), p. 461.

22. Hans Bernd Gisevius, *Wo ist Nebe? Erinnerungen an Hitlers Reichskriminaldirektor* (Zurich, 1966), p. 244.

23. Fabian von Schlabrendorff, *The Secret War against Hitler*, trans. Hilda Simon (New York: Pitman, 1965), pp. 137, 174.

24. Peter Hoffmann, *The History of the German Resistance, 1933–1945* (Cambridge, Mass., 1977), pp. 328, 334–36; Harold C. Deutsch, *The Conspiracy against Hitler in the Twilight War* (Minneapolis, 1968), pp. 123, 177; Allan Welsh Dulles, *Germany's Underground* (New York, 1947), pp. 4, 45.

25. Heinz Höhne, *The Order of the Death's Head: The Story of Hitler's SS* (New York, 1970), p. 356.

26. Quoted in Höhne, *Order of the Death's Head*, p. 357.

27. *Trials of War Criminals*, 4:102–13. See also the discussion in Ronald Headland, *Messages of Murder: A Study of the Reports of the Einsatzgruppen of the Security Police and the Security Service, 1941–1943* (Rutherford, N.J., 1992), pp. 171–74.

28. Rudolf-Christoph Freiherr von Gersdorff, *Soldat im Untergang* (Frankfurt/ Main, 1977), p. 99.

29. Quoted in Helmut Krausnick, "Hitler und die Befehle an die Einsatzgruppen im Sommer 1941," in *Der Mord an den Juden im Zweiten Weltkrieg: Entschlussbildung und Verwirklichung*, ed. Eberhard Jäckel and Jürgen Rohwer (Stuttgart, 1985), p. 95.

30. Ogorreck, *Einsatzgruppen*, p. 178. See also the assessment of Peter Black, "Arthur Nebe: Nationalsozialist im Zwielicht," in *Die SS-Elite*, ed. R. Smelser and Enrico Syring (Paderborn, 1999).

31. Hilberg's account is based on participants' recollections and postwar trial records. See *Destruction of the European Jews*, 2d ed. (New York, 1985), 1:332–33.

32. This summary of events is based on evidence brought out at the trial of Widmann in 1959, ZSL Ludwigsburg, 439 AR-Z 18a/60, 3:12–14.

33. Ibid., pp. 15–16. See also Eugen Kogon et al., eds., *Nazi Mass Murder: A Documentary History of the Use of Poison Gas* (New Haven, Conn. 1993), pp. 52–53, and Christian Gerlach, "Failure of Plan for an SS Extermination Camp in Mogilev, Belorussia," *Holocaust and Genocide Studies* 11 (1997): 65. Gerlach suggests that the idea of killing by motor exhaust gas may have been developed earlier.

34. BA-MA Freiburg, RH 22-225, p. 70; Streit, *Keine Kameraden*, p. 122; Hannes Heer, "Die Logik des Vernichtungskrieges: Wehrmacht und Partisanenkampf," in, *Vernichtungskrieg: Verbrechen der Wehrmacht, 1941–1944*, ed. Hannes Heer and Klaus Naumann, (Hamburg, 1995), p. 135.

35. Grawitz to Himmler, June 28, 1944, NA Washington, Nuremberg document NO-179, RG 238, box 4.

36. Wehner, *Dem Täter auf der Spur*, pp. 202, 204. See also the interview of Wehner by public prosecutor Schneider on January 26, 1960, IfZ Munich, ZS 3119. Rudolf Diels, the deputy chief of the Geheimes Staatspolizeiamt and Nebe's superior, speaks of Nebe in 1933 as a careerist without moral scruples (*Lucifer ante Portas: Zwischen Severing und Heydrich* [Zurich, n.d.], p. 281).

37. Smolen, "Das Schicksal der Sinti und Roma," p. 153.

38. DÖW Vienna, Nr. 9626.

39. *Trials of War Criminals*, 4:16–21, 415.

40. Manoschek, "*Serbien ist judenfrei*," p. 24.

41. Hilberg, *Destruction of the European Jews*, p. 714.

42. Hans-Heinrich Wilhelm, *Die Einsatzgruppe A der Sicherheitspolizei und des SD, 1941–42* (Frankfurt/Main, 1996), p. 468.

43. ZSL Ludwigsburg, II 207 AR-Z 497/1967, Bd. 4; Hilberg, *Destruction of the European Jews*, p. 708.

44. Eiber, "*Ich wusste es wird schlimm*," p. 133.

45. Klamper, "Persecution and Annihilation of Roma and Sinti in Austria, 1938–1945," p. 63, n. 11.

46. Gideon Hausner, *Justice in Jerusalem* (New York, 1966), p. 424.

47. Memo of Staatsanwaltschaft Stuttgart, January 29, 1982, pp. 4–6, HSTA Wiesbaden, Abt. 461, Nr. 3412, Bd. 2.

48. Ibid., pp. 6–7.

49. Ritter, "Arbeitsbericht," BA Koblenz, R 73, Nr. 14005, p. 1.

50. Ritter, "Bestandaufnahme," p. 481.

51. Ritter, "Arbeitsbericht," BA Koblenz, R 73, Nr. 14005, p. 7.

52. Ritter made this claim in a statement composed when he applied for a position in the municipal health service in 1947, "Erläuterungen zu unseren Asozialen- und Zigeunerforschungen," p. 40, quoted in Gilad Margalit, "The Justice System of the Federal Republic of Germany and the Nazi Persecution of the Gypsies," *Holocaust and Genocide Studies* 11 (1997): 339.

53. Ritter described this episode in a letter of April 28, 1949, to Hermann Arnold, a fellow Gypsy expert. The letter is quoted in Arnold, *Die NS-Zigeunerverfolgung*, p. 9. Ritter's opposition to this and similar proposals is also mentioned in testimony by Eva Justin given during the investigation of Dr. Maly (Müller-Hill, *Murderous Science*, p. 59).

54. Hermann Arnold, *Die Zigeuner: Herkunft und Leben der Stämme im deutschen Sprachgebiet* (Olten, 1965), p. 295; Döring, *Zigeuner im Nationalsozialistischen Staat*, p. 82.

55. "*Gründe*" for ending the investigation of Eva Justin, HSTA Wiesbaden, Abt. 461, Nr. 34141.

56. IV. Zivilsenat des Bundesgerichtshofes, May 16, 1962, IfZ Munich, Gx 30.

57. LHA Potsdam, Rep. 30 Berlin C, Nr. 106.

58. Eva Justin, *Lebensschicksale artfremd erzogener Zigeunerkinder und ihrer Nachkommen* (Berlin, 1944), pp. 120–21.

59. Hermann Arnold, "Ein Menschenalter danach: Anmerkungen zur Geschichtsschreibung der Zigeunerverfolgung," *Mitteilungen zur Zigeunerkunde*, Beiheft Nr. 4 (1977): 9. The article is reproduced in ZSL Ludwigsburg, 414 AR-Z 42/83, p. 69 ff.

60. Staatsanwaltschaft Stuttgart, January 29, 1982, HSTA Wiesbaden, Abt. 461, Nr. 3412, Bd. 2.

61. Müller-Hill, *Murderous Science*, p. 144.

62. ZLS Ludwigsburg, 414 AR 540/83, Bd. 4. See also " 'Die nette alte Dame,' " *Mitteilungen der Dokumentationsstelle zur NS-Sozialpolitik* 2, no. 12 (April 1986): 114–35.

63. Rüdiger Vossen, *Zigeuner: Roma, Sinti, Gytanos—Zwischen Verfolgung und Romantisierung* (Frankfurt/Main, 1983), p. 158; Feuerhelm, *Polizei und "Zigeuner,"* p. 9.

64. Grattan Puxon, *Roma: Europe's Gypsies* (London, 1987), p. 13.

65. Katrin Reemtsma, *Sinti und Roma: Geschichte, Kultur und Gegenwart* (Munich, 1996), p. 57.

66. Vossen, *Zigeuner*, pp. 112–14.

67. Michael H. Schenk, *Rassismus gegen Sinti und Roma: Zur Kontinuität der Zigeunerverfolgung innerhalb der deutschen Gesellschaft von der Weimarer Republik bis in die Gegenwart* (Frankfurt/Main, 1994), p. 486.

68. Josef Bura, "Die unbewältigte Vergangenheit: Zigeunerpolitik und alltäglicher Rassismus in der Bundesrepublik," in *Sinti in der Bundesrepublik: Beiträge zur sozialen Lage einer verfolgten Minderheit*, ed. Rudolph Bauer et al. (Bremen, 1984), pp. 62–63.

69. Rainer Münz and Ralf Ulrich, "Changing Patterns of Immigration to Germany, 1945–1995: Ethnic Origins, Demographic Structure, Future Prospects," in *Migration Past, Migration Future: Germany and the United States*, ed. Klaus J. Bade and Myron Weiner (Providence, R.I., 1997), pp. 84–87, 97.

70. Gilad Margalit, "Antigypsism in the Political Culture of the Federal Republic of Germany: A Parallel with Antisemitism?" *Acta: Analysis of Current Trends in Antisemitism* 9 (1996): 23–25.

71. Alan Cowell, "Attack on Austrian Gypsies Deepens Fear of Neo-Nazis," *New York Times*, February 21, 1995.

72. Wilfried Schubarth, "Fremde als Sündenböcke," *Spiegel Spezial* 1 (1991): 47, cited by Susan Tebbutt, ed., *Sinti and Roma in German-Speaking Society and Literature* (Providence, R.I., 1998), p. x.

73. EMNID Institut survey, January 12–31, 1994, discussed in Reemtsma, *Sinti und Roma*, p. 173.

74. Tilman Zülch, ed., *In Auschwitz vergast; bis heute verfolgt: Zur Situation der Roma (Zigeuner) in Deutschland und Europa* (Reinbek bei Hamburg, 1979).

75. Reemtsma, *Sinti und Roma*, p. 143. See also the discussion in Gilad Margalit, "Sinti und andere Deutsche—Über ethnische Spiegelungen," *Tel Aviver Jahrbuch für deutsche Geschichte* 26 (1997): 304–5; and Yaron Matras, "The Development of the Romani Civil Rights Movement in Germany 1945–1996," in *Sinti and Roma in German-Speaking Society and Literature*, pp. 60–63.

76. Report of January 31, 1944, BA Koblenz, R 73, Nr. 14005.

77. The long and involved saga of the files is discussed by Josef Henke, "Quellenschicksale und Bewertungsfragen: Archivische Probleme bei der Überlieferungsbildung zur Verfolgung der Sinti und Roma im Dritten Reich," *Vierteljahrshefte für Zeitgeschichte* 41 (1993): 64–71. See also Karola Fings and Frank Sparing, "Vertuscht, Verleugnet, Versteckt: Akten zur NS-Verfolgung von Sinti und Roma," in *Besatzung und Bündnis: Deutsche Herrschaftsstrategieen in Ost- und Südosteuropa, Beiträge zur nationalsozialistischen Gesundheits- und Sozialpolitik* 12 (1995): 181–201.

78. Barbara Distel, "Die Verfolgung und Ermordung der Sinti und Roma in der Arbeit der KZ-Gedenkstätte Dachau," in *Der Völkermord an den Sinti und Roma in der Gedenkstättenarbeit*, ed. Edgar Bamberger (Heidelberg, 1994), pp. 40–41.

79. Romani Rose and Walter Weiss, *Sinti und Roma im "Dritten Reich": Das Programm der Vernichtung durch Arbeit* (Göttingen, 1991), p. 22; Rose, ed., *Der Nationalsozialistische Völkermord*, p. 189.

80. Preface to Kirsten Martins-Heuss, *Zur mythischen Figur der Zigeuner in der deutschen Zigeunerforschung* (Frankfurt/Main, 1983), p. 28.

81. Joachim S. Hohmann, *Bravo Sinto! Auf den Spuren eines geächteten Buches: Eine Dokumentation* (Fernwald, 1986), p. 62.

82. "Differenzen um Sicht auf die NS-Geschichte," *Thüringer Allgemeine*, August 21, 1997; Stellungnahme by the Gedenkstätte Buchenwald, September 9, 1997. The relevant correspondence and position papers are available from the Gedenkstätte Buchenwald, Direktion-Haus 2, 99427 Weimar-Buchenwald.

83. Reemtsma, *Sinti und Roma*, p. 143.

84. Michael Zimmermann, "Das Stigma des Fremden: Zu einigen Neuerscheinungen über Geschichte, Kultur und Verfolgung der Roma und Sinti," *Die Zeit*, October 11, 1996, p. 58.

Chapter 14

1. RKPA, *Auswertung der rassenbiologischen Gutachten über zigeunerische Personen*, September 20, 1941, *Erlasssammlung Nr. 15*.

2. STA Munich, Pol Dir München, Nr. 7033.

3. I have found one such case in a Kripo file for Gypsies: Korseda M., said to belong to a family of Gypsy-like itinerants and considered asocial, was sent to Ravensbrück in June 1939 and to the woman's camp of Auschwitz in March 1942 (LHA Potsdam, Rep. 30, Berlin C, Nr. 90).

4. Report of rural police post Wildshut, DÖW Vienna, Nr. 1506/8.

5. Heinz Caprez, "Jenische als Naziopfer: Beschwerliche Suche nach Überleben-den," *Beobachter*, November 28, 1997, p. 49.

6. See most recently Thomas Sandkühler, *"Endlösung" in Galizien: Der Judenmord in Ostpolen und die Rettungsinitiativen von Berthold Beitz, 1941–1944* (Bonn, 1996); and Burleigh and Wippermann, *Racial State*, p. 59. In his diary entry of March 27, 1942, Goebbels mentioned the window of opportunity opened up by the war.

7. Kenrick and Puxon, *Destiny of European Gypsies*, give a figure of 21,500 (p. 183). Zimmerman, *Rassenutopie und Genozid*, estimates the number of dead as about 23,000 (pp. 381–382).

8. Kenrick and Puxon, *Destiny of European Gypsies*, pp. 83–84; Donald Kenrick, letter to the editor, *Holocaust and Genocide Studies* 4 (1989): 253.

9. Letter to the editor, *Frankfurter Rundschau*, February 20, 1997.

10. Rose and Weiss, *Sinti und Roma im "Dritten Reich,"* p. 176; Rose, *Der National-sozialistische Völkermord*, p. 189.

11. For example, Roman Herzog, president of the Federal Republic, on March 16, 1997, condemned the crimes against the Gypsies as "genocide" (*Tagesspiegel*, March 17, 1997).

12. Brenda Davis Lutz and James M. Lutz, "Gypsies as Victims of the Holo-caust," *Holocaust and Genocide Studies* 9 (1995): 356.

13. *Convention on the Prevention and Punishment of the Crime of Genocide, 9 Decem-ber 1948* (London: Her Majesty's Stationery Office, March 1966), cited by George Andreopoulos, ed., *Genocide: Conceptual and Historical Dimensions* (Philadelphia, 1994), p. 48.

14. This important point is raised by Steven T. Katz, *The Holocaust in Historical Context* (New York, 1994), 1:128.

15. Ibid., pp. 20–21.

16. ZSL Ludwigsburg, 402 AR-Z 47/84, Bd. 3, p. 576.

17. ZSL Ludwigsburg, 414 AR 540/83, Bd. 4, p. 233 (799).

18. Döring, *Zigeuner im nationalsozialistischen Staat*, p. 168.

19. Eiber, *"Ich wusste es wird schlimm,"* p. 94.

20. Zimmermann, *Rassenutopie und Genozid*, p. 383.

21. Rose, ed., *Der Nationalsozialistische Völkermord*, p. 8.

22. Donald Kenrick and Grattan Puxon, *Gypsies under the Swastika* (Hatfield, U.K., 1995), p. 7. This new edition not only is far shorter than the original book but also omits all documentation. In a publicity release, the publisher claims that "the deliberate omission of footnotes and references make it a compelling read for older schoolchildren as well as the most comprehensive and up to date single volume account of the fate of the Gypsies in the Holocaust."

23. Sybil Milton, "Gypsies and the Holocaust" (an exchange with Yehuda Bauer), *History Teacher* 25 (1992): 516.

24. Yehuda Bauer, "Gypsies and the Holocaust," p. 513.

25. For a review of the state of scholarship on this question, see Ulrich Herbert, "Vernichtungspolitik: Neue Antworten und Fragen zur Geschichte des 'Holo-caust,'" in *Nationalsozialistische Vernichtungspolitik 1939–1945: Neue Fragen und Kon-troversen*, ed. Ulrich Herbert (Frankfurt/Main, 1998), pp. 9–66.

26. Several such utterances are quoted in Christian Gerlach, "Die Wannsee-Kon-ferenz, das Schicksal der deutschen Juden und Hitlers politische Grundsatzentschei-dung, alle Juden zu ermorden," *Werkstatt-Geschichte* 18 (1997): 24–25, 35–37. For other examples, see Götz Aly and Susanne Heim, *Vordenker der Vernichtung: Auschwitz und die deutschen Pläne für eine neue europäische Ordnung* (Hamburg, 1991).

27. Steven T. Katz, "Essay: Quantity and Interpretation—Issues in the Comparative Historical Analysis of the Holocaust," *Holocaust and Genocide Studies* 4 (1989): 145.

28. Lucy S. Dawidowicz, "Thinking about the Six Million: Facts, Figures, Perspectives," in *Holocaust: Religious and Philosophical Implications*, ed. John K. Roth and Michael Berenbaum (New York, 1989), p. 60.

29. Steven T. Katz, "The Uniqueness of the Holocaust: The Historical Dimension," in *Is the Holocaust Unique? Perspectives on Comparative Genocide*, ed. Alan S. Rosenbaum, (Boulder, Colo., 1996), p. 19.

30. Elie Wiesel, preface to *Report to the President* [Carter], President's Commission on the Holocaust (Washington, D.C., 1979), p. iii, quoted in *A Mosaic of Victims: Non-Jews Persecuted and Murdered by the Nazis*, ed. Michael Berenbaum (New York, 1990), p. xii.

31. Ian Hancock, "Uniqueness, Gypsies and Jews," in *Remembering for the Future*, ed. Yehuda Bauer et al. (Oxford, 1989), 2:2017–25. See also Edward T. Linenthal, *Preserving Memory: The Struggle to Create America's Holocaust Museum* (New York, 1995), pp. 243–44.

32. Gabrielle Tyrnauer, "The Fate of the Gypsies during the Holocaust: Report to the U.S. Holocaust Memorial Council," February 1985. The report was considered a planning document and was never published.

33. Ibid., p. 27.

34. Linenthal, *Preserving Memory*, p. 247.

35. Ian Hancock, "Responses to the Porrajmos: The Romani Holocaust," in *Is the Holocaust Unique?* p. 40.

36. Ian Hancock, "Communication: A Response to Raymond Pearson's Review of Ian Hancock—the Pariah Syndrome," *Nationalities Papers* 19 (1991): 434.

37. Quoted in Linenthal, *Preserving Memory*, p. 245.

38. Milton, "Correspondence: 'Gypsies and the Holocaust,' " p. 516. The charge was repeated in a lecture given in Berlin on December 12, 1994, "Der Weg zur 'Endlösung' der Sinti und Roma: Von der Ausgrenzung zur Ermordung," p. 3.

39. Niedersächsischer Verband Deutscher Sinti, *"Es war menschenunmöglich,"* p. 3.

40. Hancock, "Responses to the Porrajmos," p. 47.

41. Bamberger, ed., *Der Völkermord an den Sinti und Roma*, p. 13.

Bibliography

─────

Unpublished Sources

Archives in the Federal Republic of Germany

Bundesarchiv Berlin
Bundesarchiv Dahlwitz-Hoppegarten
Nordrhein-Westfälisches Staatsarchiv Detmold
Nordrhein-Westfälisches Hauptstaatsarchiv Düsseldorf
Stadtarchiv Frankfurt/Main
Bundesarchiv Militärarchiv Freiburg i.Br.
Staatsarchiv Freiburg
Stadtarchiv Giessen
Stadtarchiv Hannover
Niedersächsisches Hauptstaatsarchiv Hannover
Stadtarchiv Karlsruhe
Generallandesarchiv Karlsruhe
Bundesarchiv Koblenz
Landeshauptarchiv Koblenz
Staatsarchiv Ludwigsburg
Zentrale Stelle der Landesjustizverwaltungen Ludwigsburg
Landeshauptarchiv Magdeburg
Stadtarchiv München
Staatsarchiv München
Bayerisches Hauptstaatsarchiv München
Institut für Zeitgeschichte München
Nordrhein-Westfälisches Staatsarchiv Münster
Staatsarchiv Nürnberg
Brandenburgisches Landeshauptarchiv Potsdam
Hauptstaatsarchiv Stuttgart
Hessisches Hauptstaatsarchiv Wiesbaden

Archives in Austria

Archiv des Öffentlichen Denkmals und Museums Mauthausen Wien
Österreichisches Staatsarchiv Wien
Dokumentationsarchiv des Österreichischen Widerstandes Wien

Archives in the United States

National Archives, Washington, D.C.
U.S. Holocaust Memorial Museum, Washington, D. C.

Printed Sources

Pre-1945 Literature

Ammon, Kurt. "Die Zigeunerfrage in Deutschland: Verantwortungsbewusste Zusammenarbeit von Forschung und Praxis." *Völkischer Wille* 9, no. 11–12 (March 1941): 3.

Bader, [Karl Siegfried]. "Bekämpfung des Zigeunerunwesens." *Kriminalistische Monatshefte* 9 (1935): 265–68.

Baur, Erwin, et al. *Grundriss der menschlichen Erblichkeitslehre und Rassenhygiene.* Munich: J. F. Lehmann, 1921.

Behrendt. "Die Wahrheit über die Zigeuner." *Nationalsozialistische Partei-Korrespondenz* (Beilage "Volk und Familie") 35 (February 1939): 1–2.

Bercovici, Konrad. *Singing Winds: Stories of Gypsy Life.* Garden City, N.Y.: Doubleday, 1926.

Block, Martin. *Gypsies: Their Life and Their Customs.* Translated by Barbara Kuczynski and Duncan Taylor. London: Methuen, 1938.

Brandis, Ernst. *Die Ehegesetze von 1935 erläutert.* Berlin: Verlag für Standesamtwesen, 1936.

Dubitscher, Fred. "Der moralische Schwachsinn, unterer besonderer Berücksichtigung des Gesetzes zur Verhütung erbkranken Nachwuchses." *Zeitschrift für die Gesamte Neurologie und Psychiatrie* 12 (1936):422–57.

"Echte und Unechte Zigeuner, ihre Stellung in der Volksgemeinschaft." *Nachrichtendienst des Deutschen Vereins für öffentliche und private Fürsorge* 18 (1937): 345–48.

Ehrhardt, Sophie. "Zigeuner und Zigeunermischlinge in Ostpreussen." *Volk und Rasse* 17 (1942): 52–57.

Feldscher, Werner. *Rassen- und Erbpflege im Deutschen Recht.* Berlin: Deutscher Rechtsverlag, 1943.

Ferst, Elisabeth. *Fertilität und Kriminalität der Zigeuner: Eine statistische Untersuchung.* Munich, 1943.

Fickert, Hans. *Rassenhygienische Verbrechensbekämpfung.* Leipzig: Ernst Wiegandt, 1938.

Finger, Otto. *Studien an zwei asozialen Zigeunermischlings-Sippen: Ein Beitrag zur Asozialen- und Zigeunerfrage.* 2d ed. Giessen: Justus Christ, 1937.

Fraenkel, Ernst. *The Dual State: A Contribution to the Theory of Dictatorship.* Translated by E. A. Shils et al. New York: Oxford University Press, 1941.

Frick, Wilhelm. "Das Reichsbürgergesetz und das Gesetz zum Schutze des deutschen Blutes und der deutschen Ehre." *Deutsche Juristen-Zeitung* 23 (December 1935): 1390.

Greiner. "Verbrechensbekämpfung im nationalsozialistischen Staat." *Kriminalistische Monatshefte* 8 (1934): 121–24, 151–54.

Grellmann, Heinrich Moritz. *Dissertation on the Gypsies*. Translated by Matthew Raper. London: G. Bigg, 1787.

Günther. "Die Zigeunerverhältnisse in Berleburg." *Ziel und Weg* 7 (1937): 262–68.

———. "Sesshafte Zigeuner." *Reichsverwaltungsblatt* 58 (1937): 193–97.

Günther, Hans F. K. *The Racial Elements of European History*. Translated by G. C. Wheeler. London: Methuen, 1927.

Gütt, Arthur, et al. *Blutschutz- und Ehegesundheitsgesetz*. Munich: J. F. Lehmann, 1937.

Haag, F. E. "Zigeuner in Deutschland." *Volk und Rasse* 9 (1934): 190.

Haarer, Johann. "Unterirdische Filmtendenzen? Zigeuner im Film und in der Wirklichkeit." *Ziel und Weg* 7 (1937): 554–56.

Helbig, Adolf. "Bekämpfung des Zigeunerunwesens." *Der Deutsche Verwaltungsbeamte* 16 (1936): 494–96.

Herz, Hugo. *Verbrechen und Verbrechertum in Österreich: Kritische Untersuchungen über Zusammenhänge von Wirtschaft und Verbrechen*. Tübingen: H Laup'sche Buchhandlung, 1908.

Höhne, Werner Kurt. "Die Vereinbarkeit der deutschen Zigeunergesetze und -verordnungen mit dem Reichsrecht, insbesonder der Reichsverfassung." Ph.D. diss. University of Heidelberg, 1929.

Eva Justin. *Lebensschicksale artfremd erzogener Zigeunerkinder und ihrer Nachkommen*. Berlin: Schuetz, 1944.

———. "Die Rom-Zigeuner." *Neues Volk* 11, no. 5 (1943): 21–24.

Kopp, Walter. "Die Unfruchtbarmachung der Asozialen." *Der Erbarzt* 6, no. 6 (1939): 66–69.

Krämer, Robert. "Rassische Untersuchungen an den 'Zigeuner'-Kolonien Lause und Altengraben bei Berleburg (Westf.)." *Archiv für Rassen- und Gesellschaftsbiologie* 31 (1937–38): 33–56.

Kranz, Heinrich Wilhelm. "Zigeuner, wie sie wirklich sind." *Neues Volk* 5, no. 9 (1937): 21–27.

———. "Zur Entwicklung der Rassenhygienischen Institute an unseren Hochschulen." *Ziel und Weg* 9 (1939): 286–90.

Kranz, Heinrich Wilhelm, and Siegfried Koller. *Die Gemeinschaftsunfähigen*. Giessen: Karl Christ, 1939–41.

Küppers, G. A. "Begegnung mit Balkanzigeunern." *Volk und Rasse* 13 (1938): 183–93.

Küppers, H. "Die Beschäftigung von Zigeunern." *Reichsarbeitsblatt* 22 (1942): 176–78.

Kürten, H. "Die 'deutschen' Zigeuner." *Ziel und Weg* 7 (1937): 474–75.

Leibig, Carl. "Die Bekämpfung des Zigeunerunwesens." *Bayerische Gemeinde- und Verwaltungszeitung* 48 (1938): 159–62, 178–82.

Lombroso, Cesare. *Die Ursachen und Bekämpfung des Verbrechens*. Translated by Hans Kurella and E. Jentsch. Berlin: Hugo Bermühler, 1902.

Nebe, Arthur. "Aufbau der Deutschen Kriminalpolizei." *Kriminalistik* 12 (1938): 4–8.

Neureiter, Ferdinand von. *Kriminalbiologie*. Berlin: Carl Hymann, 1940.

Palitzsch. "Die Zusammenarbeit der deutschen Kriminalpolizeien im Kampf gegen das Verbrechertum." *Kriminalistische Monatshefte* 8 (1934): 217–20.

Reichskriminalpolizeiamt. *Organisation und Meldedienst der Reichskriminalpolizei*. Berlin: Elise Jaedicke, 1941.

Reichorganisationsleiter der NSDAP, ed. *Organisationsbuch der NSDAP*. 4th ed. Munich: Franz Eher, 1937.

Reiter, Hans. *Das Reichsgesundheitsamt, 1933–1939: Sechs Jahre nationalsozialistische Führung*. Berlin: Julius Springer, 1939.

Riedl, Martin. "Studie über Verbrecherstämmlinge, Spätkriminelle und Frühkriminelle und über deren sozialprognostische and rassehygienische Bedeutung." *Archiv für Kriminalogie* 93 (1933): 7–13, 125–35, 238–57.

Ritter, Robert. "Die Asozialen, ihre Vorfahren und ihre Nachkommen." *Fortschritte der Erbpathologie, Rassenhygiene und ihrer Grenzgebiete* 5 (1941): 137–55.

——— . "Die Aufgaben der Kriminalbiologie und der kriminalbiologischen Bevölkerungsforschung." *Kriminalistik* 15 (1941): 38–41.

——— . "Die Bestandaufnahme der Zigeuner und Zigeunermischlinge in Deutschland." *Der öffentliche Gesundheitsdienst* 6/B (1941): 477–89.

——— . "Erbärztliche Verbrechensverhütung." *Deutsche medizinische Wochenschrift* 681 (1942): 535–39.

——— . "Erbiologische Untersuchungen innerhalb eines Züchtungskreises von Zigeunermischlingen und 'asozialen Psychopathen.' " In *Bevölkerungsfragen: Bericht des internationalen Kongresses für Bevölkerungswissenschaft . . . 1935*, edited by Hans Harmsen and Franz Lohse, pp. 713–18. Munich: J. F. Lehmann, 1936.

——— . "Das Kriminalbiologische Institut der Sicherheitspolizei." *Kriminalistik* 16 (1942): 117–19.

——— . *Ein Menschenschlag: Erbärztliche und erbgeschichtliche Untersuchung über die— durch 10 Geschlechterfolgen erforschten—Nachkommen von Vagabunden, Jaunern und Räubern*. Leipzig: Georg Thieme, 1937.

——— . "Mitteleuropäische Zigeuner: Ein Volksstamm oder eine Mischlingspopulation?" *Congrès International de la Population, Paris 1937, Extrait VIII*, pp. 51–60. Paris: Hermann, 1938.

——— . "Primitivität und Kriminalität." *Monatsschrift für Kriminalbiologie und Strafrechtsreform* 31 (1940): 197–210.

——— . "Untergruppe L3 (Rassenhygienische- und bevölkerungsbiologische Forschungsstelle." In *Das Reichsgesundheitsamt 1933–1939: Sechs Jahre nationalsozialistische Führung*, edited by Hans Reiter, pp. 356–58. Berlin: Julius Springer, 1939.

——— . "Zigeuner und Landfahrer." In *Der nicht sesshafte Mensch: Ein Beitrag zur Neugestaltung der Raum- und Menschenordnung im Grossdeutschen Reich*, edited by Bayerischer Landesverband für Wanderdienst, pp. 71–88. Munich: C. H. Beck, 1938.

——— . "Die Zigeunerfrage und das Zigeunerbastardproblem." *Fortschritte der Erbpathologie, Rassenhygiene und ihrer Grenzgebiete* 3 (1939): 2–20.

——— . "Zur Frage der Rassenbiologie und Rassenpsychologie der Zigeuner in Deutschland." *Reichs-Gesundheitsblatt* 13 (1938): 425–26.

Rodenberg, Carl–Heinz. "Die Zigeunerfrage." *Der öffentliche Gesundheitsdienst* 3/B (1937): 437–46.

Rohne. "Zigeunerpolizei." *Reichsverwaltungsblatt* 58 (1937): 197–99.

Römer, Joachim. "Fremdrassen in Sachsen (Aus der Erhebung des Rassenpolitischen Amtes der NSDAP)." *Volk und Rasse* 12 (1937): 281–88, 321–28.

——— . "Zigeuner in Deutschland." *Volk und Rasse* 9 (1934): 112–13.

Rüdiger, Karlheinz. "Parasiten der Gemeinschaft." *Volk und Rasse* 13 (1938): 87–89.

Scott, Macfie. "Gypsy Persecution: Survey of a Black Chapter in European History." *Journal of the Gypsy Lore Society*, 3d ser. 3, 22 (1943): 65–78.

Stein, Gerhard. "Zur Physiologie und Anthropologie der Zigeuner in Deutschland." *Zeitschrift für Ethnologie* 72 (1940): 74–114.

Stuckart, Wilhelm, and Hans Globke. *Kommentar zur deutschen Rassengesetzgebung*. Vol. 1. Munich: C. Beck, 1936.

Stuckart, Wilhelm, and Rolf Schiedermair. *Rassen- und Erbpflege in der Gesetzgebung des Reiches*. 3d ed. Leipzig: W. Kohlhammer, 1942.

Thiele, H. "Zur Frage der asozialen Psychopathen." *Der öffentliche Gesundheitsdienst* 4/A (1938–39): 394–96.

"Über das Königsberger Zigeunerlager." *Ziel und Weg* 13 (1938): 360.

Verschuer, Otmar Freiherr von. *Leitfaden der Rassenhygiene*. Stuttgart: Georg Thiem, 1941.

Weissenbruch, Johann Benjamin. *Ausführliche Relation von der Famosen Zigeuner-Diebs-Mord und Rauber Bande*. Frankfurt: Joh. Pil. Krieger, 1727.

Werner, Paul. "Die vorbeugende Verbrechensbekämpfung durch die Polizei." *Kriminalistik* 12 (1938): 58–61.

Wittich, Engelbert. *Blicke in das Leben der Zigeuner*. Rev. ed. Hamburg: Advent, 1927.

Würth, A. "Bemerkungen zur Zigeunerfrage und Zigeunerforschung in Deutschland." *Verhandlungen der deutschen Gesellschaft für Rassenforschung* 9 (1938): 95–98.

——— . "Die Zigeuner- und Zigeunermischlingsfrage in Deutschland." *Der Öffentliche Gesundheitsdienst* 5 (1939/40): 36–37.

Wüst, Walther. *Indogermanisches Bekenntnis: Sieben Reden*. Berlin: Ahnenerbe-Stiftung, 1943.

"Die Zigeuner als asoziale Bevölkerungsgruppe." *Deutsches Ärzteblatt* 69 (1939): 246–47.

"Zigeunerfrage im Burgenland." *Ziel und Weg* 13 (1938): 572.

"Die Zigeunerfrage in der Ostmark." *Neues Volk* 6, no. 9 (1938): 22–27.

Post-1945 Literature

Ackermann, Josef. *Heinrich Himmler als Ideologe*. Göttingen: Musterschmidt, 1970.

Ackovic, Dragoljub. "Suffering of Roma in Yugoslavia in Second World War." *Giessener Hefte für Tsiganologie* 3 (1986): 128–34.

Acton, Thomas A. "Zigeunerkunde—ein Begriff dessen Zeit vorüber ist." *Zeitschrift für Kulturaustausch* 31 (1981): 380–84.

Adelsberger, Lucie. *Auschwitz: Ein Tatsachenbericht*. Berlin: Leitner, 1956.

Adler, Hans Guenter. *Theresienstadt 1941–1945: Das Antlitz einer Zwangsgemeinschaft*, 2nd ed. Tübingen: J. C. B. Mohr, 1960.

Adler, Marta. *My Life with the Gypsies*. London: Souvenir, 1960.

Alt, Betty, and Silvia Folts. *Weeping Violins: The Gypsy Tragedy in Europe*. Kirksville, Mo.: Thomas Jefferson University Press, 1996.

Aly, Götz. *"Endlösung," Völkerwanderung und der Mord an den europäischen Juden*. Frankfurt/Main: S. Fischer, 1995.

Aly, Götz, et al. *Cleansing the Fatherland: Nazi Medicine and Racial Hygiene*. Trans. Belinda Cooper. Baltimore: Johns Hopkins University Press, 1994.

Aly, Götz, and Susanne Heim. *Vordenker der Vernichtung: Auschwitz und die deutschen Pläne für eine neue europäische Ordnung*. Hamburg: Hoffmann and Campe, 1991.

Aly, Götz, and Karl Heinz Roth. *Die restlose Erfassung: Volkszählen, Indentifizieren, Aussondern im Nationalsozialismus*. Berlin: Rotbuch, 1984.

Andreopoulos, George, ed. *Genocide: Conceptual and Historical Dimensions*. Philadelphia: University of Pennsylvania Press, 1994.

Annas, George J., and Michael A. Grodin. *The Nazi Doctors and the Nuremberg Code: Human Rights in Human Experimentation*. New York: Oxford University Press, 1992.

Arnold, Hermann. "Ein Menschenalter danach: Anmerkungen zur Geschichtsschreibung der Zigeunerverfolgung." *Mitteilungen zur Zigeunerkunde* Beiheft no.4
(1977): 1–15.

——— . *Randgruppen des Zigeunervolkes*. Neustadt/Weinstrasse: Pfälzische Verlagsanstalt, 1975.

———. *Die Zigeuner: Herkunft und Leben der Stämme im deutschen Sprachgebiet*. Olten:
Walter, 1965.

———. *Die NS-Zigeunerverfolgung: Ihre Ausdeutung und Ausbeutung*. Aschaffenburg:
Antiquariat Karl-Heinz Gerster, n.d. [1989].

Aronson, Shlomo. *Reinhard Heydrich und die Frühgeschichte von Gestapo und SD*.
Stuttgart: Deutsche Verlags-Anstalt, 1971.

Auerbach, Hellmuth. "Die Einheit Dirlewanger." *Vierteljahrshefte für Zeitgeschichte*
10 (1962): 250–63.

———. "Konzentrationslagerhäftlinge im Fronteinsatz." In *Miscellanea: Festschrift für
Helmut Krausnick zum 75*. Geburtstag, edited by Wolfgang Benz, pp. 63–83.
Stuttgart: Deutsche Verlagsanstalt, 1980.

Ayass, Wolfgang. *"Asoziale" im Nationalsozialismus*. Stuttgart: Klett-Cotta, 1995.

——— . "Vagrants and Beggars in Hitler's Reich." In *The German Underworld:
Deviants and Outcasts in German History*, edited by Richard J. Evans, pp. 210–37.
London: Routledge, 1988.

Ayass, Wolfgang, et al. *Feinderklärung und Prävention: Kriminalbiologie, Zigeunerforschung und Asozialenpolitik. Beiträge zur nationalsozialistischen Gesundheits- und
Sozialpolitik*, no. 6. Berlin: Rotbuch, 1988.

Bamberger, Edgar, ed. *Der Völkermord an den Sinti und Roma in der Gedenkstättenarbeit*. Heidelberg: Dokumentations- und Kulturzentrum Deutscher Sinti, 1994.

Bamberger, Edgar, and Annegret Ehmann, eds. *Kinder und Jugendliche als Opfer des
Holocaust*. Heidelberg: Dokumentationszentrum Deutscher Sinti und Roma,
1995.

Bankier, David. *The Germans and the Final Solution: Public Opinion under Nazism*.
Oxford: Blackwell, 1992.

Bartov, Omer. *The Eastern Front, 1941–45: German Troops and the Barbarization of
Warfare*. London: Macmillan, 1995.

——— . *Hitler's Army: Soldiers, Nazis and War in the Third Reich*. New York: Oxford
University Press, 1991.

Bauer, Yehuda. "Correspondence: 'Gypsies and the Holocaust.' " *History Teacher* 25
(1992): 513–15.

———. "Gypsies." In *Anatomy of the Auschwitz Death Camp*. Edited by Yisrael Gutman and Michael Berenbaum, pp. 441–53. Bloomington, Ind.: Indiana University
Press, 1994.

———. "Gypsies." In *Encyclopedia of the Holocaust*, vol. 2, pp. 634–38. New York:
MacMillan, 1990.

———. "Jews, Gypsies and Slavs: Policies of the Third Reich." *UNESCO Yearbook on
Peace and Conflict Studies 1985*, pp. 73–100. Westport, Conn.: Greenwood Press,
1987.

Baumgartner, Andreas. *Frauen im Konzentrationslager Mauthausen: Dokumentation,
Quellensammlung und Datenbank*. Vienna: Bundesministerium des Innern, 1996.

Behrens, P. " 'Vollzigeuner' und 'Mischlinge': Die ehemalige Rassenforscherin Ruth
Kellermann verteidigt ihren Ruf," *Die Zeit*, February 7, 1986, p. 36.

Benz, Wolfgang. "Das Lager Marzahn: Zur nationalsozialistischen Verfolgung der
Sinti und Roma und ihrer anhaltenden Diskriminierung." In *Die Normalität des*

Verbrechens: Bilanz und Perspektive der Forschung zu den nationalsozialistischen Gewaltverbrechen, edited by Helge Grabitz et al., pp. 260–79. Berlin: Edition Hentrick, 1994.

Berenbaum, Michael, ed. *A Mosaic of Victims: Non-Jews Persecuted and Murdered by the Nazis*. New York: New York University Press, 1990.

Bernadac, Christian. *L'Holocauste Oublié: Le Massacre de Tsiganes*. Paris: Editions France-Empire, 1979.

Beuys, Werner. "Permanente Kriminalität durch Landfahrer." In *Kriminalpolizeiliche Tagespraxis*. Beilage zu *Die Polizei* 1 (February 1967): 49–52.

Bezwinska, Jadwiga, and Danuta Czech. *KL Auschwitz Seen by the SS*. Auschwitz: Pantwowe Museum, 1978.

Birnbaum, Mariana D. "On the Language of Prejudice." *Western Folklore* 30 (1971): 247–68.

Black, Peter. "Forced Labor in the Concentration Camps, 1942–1944." In *A Mosaic of Victims*, edited by Michael Berenbaum, pp. 46–63. New York: New York University Press, 1990.

———. "Arthur Nebe: Nationalsozialist im Zwielicht." In *Die SS-Elite*. Edited by R. Smelser and Enrico Syring. Paderborn: Schöningh, 1999.

Boberach, Heinz, ed. *Meldungen aus dem Reich, 1938–1945: Die geheimen Lageberichte des Sicherheitsdienstes der SS*. Herrsching: Pawlak, 1984.

Bock, Gisela. *Zwangssterilisation im Nationalsozialismus: Studien zur Rassenpolitik und Frauenpolitik*. Opladen: Westdeutscher Verlag, 1986.

Bodlée, Hans. "Landfahrer: Ein Beitrag über ihre Kriminalität." *Kriminalistik* 16 (1962): 575–78.

Boström, Jörg. *Das Buch der Sinti: "Nicht länger stillschweigend das Unrecht hinnehmen!"* Berlin: Elefanten, 1981.

Bott-Bodenhausen, Karin, and Hubertus Tammen, eds. *Erinnerungen an "Zigeuner": Menschen aus Ostwestfalen-Lippe erzählen von Sinti und Roma*. Düsseldorf: Kleine, 1988.

Bracher, Karl Dietrich. *The German Dictatorship: The Origins, Structure and Effects of National Socialism*. Translated by Jean Steinberg. New York: Praeger, 1970.

Braham, Randolph L. "Hungarian Jews." In *Anatomy of the Auschwitz Death Camp*, edited by Yisrael Gutman and Michael Berenbaum, pp. 456–68. Bloomington: Indiana University Press, 1994.

Breitman, Richard. *The Architect of Genocide: Himmler and the Final Solution*. New York: Alfred Knopf, 1991.

Brennan, Patricia A. "Biomedical Factors in Crime." In *Crime*, edited by James Q. Wilson and Joan Petersilia, pp. 65–90. San Francisco: ICS Press, 1995.

Broszat, Martin. *The Hitler State: The Foundation and Development of the Internal Structure of the Third Reich*. Translated by John W. Hiden. London: Longman, 1981.

———. "Nationalsozialistische Konzentrationslager 1933–1945." In *Anatomie des SS Staates*, Vol. 2. Munich: Deutscher Taschenbuchverlag, 1967.

Browder, George C. *Hitler's Enforcers: The Gestapo and the SS Security Service in the Nazi Revolution*. New York: Oxford University Press, 1996.

Browning, Christopher. *Fateful Months: Essays on the Emergence of the Final Solution*. New York: Holmes and Meier, 1985.

———. "Harald Turner und die Militärverwaltung in Serbien 1941–1942." In *Verwaltung contra Menschenführung im Staat Hitler: Studien zum politisch-administrativen System*, edited by Dieter Rebentisch and Karl Teppe, pp. 351–73. Göttingen: Vandenhoeck and Ruprecht, 1986.

Browning, Christopher. "Nazi Resettlement Policy and the Search for a Solution of the Jewish Question, 1939–1941." *German Studies Review* 9 (1986): 497–519.
———. *Path to Genocide: Essays on Launching the Final Solution*. New York: Cambridge University Press, 1992.
———. "Wehrmacht Reprisal Policy and the Mass Murder of Jews in Serbia." *Militärgeschichtliche Mitteilungen* 33 (1983): 31–47.
Brucker-Boroujerdi, Ute. "Die 'Rassenhygienische und Erbbiologische Forschungsstelle' im Reichsgesundheitsamt." *Bundesgesundheitsblatt* 32 (Sonderheft March 1989): 13–19.
Buchheim, Hans. "Die Aktion 'Arbeitsscheu Reich'." *Gutachten des Instituts für Zeitgeschichte*, 2:189–95. Munich: Institut für Zeitgeschichte, 1966.
———. "Die Zigeunerdeportation vom Mai 1940." In *Gutachten des Instituts für Zeitgeschichte*, 1: 51–60. Munich: Institut für Zeitgeschichte, 1958.
Buchmann, Erika. *Die Frauen von Ravensbrück*. Berlin: Kongress, 1961.
Bura, Josef. "Die unbewältigte Vergangenheit: Zigeunerpolitik und alltäglicher Rassismus in der Bundesrepublik." In *Sinti in der Bundesrepublik: Beiträge zur sozialen Lage einer verfolgten Minderheit*, edited by Rudolph Bauer et al., pp. 9–85. Bremen: Universität, 1984.
Burleigh, Michael, and Wolfgang Wippermann. *The Racial State: Germany, 1933–1945*. Cambridge: Cambridge University Press, 1991.
Calvelli-Adorno, Franz. "Die rassische Verfolgung der Zigeuner vor dem 1. März 1943." *Rechtssprechung zum Wiedergutmachungsrecht* 12 (1961): 529–39.
Clébert, Jean-Paul. *The Gypsies*. Translated by Charles Duff. New York: Dutton, 1963.
Cohn, Werner. *The Gypsies*. Reading, Mass.: Addison-Wesley, 1973.
Cooper, Matthew. *The Phantom War: The German Struggle against Soviet Partisans*. London: MacDonald and James, 1979.
Crowe, David, and John Kolsti, eds. *The Gypsies of Eastern Europe*. New York: M. E. Sharpe, 1991.
Czech, Danuta. *Auschwitz Chronicle, 1939–1945*. New York: Henry Holt, 1990.
Dambrowski, Amanda. "Das Schicksal einer vertriebenen ostpreussischen Sinti-Familie im NS-Staat." *Pogrom* 12, no. 80–81 (March–April 1981): 72–75.
Daum, Monika, and Hans-Ulrich Deppe. *Zwangssterilisation in Frankfurt am Main*. Frankfurt/Main: Campus, 1991.
Dawidowicz, Lucy S. "Thinking about the Six Million: Facts, Figures, Perspectives." In *Holocaust: Religious and Philosophical Perspectives*, edited by John K. Roth and Michael Berenbaum, pp. 51–70. New York: Paragon House, 1989.
Deutsch, Harold C. *The Conspiracy against Hitler in the Twilight War*. Minneapolis: University of Minnesota Press, 1968.
Diels, Rudolf. *Lucifer ante Portas: Zwischen Severing und Heydrich*. Zurich: Interverlag, n.d.
Djuric, Rajko. *Roma und Sinti im Spiegel der deutschen Literatur: Ein Essay*. Frankfurt/Main: Lang, 1995.
Dlugoborski, Waclaw. "On the History of the Gypsy Camp at Auschwitz-Birkenau." In *Memorial Book: The Gypsies at Auschwitz*, edited by State Museum of Auschwitz-Birkenau, 1:1–5. Munich: Saur, 1993.
———. *Der 50. Jahrestag der Vernichtung der Roma im KL Auschwitz-Birkenau*. Oswiecim: Vereinigung der Roma in Polen, 1994.
Dobroszycki, Lucjan, ed. *The Chronicle of the Lodz Ghetto, 1941–1944*. New Haven: Yale University Press, 1984.

Dokumentationsarchiv des Österreichischen Widerstandes. *Widerstand und Verfolgung im Burgenland, 1934–1945: Eine Dokumentation*. Vienna: Österreichischer Bundesverlag, 1983.

——. *Widerstand und Verfolgung in Niederösterreich, 1934–1945*. Vol. 3. Vienna: Österreichischer Bundesverlag, 1987.

——. *Widerstand und Verfolgung in Wien, 1934–1945: Eine Dokumentation*. Vienna: Österreichischer Bundesverlag, 1975.

Döring, Hans-Joachim. "Die Motive der Zigeuner-Deportation vom Mai 1940." *Vierteljahrshefte für Zeitgeschichte* 7 (1959): 418–28.

——. *Die Zigeuner im Nationalsozialistischen Staat*. Hamburg: Kriminalistik Verlag, 1964.

Dorsch and Vaas. *Die polizeiliche Überwachung der Zigeuner und nach Zigeunerart umherziehenden Personen: Eine Sammlung von Rechtsvorschriften*. Ravensburg, 1948–1949.

Dostal, Walter. "Die Zigeuner in Österreich." *Archiv für Völkerkunde* 10 (1955): 1–15.

Dulles, Allan Welsh. *Germany's Underground*. New York: Macmillan, 1947.

Ebbinghaus, Angelika, et al., eds. *Heilen und Vernichten im Mustergau Hamburg: Bevölkerungs- und Gesundheitspolitik im Dritten Reich*. Hamburg: Konkret Literatur, 1984.

Eiber, Ludwig. *"Ich wusste es wird schlimm:" Die Verfolgung der Sinti und Roma in München, 1933–1945*. Munich: Buchendorfer, 1993.

Eine Schuld die nicht erlischt: Dokumente über deutsche Kriegsverbrechen in der Sovietunion. Cologne: Pahl-Rugenstein, 1987.

Eller, Hanns. "Die Zigeuner—ein Problem." *Kriminalistik* 8 (1954): 124–26.

Engbring-Romano, Udo. *Fulda-Auschwitz: Zur Verfolgung der Sinti in Fulda*. Darmstadt: Verband deutscher Sinti und Roma, 1996.

——. *Wiesbaden-Auschwitz: Zur Verfolgung der Sinti in Wiesbaden*. Darmstadt: Verband deutscher Sinti und Roma, 1997.

Evans, Richard J. *In Hitler's Shadow: West German Historians and the Attempt to Escape the Nazi Past*. New York: Pantheon, 1989.

Ezergailis, Andrew. *The Holocaust in Latvia, 1941–1944: The Missing Center*. Riga: Historical Institute of Latvia, 1996.

Fedkiel, Wladyslaw. "Starvation in Auschwitz." In *From the History of KL. Auschwitz*, edited by Kazimierz Smolen et al. pp. 119–34. Translated by Krystyna Michalik. New York: Howard Fertig, 1982.

Fenner, Elisabeth. *Zwangssterilisation im Nationalsozialismus: Zur Rolle der Hamburger Sozialverwaltung*. Ammersbek bei Hamburg: An der Lottbek, 1990.

Feuerhelm, Wolfgang. *Polizei und "Zigeuner;" Strategien, Handlungsmuster und Alltagstheorien im polizeilichen Umgang mit Sinti und Roma*. Stuttgart: Ferdinand Euke, 1987.

Ficowski, Jerzy. *The Gypsies in Poland: History and Customs*. Translated by Eileen Healey. Warsaw: Interpress, n.d.

Fings, Karola et al. *"Einziges Land, in dem die Judenfrage und Zigeunerfrage gelöst;" Die Verfolgung der Roma im faschistisch besetzten Jugoslawien, 1941–1945*. Cologne: Rom, n.d.

Fings, Karola, and Frank Sparing. " 'Eine erziehende Tätigkeit kommt nicht in Betracht': Die nationalsozialistische Verfolgung Düsseldorfer Zigeunerkinder durch die Fürsorgeerziehungsbehörde." *Augenblick* 6 (1994): 2–6.

——. " 'Regelung der Zigeunerfrage.' " *Konkret* 11/93: 26–29.

Fings, Karola, and Frank Sparing. " 'Tunlichst als erziehungsunfähig hinzustellen':
    Zigeunerkinder und Jugendliche—Aus der Fürsorge in die Vernichtung."
    Dachauer Hefte, vol. 9, no. 9 (November 1993): 159–180.

———. "Vertuscht, Verleugnet, Versteckt: Akten zur NS-Verfolgung von Sinti und
    Roma." In *Besatzung und Bündnis: Deutsche Herrschaftsstrategien in Ost- und Südeu-
    ropa*. Beiträge zur nationalsozialistischen Gesundheits- und Sozialpolitik, vol. 12.
    Berlin: Rotbuch, 1995.

———. "Das Zigeunerlager in Köln-Bickendorf, 1935–1958." *1999* 6, no. 3 (July
    1991): 11–40.

———. "z.Zt. Zigeunerlager:" *Die Verfolgung der Düsseldorfer Sinti und Roma im
    Nationalsozialismus*. Cologne: Volksblatt, 1992.

Fonseca, Isabel. *Bury Me Standing: The Gypsies and Their Journey*. New York: Knopf,
    1995.

Franz, Philomena. *Zwischen Liebe und Hass: Ein Zigeunerleben*. Freiburg: Herder, 1992.

Fraser, Angus. *The Gypsies*. Oxford: Blackwell, 1992.

Friedlander, Henry. *The Origins of Nazi Genocide: From Euthanasia to the Final Solu-
    tion*. Chapel Hill: University of North Carolina Press, 1995.

Friedländer, Saul. *Nazi Germany and the Jews*. Vol. 1. New York: HarperCollins, 1997.

Füllberg-Stolberg, Claus, et al., eds. *Frauen in Konzentrationslagern: Bergen-Belsen,
    Ravensbrück*. Bremen: Temmen, 1994.

Galinski, Heinz. "Dieses Gedenken sei uns Mahnung zum Handeln." In *Sinti und
    Roma im ehemaligen KZ Bergen-Belsen*. Göttingen: Gesellschaft für bedrohte
    Völker, 1980.

Geigges, Anita, and Bernard W. Wette. *Zigeuner heute: Verfolgung und Diskrim-
    inierung in der BRD*. Bornheim-Merten: Lamuv, 1979.

Gellately, Robert. *The Gestapo and German Society: Enforcing Racial Policy, 1933–1945*.
    Oxford: Clarendon 1990.

Gerlach, Christian. "Failure of Plans for an SS Extermination Camp in Mogilev."
    Holocaust and Genocide Studies 11 (1997): 60–78.

———. "Die Wannsee-Konferenz, das Schicksal der deutschen Juden und Hitlers
    politische Grundsatzentscheidung, alle Juden Europas zu ermorden." *Werkstatt-
    Geschichte* 18 (1997): 7–44.

Gersdorff, Rudolf-Christoph Freiherr von. *Soldat im Untergang*. Frankfurt/Main:
    Ullstein, 1977.

Giere, Jacqueline. *Die gesellschaftliche Konstruktion des Zigeuners: Zur Genese eines
    Vorurteils*. Frankfurt/Main: Campus, 1996.

Gilbert, Martin. *Atlas of the Holocaust*. New York: William Morrow, 1993.

Gilsenbach, Reimar. *Oh Django, sing deinen Zorn: Sinti und Roma unter den Deutschen*.
    Berlin: Basis, 1993.

———. "Wie Alfred Lora den Wiesengrund überlebte: Aus der Geschichte einer
    deutschen Sinti-Familie." *Pogrom* 21, no. 151 (January-February 1990): 13–18.

Gisevius, Hans Bernd. *To the Bitter End*. Translated by Richard and Clara Winston.
    Westport, Conn.: Greenwood, 1975.

———. *Wo ist Nebe? Erinnerungen an Hitler's Reichskriminaldirektor*. Zurich: Droemer,
    1966.

Grode, Walter. *Die "Sonderbehandlung 14 f 13" in den Konzentrationslagern des Dritten
    Reiches: Ein Beitrag zur Dynamik faschistischer Vernichtungspolitik*. Frankfurt/Main:
    Peter Lang, 1987.

Gronemeyer, Reimer. "Warum Tsiganologie? Bemerkungen zu einer Wissenschaft
    mit Blutspuren." *Giessener Hefte zur Tsiganologie* 2, no. 1 (1985): 3–7.

Gronemeyer, Reimer. *Zigeuner im Spiegel früherer Chroniken und Abhandlungen: Quellen vom 15. bis 18. Jahrhundert.* Giessen: Focus, 1987.

Gross, Jan Tomasz. *Polish Society under German Occupation: The Generalgouvernement, 1939–1944.* Princeton, N.J.: Princeton University Press, 1979.

Günther, Wolfgang. *"Ach Schwester, ich kann nicht mehr tanzen": Sinti und Roma im KZ Bergen-Belsen.* Hannover: Niedersächsischer Verband deutscher Sinti, 1990.

———. *Die preussische Zigeunerpolitik seit 1871 in Widerspruch zwischen zentraler Planung und lokaler Durchführung: Eine Untersuchung am Beispiel des Landkreises Neustadt am Rübenberge und der Hauptstadt Hannover.* Hannover: ANS Verlag, 1985.

Gutman, Yisrael, and Michael Berenbaum, eds. *Anatomy of the Auschwitz Death Camp.* Bloomington: Indiana University Press, 1994.

Guttenberger, Elisabeth. "Das Zigeunerlager." In *Auschwitz: Zeugnisse und Berichte,* edited by H. G. Adler, pp. 131–34. Frankfurt/Main: Europäische Verlagsanstalt, 1962.

Hackett, David A., ed. and trans. *The Buchenwald Report.* Boulder, Colo.: Westview, 1995.

Hancock, Ian F. "Communication: A Response to Raymond Pearson's Review of Ian Hancock: The Pariah Syndrome." *Nationalities Papers* 19 (1991): 433–36.

———. *The Pariah Syndrome: An Account of Gypsy Slavery and Persecution.* Ann Arbor, Mich.: Karoma, 1987.

———. "Responses to the Porrajmos: The Romani Holocaust." In *Is the Holocaust Unique?* Edited by Alan S. Rosenbaum, pp. 36–64. Boulder, Col.: Westview, 1996.

———. "Uniqueness, Gypsies and Jews." in *Remembering for the Future,* edited by Yehuda Bauer et al., vol. 2, pp. 2017–25. Oxford: Pergamon, 1989.

Harder, Alexander. *Kriminalzentrale Werderscher Markt: Die Geschichte des "Deutschen Scotland Yard."* Bayreuth: Hestia, 1963.

Hase-Mihalik, Eva von, and Doris Kreuzkamp. *"Du kriegst auch einen schönen Wohnwagen": Zwangslager für Sinti und Roma während des Nationalsozialismus in Frankfurt am Main.* Frankfurt/Main: Brandes and Apsel, 1990.

Hausner, Gideon. *Justice in Jerusalem.* New York: Harper and Row, 1966.

Headland, Donald. *Messages of Murder: A Study of the Reports of the Einsatzgruppen of the Security Police and the Security Service, 1941–1943.* Rutherford, N.J.: Fairleigh Dickinson University Press, 1992.

Heer, Hannes, and Naumann, Klaus. *Vernichtungskrieg: Verbrechen der Wehrmacht 1941–1944.* Hamburg: Hamburger Edition, 1995.

Hehemann, Rainer. *Die "Bekämpfung des Zigeunerunwesens" im Wilhelminischen Deutschland und in der Weimarer Zeit, 1871–1933.* Frankfurt/Main: Hang and Herchen, 1987.

Hemmerlein, Astrid. *Sinti und Roma im System Himmlers.* Diplomarbeit. Free University, Berlin, 1994.

Hendsch, Gerhard. "Der Zigeuner, vom Standpunkt des Polizeibeamten betrachtet." *Polizeipraxis* 4 (1950): 144–45.

Henke, Josef. "Quellenschicksale und Bewertungsfragen: Archivische Probleme bei der Überlieferungsbildung zur Verfolgung der Sinti und Roma im Dritten Reich." *Vierteljahrshefte für Zeitgeschichte* 41 (1993): 61–77.

Herbert, Ulrich. "Arbeit und Vernichtung: Ökonomisches Interesse und Primat der 'Weltanschauung' im Nationalsozialismus." In *Ist der Nationalsozialismus Geschichte? Zu Historisierung und Historikerstreit,* edited by Dan Diner, pp. 198–236. Frankfurt/Main: Fischer, 1987.

Herbert, Ulrich, ed. *Nationalsozialistische Vernichtungspolitik, 1939–1945: Neue Forschungen und Kontroversen.* Frankfurt/Main: Fischer Taschenbuch Verlag, 1998.

Hess, Gerhard. " 'Zigeunerromantik' oder Bekämpfung des Landfahrerunwesens." *Der Kriminalist* 11 (1979): 343–44.

Hesse, Hans. "Wilhelm Mündrath: Kriminalsekretär des Bremer 'Zigeunerdezernats.' " In *Historische Rassismusforschung: Ideologen—Täter—Opfer,* edited by Barbara Danckwortt et al. Hamburg: Argument, 1995.

Heuss, Herbert. *Darmstadt-Auschwitz: Die Verfolgung der Sinti in Darmstadt.* Frankfurt/Main: Verband deutscher Sinti und Roma, 1995.

———. *Die Verfolgung der Sinti in Mainz und Rheinhessen: 1933–1945.* Landau: Verband deutscher Sinti, 1996.

———. "Wissenschaft und Völkermord: Zur Arbeit der 'Rassenhygienischen Forschungsstelle' beim Reichsgesundheitsamt." *Bundesgesundheitsblatt* 32, Sonderheft (March 1989): 20–24.

Heuss, Peter. "Kulturpolitik im Dritten Reich: Das 'Ahnenerbe' der SS und seine Funktion für Himmler's Rassenpolitik." In *Die Sinti/Roma Erzählungskunst im Kontext europäischer Märchenkultur.* Edited by Daniel Strauss. Heidelberg: Dokumentations- und Kulturzentrum deutscher Sinti und Roma, 1992.

Heuzeroth, Günter, ed. *Unter der Gewaltherrschaft des Nationalsozialismus 1933–1945: Dargestellt an den Ereignissen im Oldenburger Land.* Vol. 2. Oldenburg: Universität Oldenburg, 1985.

Hilberg, Raul. *The Destruction of the European Jews.* Chicago: Quadrangle, 1961.

Hoffmann, Peter. *The History of the German Resistance.* Translated by Richard Barry. Cambridge, Mass.: MIT Press, 1977.

Hohmann, Joachim Stephan. *Bravo Sinto!* Frankfurt/Main: Fischer, 1984.

———. *Bravo Sinto! Auf den Spuren eines geächteten Buches: Eine Dokumentation.* Fernwald: Litblockin, 1986.

———. *Geschichte der Zigeunerverfolgung in Deutschland.* Frankfurt/Main: Campus, 1981.

———. *Robert Ritter und die Erben der Kriminalbiologie: 'Zigeunerforschung' im Nationalsozialismus und in Westdeutschland im Zeichen des Rassismus.* Frankfurt/Main: Peter Lang, 1991.

———. *Verfolgte ohne Heimat: Geschichte der Zigeuner in Deutschland.* Frankfurt/Main: Peter Lang, 1990.

———. *Zigeuner und Zigeunerwissenschaft: Ein Beitrag zur Grundlagenforschung und Dokumentation des Völkermords im "Dritten Reich."* Marburg: Guttandin und Hoppe, 1980.

Hohmann, Joachim Stephan, and Roland Schopf, eds. *Zigeunerleben: Beiträge zur Sozialgeschichte einer Verfolgung.* 2nd ed. Darmstadt: MS Edition, 1979.

Höhne, Heinz. *The Order of the Death's Head: The Story of Hitler's SS.* Translated by Richard Barry. New York: Coward-McCann, 1970.

Horwitz, Gordon J. *In the Shadow of Death: Living Outside the Gates of Mauthausen.* New York: Free Press, 1990.

Höss, Rudolf. *Commandant of Auschwitz: The Autobiography of Rudolf Höss.* Translated by Constantin FitzGibbon. Cleveland: World, 1959.

Hundsalz, Andreas. *Soziale Situation der Sinti in der Bundesrepublik Deutschland: Endbericht.* Stuttgart: W. Kohlhammer, 1982.

Huttenbach, Henry R. "The Romani Porajmos: The Nazi Genocide of Europe's Gypsies." *Nationalities Papers* 19 (1991): 373–96.

International Auschwitz Committee. *Nazi Medicine: Doctors, Victims and Medicine in Auschwitz.* New York: Howard Fertig, 1986.

International Military Tribunal. *Trial of the Major War Criminals before the International Military Tribunal.* 42 vols. Nuremberg: 1946–49.

Jäckel, Eberhard. *Hitler's Weltanschauung: A Blueprint for Power.* Rev. ed. Translated by Herbert Arnold. Middletown, Conn.: Wesleyan University Press, 1972.

Jäckel, Eberhard and Rohwer, Jürgen, eds. *Der Mord an den Juden im zweiten Weltkrieg: Entschlussbildung und Verwirklichung.* Stuttgart: Deutsche Verlags-Anstalt, 1985.

Kaienburg, Hermann. *"Vernichtung durch Arbeit": Der Fall [Neuengamme.]* Bonn: J. H. W. Dietz, 1990.

Kater, Michael H. *Das "Ahnenerbe" der SS, 1935–1945: Ein Beitrag zur Kulturpolitik des Dritten Reiches.* Stuttgart: Deutsche Verlags-Anstalt, 1974.

———. *Doctors under Hitler.* Chapel Hill: University of North Carolina Press, 1989.

Katz, Steven T. "Essay: Quantity and Interpretation—Issues in the Comparative Historical Analysis of the Holocaust." *Holocaust and Genocide Studies* 4 (1989): 127–48.

———. *The Holocaust in Historical Context.* Vol. 1, *The Holocaust and Mass Death before the Modern Age.* New York: Oxford University Press, 1994.

———. "The Uniqueness of the Holocaust: The Historical Dimension." In *Is the Holocaust Unique? Perspectives on Comparative Genocide.* Edited by Alan S. Rosenbaum, pp. 19–38. Boulder, Colo.: Westview, 1996.

Kenrick, Donald. Letter to the editor. *Holocaust and Genocide Studies* 4 (1989): 251–54.

Kenrick, Donald, and Grattan Puxon. *The Destiny of Europe's Gypsies.* New York: Basic Books, 1972.

———. *Gypsies under the Swastika.* Hatfield, U.K.: University of Hertfordshire Press, 1995.

Keren, Nili. "The Family Camp." In *Anatomy of the Auschwitz Death Camp.* Edited by Yisrael Gutman and Michael Berenbaum, pp. 428–40. Bloomington: Indiana University Press, 1994.

Kettenacker, Lothar. *Nationalsozialistische Volkstumpolitik im Ellsass.* Stuttgart: Deutsche Verlags–Anstalt, 1973.

Kielar, Wieslaw. *Anus Mundi: 1,500 Days in Auschwitz.* Translated by Susanne Flatauer. New York: Times Books, 1979.

Klamper, Elisabeth, ed. *Archives of the Holcaust.* Vol. 19, *Dokumentationsarchiv des Österreichischen Widerstandes.* New York: Garland, 1991.

———. "Persecution and Annihilation of Roma and Sinti in Austria, 1938–1945." *Journal of the Gypsy Lore Society*, 5th ser., 3, no. 2 (August 1993): 55–65.

Klausch, Hans-Peter. *Antifaschisten in SS-Uniform: Schicksal und Widerstand der deutschen politischen KZ-Häftlinge, Zuchthaus- und Wehrmachtsstrafgefangene in der SS-Sonderformation Dirlewanger.* Bremen: Edition Temmen, 1993.

Klee, Ernst. *Auschwitz, die NS-Medizin und ihre Opfer.* Frankfurt/Main: S. Fischer, 1997.

———. *"Euthanasie" im NS-Staat: Die Vernichtung lebensunwerten Lebens.* Frankfurt/Main: Fischer Taschenbuch Verlag, 1985.

Klein, Nikolaus, ed. *Sinti und Roma: Ein Volk auf dem Wege zu sich selbst.* Stuttgart: Institute für Auslandsbeziehungen, 1981.

Koch, Thomas. *Zwangssterilisation im Dritten Reich: Das Beispiel der Universitätsklinik Göttingen.* Frankfurt/Main: Mabuse, 1994.

Kochanowski, Vanya. "Some Notes on the Gypsies of Latvia by one of the Survivors." *Journal of the Gypsy Lore Society*, 3d ser., 25 (1946): 112–16.

Koehl, Robert L. *RKFDV: German Resettlement and Population Policy: A History of the Reich Commission for the Strengthening of Germandom.* Cambridge: Harvard University Press, 1957.

Kogon, Eugen. *The Theory and Practice of Hell.* Translated by Heinz Norden. New York: Berkley, n.d.

Kogon, Eugen et al., eds. *Nazi Mass Murder: A Documentary History of the Use of Poison Gas.* Translated by Mary Scott and Caroline Lloyd-Morris. New Haven: Yale University Press, 1993.

König, Ulrich. *Sinti und Roma unter dem Nationalsozialismus: Verfolgung und Widerstand.* Bochum: Brockmeyer, 1989.

Kotze, Hildegard von, ed. *Heeresadjutant bei Hitler, 1938–1943: Aufzeichnungen des Majors Engel.* Stuttgart: Deutsche Verlagsanstalt, 1974.

Kraus, Ota Benjamin, and Erich Kulka. *Death Factory: Document on Auschwitz.* Oxford: Pergamon, 1966.

Krausnick, Helmut, and Hans-Heinrich Wilhelm. *Die Truppe des Weltanschauungskrieges: Die Einsatzgruppen der Sicherheitspolizei und des SD, 1938–1942.* Stuttgart: Deutsche Verlags-Anstalt, 1981.

Krausnick, Michail. *Abfahrt Karlsruhe: Die Deportation in den Völkermord, ein unterschlagenes Kapitel aus der Geschichte unserer Stadt.* Karlsruhe: Verband der Sinti und Roma Karlsruhe, 1991.

———. *"Da wollten wir frei sein!" Eine Sinti Familie erzählt.* Weinheim-Basel: Beltz and Gelberg, 1993.

———. *Wo sind sie hingekommen? Der unterschlagene Völkermord an den Sinti und Roma.* Gerlingen: Bleicher, 1995.

Kühl, Stefan. *The Nazi Connection: Eugenics, American Racism and German National Socialism.* New York: Oxford University Press, 1994.

Langbein, Hermann. *Der Auschwitzprozess: Eine Dokumentation.* 2 vols. Vienna: Neue Kritik, 1995.

———. *Menschen in Auschwitz.* Vienna: Europa, 1972.

Leidgeb, Ellen, and Nicole Horn. *Opre Roma! Erhebt euch: Eine Einführung in die Geschichte und Situation der Roma.* Munich: AG-Spak, 1994.

Lengyel, Olga. *Five Chimneys: The Story of Auschwitz.* Chicago: Ziff-Davis, 1947.

Lerch, Hans-Günter. *"Tschü lowi . . ." Das Manische in Giessen.* Giessen: Anabus, 1976.

Lessing, Alfred. *Mein Leben im Versteck: Wie ein deutscher Sinti den Holocaust überlebte.* Düsseldorf: Zebulon, 1993.

Liégeois, Jean-Pierre. *Gypsies and Travellers.* Strassbourg: Council for Cultural Cooperation, 1987.

Lifton, Robert Jay. *The Nazi Doctors: Medical Killing and the Psychology of Genocide.* New York: Basic Books, 1986.

Linenthal, Edward T. *Preserving Memory: The Struggle to Create America's Holocaust Museum.* New York: Viking, 1995.

Longerich, Peter. *Hitler's Stellvertreter: Führung der Partei und Kontrolle des Staatsapparates durch den Stab Hess und die Partei-Kanzlei Bormanns.* Munich: K. G. Saur, 1992.

Lucassen, Leo. *Zigeuner: Die Geschichte eines polizeilichen Ordnungsbegriffes in Deutschland, 1700–1945.* Cologne: Böhlau, 1996.

Lustig, Oliver. *"Das 'Zigeunerlager' von Auschwitz-Birkenau," Aus den Erinnerungen eines Rumänen." Giessener Hefte für Tsiganologie* 2, no. 4 (1985): 16–19.

Lutz, Brenda Davis, and James M. Lutz. *"Gypsies as Victims of the Holocaust." Holocaust and Genocide Studies* 9 (1995): 346–59.

Maier, Dieter. *Arbeitseinsatz und Deportation: Die Mitwirkung der Arbeitsverwaltung bei der nationalsozialistischen Judenverfolgung in den Jahren 1938–1945.* Berlin: Edition Hentrich, 1994.

Maislinger, Andreas. " 'Zigeuneranhaltelager' und 'Arbeitserziehungslager' Weyer: Ergänzung einer Ortschronik." *Pogrom* 18, no. 137 (December 1987): 33–36.

Majer, Diemut. *'Fremdvölkische' im Dritten Reich: Ein Beitrag zur nationalsozialistischen Rechtssetzung und Rechtspraxis in Verwaltung und Justiz unter besonderer Berücksichtigung der eingegliederten Ostgebiete und des Generalgouvernement.* Boppard: Harald Boldt, 1981.

Manoschek, Walter. *"Serbien ist judenfrei": Militärische Besatzungspolitik und Judenvernichtung in Serbien 1941/42.* Munich: R. Oldenbourg, 1993.

Margalit, Gilad. "Antigypsism in the Political Culture of the Federal Republic of Germany: A Parallel with Antisemitism?" *Acta: Analysis of Current Trends in Antisemitism* 9 (1996): 1–29.

———. "Die deutsche Zigeunerpolitik nach 1945." *Vierteljahrshefte für Zeitgeschichte* 45 (1997): 557–88.

———. "The Justice System of the Federal Republic of Germany and the Nazi Persecution of the Gypsies." *Holocaust and Genocide Studies* 11 (1997): 330–50.

———. "Sinti und andere Deutsche—Über ethnische Spiegelungen." *Tel Aviver Jahrbuch für deutsche Geschichte* 26 (1997): 281–306.

Martins-Heuss, Kirsten. "Reflections on the Collective Identity of German Roma and Sinti (Gypsies) after National Socialism." *Holocaust and Genocide Studies* 4 (1989): 193–211.

———. *Zur mythischen Figur des Zigeuners in der deutschen Zigeunerforschung.* Frankfurt/Main: Haag and Herchen, 1983.

Matalon Lagnado, Lucette, and Sheila Cohn Dekel. *Children of the Flames: Dr. Josef Mengele and the Untold Story of the Twins of Auschwitz.* New York: William Morrow, 1991.

Matl, Wolfgang. "Ein Albtraum vom reinen Schweden." *Die Zeit,* September 5, 1997, pp. 13–15.

Matras, Yaron. "The Development of the Romani Civil Rights Movement in Germany, 1945–1996." In *Sinti and Roma in German-Speaking Society and Literature,* edited by Susan Tebbutt, pp. 49–63. Providence, R.I.: Berghahn, 1998.

Matthäus, Jürgen. "What about the 'Ordinary Men'? The German Order Police and the Holocaust in the Occupied Soviet Union." *Holocaust and Genocide Studies* 10 (1996): 134–50.

Maur, Wolf in der. *Die Zigeuner: Wanderer zwischen den Welten.* Vienna: Molden, 1969.

Maximoff, Matéo. "Germany and the Gypsies: From the Gypsy's Point of View." *Journal of the Gypsy Lore Society,* 3d ser., 25 (1946): 104–8.

Mayerhofer, Claudia. *Dorfzigeuner: Kultur und Geschichte der Burgenland-Roma von der ersten Republik bis zur Gegenwart.* Vienna: Picus, 1987.

Meier, Heinrich Christian. *So war es: Das Leben im KZ Neuengamme.* Hamburg: Phönix, 1946.

Meister, Johannes. "Schicksale der 'Zigeunerkinder' aus der St. Josefspflege in Mulfingen." *Jahrbuch des Historischen Vereins Württembergisch-Franken,* May 1984, pp. 197–229.

Mergen, Armand. *Die Tiroler Karner: Kriminologische und kriminalbiologische Studien an Landfahrern (Jenischen).* Mainz: Internationaler Universum Verlag, 1949.

Messerschmidt, Manfred. *Die Wehrmacht im NS-Staat: Zeit der Indoktrination.* Hamburg: R.v. Decker, 1969.

Michalczyk, John J., ed. *Medicine, Ethics and the Third Reich: Historical and Contemporary Issues.* Kansas City: Sheed and Ward, 1994.

Milton, Sybil. "Antechamber to Birkenau." In *Die Normalität des Verbrechen,* edited by Helge Grabitz et al., pp. 241–59. Berlin: Edition Hentrich, 1994.

Milton, Sybil. "The Context of the Holocaust." *German Studies Review* 13 (1990): 269–83.
———. "Correspondence: 'Gypsies and the Holocaust.'" *History Teacher* 25 (1992): 515–21.
———. "Gypsies and the Holocaust." *History Teacher* 24 (1991): 375–87.
———. "Holocaust: The Gypsies, Eyewitness Accounts." In *Genocide in the Twentieth Century: Critical Essays and Eyewitness Accounts*, edited by Samuel Totten et al., pp. 209–64. New York: Garland, 1995.
———. "Nazi Policies toward Roma and Sinti." *Journal of the Gypsy Lore Society*, 5th ser., 2, no. 1 (1992): 1–18.
———. "Non-Jewish Children in the Camps." In *A Mosaic of Victims*, edited by Michael Berenbaum, pp. 150–60. New York: New York University Press, 1990.
Milton, Sybil, ed. *The Story of Karl Stojka: A Childhood in Birkenau*. Washington, D.C.: U.S. Holocaust Memorial Council, 1992.
Mitscherlich, Alexander, and Fred Mielke. *Medizin ohne Menschlichkeit: Dokumente des Nürnberger Ärzteprozesses*. Frankfurt/Main: Fischer, 1960.
Mode, Heinz, and Siegfried Wölffling. *Zigeuner: Der Weg eines Volkes in Deutschland*. Leipzig: Koehler and Amelang, 1968.
Molitor, Jan. "The Fate of a German Gypsy." *Journal of the Gypsy Lore Society*, 3d ser., 26 (1947): 48–52.
Moser, Jonny. "Nisko: The First Experiment in Deportation." *Simon Wiesenthal Center Annual* 2 (1985): 1–30.
Mosse, Georg. *The Crisis of German Ideology: Intellectual Origins of the Third Reich*. New York: Grosset and Dunlap, 1964.
———. *Toward the Final Solution: A History of European Racism*. New York: Howard Fertig, 1978.
Mozes-Kor, Eva. "The Mengele Twins and Human Experimentation: A Personal Account." In *The Nazi Doctors and the Nuremberg Code*, edited by George J. Annas and Michael A. Grodin, pp. 53–59. New York: Oxford University Press, 1992.
Müller-Hill, Benno. *Murderous Science: Elimination by Scientific Selection of Jews, Gypsies, and Others*. Translated by George R. Fraser. New York: Oxford University Press, 1988.
———. "Human Genetics in Nazi Germany." In *Medicine, Ethics and the Third Reich*. Edited by John J. Michalczyk. Kansas City: Sheed and Ward, 1994.
Münz, Rainer, and Ralf Ulrich. "Changing Patterns of Immigration to Germany, 1945–1995: Ethnic Origins, Demographic Structure, Future Prospects." In *Migration Past, Migration Future: Germany and the United States*. Edited by Klaus J. Bade and Myron Weiner. Providence, R.I.: Berghahn, 1997.
Münzel, Mark, and Bernard Streck. *Kumpania und Kontrolle: Moderne Behinderungen zigeunerischen Lebens*. Giessen: Focus, 1981.
Necas, Ctibor. "Das Schicksal und die Vernichtung der Roma im Protektorat Böhmen und Mähren." In *Der 50.Jahrestag der Vernichtung der Roma im KL Auschwitz-Birkenau*, edited by Waclaw Dlugoborski, pp. 66–73. Oswiecim: Vereinigung der Rom in Polen, 1994.
———. "Die Tschechischen und die slowakischen Roma im Dritten Reich." *Pogrom* 12, no. 80–81 (March–April 1981): 62–64.
" 'Die Nette Alte Dame': Dokumentation zum Fall Kellermann." *Mitteilungen der Dokumentationsstelle zur NS-Sozialpolitik* 2, no. 12 (April 1986): 114–135.
Niedersächsischer Verband deutscher Sinti. *"Es war menschenunmöglich": Sinti aus Niedersachsen erzählen*. Hannover: NVDS, 1995.
Noakes, Jeremy. "Social Outcasts in the Third Reich." In *Life in the Third Reich*, edited by Richard Bessel, pp. 83–96. Oxford: Oxford University Press, 1987.

Nolte, Ernst. *Streitpunkte: Heutige und künftige Kontroversen um den Nationalsozialismus.* Berlin: Prophyläen, 1993.

Nomberg-Przytyk, Sara. *Auschwitz: True Tales from a Grotesque Land.* Translated by Roslyn Hirsch. Chapel Hill: University of North Carolina Press, 1985.

Nyiszli, Miklos. *Auschwitz: An Eyewitness Account of Mengele's Infamous Death Camp.* New York: Seaver Books, 1986.

Ogorreck, Ralf. *Die Einsatzgruppen und die "Genesis der Endlösung."* Berlin: Metropol, 1996.

Okely, Judith. *The Traveller-Gypsies.* Cambridge: Cambridge University Press, 1983.

Opfermann, Ulrich Friedrich. *"Das sie den Zigeuner-Habit ablegen": Die Geschichte der 'Zigeuner-Kolonien' zwischen Wittgenstein und Westerwald.* Frankfurt/Main: Peter Lang, 1996.

Perl, Gisella. *I Was a Doctor in Auschwitz.* New York: Arno, 1979.

Petersen, P., and U. Liedtke. "Zur Entschädigung zwangssterilisierter Zigeuner (Sozialpsychologische Einflüsse auf psychische Störungen nationalsozialistisch Verfolgter)." *Der Nervenarzt* 42 (1971): 197–205.

Peukert, Detlev J. K. *Inside Nazi Germany: Conformity, Opposition, and Racism in Everyday Life.* Translated by Richard Deveson. New Haven: Yale University Press, 1987.

Pingel, Falk. *Häftlinge unter SS-Herrschaft: Widerstand, Selbstbehauptung und Vernichtung im Konzentrationslager.* Hamburg: Hoffmann und Campe, 1978.

Piper, Franciczek. "Die Familienlager in Auschwitz-Birkenau (Genesis, Funktione, Ähnlichkeiten und Unterschiede)." In *Theresienstadt in der "Endlösung der Judenfrage,"* edited by Miroslav Karney, pp. 245–51. Prague: Panorama, 1992.

———. "The Number of Victims." In *Anatomy of the Auschwitz Death Camp*, edited by Yisrael Gutman and Michael Berenbaum, pp. 61–76. Bloomington: Indiana University Press, 1994.

Porter, Jack N., ed. *Genocide and Human Rights: A Global Anthology.* Lanham, Md.: University Press of America, 1982.

Proctor, Robert. "Nazi Doctors, Racial Medicine and Human Experimentation." In *The Nazi Doctors and the Nuremberg Code*, edited by George J. Annas and Michael A. Grodin, pp. 17–31. New York: Oxford University Press, 1992.

———. *Racial Hygiene: Medicine under the Nazis.* Cambridge: Harvard University Press, 1988.

Pross, Christian. *Wiedergutmachung: Der Kleinkrieg gegen die Opfer.* Frankfurt/Main: Athenaum, 1988.

Puxon, Grattan. *Roma, Europe's Gypsies.* London: Minority Rights Group, 1987.

Rahe, Thomas. "Aus 'rassischen' Gründen verfolgte Kinder im Konzentrationslager Bergen-Belsen: Eine erste Skizze." In *Kinder und Jugendliche als Opfer des Holocaust*, edited by Edgar Alexander and Annegret Ehmann, pp. 129–43. Heidelberg: Dokumentationszentrum deutscher Sinti und Roma, 1995.

Ramati, Alexander. *And the Violins Stopped Playing: A Story of the Holocaust.* London: Hodder and Stoughton, 1985.

Reemtsma, Katrin. *Sinti und Roma: Geschichte, Kultur und Gegenwart.* Munich: C. H. Beck, 1996.

Renner, Erich, ed. *Zigeunerleben: Der Lebensbericht des Sinti-Musikers und Geigenbauers Adolf Boko Winterstein.* Frankfurt/Main: Büchergilde Guttenberg, 1988.

Riechert, Hansjörg. "Im Gleichschritt . . . : Sinti und Roma im Feldgrau." *Militärgeschichtliche Mitteilungen* 53 (1994): 377–97.

———. *Im Schatten von Auschwitz: Die nationalsozialistische Sterilisationspolitik gegenüber Sinti und Roma.* Münster: Waxmann, 1995.

Rose, Romani. "Dreieinhalb Jahrzehnte Verlassen: Zur Entstehung des neuen Selbst-bewusstseins der Sinti." *Zeitschrift für* Kulturaustausch 31 (1981): 411–22.

Rose, Romani, ed. *Der nationalsozialistische Völkermord an den Sinti und Roma.* 2d ed. Heidelberg: Dokumentations- und Kulturzentrum deutscher Sinti und Roma, 1995.

Rose, Romani and Walter Weiss. *Sinti und Roma im "Dritten Reich": Das Programm der Vernichtung durch Arbeit.* Göttingen: Lamuv, 1991.

Roth, Byron M. "Crime and Child Rearing." *Society* 34, no. 1 (November–December 1996): 39–45.

Rüdiger, Gerhard F. " 'Jeder Stein ist ein Blutstropfen': Zigeuner in Auschwitz-Birkenau." In *In Auschwitz vergast, bis heute verfolgt,* edited by Tilman Zülch, pp. 135–46. Reinbek: Rowohlt, 1979.

Sandkühler, Thomas. *"Endlösung" in Galizien: Der Judenmord in Ostpolen und die Rettungsinitiativen von Berthold Beitz.* Bonn: J. H. W. Dietz, 1996.

Sandner, Peter. *Frankfurt, Auschwitz: Die nationalsozialistische Verfolgung der Sinti und Roma in Frankfurt am Main.* Frankfurt/Main: Brandes und Apsel, 1998.

Scherer, Klaus. *"Asozial" im Dritten Reich: Die vergessenen Verfolgten.* Münster: Votum, 1990.

Schlabrendorff, Fabian von. *The Secret War against Hitler.* Translated by Hilda Simon. New York: Pitman, 1965.

Schleiermacher, Sabine. "Die SS-Stiftung 'Ahnenerbe': Menschen als Material für 'exakte' Wissenschaft." In *Menschenversuche: Wahnsinn und Wirklichkeit,* edited by Rainer Osnowski, pp. 70–87. Cologne: Kölner Volksblatt, 1988.

Schmacke, Norbert. *Zwangssterilisiert, verleugnet, vergessen: Zur Geschichte der nationalsozialistischen Rassenhygiene am Beispiel Bremen.* Bremen: Brockkamp, 1984.

Schmitz, Hubert. *Die Bewirtschaftung der Nahrungsmittel und Verbrauchsgüter, 1939–1950: Dargestellt an dem Beispiel der Stadt Essen.* Essen: Stadtverwaltung, 1956.

Schmuhl, Hans-Walter. *Rassenhygiene, Nationalsozialismus, Euthanasie: Von der Verhütung zur Vernichtung 'lebensunwerten Lebens', 1890–1945.* Göttingen: Vandenhoeck und Ruprecht, 1987.

Seible, Theresa. "Sintezza und Zigeunerin." In *Opfer und Täterinnen: Frauenbiographien des Nationalsozialismus,* edited by Angelika Ebbinghaus, pp. 302–16. Nördlingen: Delphi Politik, 1987.

Seipolt, Harry. *Kann der Gnadentod gewährt werden: Zwangssterilisation und NS-"Euthanasie" in der Region Aachen.* Aachen: Alano, 1995.

Shelach, Menachem. "Sajmiste: An Extermination Camp in Serbia." *Holocaust and Genocide Studies* 2 (1987): 243–60.

Simon, Jürgen. "Die Erbgesundheitsgerichtbarkeit im OLG-Bezirk Hamm: Rechtsprechung zwischen juristischen Vorgaben und ideologischer Anforderung." *Juristische Zeitgeschichte.* Vol. 1, Justiz und Nationalsozialismus, pp. 131–67. Düsseldorf: Justizministerium des Landes Nordrhein-Westfalen, 1993.

Smith, Bradley F., and Agnes F. Peterson, eds. *Heinrich Himmler Geheimreden 1933 bis 1945 und andere Ansprachen.* Frankfurt/Main: Prophyläen, 1974.

Smolen, Kazimierz. "Das Schicksal der Sinti und Roma im KL Auschwitz-Birkenau." In *Das Schicksal der Sinti und Roma im KL Auschwitz-Birkenau,* edited by Jan Parcer, pp. 129–75. Warsaw: Kanzlei des Sejm, 1994.

Sofsky, Wolfgang. *The Order of Terror: The Concentration Camp.* Translated by William Templer. Princeton, N.J.: Princeton University Press, 1997.

Solms, Wilhelm. "On the Demonizing of Jews and Gypsies in Fairy Tales." In *Sinti and Roma in German-Speaking Society and Literature,* edited by Susan Tebbutt, pp. 91–106. Providence, R.I.: Berghahn, 1998.

Spitta, Arnold. "Entschädigung für Zigeuner? Geschichte eines Vorurteils." In *Wiedergutmachung in der Bundesrepublik*, edited by Ludolf Herbst and Constantin Goschler, pp. 385–401. Munich: R. Oldenbourg, 1989.

State Museum of Auschwitz-Birkenau, ed. *Gedenkbuch: Die Sinti und Roma im Konzentrationslager Auschwitz-Birkenau*. 2 vols. Munich: K. G. Saur, 1993.

———. *Sterbebücher von Auschwitz: Fragmente*. Vol. 1. Munich: K. G. Saur, 1995.

Steinberger, Lila. "Das Leben des Herrn Steinberger." *Aus Politik und Zeitgeschichte* 31, no. 12 (1981): 18–31.

Steinmetz, Selma. *Österreichs Zigeuner im NS-Staat*. Vienna: Europa, 1966.

Stojka, Ceija. *Wir leben im Verborgenen: Erinnerungen einer Rom-Zigeunerin*. Vienna: Picus, 1988.

Strauss, Eva. "Die Zigeunerverfolgung in Bayern: 1855–1926." *Giessener Hefte zur Tsiganologie* 3 (1986): 31–108.

Streck, Bernhard. "Die 'Bekämpfung des Zigeunerunwesens': Ein Stück moderner Rechtsgeschichte." In *In Auschwitz vergast, bis heute verfolgt*, edited by Tilmann Zülch, pp. 64–87. Reinbek: Rowohlt, 1979.

———. "Nationalsozialistische Methoden zur Lösung der 'Zigeunerfrage.' " *Politische Didaktik* 1 (1981): 26–37.

———. "Zigeuner in Auschwitz: Chronik des Lagers B II e." In *Kumpania und Kontrolle*, edited by Mark Münzel and Bernhard Streck, pp. 69–128. Giessen: Focus, 1981.

Streit, Christian. *Keine Kameraden: Die Wehrmacht und die sowietischen Kriegsgefangenen, 1941–1945*. Stuttgart: Deutsche Verlagsanstalt, 1978.

Strom, Yale. *Uncertain Roads: Searching for the Gypsies*. New York: Four Winds, 1993.

Sutherland, Anne. *Gypsies: The Hidden Americans*. New York: Free Press, 1975.

Sway, Marlene B. "Simmel's Concept of the Stranger and the Gypsies." *Social Science Journal* 18, no. 1 (1981): 41–50.

Szymanski, Tadeusz. "The 'Hospital' in the Family Camp for Gypsies in Auschwitz-Birkenau." In *Nazi Medicine*, edited by International Auschwitz Committee, pt. 3, pp. 1–45. New York: Howard Fertig, 1986.

Tebbutt, Susan, ed. *Sinti and Roma in German-Speaking Society and Literature*. Providence, R.I.: Berghahn, 1998.

Terhorst, Karl-Leo. *Polizeiliche planmässige Überwachung und polizeiliche Vorbeugungshaft im Dritten Reich: Ein Beitrag zur Rechtsgeschichte vorbeugender Verbrechensbekämpfung*. Heidelberg: C. F. Müller, 1985.

Thurner, Erika. *Kurzgeschichte des nationalsozialistischen Zigeunerlagers in Lackenbach (1940 bis 1945)*. Eisenstadt: Rötzer, 1984.

———. *Nationalsozialismus und Zigeuner in Österreich*. Vienna: Geyer, 1983.

Tillion, Germaine. *Ravensbrück*. Garden City, N.Y.: Doubleday, 1975.

Trials of War Criminals before the Nuernberg Military Tribunals under Control Council Law no. 10. 15 vols. Washington, D.C.: GPO, 1946–49.

Trumpener, Katie. "The Time of the Gypsies: A 'People without History' in the Narratives of the West." *Critical Inquiry* 18 (1992): 843–84.

Trunk, Isaiah. *Judenrat: The Jewish Councils in Eastern Europe under Nazi Occupation*. New York: MacMillan, 1972.

Tyrnauer, Gabrielle. "Scholars, Gypsies and the Holocaust." In *Papers from the Sixth and Seventh Annual Meetings, Gypsy Lore Society, North American Chapter*, edited by Joanne Grumet, pp. 157–64. New York: Gypsy Lore Society, 1986.

Uschold, Rudolf. "Das Zigeunerproblem." *Die Neue Polizei* 5, no. 3 (1951): 38–40.

———. "Das Zigeunerproblem." *Die Neue Polizei* 5, no. 4 (1951): 60–62.

Vermehren, Isa. *Reise durch den letzten Akt: Ein Bericht (10.2.44 bis 29.6.45)*. Hamburg: Christian Wegner, 1948.

Volk, Ludwig, ed. *Akten deutscher Bischöfe über die Lage der Kirche 1933 bis 1945. Vol. 6: 1943–1945*. Mainz: Matthias-Grünewald, 1985.

Völklein, Ulrich. *Zigeuner: Das verachtete Volk*. Oldenburg: Stalling, 1981.

Vossen, Rüdiger. *Zigeuner: Roma, Sinti, Gitanos, Gypsies, zwischen Verfolgung und Romantisierung*. Frankfurt/Main: Ullstein, 1983.

Wagner, Patrick. "Das Gesetz über die Behandlung Gemeinschaftsfremder: Die Kriminalpolizei und die 'Vernichtung des Verbrechertums.'" In *Feinderklärung und Prävention*, pp. 75–100. Berlin: Rotbuch, 1988.

——. *Volksgemeinschaft ohne Verbrecher: Konzeptionen und Praxis der Kriminalpolizei in der Zeit der Weimarer Republik und des Nationalsozialismus*. Hamburg: Christians, 1996.

[Wehner, Bernd]. "'Das Spiel ist aus—Arthur Nebe': Glanz und Elend der deutschen Kriminalpolizei." *Der Spiegel*, September 29, 1949–April 20, 1950 (not consecutive).

——. *Dem Täter auf der Spur: Die Geschichte der deutschen Kriminalpolizei*. Bergisch-Gladbach: Gustav Lübbe, 1983.

Weindling, Paul. *Health, Race and German Politics between National Unification and Nazism, 1870–1945*. Cambridge: Cambridge University Press, 1989.

Weingart, Peter. *Rasse, Blut und Gene: Geschichte der Eugenik und Rassehygiene in Deutschland*. Frankfurt/Main: Suhrkamp, 1988.

Weinreich, Max. *Hitler's Professors: The Part of Scholarship in Germany's Crimes against the Jewish People*. New York: Yiddish Scientific Institute—YIVO, 1946.

Weiss, Sheila Faith. *Race Hygiene and National Efficiency: The Eugenics of Wilhelm Schallmayer*. Berkeley: University of California Press, 1987.

Wilhelm, Hans-Heinrich. *Die Einsatzgruppe A der Sicherheitspolizei und des SD 1941/42*. Frankfurt/Main: Peter Lang, 1996.

Willems, Wim. *In Search of the True Gypsy: From Enlightenment to Final Solution*. London: Frank Cass, 1997.

Wilson, James Q., and Richard J. Herrnstein. *Crime and Human Nature*. New York: Simon and Schuster, 1985.

Winter, Mathias. "Kontinuitäten in der deutschen Zigeunerforschung und Zigeunerpolitik." In *Feinderklärung und Prävention*, pp. 135–52. Berlin: Rotbuch, 1988.

Wippermann, Wolfgang. "Christine Lehmann und Mazurka Rosa: Two 'Gypsies' in the Grip of the German Bureaucracy, 1933–60." In *Confronting the Nazi Past: New Debates in Modern German History*, edited by Michael Burleigh, pp. 112–24. New York: St. Martin's, 1996.

——. *Das Leben in Frankfurt zur NS-Zeit*. Vol. 2: *Die nationalsozialistische Zigeunerverfolgung: Darstellung, Dokumente, didaktische Hinweise*. Frankfurt/Main: Waldemar Kramer, 1986.

——. "Nur eine Fussnote? Die Verfolgung der sowjetischen Roma: Historiographie, Motive, Verlauf." In *Gegen das Vergessen: Der Vernichtungskrieg gegen die Sowjetunion 1941–1945*, pp. 75–90. Frankfurt: Haag und Herchen, 1992.

——. *Wie die Zigeuner: Antisemitismus und Antitsiganismus im Vergleich*. Berlin: Elefanten, 1997.

Wippermann, Wolfgang, and Ute Brucker-Boroujerdi. "Nationalsozialistische Zwangslager in Berlin III: Das 'Zigeunerlager' Marzahn." *Berliner Forschungen* 2 (1987): 189–201.

Wirbel, Franz. "Die Rückkehr von Auschwitz." *Zeitschrift für Kulturaustausch* 31 (1981): 468–70.

Wölffling, Siegfried. "Zur Verfolgung und Vernichtung der Mitteldeutschen Zigeuner unter dem Nationalsozialismus." *Wissenschaftliche Zeitschrift der Martin-Luther-Universität Halle-Wittenberg* 14 (1965): 501–08.

Wood, Manfri Frederick. *In the Life of a Romany Gypsy*. London: Routledge and Kegan Paul, 1973.

Yates, Dora E. *My Gypsy Days: Recollections of a Romani Rawnie*. London: Phoenix House, 1953.

Yoors, Jan. *Crossing*. New York: Simon and Schuster, 1971.

———. *The Gypsies*. New York: Simon and Schuster, 1967.

Ziegler, Jürgen. *Mitten unter uns, Natzweiler-Struthof: Spuren eines Konzentrationslagers*. Hamburg: VSA, 1986.

Zimmermann, Michael. "Ausgrenzung, Ermordung, Ausgrenzung: Normalität und Exzess in der polizeilichen Zigeunerverfolgung in Deutschland (1870–1980)." In *"Sicherheit" und "Wohlfahrt": Polizei, Gesellschaft und Herrschaft im 19. und 20. Jahrhundert*. Edited by Alf Lüdtke, pp. 344–370. Frankfurt/Main: Suhrkamp, 1992.

———. "Die Deportation der Sinti und Roma nach Auschwitz-Birkenau." In *Das Schicksal der Sinti und Roma im KL Auschwitz-Birkenau*, edited by Jan Parcer, pp. 45–83. Warsaw: Kanzlei des Sejm, 1994.

———. "Deportation ins 'Generalgouvernement': Zur nationalsozialistischen Verfolgung der Sinti und Roma aus Hamburg." In *Hamburg in der NS-Zeit: Ergebnisse neuerer Forschungen*, edited by Frank Bajohr and Joachim Szodrzynski, pp. 151–73. Hamburg: Ergebnisse Verlag, 1995.

———. "Eine Deportation nach Auschwitz: Zur Rolle des Banalen bei der Durchsetzung des Monströsen." In *Normalität oder Normalisierung? Geschichtsmarkstätten und Faschismusanalyse*, edited by Heide Gerstenberger and Dorothea Schmidt, pp. 84–96. Münster: Westfälisches Dampfboot, 1987.

———. "Emscherstr. 9 und Emscherstr. 20: Zwei Zigeunerplätze in Recklinghausen 1939 bis 1943." *Vestische Zeitschrift* 90/91 (1991/1992): 245–67.

———. " 'Jetzt' und 'Damals' als imaginäre Einheit: Erfahrungen in einem lebensgeschichtlichen Projekt über die nationalsozialistische Verfolgung von Sinti und Roma." *Bios* 4 (1991): 225–42.

———. "Der nationalsozialistische Genozid an den Zigeunern und der Streit zwischen 'Intentionalisten' und 'Funktionalisten.' " In *Von der Aufgabe der Freiheit: Festschrift für Hans Mommsen zum 5. November 1995*, edited by Christian Jansen, pp. 413–26. Berlin: Akademie Verlag, 1995.

———. "Die nationalsozialistische 'Lösung der Zigeunerfrage.' " In *Nationalsozialistische Vernichtungspolitik 1939–1945: Neue Forschungen und Kontroversen*, edited by Ulrich Herbert, pp. 235–262. Frankfurt/Main: Fischer Taschenbuch Verlag, 1998.

———. *Rassenutopie und Genozid: Die nationalsozialistische 'Lösung der Zigeunerfrage.'* Hamburg: Christians, 1996.

———. "Robert Ritter und die Utopie einer 'verbrecherfreien Volksgemeinschaft.' " In *Fürsteberg-Drögen: Schichten eines verlassenen Ortes*, edited by Florian von Buttlar, pp. 143–52. Berlin: Edition Hentrich, 1994.

———. "Utopie und Praxis der Vernichtungspolitik in der NS-Diktatur: Überlegungen in vergleichender Absicht." *Werkstatt Geschichte* 13 (1996): 60–71.

———. *Verfolgt, vertrieben, vernichtet: Die nationalsozialistische Vernichtungspolitik gegen Sinti und Roma*. 2d ed. Essen: Klartext, 1993.

———. "Von der Diskriminierung zum 'Familienlager' Auschwitz: Die nationalsozialistische Zigeunerverfolgung." *Dachauer Hefte* 5 (1989): 87–114.

Zimmermann, Michael. "Wer schützt das Leben eines Menschen?" In *Auschwitz: Geschichte, Rezeption und Wirkung*, edited by Fritz Bauer Institute, pp. 75–97. Frankfurt/Main: Campus, 1996.

Zülch, Tilman, ed. *In Auschwitz vergast, bis heute verfolgt: Zur Situation der Roma (Zigeuner) in Deutschland und Europa*. Reinbek: Rowohlt, 1979.

———. *Sinti und Roma in Deutschland: 600 Jahre Geschichte einer verfolgten Minderheit*. Bonn: Bundeszentrale für politische Bildung, 1983.

Zywulska, Krystyna. *I Came Back*. Trans. Krystyna Cenkalska. London: Dennis Dobson, 1951.

Index

Aachen, 30
Adelsberger, Lucie, 156
Adler, Herbert, 92
Adler, Marta, 191
Adolph Frederick (of Mecklenburg-Strelitz), 3
Ahnenerbe, 136, 138–39, 176
Allied Control Commission, 200
Alsace and Lorraine, expulsions from, 81–82
American Model Eugenic Sterilization Law (1922), 39
Anschluss, 29, 56
Anus Mundi (Kielar), 156–57
Arajs, Viktor, 123
Arbeitsbuch, conditions for issuing, 67
Army Group Rear Area North, 120–21, 124
Arnold, Hermann, 212
Arnsberg, 97
"Aryan race," 4, 49, 135–36
Asocials:
    arrested during Operation Work-Shy, 28–31
    and crime, 219
    in concentration camps, 30, 35, 167–68
    deported to Auschwitz, 150
    and "extermination by work," 168
    and preventive police custody, 25–26, 59
    in Soviet Union, 119
    and sterilization law, 40–41
Augustus I (elector of Saxony), 3
Auschwitz decree (1942), 135, 141, 203, 216, 233
    implementing regulations for, 141–42
    exemption from, 141–42, 148–49, 181–82
Auschwitz Gypsy family camp, 83, 220–21, 223
    children in, 160–61, 164
    description of, 152–58
    food rations in, 155
    Hungarian Jews in, 164
    liquidation of, 162–66
    medical experiments in, 158–62
    number of victims, 166
    transfers from, 162–64
Auschwitz trial, 164–65
Austria, annexation of, 26, 29, 56

Bach-Zelewski, Erich von dem, 206
Bader, Karl Siegfried, 18
Bad Vilbel, 10
Baltic states, 120

Bankier, David, 145
Bartov, Omar, 118, 121
Bauer, Ignaz, 173
Bauer, Yehuda, 152, 224–25
Baur, Erwin, 38
Becker-Freysing, Hermann, 173
Beggars, 2–3, 19–20
Beiglböck, Wilhelm, 173
Belgrade, 129, 131
Belzec, 77–78
Berleburg, 50, 90
Berlin, 22, 25, 100
Bertram, Adolf, 145–46
Best, Werner, 87
Beverungen, 85–86
Bialystok, 82–83, 162, 166
Biology of criminality, 43, 47–48, 105
Bickenbach, Otto, 177
Birkenau, 152, 154, 163
Black triangle, 172
Bochum, 20
Boehm, Karol, 113
Boeters, Gustav, 39
Böhme, Franz, 129, 208
Bonigut, Georg, 163
Border zone, exclusion from, 53, 66, 75
Bormann, Martin, 140–41, 170, 195
Bradfisch, Otto, 206
Brandt, Rudolf, 155
Bräutigam, Otto, 125
Bravo Sinto! Lebenspuren deutscher Zigeuner (Wittich), 216
Breitscheid, 44–45
Bremen, 17
Brest-Litowsk, 83
Broad, Pery, 164
Browning, Christopher, 132
Brown triangle, 172
Brunner, Julius, 111
Buchen, 200
Buchenwald, 29–34, 163, 174–75, 215
Bundesarchiv, Gypsy files taken to, 215
Burgenland, 56–59, 107–9, 113, 116, 177

Carl Theodor (count palatine by Rhine), 3
Center for Culture and Documentation, 215

Chamberlain, Houston Stewart, 4, 37
Chelmno (Kulmhof), 115, 223
Children, deported, 145–47
Christian, V., 136
Clauberg, Carl, 161–62, 176
Cloppenburg, 31, 192
Cologne, 33, 73, 80, 89
Combating the Gypsy Plague decree (1938), 36, 52–55, 66, 68, 135
Communists, killing of, 118–19, 128–30
Compulsory labor, 90–93
Concentration camps, 171–72
    death rates in, 167
    hierarchy of prisoners, 30
    medical experiments in, 172, 176–77, 179
    number of victims, 167
    purpose of, 168
    See also names of specific camps
Conti, Leonardo, 71
Crimea, 121
Crime is Destiny (Lange), 48
Crime, causes of, 25, 48
Criminal Police (Kripo):
    political outlook of, 25–26
    reorganization of, 26–28
Croatia, 128

Dachau, 19, 24, 30–32, 34, 59, 172–73, 215
Dawidowicz, Lucy, 225–26
Deportations of Gypsies:
    from Austria (1941), 108–9, 112–16
    from East Prussia (1942), 82–83
    to the General Government (1940), 70–77, 108, 203, 220
    to Auschwitz (1943), 143–48
Destiny of Europe's Gypsies, The (Kenrick and Puxon), 165, 224
Deutsch, Harold C., 205
Deutsches Ärzteblatt, 51
Dietrich, Fritz, 123
Dillmann, Alfred, 5
Dirlewanger, Oskar, 180
"Disguised mental retardation," 40
Donaueschingen, district of, 66
Dora-Mittelbau, 174–75
Döring, Hans-Joachim, 106
Dortmund, 19, 30, 85
Dubitscher, Fred, 40

Duisburg, 78–80
Dulles, Allan, 205
Duna, William, 226–27
Düsseldorf, 31, 90

East Prussia, expulsion from, 82–83
Ehrhardt, Sophie, 44, 212, 215
Eichberger, Josef, 20
Eichmann, Adolf, 68–69, 112, 209
18th Panzer Division, 118
Einsatzgruppe A, 114, 123, 150
Einsatzgruppe B, 14, 119, 121–22, 205–6
Einsatzgruppe C, 123
Einsatzgruppe D, 118, 120–22
Einsatzgruppe Gottenberg, 121–22
Einsatzgruppen:
    creation of, 117
    in Polish campaign, 117
    in Serbia, 128
    instructions to, 118–19
    in war against Soviet Union, 119
Einsatzkommando 8, 206
Einsatzkommando 4a, 119
Einsatzkommando 9, 114
Eisenstadt, 57
Eller, Hans, 201–2
EMNID survey, 214
Engel, Gerhard, 95
Epp, Franz von, 19
Epstein, Bertold, 160
Ernst Ludwig (landgrave of Hesse-
    Darmstadt), 3
Essai sur l'inégalité des races humaines
    (Gobineau), 4
Esslingen, 19, 50
Ethnic Germans, resettlement of, 69,
    71, 109
Eugenics, 37
"Euthanasia" program, 41, 87, 127, 146,
    167, 188
Evangelical church synod of Berlin, 47
"Extermination by work," 168–70

Family camps in Auschwitz, 152
Festsetzungserlass. See Freeze on Mobility
    decree
Fight against the Gypsy Plague decree
    (1936), 18
Final Solution of the Jewish Question,
    221, 223, 225

Finger, Otto, 51
Fischer, Eugen, 38
Fischer, Werner, 179
Flossenbürg, 30, 163
Fonseca, Isabel, 12–13
Fortune-telling, 2, 12, 67
Four Year Plan, 29–30
Fraenkel, Ernst, 101
Frank, Hans, 71, 77, 89, 225
Frankfurt/Main, 9, 90
Franz, Philomena, 94
Fraser, Angus, 2
Frauenburg, 125
Frederick William I (king of Prussia), 3
Freeze on Mobility decree (1939),
    67–70, 85–86, 194, 108
Frerks, 60
Frick, Wilhelm, 25–26, 40, 42, 170
Friedländer, Saul, 49
Friesythe, 192
Fuchs, Wilhelm, 128
Fulda, 68
Fuldaer Zeitung, 49

Gadzé, 11
Galton, Francis, 37
Gas vans, 115
Gaunersprache (or *Rotwelsch*), 5
Gaupp, Robert, 39
Gelderari, 102
Gemeinschaftsfremdengesetz. See Law for
    Aliens to the Community
General Government, 68, 70–72
    administration of, 71,
    German Gypsies in, 76–81
    German Gypsies' return from, 79–80,
    220
Genetic health courts, 39, 89, 189
Genocide convention (1948), 222–24, 226
Genocide, crime of, 222–24
George I (elector of Saxony), 3
German constitution, 7
German Criminal Police Commission
    (DKK), 9
German Labor Front (DAF), 100, 185
German Research Foundation (DFG),
    105
German Society for Racial Hygiene, 51
Gersdorff, Rudolf-Christoph Freiherr
    von, 206

Gesellschaft für bedrohte Völker. See
    Society for Endangered People
Gestapo, 25–30, 40, 65
Geyer, Georg, 202
Giessen, 50, 144, 216
Gisevius, Hans, 205
Globocnik, Odilo, 77–78
Gobineau, J.-A., Count, 4, 37
Goebbels, Joseph, 168, 223
Göring, Hermann, 71, 89, 96
Gottberg, Kurt von, 121
Gottlieb, Dina, 158
Gravenhorst (German officer in Serbia),
    128
Grawitz, Ernst Robert von, 172, 179, 207
Greifelt, Ulrich, 29–30
Greiser, Artur, 112
Grundlagen des neunzehnten Jahrhunderts
    (Chamberlain), 4
Gürtner, Franz, 89
Gypsies:
    agitation against, 49–52, 84–86, 107–8
    as "Aryans," 49, 135
    assistance to, 194
    attitude toward *gadzé*, 11–12
    called Egyptians, 2
    and charge of espionage, 2, 65, 107,
        118, 128, 130–132
    crime rates of, 14, 213
    denunciations of, 194–95
    fingerprinting of, 5, 9, 59
    in Holy Roman Empire, 2
    hostility toward, roots of, 10–14
    Indian origins of, 1, 36, 49, 135, 139
    name changes among, 11, 104, 250 *n*
        108
    nomadic way of life of, 2, 6–7, 10, 15, 62
    number of victims, 128, 132, 166,
        221–22
    "racially pure" Gypsies, 47, 52, 55, 87,
        102, 106, 128, 135–41, 148, 181–82
    and ritual purity, 13
    size of population, 15, 43, 84, 109,
        116, 148–50, 181, 213
    treated like Jews, 99–100, 125
    during Weimar Republic, 7–10, 17
    after World War II, 199–202
Gypsy law, plans for, 46, 54, 86–87
"Gypsy marriage" (*Zigeunerehe*), 98
Gypsy music, 4, 57

Haagen, Eugen, 176–77
Hague Convention, 130
Hamburg, 23, 31, 77, 89–90
Hancock, Ian, 11, 226–27
Hansk, 78
Hasenputh, district of, 124
Hechingen, 98
Hecht, Gerhard, 70
Heinsheim, 84
Hereditary mental retardation, 41
Herford, 214
Hess, Rudolf, 140
Heterochromia, 160
Heydrich, Reinhard, 26, 34, 70, 95, 205
    appointed head of Security Police, 27
    death of, 204
    establishes border zone, 66
    forbids fortune-telling, 67
    issues implementing regulations for
        Combating the Gypsy Plague
        decree, 54–55, 87
    issues shooting order in 1941, 118
    orders freeze on mobility, 67
    orders Operation Work–Shy, 29–30
    plans expulsion of Gypsies, 67–68, 72
    sets up *Einsatzgruppen*, 117
Hilberg, Raul, 71, 206
Himmler, Heinrich, 26–27, 29, 55,
    66–67, 77, 86, 91, 95, 100, 127, 138,
    140, 148, 225
    and "Aryan" race, 135
    appointed Reich Commissioner for
        the strengthening of German
        nationhood, 70
    appoints Senior SS and Police
        Leaders, 119
    and Austrian Gypsies, 58–59
    differentiates between Jews and
        Gypsies, 196
    establishes *SS Sonderkommando
        Dirlewanger*, 180
    and "extermination by work," 168–69
    fascination with "pure Gypsies," 120,
        135, 139
    and Frank, 71
    issues Auschwitz decree, 135, 220
    issues Combating the Gypsy Plague
        decree, 38, 52–54
    and Litzmannstadt Gypsy camp,
        112–13

meetings with Hitler and Bormann on December 6, 1941, 141
named head of German police, 26
orders Operation Work-Shy, 28
orders special rations for Gypsy women and children, 155
and resettlement policy, 69–70
rivalry with Rosenberg, 126
protects "racially pure" Gypsies, 136–37
suicide of, 204,
visits Auschwitz, 164–65
visits Minsk, 206
and *Wiedereindeutschung*, 139
and "work education camps," 91
Hitler, Adolf, 15, 20, 29, 37, 225
attitude toward Gypsies, 38
birthday amnesty of 1939, 32
and Bormann, 140
and "extermination by work," 169
and Jews, 38
and killing of partisans, 122
Mein Kampf, 38
objects to Gypsies' military service, 95
and racial hygiene, 38
Hodonin, 150–51
Hoffmann, Peter, 205
Hohenasperg prison, 72–73, 77
Höhere SS- und Polizeiführer. See Senior SS and Police Leaders
Hohmann, Joachim S., 216
Höhne, Heinz, 205
Holocaust (Shoah), 224, 226
Homosexuals, 30
"Hordes," traveling in, 6–7, 53
Horwitz, Gordon J., 177
Höss, Rudolf, 138, 154–55, 157, 164–65
Hostage case, 130
Hostages, shooting of, 129–32

Identitätshaft, 52
In Auschwitz vergast, bis heute verfolgt (Zülch), 215
Indian Legion, 138
Ingelheim, 72
Institut für wehrwissenschaftliche Zweckforschung (IWZ), 176
Institut für Erb- und Rassenpflege, 50
International Central Office for Combating the Gypsy Nuisance, 28

International Congress on Population (1937), 45
International Criminal Police Commission, 18
International Romani Union, 226

Jansen, Eugenius, 113
Jeckeln, Friedrich, 124, 208
Jedicke, Bruno, 124
Jedrzejow, 77
Jenische, 5, 16, 47–48, 52, 54, 70, 92, 104, 201, 219
Jesus, 2, 12
Jews, 37
in Auschwitz, 152
in Austria, 59
as an alien race, 43, 51
compared with fate of Gypsies, 224–26
in concentration camps, 30
confiscation of property, 147
demands for anti-Jewish measures, 49
deportation to General Government, 67–68, 70, 72
employment during wartime, 145
Final Solution, 221, 223, 225
Hitler's hatred of, 38
killings in Soviet Union, 118–22, 125–26, 128, 205, 207
in Lodz ghetto, 112–13
and Nuremberg Laws, 42–43
prejudice against, 10
"racially pure" as worst-treated, 55, 225
in Siedlce ghetto, 78
status for social legislation, 100
shot as hostages in Serbia, 128–32
treatment of Jewish *Mischlinge*, 188, 225
Joachimowski, Tadeusz, 163
Joseph II (emperor), 56
Justin, Eva, 44, 46, 137–38, 141, 146, 210–11

Kaienburg, Hermann, 168
Kaiser Wilhelm Institut of Anthropology, 158
Kapos, 109, 111, 154, 156, 173
Karlowitsche, Alberts, 124
Karlsruhe, 66, 85

Kassel, 68
Katz, Steven, 225
Keitel, Wilhelm, 95, 122, 129
Kellermann, Ruth, 212–13, 223
Kenrick, Donald, 165, 222, 224
Kielar, Wieslaw, 156–57
Knobloch, Johann, 136, 139
Koch, Karl, 174
Koeppen, Werner, 95
Kogon, Eugen, 174
Koller, Siegfried, 187
Kollross, Hans, 110
König, Ernst-August, 156, 208, 223
Königsberg, 93
Krämer, Robert, 50
Kranz, Heinrich Wilhelm, 50–51, 187
Krimchaks, 121
Kripo. *See* Criminal Police
Krüger, Kurt, 60
Krychow, 78–79
Kulmhof. *See* Chelmno

Labor Corps (*Arbeitsdienst*), expulsion
    from, 97
Lackenbach camp, 110–11, 113, 136
Lalleri, 102, 137–38, 141, 183
Landfahrer (Gypsy-like itinerants), 7, 200–
    201. See also Jenische
Landfahrerzentrale, 202
Lange, Herbert, 115
Langmüller, Franz, III, 208
Latvia, 123–26
Latvian Auxiliary Security Police, 123
Law against Dangerous Career
    Criminals (1933), 24, 170, 24, 170
Law for Aliens to the Community, 87–89
Law for the Combating of Gypsies,
    Travelers and the Work-Shy (1926),
    7, 9, 17–18, 200, 203
Law for the Compensation of Nazi
    Victims (1953 and 1965), 203
Law for the Determination of
    Citizenship (1935), 42, 61, 94, 195
Law for the Fight against the Gypsy
    Nuisance (1929), 9
Law for the Prevention of Genetically
    Diseased Offspring (1933), 38–41,
    48, 58, 188
Law for the Protection of German Blood
    and Honor (1935), 42, 53, 99, 189

Law for the Protection of the
    Hereditary Health of the German
    People (1935), 42
Law for the Protection of the
    Population against Molestation by
    Gypsies, Travelers, and Work-
    Shy (1933), 17
Lehmann, Gregor, 183
Lehmann, Johann, 38
Lehmann, Julius, 38
Lemkin, Raphael, 222
Lengyel, Olga, 156
Lenz, Adolf, 48
Lenz, Fritz, 37–38
Leopoldskron camp, 110
Lety, 150–51
Libau, 123–24
Lifton, Robert, 155
Litzmannstadt. *See* Lodz
Lodz (Litzmannstadt), 86, 112–16, 220
Lohse, Hinrich, 123–25, 208
Lombroso, Cesare, 4
Lowari, 102
Lucas, Franz, 176
Ludwigsburg, 85

Machens, Josef Godehard, 145
Magdeburg, 31, 33–35, 90–91, 144
Mainz, 72
Maly, Hans, 209
Maria Theresa (empress), 56
Marriages and sexual relations, regula-
    tion of, 54, 59, 97–99, 184, 189
Marriage suitability, certificate of, 53
Marzahn, 22, 80
Mauthausen, 30–31, 59, 177–79
Medical experiments:
    in Auschwitz, 158–62
    in Dachau, 172
    in Natzweiler-Struthof, 176–77
    in Ravensbrück, 176
    in Sachsenhausen, 179
Mein Kampf (Hitler), 23
Meissner (chief public prosecutor,
    Graz), 107
Mengele, Josef, 158–62
Military government, 199
Military service, dismissal from, 93–97
Milton, Sybil, 224–25, 227
Minden, 101

Ministry for the Occupied Eastern
    Territories, 123, 125–27, 225
Minsk, 127
Mogilev, 207
Mosse, George, 37
Müller, Heinrich, 208
Munich, 23, 90, 93, 144
Munich-Riem, 172
Municipal Gyspy camps:
    in Berlin-Marzahn, 22, 93
    in Cologne, 21, 93
    in Düsseldorf, 21–22, 93
    in Frankfurt/Main, 10, 20–21, 92, 145
    in Karlsruhe, 22–23
    in Königsberg, 93
    in Salzburg, 110
Nationalsozialistische Volkswohlfahrt
    (NSV), 100
Natzweiler-Struthof, 31–33, 76–77
Nebe, Arthur, 25, 28, 54, 106, 138
    and *Ahnenerbe*, 136
    appointed head of RKPA, 28, 205
    and Auschwitz decree, 142
    career of, 204–5
    commands *Einsatzgruppe B*, 205–6, 208
    death of, 204–5
    and experiments in Mogilev, 207
    and expulsion of Gypsies from Berlin, 68
    and German resistance, 205
    and interest in preventive crime fight-
        ing, 25
    and medical experiments in concen-
        tration camps, 163, 172, 207–8
    and "racially pure" Gypsies, 138
    and shooting in Minsk, 206
Nedvedova-Nejedla, Zdonka, 176
Negroes, 40, 42
Neuengamme, 171
Neues Volk, 51, 57
Neusiedler, lake, 138
Nisko, 68–69
Noma, 160–61
Norwoshew, 120
Nuremberg Laws (1935), 42–43, 46, 93,
    98
Nyiszli, Miklos, 159–60, 164

Oberwart, 60, 111, 116, 214
Office of Racial Policy of the NSDAP,
    42, 70

Ohlendorf, Otto, 118, 122, 208
OKW. *See* Supreme Command of the
    Armed Forces (OKW)
Oldenburg, 144
Olympic Games in Berlin, 25
Operation Work-Shy, 28–35, 35, 167,
    174
Order Police, 26
Organisation Todt, 196

Pancke, Günther, 87
Partisans, killing of, 118, 122, 130, 207
Pfeffer, von, 66
Pfundtner, Hans, 87
Ploetz, Alfred, 37
Poachers, 180
Pohl, Oswald, 29, 155, 167
Police, reorganization of, 26–28, 53
Poles:
    expulsion of, 69
    and "extermination by work," 169
Porrajmos (Great Devouring), 226
Portschy, Tobias, 57–58, 60, 208
Poulson (Norwegian doctor), 177
Preventive Crime Fighting by the Police
    decree (1937), 25, 81, 98
Preventive police custody, 24, 58
"Projekt Tsiganalogie," 216
Property, confiscation of, 75, 147
Protective custody, 24
Protectorate of Bohemia and Moravia,
    137, 149–51, 157, 166
Public transportation, forbidden use of,
    91, 111
Puxon, Grattan, 165, 222, 224
Puzyna, Martyna, 158

Quedlinburg, 32–34

Racial hygiene, 36
Racial assessments, 102–5
Radicalization of Nazi policy, reasons
    for, 221
Radom, 77
Rapp, Albert, 122
Rascher, Sigmund, 172
*Rassenhygienische and bevölkerungsbiologis-
    che Forschungsstelle. See* Research
    Institute for Racial Hygiene and
    Population Biology

Rassenpolitisches Amt der NSDAP. See
Office of Racial Policy of the
NSDAP
Rassenschande (racial defilement), 42, 58
Rasse- und Siedlungshauptamt (RuSHA),
70, 87, 141
Rau, Johannes, 149
Ravensbrück, 59, 67, 79, 163, 175–76, 215
Reformation, age of the, 2
*Reichsausschuss zur wissenschaftlichen
Erfassung von erb- und anlagebed-
ingten schweren Leiden*, 188
*Reichskommissar für die Festigung
Deutschen Volkstums (RKF)*, 70
Reichskommmissariat Ostland, 123, 125
Reichskriminalpolizeiamt (RKPA), estab-
lishment of, 27
Reichssicherheitshauptamt (RSHA), 27,
126
*Reichszentrale zur Bekämpfung des
Zigeunerunwesens*, 28, 52
Reinhardt, Jakob, 138, 183–84
Reinhardt, Jakob (died 1787), 3
Reinhardt, Konrad, 138, 184
Research Institute for Criminal Biology,
43–45, 105
Research Institute for Racial Hygiene
and Population Biology, 43–47, 52,
102
Restitution, 202–4
Rheinlandbastarde, 40
Riechert, Hansjörg, 192–93
Riefenstahl, Leni, 110
Ritter, Robert, 33, 43, 45, 49, 54–55,
106, 185
and *Ahnenerbe*, 138
attitude toward "racially pure"
Gypsies, 47, 137, 209–10
and biology of criminality, 48
collaboration with Nebe, 142, 210
considers *Mischlinge* as asocial, 47
and deportation to Auschwitz, 142
and Gypsy law, 87–88.
and Indian origins of Gypsies, 49, 135
investigated for Nazi crimes, 209–10
professional career of, 43
research on racial characteristics of
Gypsies, 47
and sterilization of Gypsies, 71,
141–42, 187, 193

work on racial assessments, 43–46,
102–5
Rittersbach, 84
Ritual purity, 13
Rodenberg, Carl-Heinz, 51
Roma, 4, 102, 215
Romani language, 1, 4, 61, 136
Rom e.V. (Cologne), 215
Rom Union (Frankfurt/Main), 215
Rose, Romani, 216
Rosenberg, Alfred, 122–23, 126
Rostock, 214
Rotwelsch (or *Gaunersprache*), 5
Rural police in German-occupied Soviet
Union, 120
Ruthenia, 149

Sabac, 129
Sachsenhausen, 29–33, 35, 79, 179–80
Sajmiste (Semlin), 132
Salzburg, 108, 110
St. Johann, 61
St. Josephspflege, 146
Sanskrit, 1, 49, 135
Schallmeyer, Wilhelm, 37
Schlabrendorff, Fabian von, 205
Schmundt, Rudolf, 95
School attendance, 59–62, 89–90
Schwarzach, 108
SD (*Sicherheitsdienst*), 2, 67
Secret Field Police (GFP), 120
Security Police, establishment of, 26–27
Security Service. *See* SD
Sedentary Gypsies, 120–21, 124–126,
128–29, 150, 225
Seldte, Franz, 100
Senior SS and Police Leaders, 119
Serbia, killing of Gypsies in, 128–32, 220
Shooting order of 1941, 118
Siebert, Eduard, 183
Siedlce, 78
Siegen, 192
Sievers, Wolfram, 136, 138–39
Sigismund (emperor), 2
Sinti, 4, 102, 141
Six, Franz, 206
Social Darwinism, 37
Social legislation, 99–102, 106
"Socially adjusted" Gypsies, 128,
141–42, 184–87, 189, 219–20, 225

Society for Endangered People, 214
Solobjewa, P.W., 176
Sonderkommando Lange, 115
Sonderkommando 7a, 122
Soviet Union, killing of Gypsies in,
  117–28, 220
Sozialausgleichsabgabe, 100
Speer, Albert, 29
Spokesmen, 137–38, 142, 182–84
SS Sonderkommando Dirlewanger, 179–80
Stahlecker, Franz, 150
"Staircase of death" (Mauthausen), 178
Standesämter, 5, 53
Stein, Gerhard, 44
Steinbach, Heinrich, 138
Sterilization, 73, 88, 221
  and Auschwitz decree, 141–42, 188,
    192–93
  and Clauberg experiments, 161–62,
    176
  compensation for, 204
  as condition for release from
    Auschwitz, 163
  consequences of, 193, 199
  demands for, 38–39, 50–52, 62, 71,
    187
  for "disguised mental retardation," 40
  for hereditary mental retardation, 41
  for "moral mental retardation," 40
  number of Gypsies subjected to,
    39–41, 192–93
  in Sweden, 39
  in the U.S.A., 39
  in wartime, 41, 189–93
Strasburg, 65
Streck, Bernhard, 216
Streckenbach, Bruno, 117
Struggle against the Gypsy Nuisance
  decree (1903), 6
Supreme Command of the Armed
  Forces (OKW), 75, 94, 96, 113, 196
Sutherland, Anne, 11
Szymanski, Tadeusz, 154–55, 162

Tattars, 39
Taylor, Telford, 131
Themel, Karl, 46–47
Theresienstadt, 152
Thielo, Heinz, 161
Thierack, Otto, 89, 68–70, 195

Thirty Years' War, 3
Thomasius, Jacobus, 2
Tiefland, film (Riefenstahl), 110
Tillion, Germaine, 175
Topola, 129
Travelers, 8–9, 18–19, 47, 70, 200. *See
  also Jenische*
Trunk, Isaiah, 114
Turner, Harald, 128–29, 131–32, 208
Twin studies, 48
281st Security Division, 120–21
Typhus, 110, 113–14, 156, 162
Tyrnauer, Gabrielle, 226–27

Uebelhör, Friedrich, 112
L'uomo delinquente (Lombroso), 4
Ursachen und Bekämpfung des Verbrechens
  (Lombroso), 4
U.S. Holocaust Memorial Council, 226
U.S. Holocaust Memorial Museum,
  226–27
Uschold, Rudolf, 201

Vaihingen, 86
Ventzki, Werner, 112
Verden, district of, 30
Vermehren, Isa, 175
Verschuer, Otmar von, 158
Vexler, Iancu, 161
Vienna, 61, 69
Villingen, district of, 66
Volhynia Germans, 71
Völkischer Beobachter, 59, 89
Volkssturm, 196
Volk und Rasse, 51

Wagner, Georg, 139–40
Wagner, Robert, 82
Walther, Hans-Dietrich, 130
Wandergewerbeschein, 4, 8, 19, 53, 66–67,
  92
Wannsee Conference, 188
Warthegau, 69
Wehner, Bernd, 208
Werner, Paul, 209
Westwall, 66
Wetzel, Erhard, 70
Weyer, 219
"White Gypsies." *See Jenische*
Widmann, Albert, 206–07

Wiedereindeutschung, 139
Wiesbaden, 90
Wiesel, Elie, 226
Wilson, James Q., 52, 61
Witte (Reverend), 35
Wittich, Engelbert, 12, 216
Wo ist Nebe? (Gisevius), 205
Wolff, Karl, 206
Wolmirstedt, 139
Wood, Manfri, 12
"Work education camps," 91
Work-Shy. *See* Operation Work-Shy
World Romani Congress, 214
Worms, 72
Würth, Adolf, 44, 49–50, 73
Württemberg, Gypsies in, 181

Wüst, Walther, 136

Yoors, Ian, 11–12
Youth Corps (*Jugenddienstpflicht*), 104
Yugoslavia, 128

Zentralrat deutscher Sinti und Roma, 215, 222, 224
Zigeunerbuch (Dillmann), 5
Zigeunermischlinge, definition of, 102
Zigeunerzentrale (Central Office of Gypsy Affairs), 5, 9, 18, 28, 45, 201
Zimmermann, Michael, 216–17, 222, 224
Zindel, Karl, 86
Zörner, Ernst, 78

PUBLIC LIBRARY
CATALOG
12TH EDITION